Adolescence
Development, Diversity, and Context

Series Editor

Richard M. Lerner
Tufts University

A GARLAND SERIES

Series Contents

The Editors of this series are grateful to the several colleagues who facilitated our work on this series. Foremost, we are grateful to the authors of the selections reprinted in this volume. Their scholarship has shaped the study of adolescent development and we appreciate greatly their allowing us to include their work in this book.

We are especially grateful to Sofia T. Romero, Editor at the Boston College Center for Child, Family, and Community Partnerships, and to Imma De Stefanis, Graduate Research Assistant at the Center, for all their many contributions. Ms. Romero provided us with sage and professional editorial advice. Her wisdom, judgment, and skills enhanced the quality of our work and made it much more productive. Sr. De Stefanis collaborated extensively with us in the selection and organization of the scholarship included in the series. Her knowledge of and enthusiasm for the study of adolescence was an invaluable asset in our work.

We appreciate as well the excellent work of Carole Puccino, Editor at Garland Publishing. Her productivity and organizational skill enabled the volume to be produced with efficiency and quality. Finally, we thank Leo Balk, Vice President of Garland, for his enthusiasm for this project and for his support, encouragment, and guidance.

Cognitive and Moral Development and Academic Achievement in Adolescence

Edited, with an introduction by

Richard M. Lerner
Tufts University

Jasna Jovanovic
University of Illinois, Urbana-Champaign

GARLAND PUBLISHING, INC.
A MEMBER OF THE TAYLOR & FRANCIS GROUP
New York & London
1999

Library of Congress Cataloging-in-Publication Data

Cognitive and moral development and academic achievement in
  adolescence / edited, with an introduction by Richard M. Lerner,
  Jasna Jovanovic.
        p.   cm. — (Adolescence : development, diversity, and context
  ; 2)
      Includes bibliographical references.
      ISBN 0-8153-3291-2 (alk. paper)
      1. Cognition in adolescence. 2. Academic achievement.
  3. Teenagers—Conduct of life. I. Lerner, Richard M.
  II. Jovanovic, Jasna. III. Series: Adolescence (New York, N.Y.) ; 2.
  BF724.3.C58C64 1999
  155.5—dc21   99-33731
                                                      CIP

Printed on acid-free, 250-year-life paper
Manufactured in the United States of America

Contents

Introduction

Cognitive and Moral Development and Academic Achievement in Adolescence: A View of the Issues

*Richard M. Lerner, **Jasna Jovanovic*

The volumes in *Adolescence: Development, Diversity, and Context* stress that adolescent life is embedded in a complex developmental system involving multiple features of the individual (e.g., biology, personality, and cognition) and multiple levels of his or her ecology (e.g., family, peers, school, and culture). The present volume presents an array of perspectives that have been used to understand changes during adolescence in cognitive functioning and their relations to moral development, the connection between cognitive changes and academic performance, and the impact of the school environment on intellectual development and achievement. Consistent with the ideas of a developmental-systems perspective stressed in this series, the relationship between the developing person and features of his/her setting are seen as essential in all areas of scholarship reviewed in this volume. Nevertheless, variation in theoretical perspectives present in the articles show that, when trying to understand intellectual development and achievement in adolescence, scholars differ in the extent to which they place primary emphasis on the individual, on the context, or on the relationship between the two.

Organismic and Relational Views of Cognitive and Moral Development

The first two sections of this volume focus on cognitive and moral development, respectively. Articles by Piaget (1972) and by Kohlberg (1963, 1978) illustrate the organismic theoretical idea that development occurs through a process that engages actions of the person on the context and, in turn, the action of the context on the person. Nevertheless, stage-related changes in the organism are given primary importance in these instances of organismic theory.

However, and despite the influence of "Piagetian" and/or "Kohlbergian" theory on their work, the authors of the other articles in these sections present scholarship that represents a broad range of interests in the social ecology within which cognitive and moral development occur. These articles point to the role of cognitive and moral development in regulating the exchanges adolescents have with their social and physical worlds (Keating and Clark, 1980; Kuhn and Adams, 1979; Overton et al., 1992), and the importance of cognitive and moral development for the furtherance of civil society, for instance in regard to interpersonal relationships and prosocial behavior (Eisenberg et al., 1995; Smetana et al., 1991).

Indeed, a fully relational adolescent-context relational view of such development is presented by Damon and Gregory (1997). They stress the importance of community in providing guidance and social support, assets that may promote the moral development of young people.

Academic Achievement and School Effects

The person-context relational emphasis within developmental systems theory frames the range of research presented in the third section of the volume on academic achievement and school effects. For instance, there appear to be no global and pervasive effects of puberty on cognitive development; instead pubertal changes interact with contextual and experiential factors (e.g., the transition to junior high school) to influence academic achievement. Other contextual variables, for instance, those related to race, ethnicity, gender, family, and culture, also have important influences on academic achievement (Jovanovic and Lerner, 1994; Leadbeater, 1996; Rosenthal and Feldman, 1991; Sameroff et al., 1993; Steinberg et al., 1992; Taylor et al., 1994). In addition, the nature of the curriculum of the academic program offered to the student (Epstein and Dauber, 1995); the presence in the school of a full set of social and family services, as well as of course educational support programs (Dryfoos, 1995); and the linkage between the support present in the school for the adolescent with the care and nurturance received after school within the community (Damon and Gregory, 1997; Galambos and Maggs, 1991) all impact the young person's school achievement and broader, psychosocial development.

Thus, the articles in this section highlight the importance of the multiple levels of the human ecology of development for adolescents' academic achievement and personal development. Accordingly, individual-psychological characteristics relevant to adolescents' academic development (e.g., ability appraisals, expectations for success, attitudes toward learning; Eccles and Wigfield, 1995) may have a different impact depending on the relations that exist between the youth and his or her context. The implication of the scholarship in this section, then, is that there is potential for great individual variation both in the system of individual-context relationships associated with academic development and also in the outcomes the system effects.

Enhancing Achievement and Promoting Positive Development

The significance of the implications of the relational, developmental systems-oriented scholarship in this volume lies in its import for interventions aimed at improving the achievement and enhancing the healthy development of adolescents. Consider the variation in the achievement trajectories seen among our nation's youth. On all major indicators of academic achievement (e.g., graduation rates, proficiency exams, higher education enrollment patterns), minority youth in the U.S. today continue to fall behind their majority youth counterparts (U.S. Department of Education, 1995a, 1995b). At the same time, among the majority group a gender inequity persists (AAUW, 1998).

Historically in the United States the responsibility of ensuring that all of our young people are educated has fallen mostly on our educational institutions. However, as stressed by Dryfoos (1995), the school must become a collaborative part of the broader, community system in order to successfully educate and enhance equity for diverse youth. Eccles and Wigfield (1995) propose youth will be engaged in school if they see value and utility to what they are learning. But, perceiving the value and utility of learning is dependent on the multiple (and sometimes conflicting messages) students receive from the social milieu in which they learn. The articles in this volume suggest, then, that several different levels of the context may be appropriate targets for intervention, i.e., for policies and programs aimed at enhancing youth achievement and development.

For example, Steinberg et al. (1992) found that across ethnic groups, adolescents whose friends and parents both support achievement perform better than those youth who receive support only from one source but not the other. Their findings — that African American youth cannot easily find support from peers for achievement — illustrates why one contextual influence (in this case parents) must be evaluated in terms of the other contexts in which adolescents are expected to perform. Taylor et al. (1994) provide a critical example of how among African American youth a societal barrier of a job ceiling gives rise to disillusionment about the real value of schooling. In turn, the articles by Jovanovic and Lerner (1994) and Rosenthal and Feldman (1991) demonstrate that when we consider adolescent academic development at the contextual level of culture, individual variation in achievement outcomes are better understood. Culture can determine the degree of importance that is attached to academic achievement and can endorse different social models concerning who should achieve (e.g., who is predisposed to do better at math or science, women or men).

Conclusions

The papers in this volume demonstrate that the methods by which we educate youth need to incorporate both individual (e.g., ethnicity, gender, pubertal status) and contextual factors. These contextual factors should include both proximal contexts, such as family and school, along with more distal settings, such as the broader community, and the societal and cultural context in which young persons are embedded. This integration is critical to ensuring equity in our educational system, since our society and culture have firmly embedded gender- and race-related expectations that are closely linked to the variation in academic outcomes among the youth in our nation's schools (Bailey and Campbell, 1992; Ogbu, 1986).

When we do consider integratively individual differences and contextual diversity, we increase the potential for quality education. We enhance our understanding of the key relations involved in the developmental system producing variation in intellectual development and achievement, and we develop theory-predicated ideas about the ways in which we may intervene in the complex person-social ecology system to reach the goal of helping healthy youth develop.

*Richard M. Lerner holds the Bergstrom Chair in Applied Developmental Science at Tufts University. A developmental psychologist, Lerner received a Ph.D. in 1971 from the City University of New York. He has been a fellow at the Center for Advanced Study in the Behavioral Sciences and is a fellow of the American Association for the Advancement of Science, the American Psychological Association, the American Psychological Society, and the American Association of Applied and Preventive Psychology. Prior to joining Tufts University, he was on the faculty and held administrative posts at Michigan State University, Pennsylvania State University, and Boston College, where he was the Anita L. Brennan Professor of Education and the director of the Center for Child, Family, and Community Partnerships. During the 1994–95 academic year Lerner held the Tyner Eminent Scholar Chair in the Human Sciences at Florida State University. Lerner is the author or editor of 40 books and more than 275 scholarly articles and chapters, including his 1995 book, *America's Youth in Crisis: Challenges and Options for Programs and Policies.* He edited Volume 1, on "Theoretical models of human development," for the fifth edition of the *Handbook of Child Psychology.* He is known for his theory of, and research about, relations between life-span human development and contextual or ecological change. He is the founding editor of the *Journal of Research on Adolescence* and of the new journal, *Applied Developmental Science.*

**Jasna Jovanovic is an assistant professor in the Department of Human and Community Development at the University of Illinois, Urbana-Champaign. In 1991 she completed her doctoral degree in Human Development and Family Studies from the Pennsylvania State University. Subsequently, she did postdoctoral work in the Graduate School of Education at the University of California, Santa Barbara. Her research examines the psychosocial factors that lead to successful or unsuccessful academic achievement outcomes among adolescents, particularly adolescent girls. In her most recent published work. Dr. Jovanovic examines how the classroom environment plays a role in influencing girls' interest and confidence in science.

References[1]

American Association of University Women. (1998). *Gender gaps: Where schools still fail our children.* Washington, DC: Author.

Bailey, S.M. and Campbell, P.B. (1992). *Gender equity: The unexamined basic of school reform.* Stanford Law and Policy Review, 73–86.

Ogbu, J. (1986). The consequences of the American caste system. In U. Neisser (Ed.), *The school achievement of minority children: New perspectives* (pp. 19–56). Hillsdale, NJ: Erlbaum.

U.S. Department of Education National Center for Education Statistics. (1995a). *Findings from the Condition of Education 1994: The educational progress of black students,* NCES 95≠765. Washington DC: Author.

U.S. Department of Education National Center for Education Statistics. (1995b). *Findings from the Condition of Education 1994: The educational progress of Hispanic students,* NCES 95–767. Washington DC: Author.

Footnote

[1]This list provides reference only to citations not included in this volume.

Human Develop. *15:* 1–12 (1972)

Intellectual Evolution from Adolescence to Adulthood[1]

J. Piaget

Université de Genève, Ecole de Psychologie et des Sciences de l'Education, Genève

Abstract. Growing out of a child's cognitive developmental history, formal operations become established at about the age of 12–15 years. Reflected in his ability to reason hypothetically and independently on concrete states of affairs, these structures may be represented by reference to combinatorial systems and to 4-groups. The essence of the logic of cultured adults and the basis for elementary scientific thought are thereby provided. The rate at which a child progresses through the developmental succession may vary, especially from one culture to another. Different children also vary in terms of the areas of functioning to which they apply formal operations, according to their aptitudes and their professional specializations. Thus, although formal operations are logically independent of the reality content to which they are applied, it is best to test the young person in a field which is relevant to his career and interests.

Key Words
Cognitive development
Adolescence
Adulthood
Logic
Environmental differences
Individual differences

We are relatively well informed about the important changes that take place in cognitive function and structure at adolescence. Such changes show how much this essential phase in ontogenic development concerns all aspects of mental and psychophysiological evolution and not only the more 'instinctive', emotional or social aspects to which one often limits one's consideration. In contrast, however, we know as yet very little about the period which separates adolescence from adulthood and we feel that the decision of the

[1] A French version of the article was presented at *FONEME,* 3rd International Convention, Milan 1970, and published in the proceedings (FONEME, Institution for Studies and Research in Human Formation, 20135, Via Bergamo 21, Milan, Italy). The English translation was prepared by Joan Bliss and Hans Furth, to whom special thanks are due. The editors of Human Development gratefully acknowledge permission by the author and FONEME to publish the English version.

1

Institution FONEME to draw the attention of various research workers to this essential problem is extremely well founded.

In this paper we would first like to recall the principal characteristics of the intellectual changes that occur during the period from 12–15 years of age. These characteristics are too frequently forgotten as one tends to reduce the psychology of adolescence to the psychology of puberty. We shall then refer to the chief problems that arise in connection with the next period (15–20 years); firstly, the diversification of aptitudes, and secondly, the degree of generality of cognitive structures acquired between 12 and 15 years and their further development.

The Structures of Formal Thought

Intellectual structures between birth and the period of 12–15 years grow slowly, but according to stages in development. The order of succession of these stages has been shown to be extremely regular and comparable to the stages of an embryogenesis. The speed of development, however, can vary from one individual to another and also from one social environment to another; consequently, we may find some children who advance quickly or others who are backward, but this does not change the order of succession of the stages through which they pass. Thus, long before the appearance of language, all normal children pass through a number of stages in the formation of sensorimotor intelligence which can be characterized by certain 'instrumental' behavior patterns; such patterns bear witness to the existence of a logic which is inherent to the coordination of the actions themselves.

With the acquisition of language and the formation of symbolic play, mental imagery, etc., that is, the formation of the symbolic function (or, in a general sense, the semiotic function), actions are interiorized and become representations; this supposes a reconstruction and a reorganization on the new plane of representative thought. However, the logic of this period remains incomplete until the child is 7 or 8 years old. The internal actions are still 'preoperatory' if we take 'operations' to mean actions that are entirely reversible (as adding and subtracting, or judging that the distance between A and B is the same as the distance between B and A, etc.). Due to the lack of reversibility, the child lacks comprehension of the idea of transitivity ($A \leq C$, if $A \leq B$ and $B \leq C$) and of conservation (for a preoperatory child, if the shape of an object changes, the quantity of matter and the weight of the object change also).

2

Between 7–8 and 11–12 years a logic of reversible actions is constituted, characterized by the formation of a certain number of stable and coherent structures, such as a classification system, an ordering system, the construction of natural numbers, the concept of measurement of lines and surfaces, projective relations (perspectives), certain general types of causality (transmission of movement through intermediaries), etc.

Several very general characteristics distinguish this logic from the one that will be constituted during the pre-adolescent period (between 12 and 15 years). Firstly these operations are 'concrete', that is to say, in using them the child still reasons in terms of objects (classes, relations, numbers, etc.) and not in terms of hypotheses that can be thought out before knowing whether they are true or false. Secondly, these operations, which involve sorting and establishing relations between or enumerating objects, always proceed by relating an element to its neighboring element—they cannot yet link any term whatsoever to any other term, as would be the case in a combinatorial system: thus, when carrying out a classification, a child capable of concrete reasoning associates one term with the term it most resembles and there is no 'natural' class that relates two very different objects. Thirdly, these operations have two types of reversibility that are not yet linked together (in the sense that one can be joined with the other); the first type of reversibility is by inversion or negation, the result of this operation is an annulment, for example, $+ A - A = 0$ or $+ n - n = 0$; the second type of reversibility is by reciprocity and this characterizes operations of relations, for example, if $A = B$, then $B = A$, or if A is to the left of B, then B is to the right of A, etc.

On the contrary, from 11–12 years to 14–15 years a whole series of novelties highlights the arrival of a more complete logic that will attain a state of equilibrium once the child reaches adolescence at about 14–15 years. We must, therefore, analyze this new logic in order to understand what might happen between adolescence and full adulthood.

The principle novelty of this period is the capacity to reason in terms of verbally stated hypotheses and no longer merely in terms of concrete objects and their manipulation. This is a decisive turning point, because to reason hypothetically and to deduce the consequences that the hypotheses necessarily imply (independent of the intrinsic truth or falseness of the premises) is a formal reasoning process. Consequently the child can attribute a decisive value to the logical form of the deductions that was not the case in the previous stages. From 7–8 years, the child is capable of certain logical reasoning processes but only to the extent of applying particular operations to concrete objects or events in the immediate present: in other words, the operatory form of the reasoning process, at this level, is still subordinated to the concrete content that makes up the real world. In contrast, hypothetical reasoning implies the subordination of the real to the realm of the possible, and consequently the linking of all possibilities to one another by necessary implications that encompass the real, but at the same time go beyond it.

From the social point of view, there is also an important conquest. Firstly, hypothetical reasoning changes the nature of discussions: a fruitful and constructive discussion means that by using hypotheses we can adopt the point of view of the adversary (although not necessarily believing it) and draw the logical consequences it implies. In this way, we can judge its value after having verified the consequences. Secondly, the individual who becomes capable of hypothetical reasoning, by this very fact will interest himself in problems that go beyond his immediate field of experience. Hence, the adolescent's capacity to understand and even construct theories and to participate in society and the ideologies of adults; this is often, of course, accompanied by a desire to change society and even, if necessary, destroy it (in his imagination) in order to elaborate a better one.

In the field of physics and particularly in the induction of certain elementary laws (many experiments have been carried out under the direction of B. INHELDER on this particular topic), the difference in attitude between children of 12–15 years, already capable of formal reasoning, and children of 7–10 years, still at the concrete level, is very noticeable. The 7- to 10-year-old children when placed in an experimental situation (such as what laws concern the swing of a pendulum, factors involved in the flexibility of certain materials, problems of increasing acceleration on an inclined plane) act directly upon the material placed in front of them by trial and error, without dissociating the factors involved. They simply try to classify or order what happened by looking at the results of the co-variations. The formal level children, after a few similar trials stop experimenting with the material and begin to list all the possible hypotheses. It is only after having done this that they start to test them, trying progressively to dissociate the factors involved and study the effects of each one in turn—'all other factors remaining constant'.

This type of experimental behavior, directed by hypotheses which are based on more or less refined causal models, implies the elaboration of two new structures that we find constantly in formal reasoning.

The first of these structures is a combinatorial system, an example of which is clearly seen in 'the set of all subsets', ($2n^2$ or the simplex structure).

We have, in fact, previously mentioned that the reasoning process of the child at the concrete level (7–10 years old) progresses by linking an element with a neighboring one, and cannot relate any element whatsoever to any other. On the contrary, this generalized combinatorial ability (1 to 1, 2 to 2, 3 to 3, etc.) becomes effective when the subject can reason in a hypothetical manner. In fact, psychological research shows that between 12 and 15 years the pre-adolescent and adolescent start to carry out operations involving combinatorial analysis, permutation systems, etc. (independent of all school training). They cannot, of course, figure out mathematical formulas, but they can discover experimentally exhaustive methods that work for them. When a child is placed in an experimental situation where it is necessary to use combinatorial methods (for example, given 5 bottles of colorless, odorless liquid, 3 of which combine to make a colored liquid, the fourth is a reducing agent and the fifth is water), the child easily discovers the law after having worked out all the possible ways of combining the liquids in this particular case.

This combinatorial system constitutes an essential structure from the logical point of view. The elementary systems of classification and order observed between 7 and 10 years, do not yet constitute a combinatorial system. Propositional logic, however, for two propsitions 'p' and 'q' and their negation, implies that we not only consider the 4-base associations (p and q, p and not q, not p and q, not p and not q) but also the 16 combinations that can be obtained by linking these base associations 1 to 1, 2 to 2, 3 to 3 (with the addition of all 4-base associations and the empty set). In this way it can be seen that implication, inclusive disjunction and incompatibility are fundamental propositional operations that result from the combination of 3 of these base associations.

At the level of formal operations it is extremely interesting to see that this combinatorial system of thinking is not only available and effective in all experimental fields, but that the subject also becomes capable of combining propositions: therefore, propositional logic appears to be one of the essential conquests of formal thought. When, in fact, the reasoning processes of children between 11–12 and 14–15 years are analyzed in detail it is easy to find the 16 operations or binary functions of a bivalent logic of propositions.

However, there is still more to formal thought: when we examine the way in which subjects use these 16 operations we can recognize numerous cases of the 4-group which are isomorphic to the Klein group and which reveal themselves in the following manner. Let us take, for example, the implication $p > q$, if this stays unchanged we can say it characterized the identity transformation I. If this proposition is changed into its negation N (reversibility by negation or inversion) we obtain N = p and not q. The subject can change this same proposition into its reciprocal (reversibility by reciprocity) that is R = q >p; and it is also possible to change the statement into its correlative (or dual), namely C = not p and q. Thus, we obtain a commutative 4-group such that CR = N, CN = R, RN = C and CRN = I. This group allows the subject to combine in one operation the negation and the reciprocal which was not possible at the level of concrete operations. An example of these transformations that occurs frequently is the comprehension of the relationship between action (I and N) and reaction (R and C) in physics experiments; or again, the understanding of the relationship between two reference systems, for example: a moving object can go forwards or backwards (I and N) on a board which itself can go forwards or backwards (R and C) in relation to an exterior reference system. Generally speaking the group structure intervenes when the subject understands the difference between the cancelling or undoing of an effect (N in relation to I) and the compensation of this effect by another variable (R and its negation C) which does not eliminate but neutralizes the effect.

In concluding this first part we can see that the adolescent's logic is a complex but coherent system that is relatively different from the logic of the child, and constitutes the essence of the logic of cultured adults and even provides the basis for elementary forms of scientific thought.

The Problems of the Passage from Adolescent to Adult Thought

The experiments on which the above-mentioned results are based were carried out with secondary school children, 11–15 years, taken from the better schools in Geneva. However, recent research has shown that subjects from other types of schools or different social environments sometimes give results differing more or less from the norms indicated; for the same experiments it is as though these subjects had stayed at the concrete operatory level of thinking.

Other information gathered about adults in Nancy, France, and adolescents of different levels in New York has also shown that we cannot generalize in all subjects the conclusion of our research which was, perhaps, based on a somewhat privileged population. This does not mean that our observations have not been confirmed in many cases: they seem to be true for certain populations, but the main problem is to understand why there are exceptions and also whether these are real or apparent.

A first problem is the speed of development, that is to say, the differences that can be observed in the rapidity of the temporal succession of the stages. We have distinguished 4 periods in the development of cognitive functions (see beginning of part 1): the sensorimotor period before the appearance of language; the preoperatory period which, in Geneva, seems on the average to extend from about 1½–2 to 6–7 years; the period of concrete operations from 7–8 to 11–12 years (according to research with children in Geneva and Paris) and the formal operations period from 11–12 to 14–15 years as observed in the schools studied in Geneva. However, if the order of succession has shown itself to be constant—each stage is necessary to the construction of the following one—the average age at which children go through each stage can vary considerably from one social environment to another, or from one country or even region within a country to another. In this way Canadian psychologists in Martinique have observed a systematic slowness in development; in Iran notable differences were found between children of the city of Teheran and young illiterate children of the villages. In Italy, N. Peluffo has shown that there is a significant gap between children from regions of southern Italy and those from the north; he has carried out some particularly interesting studies indicating how, in children from southern families migrating north, these differences progressively disappear. Similar comparative research is at present taking place in Indian reservations in North America, etc.

In general, a first possibility is to envisage a difference in speed of development without any modification of the order of succession of the stages. These different speeds would be due to the quality and frequency of intellectual stimulation received from adults or obtained from the possibilities available to children for spontaneous activity in their environment. In the case of poor stimulation and activity, it goes without saying that the development of the first 3 of the 4 periods mentioned above will be slowed down. When it comes to formal thought, we could propose that there will be an even greater retardation in its formation (for example, between 15 and 20 years and not 11 and 15 years); or that perhaps in extremely disadvantageous conditions, such a type of thought will never really take shape or will only develop in those individuals who change their environment while development is still possible.

This does not mean that formal structures are exclusively the result of a process of social transmission. We still have to consider the spontaneous and endogenous factors of construction proper to each normal subject. However, the formation and completion of cognitive structures imply a whole series of exchanges and a stimulating environment; the formation of operations always requires a favorable environment for 'co-operation', that is to say, operations carried out in common (e.g., the role of discussion, mutual criticism or support, problems raised as the result of exchanges of information, heightened curiosity due to the cultural influence of a social group, etc.). Briefly, our first interpretation would mean that in principle all normal individuals are capable of reaching the level of formal structures on the condition that the social environment and acquired experience provide the subject with the cognitive nourishment and intellectual stimulation necessary for such a construction.

However, a second interpretation is possible which would take into account the diversification of aptitudes with age, but this would mean excluding certain categories of normal individuals, even in favorable environments, from the possibility of attaining a formal level of thinking. It is a well-known fact that the aptitudes of individuals differentiate progressively with age. Such a model of intellectual growth would be comparable to a fully expanded hand fan, the concentric layers of which would represent the successive stages in development whereas the sectors, opening wider towards the periphery, correspond to the growing differences in aptitude.

We would go so far as to say that certain behavior patterns characteristically form stages with very general properties: this occurs until a certain level in development is reached; from this point onwards, however, individual aptitudes become more important than these general characteristics and create greater and greater differences between subjects. A good example of this type of development is the evolution of drawing. Until the stage at which the child can represent perspectives graphically, we observe a very general progress to the extent that the 'draw a man' test, to cite a particular case as an example, can be used as a general test of mental development. However, surprisingly large individual differences are observed in the drawings of 13- to 14-year-old children, and even greater differences with 19–20 year olds (e.g., army recruits): the quality of the drawing no longer has anything to do with the level of intelligence. In this instance we have a good example of a behaviour pattern which is, at first, subordinate to a general evolution in stages [cf. those described by LUQUET and other authors for children from 2–3 until about 8–9 years] and which, afterwards, gradually becomes diversified according to criteria of individual aptitudes rather than the general development common to all individuals.

This same type of pattern occurs in several fields including those which appear to be more cognitive in nature. One example is provided by the representation of space which first depends on operatory factors with the usual 4 intellectual stages—sensorimotor (cf. the practical group of displacements), preoperatory, concrete operations (measure, perspectives, etc.) and formal operations. However, the construction of space also depends on figurative factors (perception and mental imagery) which are partially subordinated to operatory factors and which then become more and more differentiated as symbolical and representative mechanisms. The final result is that for space in general, as for drawing, we can distinguish a primary evolution characterized by the stages in the ordinary sense of the term, and then a growing diversification with age due to gradually differentiating aptitudes with regard to imaged representation and figurative instruments. We know, for example, that there exist big differences between mathematicians in the way in which they define 'geometrical intuition': POINCARÉ distinguishes two types of mathematicians the 'geometricians', who think more concretely and the 'algebrists', or 'analysts', who think more abstractly.

There are many other fields in which we could also think along similar lines. It becomes possible at a certain moment, for example, to distinguish between adolescents who, on the one hand, are more talented for physics or problems dealing with causality than for logic or mathematics and those who, on the other hand, show the opposite aptitude. We can see the same tendencies in questions concerning linguistics, literature, etc.

We could, therefore, formulate the following hypothesis: if the formal structures described in part 1 do not appear in all children of 14–15 years and demonstrate a less general distribution than the concrete structures of children from 7–10 years old, this could be due to the diversification of aptitudes with age. According to this interpretation, however, we would have to admit that only individuals talented from the point of view of logic, mathematics and physics would manage to construct such formal structures whereas literary, artistic and practical individuals would be incapable of doing so. In this case it would not be a problem of under-development compared to normal development but more simply a growing diversification in individuals, the span of aptitudes being greater at the level of 12–15 years, and above all between 15 and 20 years, than at 7–10 years. In other words, our fourth period can no longer be characterized as a proper stage, but would already seem to be a structural advancement in the direction of specialization.

But there is the possibility of a third hypothesis and, in the present state of knowledge, this last interpretation seems the most probable. It allows us to reconcile the concept of stages with the idea of progressively differentiating aptitudes. In brief, our third hypothesis would state that all normal subjects attain the stage of formal operations or structuring if not between 11–12 to 14–15 years, in any case between 15 and 20 years. However, they reach this stage in different areas according to their aptitudes and their professional specializations (advanced studies or different types of apprenticeship for the various trades): the way in which these formal structures are used, however, is not necessarily the same in all cases.

In our investigation of formal structures we used rather specific types of experimental situations which were of a physical and logical-mathematical nature because these seemed to be understood by the school children we sampled. However, it is possible to question whether these situations are, fundamentally, very general and therefore applicable to any school or professional environment. Let us consider the example of apprentices to carpenters, locksmiths, or mechanics who have shown sufficient aptitudes for successful training in the trades they have chosen but whose general education is limited. It is highly likely that they will know how to reason in a hypothetical manner in their speciality, that is to say, dissociating the varia-bles involved, relating terms in a combinatorial manner and reasoning with propositions involving negations and reciprocities. They would, therefore, be capable of thinking formally in their particular field, whereas faced with our experimental situations, their lack of knowledge or the fact they have forgotten certain ideas that are particularly familiar to children still in school or college, would hinder them from reasoning in a formal way, and they would give the appearance of being at the concrete level. Let us also consider the example of young people studying law—in the field of juridical concepts and verbal discourse their logic would be far superior to any form of logic they might use when faced with certain problems in the field of physics that involve notions they certainly once knew but have long since forgotten.

It is quite true that one of the essential characteristics of formal thought appears to us to be the independence of its form from its reality content. At the concrete operatory level a structure cannot be generalized to different heterogenous contents but remains attached to a system of objects or to the properties of these objects (thus the concept of weight only becomes logically structured after the development of the concept of matter, and the concept of physical volume after weight): a formal structure seems, in contrast, generalizable as it deals with hypotheses. However, it is one thing to dissociate the form from the content in a field which is of interest to the subject and within which he can apply his curiosity and initiative, and it is another to be able to generalize this same spontaneity of research and comprehension to a field foreign to the subject's career and interests. To ask a future lawyer to reason on the theory of relativity or to ask a student in physics to reason on the code of civil rights is quite different from asking a child to generalize what he has discovered in the conservation of matter to a problem on the conservation of weight. In the latter instance it is the passage from one content to a different but comparable content, whereas in the former it is to go out of the subject's field of vital activities and enter a totally new field, completely foreign to his interests and projects. Briefly, we can retain the idea that formal operations are free from their concrete content, but we must add that this is true only on the condition that for the subjects the situations involve equal aptitudes or comparable vital interests.

Conclusion

If we wish to draw a general conclusion from these reflections we must first say that, from a cognitive point of view, the passage from adolescence to adulthood raises a number of unresolved questions that need to be studied in greater detail.

The period from 15 to 20 years marks the beginning of professional specialization and consequently also the construction of a life program corresponding to the aptitudes of the individual. We now ask the following critical question: Can one demonstrate, at this level of development as at previous levels, cognitive structures common to all individuals which will, however, be applied or used differently by each person according to his particular activities?

The reply will probably be positive but this must be established by the experimental methods used in psychology and sociology. Beyond that, the next essential step is to analyze the probable processes of differentiation: that is to say, whether the same structures are sufficient for the organization of many varying fields of activity but with differences in the way they are applied, or whether there will appear new and special structures that still remain to be discovered and studied.

It is to the credit of the FONEME Institution to have realized the existence of these problems and to have understood their importance and complexity, particularly as, generally speaking, developmental psychology believed that its work was completed with the study of adolescence. Fortunately, today, certain research workers are conscious of these facts and we can hope to know more about this subject in the near furture.

Unfortunately the study of young adults is much more difficult than the study of the young child as they are less creative, and already part of an organized society that not only limits them and slows them down but sometimes even rouses them to revolt. We know, however, that the study of the child and the adolescent can help us understand the further development of the individual as an adult and that, in turn, the new research on young adults will retroactively throw light on what we already think we know about earlier stages.

Author's address: Prof. JEAN PIAGET, Université de Genève, Ecole de Psychologie et des Sciences de l'Education, Palais Wilson, *CH-1211 Genève 14* (Switzerland)

EGOCENTRISM IN ADOLESCENCE

DAVID ELKIND

University of Rochester

This paper describes the different forms of egocentrism characteristic of each of the major stages of cognitive growth outlined by Piaget. Particular attention is paid to the egocentrism of adolescence which is here described as the failure to differentiate between the cognitive concerns of others and those of the self. This adolescent egocentrism is said to give rise to 2 mental constructions, the imaginary audience and the personal fable, which help to account for certain forms of adolescent behavior and experience. These considerations suggest, it is concluded, that the cognitive structures peculiar to a given age period can provide insights with respect to the personality characteristics of that age level.

Within the Piagetian theory of intellectual growth, the concept of egocentrism generally refers to a lack of differentiation in some area of subject-object interaction (Piaget, 1962). At each stage of mental development, this lack of differentiation takes a unique form and is manifested in a unique set of behaviors. The transition from one form of egocentrism to another takes place in a dialectic fashion such that the mental structures which free the child from a lower form of egocentrism are the same structures which ensnare him in a higher form of egocentrism. From the developmental point of view, therefore, egocentrism can be regarded as a negative by-product of any emergent mental system in the sense that it corresponds to the fresh cognitive problems engendered by that system.

Although in recent years Piaget has focused his attention more on the positive than on the negative products of mental structures, egocentrism continues to be of interest because of its relation to the affective aspects of child thought and behavior. Indeed, it is possible that the study of egocentrism may provide a bridge between the study of cognitive structure, on the one hand, and the exploration of personality dynamics, on the other

Preparation of this paper was supported in part by grant No. 6881 from the Office of Education. Author's address: Department of Psychology, University of Rochester, Rochester, New York 14627.

13

(Cowan, 1966; Gourevitch & Feffer, 1962). The purpose of the present paper is to describe, in greater detail than Inhelder and Piaget (1958), what seems to me to be the nature of egocentrism in adolescence and some of its behavioral and experiential correlates. Before doing that, however, it might be well to set the stage for the discussion with a brief review of the forms of egocentrism which precede this mode of thought in adolescence.

FORMS OF EGOCENTRISM IN INFANCY AND CHILDHOOD

In presenting the childhood forms of egocentrism, it is useful to treat each of Piaget's major stages as if it were primarily concerned with resolving one major cognitive task. The egocentrism of a particular stage can then be described with reference to this special problem of cognition. It must be stressed, however, that while the cognitive task characteristic of a particular stage seems to attract the major share of the child's mental energies, it is not the only cognitive problem with which the child is attempting to cope. In mental development there are major battles and minor skirmishes, and if I here ignore the lesser engagements it is for purposes of economy of presentation rather than because I assume that such engagements are insignificant.

Sensori-motor Egocentrism (0–2 Years)

The major cognitive task of infancy might be regarded as *the conquest of the object*. In the early months of life, the infant deals with objects as if their existence were dependent upon their being present in immediate perception (Charlesworth, 1966; Piaget, 1954). The egocentrism of this stage corresponds, therefore, to a lack of differentiation between the object and the sense impressions occasioned by it. Toward the end of the first year, however, the infant begins to seek the object even when it is hidden, and thus shows that he can now differentiate between the object and the "experience of the object." This breakdown of egocentrism with respect to objects is brought about by mental representation of the absent object.[1] An internal representation of the absent object is the earliest manifestation of the symbolic function which develops gradually during the second year of life and whose activities dominate the next stage of mental growth.

Pre-operational Egocentrism (2–6 Years)

During the preschool period, the child's major cognitive task can be regarded as *the conquest of the symbol*. It is during the preschool period that the symbolic function becomes fully active, as evidenced by the rapid

---

[1] It is characteristic of the dialectic of mental growth that the capacity to represent internally the absent object also enables the infant to cognize the object as externally existent

growth in the acquisition and utilization of language, by the appearance of symbolic play, and by the first reports of dreams. Yet this new capacity for representation, which loosed the infant from his egocentrism with respect to objects, now ensnares the preschool children in a new egocentrism with regard to symbols. At the beginning of this period, the child fails to differentiate between words and their referents (Piaget, 1952b) and between his self-created play and dream symbols and reality (Kohlberg, 1966; Piaget, 1951). Children at this stage believe that the name inheres in the thing and that an object cannot have more than one name (Elkind, 1961a, 1962, 1963).

The egocentrism of this period is particularly evident in children's linguistic behavior. When explaining a piece of apparatus to another child, for example, the youngster at this stage uses many indefinite terms and leaves out important information (Piaget, 1952b). Although this observation is sometimes explained by saying that the child fails to take the other person's point of view, it can also be explained by saying that the child assumes words carry much more information than they actually do. This results from his belief that even the indefinite "thing" somehow conveys the properties of the object which it is used to represent. In short, the egocentrism of this period consists in a lack of clear differentiation between symbols and their referents.

Toward the end of the pre-operational period, the differentiation between symbols and their referents is gradually brought about by the emergence of concrete operations (internalized actions which are roughly comparable in their activity to the elementary operations of arithmetic). One consequence of concrete operational thought is that it enables the child to deal with two elements, properties, or relations at the same time. A child with concrete operations can, for example, take account of both the height and width of a glass of colored liquid and recognize that, when the liquid is poured into a differently shaped container, the changes in height and width of the liquid compensate one another so that the total quantity of liquid is conserved (Elkind, 1961b; Piaget, 1952a). This ability, to hold two dimensions in mind at the same time, also enables the child to hold both symbol and referent in mind simultaneously, and thus distinguish between them. Concrete operations are, therefore, instrumental in overcoming the egocentrism of the preoperational stage.

Concrete Operational Egocentrism (7–11 Years)

With the emergence of concrete operations, the major cognitive task of the school-age child becomes that of *mastering classes, relations, and quantities.* While the preschool child forms global notions of classes, relations, and quantities, such notions are imprecise and cannot be combined one with the other. The child with concrete operations, on the other hand,

1027

15

can nest classes, seriate relations, and conserve quantities. In addition, concrete operations enable the school-age child to perform elementary syllogistic reasoning and to formulate hypotheses and explanations about concrete matters. This system of concrete operations, however, which lifts the school-age child to new heights of thought, nonetheless lowers him to new depths of egocentrism.

Operations are essentially mental tools whose products, series, class hierarchies, conservations, etc., are not directly derived from experience. At this stage, however, the child nonetheless regards these mental products as being on a par with perceptual phenomena. It is the inability to differentiate clearly between mental constructions and perceptual givens which constitutes the egocentrism of the school-age child. An example may help to clarify the form which egocentrism takes during the concrete operational stage.

In a study reported by Peel (1960), children and adolescents were read a passage about Stonehenge and then asked questions about it. One of the questions had to do with whether Stonehenge was a place for religious worship or a fort. The children (ages 7–10) answered the question with flat statements, as if they were stating a fact. When they were given evidence that contradicted their statements, they rationalized the evidence to make it conform with their initial position. Adolescents, on the other hand, phrased their replies in probabilistic terms and supported their judgments with material gleaned from the passage. Similar differences between children and adolescents have been found by Elkind (1966) and Weir (1964).

What these studies show is that, when a child constructs a hypothesis or formulates a strategy, he assumes that this product is imposed by the data rather than derived from his own mental activity. When his position is challenged, he does not change his stance but, on the contrary, reinterprets the data to fit with his assumption. This observation, however, raises a puzzling question. Why, if the child regards both his thought products and the givens of perception as coming from the environment, does he nonetheless give preference to his own mental constructions? The answer probably lies in the fact that the child's mental constructions are the product of reasoning, and hence are experienced as imbued with a (logical) necessity. This "felt" necessity is absent when the child experiences the products of perception. It is not surprising, then, that the child should give priority to what seems permanent and necessary in perception (the products of his own thought, such as conservation) rather than to what seems transitory and arbitrary in perception (products of environmental stimulation). Only in adolescence do young people differentiate between their own mental constructions and the givens of perception. For the child, there are no problems of epistemology.

Toward the end of childhood, the emergence of formal operational thought (which is analogous to propositional logic) gradually frees the child from his egocentrism with respect to his own mental constructions. As

1028

16

Inhelder and Piaget (1958) have shown, formal operational thought enables the young person to deal with all of the possible combinations and permutations of elements within a given set. Provided with four differently colored pieces of plastic, for example, the adolescent can work out all the possible combinations of colors by taking the pieces one, two, three and four, and none, at a time. Children, on the other hand, cannot formulate these combinations in any systematic way. The ability to conceptualize all of the possible combinations in a system allows the adolescent to construct contrary-to-fact hypotheses and to reason about such propositions "as if" they were true. The adolescent, for example, can accept the statement, "Let's suppose coal is white," whereas the child would reply, "But coal is black." This ability to formulate contrary-to-fact hypotheses is crucial to the overcoming of the egocentrism of the concrete operational period. Through the formulation of such contrary-to-fact hypotheses, the young person discovers the arbitrariness of his own mental constructions and learns to differentiate them from perceptual reality.

ADOLESCENT EGOCENTRISM

From the strictly cognitive point of view (as opposed to the psychoanalytic point of view as represented by Blos [1962] and A. Freud [1946] or the ego psychological point of view as represented by Erikson [1959]), the major task of early adolescence can be regarded as having to do with *the conquest of thought.* Formal operations not only permit the young person to construct all the possibilities in a system and construct contrary-to-fact propositions (Inhelder & Piaget, 1958); they also enable him to conceptualize his own thought, to take his mental constructions as objects and reason about them. Only at about the ages of 11–12, for example, do children spontaneously introduce concepts of belief, intelligence, and faith into their definitions of their religious denomination (Elkind, 1961a; 1962; 1963). Once more, however, this new mental system which frees the young person from the egocentrism of childhood entangles him in a new form of egocentrism characteristic of adolescence.

Formal operational thought not only enables the adolescent to conceptualize his thought, it also permits him to conceptualize the thought of other people. It is this capacity to take account of other people's thought, however, which is the crux of adolescent egocentrism. This egocentrism emerges because, while the adolescent can now cognize the thoughts of others, he fails to differentiate between the objects toward which the thoughts of others are directed and those which are the focus of his own concern. Now, it is well known that the young adolescent, because of the psysiological metamorphosis he is undergoing, is primarily concerned with himself. Accordingly, since he fails to differentiate between what others are thinking about and his own mental preoccupations, he assumes that other people are as obsessed with his behavior and appearance as he is himself. *It is this belief that others are preoccupied with his appearance and behavior that constitutes the egocentrism of the adolescent.*

One consequence of adolescent egocentrism is that, in actual or impending social situations, the young person anticipates the reactions of other people to himself. These anticipations, however, are based on the premise that others are as admiring or as critical of him as he is of himself. In a sense, then, the adolescent is continually constructing, or reacting to, *an imaginary audience.* It is an audience because the adolescent believes that he will be the focus of attention; and it is imaginary because, in actual social situations, this is not usually the case (unless he contrives to make it so). The construction of imaginary audiences would seem to account, in part at least, for a wide variety of typical adolescent behaviors and experiences.

The imaginary audience, for example, probably plays a role in the self-consciousness which is so characteristic of early adolescence. When the young person is feeling critical of himself, he anticipates that the audience —of which he is necessarily a part—will be critical too. And, since the audience is his own construction and privy to his own knowledge of himself, it knows just what to look for in the way of cosmetic and behavioral sensitivities. The adolescent's wish for privacy and his reluctance to reveal himself may, to some extent, be a reaction to the feeling of being under the constant critical scrutiny of other people. The notion of an imaginary audience also helps to explain the observation that the affect which most concerns adolescents is not guilt but, rather, shame, that is, the reaction to an audience (Lynd, 1961).

While the adolescent is often self-critical, he is frequently self-admiring too. At such times, the audience takes on the same affective coloration. A good deal of adolescent boorishness, loudness, and faddish dress is probably provoked, partially in any case, by a failure to differentiate between what the young person believes to be attractive and what others admire. It is for this reason that the young person frequently fails to understand why adults disapprove of the way he dresses and behaves. The same sort of egocentrism is often seen in behavior directed toward the opposite sex. The boy who stands in front of the mirror for 2 hours combing his hair is probably imagining the swooning reactions he will produce in the girls. Likewise, the girl applying her makeup is more likely than not imagining the admiring glances that will come her way. When these young people actually meet, each is more concerned with being the observed than with being the observer. Gatherings of young adolescents are unique in the sense that each young person is simultaneously an actor to himself and an audience to others.

One of the most common admiring audience constructions, in the adolescent, is the anticipation of how others will react to his own demise. A certain bittersweet pleasure is derived from anticipating the belated recognition by others of his positive qualities. As often happens with such universal fantasies, the imaginary anticipation of one's own demise has been realized in fiction. Below, for example, is the passage in *Tom Sawyer* where Tom sneaks back to his home, after having run away with Joe and Huck, to discover that he and his friends are thought to have been drowned:

> But this memory was too much for the old lady, and she broke entirely down. Tom was snuffling, now, himself—and more in pity of himself than anybody else. He could hear Mary crying and putting in a kindly word for him from time to time. He began to have a nobler opinion of himself than ever before. Still, he was sufficiently touched by his aunt's grief to long to rush out from under the bed and overwhelm her with joy—and the theatrical gorgeousness of the thing appealed strongly to his nature too—but he resisted and lay still.

Corresponding to the imaginary audience is another mental construction which is its complement. While the adolescent fails to differentiate the concerns of his own thought from those of others, he at the same time over-differentiates his feelings. Perhaps because he believes he is of importance to so many people, the imaginary audience, he comes to regard himself, and particularly his feelings, as something special and unique. Only he can suffer with such agonized intensity, or experience such exquisite rapture. How many parents have been confronted with the typically adolescent phrase, "But you don't know how it feels. . . ." The emotional torments undergone by Goethe's young Werther and by Salinger's Holden Caulfield exemplify the adolescent's belief in the uniqueness of his own emotional experience. At a somewhat different level, this belief in personal uniqueness becomes a conviction that he will not die, that death will happen to others but not to him. This complex of beliefs in the uniqueness of his feelings and of his immortality might be called *a personal fable*, a story which he tells himself and which is not true.

Evidences of the personal fable are particularly prominent in adolescent diaries. Such diaries are often written for posterity in the conviction that the young person's experiences, crushes, and frustrations are of universal significance and importance. Another kind of evidence for the personal fable during this period is the tendency to confide in a personal God. The search for privacy and the belief in personal uniqueness leads to the establishment of an I-Thou relationship with God as a personal confident to whom one no longer looks for gifts but rather for guidance and support (Long, Elkind, & Spilka, 1967).

The concepts of an imaginary audience and a personal fable have proved useful, at least to the writer, in the understanding and treatment of troubled adolescents. The imaginary audience, for example, seems often to play a role in middle-class delinquency (Elkind, 1967). As a case in point, one young man took $1,000 from a golf tournament purse, hid the money, and then promptly revealed himself. It turned out that much of the motivation for this act was derived from the anticipated response of "the

1031

19

audience" to the guttiness of his action. In a similar vein, many young girls become pregnant because, in part at least, their personal fable convinces them that pregnancy will happen to others but never to them and so they need not take precautions. Such examples could be multiplied but will perhaps suffice to illustrate how adolescent egocentrism, as manifested in the imaginary audience and in the personal fable, can help provide a rationale for some adolescent behavior. These concepts can, moreover, be utilized in the treatment of adolescent offenders. It is often helpful to these young people if they can learn to differentiate between the real and the imaginary audience, which often boils down to a discrimination between the real and the imaginary parents.

THE PASSING OF ADOLESCENT EGOCENTRISM

After the appearance of formal operational thought, no new mental systems develop and the mental structures of adolescence must serve for the rest of the life span. The egocentrism of early adolescence nonetheless tends to diminish by the age of 15 or 16, the age at which formal operations become firmly established. What appears to happen is that the imaginary audience, which is primarily an anticipatory audience, is progressively modified in the direction of the reactions of the real audience. In a way, the imaginary audience can be regarded as hypothesis—or better, as a series of hypotheses—which the young person tests against reality. As a consequence of this testing, he gradually comes to recognize the difference between his own preoccupations and the interests and concerns of others.

The personal fable, on the other hand, is probably overcome (although probably never in its entirety) by the gradual establishment of what Erikson (1959) has called "intimacy." Once the young person sees himself in a more realistic light as a function of having adjusted his imaginary audience to the real one, he can establish true rather than self-interested interpersonal relations. Once relations of mutuality are established and confidences are shared, the young person discovers that others have feelings similar to his own and have suffered and been enraptured in the same way.

Adolescent egocentrism is thus overcome by a twofold transformation. On the cognitive plane, it is overcome by the gradual differentiation between his own preoccupations and the thoughts of others; while on the plane of affectivity, it is overcome by a gradual integration of the feelings of others with his own emotions.

SUMMARY AND CONCLUSIONS

In this paper I have tried to describe the forms which egocentrism takes and the mechanisms by which it is overcome, in the course of mental development. In infancy, egocentrism corresponds to the impression that

1032

objects are identical with the perception of them, and this form of egocentrism is overcome with the appearance of representation. During the preschool period, egocentrism appears in the guise of a belief that symbols contain the same information as is provided by the objects which they represent. With the emergence of concrete operations, the child is able to discriminate between symbol and referent, and so overcome this type of egocentrism. The egocentrism of the school-age period can be characterized as the belief that one's own mental constructions correspond to a superior form of perceptual reality. With the advent of formal operations and the ability to construct contrary-to-fact hypotheses, this kind of egocentrism is dissolved because the young person can now recognize the arbitrariness of his own mental constructions. Finally, during early adolescence, egocentrism appears as the belief that the thoughts of others are directed toward the self. This variety of egocentrism is overcome as a consequence of the conflict between the reactions which the young person anticipates and those which actually occur.

Although egocentrism corresponds to a negative product of mental growth, its usefulness would seem to lie in the light which it throws upon the affective reactions characteristic of any particular stage of mental development. In this paper I have dealt primarily with the affective reactions associated with the egocentrism of adolescence. Much of the material, particularly the discussion of the *imaginary audience* and the *personal fable* is speculative in the sense that it is based as much upon my clinical experience with young people as it is upon research data. These constructs are offered, not as the final word on adolescent egocentrism, but rather to illustrate how the cognitive structures peculiar to a particular level of development can be related to the affective experience and behavior characteristic of that stage. Although I have here only considered the correspondence between mental structure and affect in adolescence, it is possible that similar correspondences can be found at the earlier levels of development as well. A consideration of egocentrism, then, would seem to be a useful starting point for any attempt to reconcile cognitive structure and the dynamics of personality.

REFERENCES

Blos, P. *On adolescence.* New York: Free Press, 1962.

Charlesworth, W. R. Development of the object concept in infancy: methodological study. *American Psychologist,* 1966, **21,** 623. (Abstract)

Cowan, P. A. Cognitive egocentrism and social interaction in children. *American Psychologist,* 1966, **21,** 623. (Abstract)

Elkind, D. The child's conception of his religious denomination, I: The Jewish child. *Journal of genetic Psychology,* 1961, **99,** 209–225. (a)

Elkind, D. The development of quantitative thinking. *Journal of genetic Psychology,* 1961, **98,** 37–46. (b)

Elkind, D. The child's conception of his religious denomination, II: The Catholic child. *Journal of genetic Psychology,* 1962, **101,** 185–193.

Elkind, D. The child's conception of his religious denomination, III: The Protestant child. *Journal of genetic Pschology,* 1963, **103,** 291–304.

Elkind, D. Conceptual orientation shifts in children and adolescents. *Child Development,* 1966, **37,** 493–498.

Elkind, D. Middle-class delinquency. *Mental Hygiene,* 1967, **51,** 80–84.

Erikson, E. H. Identity and the life cycle. *Psychological issues.* Vol. 1, No. 1, New York: International Universities Press, 1959.

Freud, Anna. *The ego and the mechanisms of defense.* New York International Universities Press, 1946.

Gourevitch, Vivian, & Feffer, M. H. A study of motivational development. *Journal of genetic Psychology,* 1962, **100,** 361–375.

Inhelder, Bärbel, & Piaget, J. *The growth of logical thinking from childhood to adolescence.* New York: Basic Books, 1958.

Kohlberg, L. Cognitive stages and preschool education. *Human Development,* 1966, **9,** 5–17.

Long, Diane, Elkind, D., & Spilka, B. The child's conception of prayer. *Journal for the scientific Study of Religion,* 1967, **6,** 101–109.

Lynd, Helen M. *On shame and the search for identity.* New York: Science Editions, 1961.

Peel, E. A. *The pupil's thinking.* London: Oldhourne, 1960.

Piaget, J. *The child's conception of the world.* London: Routledge & Kegan Paul, 1951.

Piaget, J. *The child's conception of number.* New York: Humanities Press, 1952. (a)

Piaget, J. *The language and thought of the child.* London: Routledge & Kegan Paul, 1952. (b)

Piaget, J. *The construction of reality in the child.* New York: Basic Books, 1954.

Piaget, J. Comments on Vygotsky's critical remarks concerning "The language and thought of the child" and "Judgment and reasoning in the child." Cambridge, Mass.: M. I. T. Press, 1962.

Weir, M. W. Development changes in problem solving strategies. *Psychological Review,* 1964, **71,** 473–490.

1034

22

Formal Reasoning among Pre- and Late Adolescents

Deanna Kuhn
Harvard University

Victoria Ho and Catherine Adams
California State University, Fullerton

KUHN, DEANNA; HO, VICTORIA; and ADAMS, CATHERINE. *Formal Reasoning among Pre- and Late Adolescents.* CHILD DEVELOPMENT, 1979, **50**, 1128–1135. The purpose of this study was to explore the sense in which older adolescents and adults may, as earlier research has suggested, lack the competence to reason at a formal operational level. 2 groups of subjects were isolated who showed no evidence of formal reasoning on isolation-of-variables assessment problems. 1 group consisted of preadolescents and the other first-year college students. Despite the initial matching of the 2 groups, when subjects were (a) administered additional kinds of assessment problems and (b) presented repeated problems over a period of months most of the college subjects showed immediate and substantial formal reasoning, while the preadolescents made only gradual, modest gains. It was concluded that the 2 groups were not at all "nonformal-operational" in an equivalent sense. The possibility was considered that the absence of a formal operational level of performance on the part of many older adolescents or adults may to a large extent reflect cognitive processing difficulties in dealing with the problem formats, rather than absence of underlying reasoning competencies.

A number of studies of Piaget's stage of formal operations have suggested that, unlike the earlier stages, this final stage in Piaget's sequence is not attained universally (Hooper & Sheehan 1977; Keating 1979; Kuhn 1979; Neimark 1975). As a result, Piaget's formal operations stage has been of special interest to educators. The educator's concerns have been focused on one of two issues. One has to do with what sorts of educational experiences children should have early in their lives in order to maximize the likelihood that they will attain the stage of formal operations (e.g., Kamii & DeVries 1977). A second issue has to do with how the apparent lack of formal reasoning ability among older adolescents and adults might be remedied.

This latter area of concern has given rise to a number of experimental educational programs aimed at promoting formal reasoning among beginning college students (Staff of Project ADAPT, Note 1). There are a number of reasons to be cautious in drawing conclusions from these educational experiments. First, we have only an intuitive understanding of the relationship between formal operational reasoning and academic performance in high school or college. There exist few empirical data in this regard. And one preliminary study (Commons, Miller, & Kuhn, Note 2) has suggested that there may be a relationship for certain academic subjects (science and mathematics) but not others.

A second, even more basic reason for caution is that we have a very incomplete understanding of the sense in which adolescents and young adults may be "nonformal operational." It is to this second concern that the present study is addressed. It may be that psychologists and educators are embarking on the task of inducing "formal operations" in college students without sufficient understanding of the particular problems and/or deficits that college-level students face in utilizing formal reasoning.

The present study focuses on two major formal operational reasoning strategies described by Inhelder and Piaget (1958)—isolation of variables and systematic combination. Rather

The authors wish to thank Noel Capon for his skilled technical assistance in constructing the chemistry problems and the Laurel School, Brea, California, for their generous cooperation. Reprints may be requested from Deanna Kuhn, Laboratory of Human Development, Graduate School of Education, Harvard University, Cambridge, Massachusetts 02138.

[*Child Development*, 1979, **50**, 1128–1135. © 1979 by the Society for Research in Child Development, Inc. 0009-3920/79/5004-0026$00.81]

than attempt to assess the formal reasoning ability of college-age subjects in some absolute sense, we thought it more meaningful to examine the performance of college subjects *relative to* the performance of younger preadolescent subjects who were just beginning to develop the competencies being investigated. Most important, in this comparative vein, we wished to compare the performance of the two groups over a period of time during which subjects were given repeated opportunities to solve problems requiring formal reasoning. It was predicted that pre- and late adolescents who showed no formal reasoning at a single initial assessment would nevertheless exhibit differences in performance over the course of a series of problem sessions.

Method

Subjects

The final sample consisted of 16 freshmen enrolled in an introductory psychology course at a large state university and 30 fourth and fifth graders from a middle-class suburban school in an adjacent community. Subjects were selected based on the absence of formal operational reasoning on the Kuhn and Brannock (1977) plant problem, designed to assess the isolation-of-variables strategy.

The manner of selection of this final sample differed in the two age groups. In the case of the college group, a preliminary screening measure was given to 701 introductory psychology students. It consisted of two written problems identical in structure (though differing in content) with the Kuhn and Brannock (1977) plant problem. Of the 701 students, 81, or 12%, showed no formal reasoning on either problem. Of the 81 students, 35 volunteered to participate in a further assessment. The plant problem was individually administered to these 35 subjects. Seventeen of these 35 showed no formal reasoning on the plant problem. Eighteen, however, showed either partial or fully formal reasoning when the problem was presented in this concrete (as opposed to the earlier written) format. (Assuming these 35 subjects were representative of the larger group of 81, it could be estimated that roughly 40, or 6%, of the entire freshman sample was nonformal operational with respect to the isolation-of-variables strategy as assessed by the plant problem.) The 17 subjects showing no formal reasoning were invited to participate in the study. One of the

17 withdrew from school shortly after the semester began and was excluded from the sample, leaving a final sample size of 16.

An initial group of 85 fourth and fifth graders was individually administered the plant problem. Of the 85, 45 exhibited no formal reasoning. Of these 45, 30 randomly selected subjects formed the present sample.

Procedure

Eleven of the 17 college subjects indicated above were assigned to an experimental group and six to a control group. The 11 experimental subjects were asked to attend a series of problem-solving sessions to take place during the remainder of the semester. Subjects were told the problems they would be presented were of a kind that would give them practice in logical reasoning skills. It was explained that they would be required to attend an individual 20–30-min session each week, scheduled at the student's convenience, during which a graduate teaching assistant would present various problems. For their participation, students were told, they would receive one unit of independent study course credit. All 11 subjects accepted the invitation and completed the project. The six control subjects were asked to participate in two assessment sessions, one immediately and another at the end of the semester. One of the six withdrew from school after the first assessment and was excluded from the sample, as indicated above.

Fifteen of the 30 preadolescent subjects were assigned to an experimental group and 15 to a control group. Experimental subjects were told that the investigator was conducting a study of children's thinking and that she would be asking them to come to her laboratory room once each week to work on some problems.

The procedure beyond this point was identical for the preadolescent and college subjects. In overview, all subjects underwent the initial assessment to be described below. Experimental subjects then participated in an 11-week series of problem-solving sessions, also described below. During the subsequent 2 weeks, the initial assessment problems were readministered to all subjects. They were administered to all subjects again 4 months later, at the beginning of the next school year.

Initial assessment.—All subjects had been administered the Kuhn and Brannock (1977) plant problem as part of the subject selection, as indicated earlier. Those subjects selected for the final sample were presented two additional assessment problems. One was the complex plant problem (Kuhn & Ho 1977), which was used as an alternative assessment of the isolation-of-variables strategy. The other problem was designed to assess the strategy of systematic combination.[1] The subject was given a supply of five kinds of candy and a supply of dishes and asked to fill as many dishes as necessary to show what all of the people at a party might choose to eat, given the conditions (a) no one was allowed to take more than one of each kind of candy, and (b) no two dishes looked exactly the same.

Problem-solving sessions.—For subjects in the experimental conditions, the problem-solving sessions began 1 week later and continued for 11 weeks. Each subject met individually with a female graduate student once a week for 20–30 min. A school vacation extended the total intervention period to 12 weeks.

The procedure was of the nondirective type used by Kuhn and Angelev (1976). Its purpose was not to teach or otherwise attempt to supply subjects with formal reasoning strategies; rather, it was simply to give subjects repeated opportunities to encounter problems requiring formal reasoning. Inhelder and Piaget's (1958) chemicals problem was used as a point of departure in constructing the series of problems. The problems required application of a combinatorial strategy and an isolation-of-variables strategy for effective solution.

The experimental material for each session consisted of (a) a supply of colorless, odorless, liquids in 2–3 dram, snap-top vials, labeled with different letters, B, C, D, E, or F; (b) a large reagent bottle labeled A and referred to as "mixing liquid"; (c) an assortment of 50–100-ml glass beakers, for mixing. In the initial problem of the series, one of the liquids (B) was sufficient when combined with the mixing liquid to produce a chemical reaction, either a color change or a precipitate. To demonstrate the reaction for the subject, the experimenter selected three vials labeled B, C, and D and emptied them into a beaker. The empty labeled vials were placed adjacent to the beaker in order to identify the components of the mixture. The experimenter then selected three vials labeled D, E, and F and mixed them in an identical manner. She then added some mixing liquid to both beakers, and the subject

observed that the first mixture turned either red or cloudy while the second mixture remained colorless.

The subject was then asked (1) What do you think makes a difference in whether it turns red (cloudy) or not? (2) How do you know? (3) Can you be sure what makes a difference? (Alternate: What makes it turn red/cloudy?) (Why/why not?) (4) (If subject mentions only some liquids as operative) Do the others have anything to do with it? Which ones? How do you know?

The subject was then invited to "try different ways of doing it" to determine what caused the reaction. The subject was encouraged to plan as many experiments as he or she wished, by setting up the appropriate vials next to a beaker. After the subject indicated he had set up as many "ways of doing it" as he desired, the following questions were asked before the actual mixing began: (5) What do you think you will find out by trying it these ways? (6) How do you think it's going to come out? Why?

The experimenter then assisted the subject in mixing the chemicals, following which she asked (7) What do you think about how it's turned out? (8) What did we find out? Questions 1–4 were then repeated.

Thus, while the experimenter asked questions that encouraged the subject to analyze and attempt to interpret what was being observed, no solutions to the problem or strategies for obtaining a solution were suggested. Nor were the subjects given any reinforcement for the strategies they did employ or for any subsequent modifications in these strategies. The only feedback subjects received was from their own actions on the physical materials.

At the next session it was explained that the liquids inside the vials were not necessarily the same ones that had been there the previous week, and therefore the subject could not be sure the results would be the same. The procedure for each of the 11 sessions was identical with that described above. The series of seven problems progressed from one in which a single one of the five liquids produced the reaction, to ones in which any of two or three could produce it, and finally to ones in which combinations of two or three liquids were necessary.

[1] We thank Barnaby Barratt for suggesting this mode of presenting the combinations problem.

The subject's own performance determined the rate of progress through the sequence. A subject was considered to have mastered a given problem type only when, in response to questions 1–4, the subject isolated the effective variable, or combination of variables, and correctly specified the remaining variables as inoperative. Each problem type was presented on successive occasions until the subject achieved mastery. For repeated presentations, the specific variable or variable combination that was effective and sometimes the nature of the chemical reaction were altered, but the underlying problem structure remained the same.

Posttest assessments.—The three initial assessment problems were readministered to both experimental and control subjects following the final problem session. Subjects were contacted 4 months later, during the early part of the next school year, and asked to participate in a final, follow-up assessment. One experimental college subject, one experimental preadolescent subject, and two preadolescent control subjects were unavailable for this follow-up assessment.

Results

Preadolescent Sample
Initial assessment.—Consistent with their concrete operational performance on the simple plant problem, preadolescent subjects showed little evidence of formal thought on the more extended assessment. Four of the 30 subjects showed some emergent formal reasoning in the complex plant problem (level 1, Kuhn & Ho 1977); the remainder reasoned at a purely concrete level. In the combinations problem, six of the 30 showed some emergent formal reasoning; the remainder reasoned at a purely concrete level.[2]

Problem-solving sessions.—Also, as would be predicted from their initial performance, subjects initially showed little ability to generate systematic combinations of liquids or to isolate the effective variable. A subject typically, for example, upon observing that $B + C + D$ produced the reaction, concluded that it was the combination of all three that had produced it (the logical error of false inclusion).

During the course of the sessions, however, 12 of the 15 subjects were successful in constructing new reasoning strategies. By the final session, one subject had mastered problem 5 in the series of seven, one had mastered problem 4, two problem 3, four problem 2 and four problem 1, while the remaining three subjects remained at problem 1. Advancement, however, tended to be slow and gradual, with many subjects showing progress only toward the end of the 12-week period, after repeated encounters with problem 1.

Posttest assessments.—Analysis of posttest scores indicated that while subjects showed significant progress from initial to subsequent assessments they did not completely generalize their newly developed reasoning schemes to the different contexts represented by the posttest problems. Of those 12 subjects who mastered problem 1 in the series, for example, five reached only a transitional level in the simple plant problem and one remained at the concrete level. Also, there was significant loss from first to second posttest, as summarized in table 1, especially on the simple plant problem. On the simple plant problem, pretest-posttest 1 difference scores were significantly different for experimentals and controls, $t(28) = 3.19$, $p < .01$, but pretest-posttest 2 difference scores were not. On the complex plant

TABLE 1

MEAN DIFFERENCE SCORES FOR
PREADOLESCENT SAMPLE

	Experimental	Control
Simple plant problem:		
Pretest-posttest 1	2.53	.33
Pretest-posttest 2	1.57	1.00
Complex plant problem:		
Pretest-posttest 1	1.80	.27
Pretest-posttest 2	1.64	.54
Combinations problem:		
Pretest-posttest 1	.73	.00
Pretest-posttest 2	.29	.00

NOTE.—These difference scores are virtually identical with the actual posttest scores, as almost all pretest scores were zero (see text). A formal level of reasoning is equivalent to a numerical score of 4 on the simple plant problem. On the other two problems a score of 3 is equivalent to early formal and a score of 4 equivalent to consolidated formal. Means are based on all 15 subjects in each condition, even though not all 15 experimental subjects progressed during the series (see text).

[2] Copies of the scoring systems for all problems, as well as a complete description of the series of problems, are available from the first author. High interscorer reliability has been established for all three assessment problems (see Kuhn and Brannock [1977] and Kuhn and Ho [1977] regarding the plant problems and Kuhn and Angelev [1976] regarding the combinations problem). Scoring in the present study was done independently and blind by two scorers and differences resolved by discussion.

27

problem, experimentals and controls differed significantly on both pretest-posttest 1 difference scores, $t(28) = 4.41$, $p < .01$, and pretest-posttest 2 difference scores, $t(25) = 2.44$, $p < .05$. On the combinations problem, the difference between experimentals and controls was significant for the pretest-posttest 1 interval, $t(28) = 3.10$, $p < .01$, and of marginal significance for the pretest-posttest 2 interval, $t(25) = 1.38$, $p < .10$.

College Sample

Initial assessment.—Inconsistent with their concrete operational performance on the simple plant problem, and in contrast to the preadolescent sample, college subjects did show a significant incidence of formal reasoning on the two additional assessment problems. On the complex plant problem, three of the 16 subjects performed at the concrete level, two at the emergent formal level, nine at the transitional level, and two at the early formal level. On the combinations problem, eight subjects performed at the concrete level, two at the emergent formal level, two at the transitional level, and four at the early formal level.

Problem-solving sessions.—The performance of the 11 experimental subjects on the series of problems is even more striking. Six of the 11 exhibited immediate experimental isolation of the variables, (liquids) and drew the appropriate inference as to the single operative variable. The remaining five did not initially (i.e., at the first session) isolate the variables experimentally but devised and tested enough combinations so as to permit them to draw an appropriate inductive inference as to which single variable was responsible for the effect, which all did correctly. In subsequent problem sessions these five subjects all went on to perform an experimental isolation of the variables to systematically test their effects; four did so by session 2 and one by session 4. Over the course of the 11 sessions, one subject achieved mastery of problem 6, four of problem 5, five of problem 4, and one subject only of problem 1.

Posttest assessments.—In contrast to the preadolescent sample, the college subjects showed a very high level of generalization of their formal reasoning performance to the posttest problems. At the initial posttest, eight of the 11 performed at a formal level on the simple plant problem, eight at a formal level on the complex plant problem, and five at a formal level on the combinations problem. Further-

more, and again in contrast to the preadolescent sample, performance either improved or remained stable between posttests; there were no declines. At the second posttest, the numbers of subjects performing at the formal level (of 10) were eight, nine, and seven on the three problems, respectively. It was also the case, however, that control subjects showed substantial improvement from initial to first posttest and from first to second posttest, again in contrast to the preadolescent sample. Thus, repeated presentation of the initial problems was evidently sufficient to enhance performance for these subjects. For each of the six comparisons (three problems and two intervals) approximately half the subjects showed improvement while half remained stable. Difference scores are given in table 2. Because of the control group improvement (but contributed to as well by ceiling effects for the experimental subjects) none of the experimental/control comparisons in table 2 was statistically significant.

Discussion

The results for the preadolescent sample substantiate those reported by Kuhn and Angelev (1976), who used a similar method with the same-age subjects: Preadolescents make significant progress in the construction of formal reasoning strategies when given the opportunity to encounter problems requiring formal reasoning over a period of months. In current work, we are examining the protocols from the sequence of problem-solving sessions for what they may reveal about the nature of the construction process (Kuhn & Phelps, in press).

Results of the present study indicated that preadolescent subjects did not completely

TABLE 2

MEAN DIFFERENCE SCORES
FOR COLLEGE SAMPLE

	Experimental	Control
Simple plant problem:		
Pretest-posttest 1........	3.27	1.20
Pretest-posttest 2,.......	3.70	1.80
Complex plant problem:		
Pretest-posttest 1........	1.55	.60
Pretest-posttest 2........	2.20	1.00
Combinations problem:		
Pretest-posttest 1........	.55	.00
Pretest-posttest 2........	.80	−.20

28

generalize their new strategies to other contexts, nor did they fully maintain their new levels of competence in the absence of continued experience in the problem-solving environment. These latter results, however, cannot be taken as evidence that the construction of new reasoning strategies that did occur was in some way not "genuine" (the sort of inference that is often made in an intervention study in which cognitive strategies have been modeled or explicitly taught), since the subject himself or herself initiated any change that occurred. These particular findings do suggest that newly developed reasoning schemes are only gradually extended to new contexts (the phenomenon commonly referred to under Piaget's term of "decalage"). And they also suggest that newly developed reasoning schemes are not necessarily maintained if the opportunities for their use diminish.

We turn now to the central issue addressed by this study—the formal operational reasoning ability of late-adolescent college students. The first result that warrants emphasis is that it was necessary to sample very widely among a college freshman population in order to obtain a group of reasonable size who showed no evidence of formal reasoning, as assessed by the plant problem. Our estimate of 6% is substantially lower than a number of previous estimates based on the traditional Inhelder and Piaget (1958) assessment problems. On the one hand this is not surprising, since the plant problem employs a concrete, familiar problem context and assesses the isolation-of-variables strategy in a form more like that in which it is likely to be utilized in a subject's real-life reasoning. Yet, it is exactly these kinds of findings that raise a very basic issue in the assessment of formal reasoning: To what extent does the absence of a formal operational level of performance reflect genuine absence of the underlying reasoning competencies, as opposed to difficulties in dealing with the format in terms of which these competencies are being assessed?

The remaining results of the present study clearly serve to underscore this issue as a fundamental one. Formal operational reasoning strategies were assessed in a variety of contexts. In none of these contexts did the preadolescent subjects initially show any significant evidence of formal operational reasoning. Some gradual development of formal operational strategies, however, was observed during the course of the problem-solving series. In the college sample, in contrast, subjects equated with the preadolescents on the basis of the absence of formal reasoning in one of the assessment contexts did show substantial formal reasoning in the remaining contexts (both on initial presentation of the remaining assessment problems and in the initial sessions of the problem-solving series). Thus, while the two samples might have been judged as equivalently nonformal operational based on the single initial assessment problem, additional evidence revealed that this was not in fact the case.

As a result of these findings, we do not think it is justified to say that the development of formal operational reasoning strategies was observed among the present college sample, in the way that one can contend that this development was observed among the preadolescent sample. Rather, our interpretation is that (a) the college subjects were already at least transitional with respect to formal reasoning competence at the outset of the study, (b) this competence did not reveal itself initially due to a variety of more superficial kinds of cognitive difficulties experienced by these college students, and (c) the repeated encounters with formal reasoning problems that occurred during the problem series enabled most of these subjects to consolidate their formal reasoning competencies and thus to exhibit a fully formal level of performance by the time of the final assessment.

It should be cautioned, however, that it is not necessarily valid to attribute the entire final-assessment difference between the pre- and late adolescents to a difference in initial competence. Initial differences may have enabled the one group to take advantage of their subsequent experience (both within and outside the problem sessions) in a way the other group could not. College coursework, for example, provides more opportunity for formal reasoning than does fourth- and fifth-grade curriculum. Thus, posttest performance differences are properly regarded as the result of an interaction between initial competence and subsequent experience.

What sorts of cognitive difficulties were responsible for the poor initial performance of these college subjects? In response to this question, we can offer only our observational impression that they had to do more with certain kinds of organizational and verbal articulation difficulties than with underlying logical competence. The best way to convey what we are referring to here is by means of an illustration from the protocol of a college subject whose initial performance seemed to be characterized by this kind of difficulty and who subsequently exhibited marked progress. The example is also nicely illustrative of the character of the progress we witnessed in general among the college subjects.

In the simple plant problem the subject is asked, "Does the leaf lotion have anything to do with it?"—it being the case that one of the two plants receiving leaf lotion is sick and the other healthy and one of the two not receiving leaf lotion is sick and the other healthy. At the first administration, this subject's reply is as follows:

Yes, it matters. (How do you know?) By the look of the two plants with lotion, it would be better to leave it off. The first came out good without it, and the second and third didn't do so well with it.

The subject distorts the data, as the third plant is in fact healthy; he nevertheless understands the need to search for correspondences between variable presence and outcome (in contrast to the approach typical of the preadolescents). At the next administration, the subject's reply is:

No, it doesn't. Whether you use white or dark food, the lotion didn't change anything compared to plants with no lotion. (How can you tell?) (Subject repeats previous statement.)

Finally, 4 months later, the subject gives his most succinct, logically precise response:

The lotion has no effect since there were two plants with it and one died and the other was healthy.[3]

In conclusion, we would contend that the cautious stance advocated at the outset of this article is supported by the results of the study. In general, assumptions about cognitive competence based on small samples of behavior can be seriously misleading. It will require a good deal of further careful research in order to ascertain the exact senses in which older adolescents or adults may in fact be nonformal operational. Recent research by Danner and Day (1977) supports this same conclusion. In their study, a series of "prompts" successfully elicited previously absent formal reasoning in late but not early adolescents. The present

results are in a sense even more dramatic, in that simple (and minimal) repeated practice, without any training procedure, was sufficient to achieve this same outcome.

As the present study has suggested, then, it is necessary to establish precisely which logical reasoning strategies an individual lacks, and, most important, *those specific situations and contexts within which the strategy is lacking*. It would appear that reasoning competencies may exist in one context and yet at the same time be absent in another, seemingly closely related, one. Especially, then, when one begins to think more broadly in terms of purely naturalistic (as opposed to psychological test) contexts, such as the college classroom, it is clear that a great deal of further study will be necessary in order to understand the extent to which students employ formal reasoning strategies in these kinds of real-life contexts.

Reference Notes

1. Staff of Project ADAPT, Multidisciplinary Piagetian-based programs for college freshmen. Monograph. Lincoln: University of Nebraska, 1977.

2. Commons, M.; Miller, P.; & Kuhn, D. The relation between formal operational reasoning in college freshmen and their academic performance. Manuscript in preparation, 1979.

References

Danner, F., & Day, M. C. Eliciting formal operations. *Child Development*, 1977, **48**, 1600–1606.

Hooper, F., & Sheehan, N. Logical concept attainment during the aging years: issues in the Neo-Piagetian research literature. In W. Overton & J. Gallagher (Eds.), *Knowledge and development: advances in research and theory*. New York: Plenum, 1977.

Inhelder, B., & Piaget, J. *The growth of logical thinking from childhood to adolescence*. New York: Basic, 1958.

Keating, D. Adolescent thinking. In J. Adelson (Ed.), *Handbook of adolescence*. New York: Wiley, 1979.

Kamii, C., & DeVries, R. Piaget for early education. In M. C. Day & R. Parker (Eds.), *The preschool in action*. Boston: Allyn & Bacon, 1977.

Kuhn, D. The significance of Piaget's formal op-

[3] This conclusion is in fact logically valid of course only under the assumption that only a single variable can be operative in a situation.

erations stage in education. *Journal of Education*, 1979, **161**, 34–50.

Kuhn, D., & Angelev, J. An experimental study of the development of formal operational thought. *Child Development*, 1976, **47**, 697–706.

Kuhn, D., & Brannock, J. Development of the isolation of variables scheme in an experimental and "natural experiment" context. *Developmental Psychology*, 1977, **13**, 9–14.

Kuhn, D., & Ho, V. The development of schemes for recognizing additive and alternative ef-

fects in a "natural experiment" context. *Developmental Psychology*, 1977, **13**, 515–516.

Kuhn, D., & Phelps, E. A methodology for observing development of a formal reasoning strategy. In D. Kuhn (Ed.), *Intellectual development beyond childhood*. San Francisco: Jossey-Bass, in press.

Neimark, E. Intellectual development during adolescence. In F. Horowitz (Ed.), *Review of child development research*. Vol. **4**. Chicago: University of Chicago Press, 1975.

28 FORMAL OPERATIONS AS REGULATORY CONTEXT IN ADOLESCENCE

WILLIS F. OVERTON, JOHN H. STEIDL, DIANA ROSENSTEIN,
AND HARVEY A. HOROWITZ

A major focus of the research project on adolescent psychopathology being pursued at the Institute of Pennsylvania Hospital has been on the construction of a developmental model of self-regulation (i.e., the self as a regulator of affect and impulses). The primary characteristics of this model are that it is relational (i.e., it asserts that regulation emerges from the ongoing interactions of self and other) and developmental (i.e., it asserts that self, as an organization, goes through a series of ontogenetic phases). In ontogenesis, the earlier forms or organizations are preserved and incorporated in later novel forms. This model is designed to account for psychological risk and common vulnerability in adolescence.

In other chapters, descriptions have been presented of the basic features of the model, the manner in which attachment theory understands the progressive internalization of a relational system (i.e., the infant-caregiver dyadic system) as the early relational precursor to self-regulation, and how family interaction functions as a context for regulation. The focus of this chapter concerns the way that cognition or, more specifically, a particular form of thinking called formal operational thought may play a role in regulating the affect and behavior of the adolescent.

Formal thought first emerges in adolescence, but it has its precursors in earlier types of thinking activities. Thus, in exploring formal thought as a regulator of adolescent affect and behavior, it is first necessary to

502

consider the general developmental course of thinking and to use that ontogenetic sequence as a framework for further examinations.

Thinking

As a first approximation to considering the ontogenetic steps to formal thought, it should be noted that we are here describing a particular type of thinking, namely, logical thought or logical reasoning. Specifically, this is the type of thought usually understood as rational thought, thought whose main hallmarks are its coherence, its consistency, its precision, and its lack of contradictions. It is this logical thought that will be understood as relevant to the regulation of affect and behavior. We are not referring to a variety of other types of thinking such as fantasy thought, creative thought, and associative thought.

Jean Piaget's theory of cognitive development presents the most influential and most thoroughly empirically supported framework for considering the ontogenesis of logical thought on the scene today (see Piaget 1980, 1987; Piaget and Garcia 1986). This framework, along with a good deal of empirical work conducted in the Adolescent Reasoning Laboratory at Temple University, and also along with some theoretical contributions from the works of Heinz Werner, Harry Stack Sullivan, and Donald Winnicott, has provided the conceptual foundation for the formulation to be discussed.

With this background, we may briefly describe the steps on the way to formal operational or formal logical thought. First, beginning at birth and proceeding into the first year of life, there is no thinking and, hence, no logical thought. In this phase—which Piaget calls the sensorimotor phase—while the infant is cognitively alert, capable of discriminating signals, and fully attuned to the caregiver, he or she lacks a system of symbols detached from the objects symbolized. Because thinking is defined as the manipulation of symbols, there is no thought proper at this time. The mode of experience in the early part of this phase is like Sullivan's "prototaxic mode," Winnicott's "object relating" as distinct from the later "object use," and Werner's "things of action." The mode is also analogous to Freud's "primary process thinking" but should more appropriately be called "primary process experiencing."

Piaget's second phase—called preoperational thought—extends from somewhere around the eighteenth month up to five or six years of

503

age. This phase begins when the child constructs the first detachable symbols. These are called protosymbols because they are composed of personal nonshared experience. Thought begins in this early period, but it is highly idiosyncratic, and objects of thought have a personalized, affectively imbued meaning. This early thinking is akin to Freud's "primary process thinking" and Sullivan's parataxic mode of experience.

As this phase proceeds, thinking, while lacking traditional signs of logic, becomes generalized and further detached from the original highly idiosyncratic meanings. Here, language comes to support generalized meanings. The child moves into the early arena of Freud's "secondary process thinking" and more solidly into Sullivan's parataxic mode. As Erikson (1980, p. 78) once noted about this period, language develops to the point that the child is capable of misunderstanding almost everything he hears. If you explore the child's thought in this period, you find a sort of illusion of logic. To the observer, there appears to be a logic, but, on close inspection, it is clear that this logic rides superficially on the syntax of language rather than being a structural feature of the thought process itself. In this and the next phase as well, the child exhibits a sense of the literal.

In the third of Piaget's four phases, genuine logic begins to emerge. This phase, called the period of concrete operational thought (see Inhelder and Piaget 1964), extends from five or six up to about ten to twelve years of age. This is very much the phase of Freud's secondary process thinking, defined as ordinary, conscious thinking that is primarily verbal and follows the usual laws of syntax and logic. However, the logical thought that emerges at this time has critical limitations. It lacks generality, and it is tied to the concrete world of actual or fantasized objects and events. The child has logical thinking, but it is logical thinking about particular concrete events and particular concrete fantasies. This logical thought is embedded in a literal context of linear causes and effects. Sullivan's syntactic mode of experience begins to emerge in this phase, but it is concretely anchored in the parataxic mode.

The sensorimotor experience, the thinking of the preoperational phase, and the logical thought of the concrete operational phase are, then, the precursor forms to the organization of thought that emerges in adolescence, in the phase of formal operational thought. What develops, here, in adolescence is a kind of universal metalogic system. That

504

is, the adolescent develops a general system of logic that allows him to think about his ordinary concrete logical thinking systematically (see Inhelder and Piaget 1958).

The emergence of this new level of thought organization can have profound influences on many dimensions of the adolescent's life. However, only a brief sketch of some of these will be presented before we undertake an equally brief consideration of how this organization can play a role in the self-regulation of affect and behavior.

Formal Operational Thought: Consequences

As a preamble to sketching some of the consequences of this new formal level in the organization of thought, we should urge you to think of this acquisition as a tool rather than as an end in itself. Like any tool, once acquired, it can be used or not used (i.e., once it becomes available, it may be accessed or not accessed). Similarly, like any tool, it may be used in some situations and not in others. Finally, like any tool, it can be used for either good or ill. Not having the tool at all, or being delayed in getting it, or perhaps getting it too early, can have negative consequences. Acquiring the tool at the appropriate time, however, still leaves open the question of how it will be used.

A considerable body of contemporary research has demonstrated that formal reasoning undergoes a transformation and a well-defined developmental progression between the ages of approximately ten to eleven and seventeen to eighteen years (Bady 1979; Bucci 1978; Byrnes and Overton 1986, 1988; Moshman 1979; Moshman and Franks 1986; O'Brien and Overton 1980, 1982; Overton, Byrnes, and O'Brien 1985; Overton, Ward, Noveck, Black, and O'Brien 1987; Pollack, Ward, and Overton 1988; Reene and Overton 1989; Ward and Overton 1990). This same body of research—as well as additional studies (Clement and Falmagne 1986; Franco and Overton 1984; Markovits 1986; Overton, Yaure, and Ward 1986)—supports the position that, prior to adolescence, the competence to reason formally is largely unavailable while, by late adolescence, adolescents as a group uniformly demonstrate the availability of this skill. This research shows that formal reasoning competence is a rather universally available tool. It does not argue that this tool must be manifested in all contexts.

We can now turn to some consequences for the adolescent of having this tool available. If formal operational thought is a generalized sys-

505

tem of logic or a logic of logic, then it functions to permit the adolescent to stand at a level above his day-to-day syntactic thought. From this new-found reflective vantage point, the everyday thought of secondary process thinking or syntactic thinking can be evaluated in terms of its coherence, consistency, lack of contradictions, and precision. In other words, formal thought permits the individual to reflect on her systems of thought systematically. This freedom psychologically to move beyond the actual world of day-to-day fantasy and commonsense experience opens the door to an array of related experiences.

Once the individual acquires the freedom of reflection, it becomes apparent that this emancipation process need not stop at this level. If, as the person discovers, he can think about his thinking, why not systematically think about his thinking about his thinking. Indeed, why not think about thinking, about thinking, about thinking, and on and on. If this sounds frivolous, consider the obsessive patient. Just as you believe that you have made some experience near contact, off he flies to the next higher level, to reflect on that experience. When you follow, he flies higher yet.

As the adolescent continues the emancipation process, an inversion of the relation between the actual world and the world of the possible takes place. In the past, the actual world led directly, in an empirical inductive fashion, to what would be possible or not possible. Now, the world of possibilities rather than actualities becomes primary. Now, utopian and counterintuitive worlds can be generated in thought, and these thought experiments can be used as standards against which to judge the actual.

The new system of logic itself permits deduction of consequences, moving from the world of possibilities to the world of the actual. Thus, thought can now evince a hypothetical-deductive quality. The adolescent can generate hypotheses and test them in a systematic, logically coherent, deductive manner.

Formal Operational Thought and Self-Regulation

What effect, then, may these consequences have on the self-regulation of affect and behavior? First, consider again the caution that the consequences just sketched do not describe what adolescents who have attained a level of reflective thought actually do. It de-

506

scribes what they become capable of, and what they may do, if they use the tool.

In considering the consequences of formal thought, it should be understood that having this new skill available may be considered a mixed blessing, for there is both an up side and a down side to the use of formal thought. Each of these will be addressed briefly.

With respect to the up side, knowing that early nonformal adolescent behavior tends to be dominated by impulses, it is not surprising that the achievement of a level of formal reflection provides the adolescent with both a method of distancing himself from the impulses and unwanted affect and a structure for their self-containment. Here, Bion's metaphor of the container and the contained is useful. It is only at the level of formal reflection that the individual can truly, herself, operate as a container for the contained impulses and affect. That is, impulses and affect can now be projected onto this level, processed there, and introjected back in a metabolized form by the self as a whole (i.e., this might be thought of as an internalized form of projective identification). It should also be noted that this new level corresponds to what classic psychoanalysis described as the "observing" or "reasonable" ego in contrast with the "experiencing" ego (Greenson 1967) that is characteristic of earlier, lower levels of operation.

The outcome of this process of developing both a distance and a containing structure is both a greater sense of self-control and the further development of self-identity. With respect to self-identity, note that research scientists working in the field of adult attachment (Main, Kaplan, and Cassidy 1985) have proposed that the achievement of formal thinking is a necessary condition for altering the status of the internal working models of relationships. That is—referencing Piaget—these researchers state that such change is possible because "these operations may permit the individual to think about thought itself, that is, to step outside a given relationship system and to see it operating" (p. 77).

If formal reflection is a mechanism for the change of internal working models, then by definition it also establishes the basis for changes of affect regulation. Movement from, for example, an "avoidant/dismissing" type of model to a "secure/free autonomous" model means a change—to quote Kobak and Sceery (1988)—in the "rules that guide individuals' responses to emotionally distressing or challenging situations" (p. 142).

507

Furthermore, if formal thinking presents a mechanism for the change of internal working models, then by the same logic it suggests a mechanism for the renegotiation of the individual's status within the actual family context. Indeed, we are aware from both the clinical and the research literature that adolescence is a period of renegotiation of status within the family context. The suggestion here is that formal reflective thought can be a critical feature both in the initiation and in the course of that renegotiation.

As a final point concerning change, self-identity, and formal thinking, it seems most probable that the reflective system of formal thought is a necessary component of therapeutic change, at least therapeutic change as understood in any psychodynamic sense. If we conceive of the point of change as the container of the formal level that receives and metabolizes affect and impulse, then psychotherapy involves the joining of therapist and patient at this juncture in the arena that Winnicott called the "playground." Here, the reflective capacities of both the individual and the therapist connect to operate as containers and process dangerous affect and impulse. At the outset, the available conflict-free area of the patient's container is severely restricted, and the therapist serves as primary container. Therapeutic progress entails the progressive transfer of the processing function to the patient's container or to the patient's "reasonable" ego.

This discussion of the up side of formal reflection has, to this point, focused on the way that this capacity entails a vantage point and a system that enables affective and impulse control in a self-regulatory context. It should also be noted that formal thinking gives the adolescent tools that are even more directly related to the regulation of overt behavior. These consist of the ability to make rational decisions and the ability to think ahead or plan in a long-range systematic and coherent fashion.

Further, the very abstractness, universality, and hypothetical quality of the systems of thought made available by movement to the level of formal reflection have a major effect on the way that the adolescent can think about a host of concepts. These include, for example, the way of thinking about personal identity, the nature of society, existence, religion, justice, morality, friendship, and knowledge itself.

As noted earlier, if there is an up side to the use of formal reflection, there is also a down side. The first potentially negative feature of formal reflection is the phenomenon of egocentrism.

Earlier the emancipation process and the freedom of reflection were

508

mentioned. This process can be a very heady experience. In its early phases, it leads the adolescent to the belief that this new experience is special and unique and, thus, because the adolescent is having this experience, that she must also be very special and unique. Here, we have the beginning of what is called adolescent egocentrism.

The quality of uniqueness itself is captured in what Elkind (1967) has called the "personal fable." This is the adolescent's complex of beliefs about his experiences: for example, "only he can suffer with such agonized intensity, or experience such exquisite rapture" (p. 1031); or about his mortality, for example, "I am so unique that I will not die." This last characteristic is particularly implicated in the high degree of risk-taking behaviors found in early adolescence.

The belief in being special also leads—particularly during the early part of this period—to the projection that others see the individual as special. One outcome of this is the adolescent's creation of what has been termed the "imaginary audience." To the extent that the individual is critical or admiring of himself or herself, so too must this projected audience be admiring or critical. As Elkind has said about this phenomenon, "The adolescent's wish for privacy and his reluctance to reveal himself may, to some extent, be a reaction to the feeling of being under the constant critical scrutiny of other people. The notion of an imaginary audience also helps to explain the observation that the affect which most concerns adolescents is not guilt, but shame, that is, the reaction to the audience" (1967, p. 1030). It also helps explain the adolescent's attempts to affect the style and behavior of the anticipated "critical and admiring audience" (see also Elkind 1985).

Another consequence of the use of formal reasoning that has a negative potential is the emergence of skepticism and dogmatism. The emancipation process of becoming capable of thinking about thinking about thinking begins to demonstrate that all knowledge involves the human activity called thinking. This opens the door to the recognition of the relativity of all knowledge (Chandler 1987). As this door opens, the adolescent tends initially to move in the direction of a complete skepticism about the validity of any knowledge or toward a dogmatic appeal to some authority for the correct answers. The formal cynical stance leads the adolescent to behavioral strategies based on "impulsivism (acting without thought), intuitionism (doing what affect demands), conformism (doing the done thing), and indifferentism (tossing a coin or acting on whim)" (p. 151). The dogmatic stance, on the other hand, provides both secular and nonsecular options. For example, the

509

secular option is illustrated in what Elkind (1967) described as the adolescent's endemic search for religious faith. The nonsecular option includes things like a blind faith in the canons of "scientism" or other ideologies. In general, both the skeptical and the dogmatic approaches tend to chase each other during the early adolescent period.

As a final down-side feature of formal thought, it should be noted that this reflective ability can operate to reinforce earlier defensive strategies. That is, formal thinking can operate as a powerful force to be put in the service of whatever defensive structure was developed earlier in life. This is the case regardless of whether the original adaptive structure was primarily externalizing or internalizing in nature. For example, the primitive form of projection becomes the systematized set of projections under the sponsorship of formal reasoning, and the isolation of affect of the obsessional neurotic becomes the intellectualization of the adolescent. In a similar vein, the avoidant regulative style of the infant and the dismissing regulative style of the adolescent, or the ambivalent style of the infant and the preoccupied style of the adolescent, represent the later reinforcement of earlier defensive strategies.

In closing, it should be noted that this combination of up-side and down-side implications of formal reflection makes the task of generating any linear predictions concerning the relation between formal operational thought and developmental psychopathology extremely complicated. We may be able to suggest that all those with disturbances of affect and impulse will show less formal reasoning, and we may be able to make suggestions about certain groups demonstrating early or late formal reasoning availability. However, we are beginning to believe that ultimately the most productive avenue will be to explore the patterning of attachment classifications, family interactions, various diagnostic groups, and formal reasoning more closely in order to arrive at a systematic and clinically useful picture of the self-regulation of affect and impulse.

Measurement of Formal Reasoning and Empirical Evidence

Ward and Overton (1990) present an overview of measurement techniques used to diagnose formal reasoning in this investigation. Essentially, this technique involves a modification of the Wason four-card or selection task. This is a task that requires that the subject test a

510

conditional (if . . . then . . .) rule. The subject does this by selecting the conditions under which he or she would be absolutely certain (i.e., it would be logically necessarily the case) that the rule was being broken.

To this point, we have data on some ninety-one hospitalized adolescents with IQ scores above 75 in our sample. The group is relatively evenly divided into a young adolescence (younger than 14.6 years), a middle adolescence (14.6–16 years), and a late adolescence (older than 16 years) group, with both males and females in each group. Thirty-six subjects have a diagnosis involving substance abuse, and these are distributed across the three age groups.

When the age-level performance for combined diagnostic groups is compared with a control group of nonhospitalized adolescents, it appears that the hospitalized adolescents have only slightly lower scores than the normal control group. When diagnosis is taken into account, the following appears. (a) The young substance abusers and a normal control group perform at identical levels, but other hospitalized subjects perform somewhat more poorly. (b) The middle-adolescent substance abusers and a normal control group also perform at identical levels, but again other hospitalized subjects perform more poorly. (c) At late adolescence, both the hospitalized substance-abusing subject and the hospitalized non-substance-abusing subject perform at identical levels, and this level is poorer than the normal control subject.

When gender is considered, the following begins to emerge. (a) In early adolescence, male substance-abusing patients perform at higher levels than nonabusing patients. (b) In middle adolescence, the same picture holds, but there is some very tentative evidence that female substance-abusing patients perform better than non-substance-abusing patients. (c) In late adolescence, it begins to appear that male substance-abusing patients perform better than male non-substance-abusing patients and female non-substance-abusing patients perform better than female substance-abusing patients.

It should be kept in mind that, given the small sample size, these reported findings are impressionistic and cannot be considered reliable at this time.

REFERENCES

Bady, R. J. 1979. Students' understanding of the logic of hypothesis testing. *Journal of Research in Science Teaching* 16:61–65.

511

41

Bucci, W. 1978. The interpretation of universal affirmation propositions. *Cognition* 6:55–77.

Byrnes, J. P., and Overton, W. F. 1986. Reasoning about certainty and uncertainty in concrete, causal, and propositional contexts. *Developmental Psychology* 22:793–799.

Byrnes, J. P., and Overton, W. F. 1988. Reasoning about logical connectives: a developmental analysis. *Journal of Experimental Child Psychology* 22:793–799.

Chandler, M. 1987. The Othello effect: essay on the emergence and eclipse of skeptical doubt. *Human Development* 30:137–159.

Clement, C. A., and Falmagne, R. J. 1986. Logical reasoning, world knowledge, and mental imagery: interconnections in cognitive processes. *Memory and Cognition* 14:299–307.

Elkind, D. 1967. Egocentrism in adolescence. *Child Development* 38:1025–1034.

Elkind, D. 1985. Egocentrism redux. *Developmental Review* 5:201–217.

Erikson, E. 1980. *Identity and the Life Cycle*. New York: Norton.

Franco, R., and Overton, W. F. 1984. Deductive reasoning in young and elderly adults: a competence-moderator-performance approach. Paper presented at the biennial Southeastern Conference on Human Development, Athens, Ga.

Greenson, R. G. 1967. *The Technique and Practice of Psychoanalysis*. New York: International Universities Press.

Inhelder, B., and Piaget, J. 1958. *The Growth of Logical Thinking from Childhood to Adolescence*. New York: Wiley.

Inhelder, B., and Piaget, J. 1964. *The Early Growth of Logic in the Child*. New York: Harper & Row.

Kobak, R. R., and Sceery, A. 1988. Attachment in late adolescence: working models, affect regulation, and representations of self and others. *Child Development* 59:135–146.

Main, M.; Kaplan, N.; and Cassidy, J. 1985. Security in infancy, childhood, and adulthood: a move to the level of representation. In I. Bretherton and E. Waters, eds. *Growing Points of Attachment Theory and Research. Monographs of the Society for Research in Child Development*, vol. 50, nos. 1–2, serial no. 209. Chicago: University of Chicago Press.

Markovits, H. 1986. Familiarity effects in conditional reasoning. *Journal of Educational Psychology* 78:492–494.

Moshman, D. 1979. Development of formal hypothesis-testing ability. *Developmental Psychology* 15:101–112.

Moshman, D., and Franks, B. A. 1986. Development of the concept of inferential validity. *Child Development* 57:153–165.

O'Brien, D., and Overton, W. F. 1980. Conditional reasoning following contradictory evidence: a developmental analysis. *Journal of Experimental Child Psychology* 30:44–60.

O'Brien, D., and Overton, W. F. 1982. Conditional reasoning and the competence-performance issue: a developmental analysis of a training task. *Journal of Experimental Child Psychology* 34:274–290.

Overton, W. F.; Byrnes, J. P.; and O'Brien, D. P. 1985. Developmental and individual differences in conditional reasoning: the role of contradiction training and cognitive style. *Developmental Psychology* 21:692–701.

Overton, W. F.; Ward, S. L.; Noveck, I.; Black, J.; and O'Brien, D. P. 1987. Form and content in the development of deductive reasoning. *Developmental Psychology* 23:22–30.

Overton, W. F.; Yaure, R.; and Ward, S. L. 1986. Deductive reasoning in young and elderly adults. Paper presented to the Conference on Human Development, Nashville.

Piaget, J. 1980. *Recent Studies in Genetic Epistemology*. Geneva: Cahiers Foundation Archives Jean Piaget.

Piaget, J. 1987. *Possibility and Necessity*. Vol. 1, *The Role of Possibility in Cognitive Development*. Vol. 2, *The Role of Necessity in Cognitive Development*. Minneapolis: University of Minnesota Press.

Piaget, J., and Garcia, R. 1986. *Vers une logique de signification*. Geneva: Editions Murionde Pierault Le-Bonniec, 1988.

Pollack, R. D.; Ward, S. L.; and Overton, W. F. 1988. Early adolescence: a transitional time in logical reasoning. Paper presented at the biennial meeting of the Society for Research on Adolescence, Alexandria, Va.

Reene, K. J., and Overton, W. F. 1989. Longitudinal investigation of adolescent deductive reasoning. Paper presented at the biennial meeting of the Society for Research in Child Development, Kansas City, Mo.

Ward, S. H., and Overton, W. F. 1990. Semantic familiarity, relevance, and the development of deductive reasoning. *Developmental Psychology* 26:488–493.

513

Developmental Psychology
1980, Vol. 16, No. 1, 23–30

Development of Physical
and Social Reasoning in Adolescence

Daniel P. Keating
Institute of Child Development
University of Minnesota

Lawrence V. Clark
Southeast Missouri State University

A theoretically important issue is the degree to which cognitive development in different domains is coordinated. Two important domains which have received considerable attention recently are physical and interpersonal reasoning, yet no adequately designed studies comparing them have been reported. We conducted a multitrait, multimethod investigation of the development of logical and interpersonal reasoning among adolescents (ages 12, 14, and 16 years) by devising group written measures of standard physical and interpersonal reasoning tasks. The results indicate that correlations between different measures within each domain were no greater than correlations between measures from different domains ($rs = .50$ and $.44$, respectively). Also, on qualitative stage comparisons, fewer subjects showed formal reasoning on the interpersonal measures than on the physical reasoning measures. Significant age effects ($p < .001$) were obtained for each measure.

A substantial body of evidence exists indicating that the cognitive abilities of individuals increase substantially during the adolescent years (Garfinkel & Thorndike, 1976; Keating, 1979a). Inhelder and Piaget (1958) have attempted to account for this growth in terms of changes in underlying logical structure and have argued that the acquisition of formal operational reasoning is the foremost cognitive accomplishment of the adolescent years. They argue further that this acquisition is universal within the species.

A number of significant problems with this formulation have been noted by critics (see Keating, 1979a, for a review). Two concerns provide the focus for the research reported here. First, the claimed universality of these logical structure changes has not proved easy to demonstrate empirically. In fact, significant proportions of college- and middle-aged adult subjects failed to show

formal reasoning in the Inhelder and Piaget (1958) tasks in a variety of studies (Keating, 1979a). Recognizing this empirical inconsistency, Piaget (1972) subsequently argued that the failure of some subjects to show formal reasoning (when they would theoretically be expected to do so) can be accounted for by their lack of familiarity with the content of the specific tasks employed. That is, although in theory formal reasoning is independent of the content of the problems addressed, in practice task unfamiliarity may prevent the individual from displaying the reasoning actually available to him/her. Piaget (1972) suggested exploring formal reasoning using tasks and content other than the physical-mathematical material employed by Inhelder and Piaget (1958).

This leads directly to the second concern, which is the generalizability of the formal reasoning construct to other domains besides the physical-mathematical. If the logical structures are in fact the most basic components of cognitive activity, then evidence for their operation should theoretically be observable across a wide variety of domains. Unfortunately, nearly all efforts at

We thank Neil Weinreb and Allen Keniston for their help in data collection and scoring.

Requests for reprints should be sent to Daniel P. Keating, Institute of Child Development, 51 East River Road, University of Minnesota, Minneapolis, Minnesota 55455.

validating Piaget's formal operations theory conducted to date have employed tasks from the physical-mathematical domain exclusively.

The domain of social or interpersonal reasoning provides a particularly interesting contrast to physical-mathematical problem solving. It can be hypothesized that individuals unable to demonstrate formal reasoning in the standard Piagetian tasks may be able to apply such reasoning to social processes to which they have had greater exposure.

The adolescent years are a particularly good time to conduct such an investigation for two reasons. It is the period during which many of the hypothesized changes are taking place, providing variance that can be readily assessed. It is a period during which there is apparently significant differentiation or specialization of abilities (Dye & Very, 1968; Horn, 1976; Keating, 1979a; Piaget, 1972), providing a reasonable test of generalizability.

Selman (1976; Selman, Note 1) has developed a system of structural analysis for the social domain based on Piaget's descriptions of cognitive-developmental stages. He studied the cognitive development of a group of preadolescents in a variety of domains, including logico-mathematical, interpersonal, and perspective taking. Selman (1976) concluded that the domains were indeed distinguishable, but that similar and correlated stage changes were evident in each area.

The data, however, seem not to support these inferences. As Shantz (1975) and Neimark (1975), among others, have pointed out, convergent and discriminant evidence is required before adequate inferences can be drawn regarding the development of reasoning in different domains of cognitive development. Selman (1976) used as discriminant evidence a pattern of correlations predicted from his logical analysis, with the highest correlation (.85) between perspective taking and logico-mathematical assessment, a lower correlation between perspective taking and interpersonal reasoning (.73), and an even lower correlation between the logico-mathematical and the moral judgment stage (.52). Within the interpersonal

reasoning assessment, however, the correlations across dilemmas ranged from .61 to .85, which Selman interpreted as moderately good internal consistency. But this is almost exactly the range of correlations used for discriminant evidence. Virtually identical sets of correlations cannot be used as evidence for convergence and for discrimination.

A major goal of the present study was to examine more thoroughly the discriminability of physical and interpersonal reasoning during adolescence. A second goal was to compare the reasoning performance of adolescents in these two domains in terms of the hypothesized underlying stages. In a stage analysis, Selman (1976) argued for significant stage concordance across domains within the preadolescent sample. Finally, the design of the study provided the opportunity for collecting some normative data on adolescent performance in these domains.

The most appropriate design for examining convergent and discriminant validity simultaneously is the Campbell and Fiske (1959) multitrait, multimethod matrix. We developed paper-and-pencil versions of the standard interview assessment procedures for physical reasoning (Inhelder & Piaget, 1958) and for interpersonal reasoning (Selman, Note 1). Each trait (physical and interpersonal reasoning) was thus assessed by each method (written test and clinical interview). This design controls for method variance, and rigorous evidence for discriminability is obtained if the within-trait, cross-method correlations significantly exceed the within-method, cross-trait and the cross-method, cross-trait correlations.

The most advantageous outcome from the Piagetian perspective, based on Piaget's (1972) position, would be significant discriminability of reasoning in the physical and the interpersonal domains, together with a substantial proportion of subjects showing formal reasoning in the interpersonal domain but not in the physical domain. The problems of nonattainment in the latter domain could then in part by attributed to differential content familiarity across subjects. (Explaining, rather than merely using such evidence for horizontal decalage, would still be required of course.) On the other hand, failure to obtain discriminant evidence would conform better to the earlier Inhelder and Piaget (1958) position of unity of formal reasoning across domains although seriously undermining the differential content familiarity justification for the failure of the universality prediction.

Method

Subjects

The subjects in this study were 151 students in the 6th-grade (tested in the spring), 9th-grade (fall testing), and 11th-grade (fall testing) classes of three schools located near each other in a middle- to upper-middle-class neighborhood. The cohorts were thus separated by approximately 2 years. The youngest group ($n = 57$; 26 males and 31 females) had a mean age of 12 years 6 months; the middle group ($n = 48$; 25 males, 23 females) had a mean age of 14 years 4 months; and the oldest group ($n = 46$; 21 males, 25 females) had a mean age of 16 years 2 months. Most of the subjects were white, and the proportion of minority students was similar at each age.

Procedure

There were five assessments for each subject: physical reasoning, interview version; physical reasoning, written version; interpersonal reasoning, interview version; interpersonal reasoning, written version; and Raven's (1960) Standard Progressive Matrices (SPM). The three paper-and-pencil tests were given to the students in a group setting in their classrooms in a single session. The order of tests for this session was SPM, physical, interpersonal. Each student was then individually interviewed within 4 weeks of this group administration. The order of interviews varied randomly across subjects. Because of scheduling problems and absences, 20 subjects did not complete both interviews. These subjects were dropped from the sample and are not included in the 151 total reported above or in the analyses that follow. These dropped subjects appeared to be a random sample of the population, since their SPM scores were similar to those of the subjects who completed all phases of the study. Different interviewers conducted the physical and interpersonal reasoning assessments, and all interviewers were blind to subjects' performances on the written tests.

Measures and Scoring

Physical reasoning interviews. Two tasks from Inhelder and Piaget (1958) were administered in the standard clinical interview format to each subject. The tasks were floating bodies, in which the subject attempts to uncover the reason for various objects' sinking or floating (displacement principle), and the pendulum, in which the subject tries to discover the controlling variable for the period of a pendulum among several possibilities (separation of variables). The tasks were presented in the order described. The experimenter scored each task immediately on completion, and an audiotape of the session was made to provide a check on scorer reliability. The scoring system used four levels: concrete = 1; advanced concrete = 2; early formal = 3; and consolidated formal = 4. These are based on Inhelder and Piaget's (1958) Levels 2A, 2B, 3A, and 3B, respectively.

Physical reasoning written test. To avoid contamination from previous exposure to the same tasks, two different tasks from Inhelder and Piaget (1958) were used for the written test. These were the balance beam task (proportionality) and conservation of momentum in an inclined plane task (separation of variables), presented in that order. For each task, a set of standard photographic slides was prepared that graphically illustrated a series of relevant experiments —eight for the balance beam and six for conservation of momentum. Subjects were given answer sheets with marked areas in which they were instructed to record anything that would help them in figuring out the problem. The nature of the task and the type of answers they were expected to give were explained for each task before its presentation.

Within each task, the subjects first saw the slides representing the experiments, presented at a pace that allowed all subjects to make as many notes as they wished. Next, subjects answered a series of questions on the answer sheet asking for their account of what happened in the experiment, why it had happened, how they figured it out, and what other experiments they would do if they did not already have an answer. This section was designed to represent the interview-type questioning of the standard format. Finally, again for each task, there was an additional set of slides presenting more situations similar to the earlier ones but requiring the subjects to make predictions about the outcome (e.g., Will the beam balance? What slot will the ball land in?). Answer sheets were scored independently in the following three sections: note taking, which indicated the degree to which the subjects recorded information from the experiments that would allow them to make the necessary inferences; explanation, which was a qualitative score from that section based on Inhelder and Piaget's (1958) descriptions; and predictions, which was simply the number of correct predictions.

Interpersonal reasoning interview. Selman (1976; Selman, Note 1) assessed interpersonal reasoning through a dilemma format. The subject is presented with a story in which the protagonist faces an interpersonal dilemma of some sort and is asked to respond to various aspects of that situation through a structured interview. We used the "puppy story" dilemma in which a child must decide whether to buy a new puppy for a friend who has recently lost a beloved dog, after the friend has said that he could never own another dog. Selman (Note 1) provides a complete description of the dilemma, structured interview questions, and scoring rules for four different categories: subjectivity, self-awareness, personality, and relations. Extensive pilot work was employed to train

47

interviewers and to develop the interview format and the scoring procedures. Interviews were recorded on audiotape and scored later by interviewers. Interviewers doubled as scorers, but they scored interviews conducted by others so that they would be blind to the age of the subject.

Two scores were obtained from each session: an overall subjective score based on Selman's levels and a weighted composite score that arithmetically combined the four category scores (Selman, Note 1). Except for one subject who scored at the egocentric perspective-taking level (Level 0), the four scoring levels we used were as follows: Level 1, subjective; Level 2, self-reflective; Level 3, third person; and Level 4, social systems. Tapes from pilot sessions and from a subset of the experimental sessions were scored independently by all scorers to establish scoring consistency and to evaluate interrater reliability.

Interpersonal reasoning written test. A filmstrip and sound recording produced by Selman portraying the puppy story dilemma was shown to all of the subjects in a group setting. The use of the same story may have contributed to shared variance, but the depth and variety of the probes minimized this problem and practical constraints necessitated this approach. Following this presentation, subjects completed a written questionnaire based on the interview questions drawn from Selman's (Note 1) manual and elaborated in our pilot testing. The questions were open-ended, and subjects were encouraged to write as much as they liked on each one. Scoring proceeded in the same way as for the interview sessions, using the same levels and the same scoring guidelines. Again a subset of questionnaires was scored by all scorers for consistency and for reliability checks.

SPM. This written test of abstract reasoning was included as a rough ability index, particularly for use in partial correlations between physical and interpersonal reasoning. There are 60 problems on this test.

Interrater and test reliabilities. Before carrying out the analyses indicated for this study, we first examined the interrater reliabilities and agreements for these data. These were calculated both for subscores (each task or category) and for the total scores that would be used in the analyses. Across the four measures, the correlations ranged from .65 to .95, with a mean of .88, and the agreements ranged from 55% to 85%, with a mean of 76%. The subscores tended to constitute the lower end of these ranges; global score reliabilities and agreements were somewhat higher. Internal homo-

geneity reliabilities were also calculated for each measure by considering each task (physical reasoning interview), section (physical reasoning written test), or category (interpersonal reasoning interview and written test) score as an item score, obtaining the average item intercorrelation, and stepping that up using the Spearman-Brown formula. This provided a lower-bound estimate of the reliability of the measure (Stanley, 1971) in addition to the interrater reliability of the scoring already reported. These reliabilities were .69 (physical reasoning interview), .74 (physical reasoning written test), .83 (interpersonal reasoning interview), and .75 (interpersonal reasoning written test). The SPM reliability was not calculated for this sample, since it is a widely used psychometric test of established reliability. Given the experimental nature of the four measures, we view both the interrater and test reliabilities as moderately to very high, justifying further analysis of the data.

Results

There are three questions that can be addressed with these data. Are physical and interpersonal reasoning coherent domains that can be empirically distinguished? Are cognitive developmental stages in different domains concordant with each other and with theoretical predictions? What are the age changes in these domains during the early and middle adolescent years?

Convergent and Discriminant Validity

The correlations among the measures in this study necessary for the convergent/discriminant validity inferences are reported in Table 1. All the correlations are positive and statistically significant. The relevant comparisons for the multitrait, multimethod matrix analysis are these: the same-trait, cross-method rs are .55 and .45; the same-method, cross-trait rs are .51 and .33; the cross-trait, cross-method rs are .60 and .32. Thus, the mean trait correlation (using Fisher's Z transformation) is .50, and the

Table 1
Intercorrelations of the Five Measures and Chronological Age

Variable	1	2	3	4	5	Age
1. Interpersonal reasoning interview	[.83]	.55	.33	.60	.45	.35
2. Interpersonal reasoning written test	(.70)	[.75]	.32	.51	.49	.40
3. Physical reasoning interview	(.44)	(.45)	[.69]	.45	.33	.30
4. Physical reasoning written test	(.77)	(.69)	(.63)	[.74]	.51	.48
5. Standard Progressive Matrices						

Note. Raw correlations are above the diagonal; estimated test reliabilities (in brackets) are on the diagonal; correlations corrected for attenuation due to test unreliability (in parentheses) are below the diagonal.

mean nontrait correlation is .44. Although this is in the predicted direction, the difference between the correlations is not statistically significant, using the test for dependent correlations ($z < 1.64$, $p > .10$). That is, physical reasoning and interpersonal reasoning measures using different methods are significantly correlated within each domain, but that convergence does not significantly exceed the correlations of performance across domains within a particular measurement method.

There is the possibility that differential reliabilities of the measures or their covariation with age or psychometric ability may obscure underlying evidence for discrimination. Thus, the same analyses were carried out using correlations corrected for attenuation due to measurement error and also using correlations with age and SPM score partialed out. The corrected correlations (which appear below the diagonal in Table 1) yield a mean same-trait correlation of .66 and a mean nontrait correlation of .59. Again, these are not significantly different from each other. After age and SPM score were partialed out, the mean same-trait correlation was .36 and the mean nontrait correlation was .28, again not significantly different from each other. Thus, physical and interpersonal reasoning development can not be empirically separated from each other in this study.

Stage Comparisons

In addition to comparing subjects' developmental levels in the correlational anal-

ysis using total scores, as in the preceding analyses, it is possible to compare them on the basis of their global stage assignment. This was done on the basis of the interview data, since that was most comparable to the previous literature. Those stage comparisons are shown in Table 2 for all subjects. Selman's (1976) structural analysis aligned concrete operations with self-reflective perspective taking, advanced concrete operations with third-person perspective taking, and early and consolidated formal operations with social systems perspective taking. In Table 2 this is represented by the figures in boldface type (i.e., Piaget Stage 1 with Selman Level 2, Piaget Stage 2 with Selman Level 3, and Piaget Stages 3 and 4 with Selman Level 4). Using this structural analysis, we computed the percentage of subjects whose stage assignment across domains was concordant, those whose interpersonal reasoning stage assignment was lower, and those whose physical reasoning stage assignment was lower. These figures were 35%, 52%, and 13%, respectively. Nearly twice as many subjects had discordant as concordant stage assignments. Also, the category that would be most supportive of Piaget's (1972) analysis is that which includes subjects who show formal reasoning with interpersonal but not physical content. In fact, there were far fewer subjects in this category (13%) than in the category with the opposite pattern (52%).

In the oldest group, for example, 63% showed early or consolidated formal reasoning on the standard physical tasks. If we add in those who showed formal reasoning

Table 2

Stage Comparisons Between Domains

	Selman level					
Piaget stage	Egocentric (0)	Subjective (1)	Self-reflective (2)	Third person (3)	Social systems (4)	Total
1. Concrete	0	3	**7**	11	1	22
2. Advanced concrete	1	2	**28**	29	7	67
3. Early formal	0	3	3	35	**13**	54
4. Consolidated formal	0	1	0	3	**4**	8
Total	1	9	38	78	25	151

Note. Entries in boldface type represent theoretically concordant stages across domains, based on Selman's (1976) structural analysis. Comparisons are based on overall score from interview data.

49

on the interpersonal reasoning dilemma (i.e., Level 4) but not on the physical tasks, this figure increases only to 70%—a total of three subjects added. Similarly, the gains in percentages of formal reasoners using this analysis are small in the younger groups —from 46% to 54% among the 14-year-olds and from 19% to 21% among the 12-year-olds. Thus, even in the oldest group, 30% do not show formal reasoning in either domain, and this figure is similar to the proportion of nonformal reasoners from studies that examined only one domain.

Age Changes

We examined the age differences in this study both quantitatively, using the total scores from the four reasoning measures, and qualitatively, using the global scores from the interview data.

Four 3 (grade) × 2 (sex) analyses of variance were computed, one for each of the reasoning total scores (physical interview, physical written, interpersonal interview, and interpersonal written). The effect of grade was highly significant for each measure ($p < .001$), with $F(2, 296) = 22.81$, 51.75, 30.43, and 47.22, respectively. There were no significant interactions and only one significant sex effect, on the interpersonal reasoning written test, $F(1, 296) = 14.41$, $p < .001$, with girls higher than boys. This may reflect higher interpersonal reasoning among girls, although if so it is not observed in the interview data, or perhaps a greater facility at written verbal expression or some other factor. The age changes are, as expected, monotonic, with the older subjects scoring at consistently higher levels on these assessments.

To examine this age difference qualitatively, it is perhaps most informative to look at the global stage assignments from the interview data. On physical reasoning tasks, the progression to formal operational reasoning (i.e., scores of 3 or 4) is most salient. From youngest to oldest groups, this figure is 19%, 46%, and 63%. On the interpersonal reasoning dilemma, Level 3 (third-person perspective taking) seems pivotal. The proportion of subjects below that level drops

rapidly, from 71% to 19% to 9%. The proportion of subjects at Level 3 increases and levels off, from 37% to 63% to 59%. Finally, the proportion of Level 4 subjects (none scored higher than Level 4) increases from 2% to 19% to 33%. If Level 4 is accurately interpreted as the formal reasoning level (Selman, 1976), then it appears that individuals apply such reasoning to interpersonal levels significantly later than to the impersonal, physical world.

Discussion

The results from this study do not support an interpretation that physical reasoning and interpersonal reasoning are separate domains of reasoning and suggest that at least as assessed here, they are more similar than different. Piaget's (1972) theoretical reinterpretation suggesting that some individuals who are nonformal on tasks from the physical domain may be able to show formal reasoning on other tasks was not evident in subjects' performances in the interpersonal domain investigated here.

Neither Piaget's original expectations nor his 1972 reinterpretation is supported by these findings. One may view the high cross-trait correlations as evidence for the unity of formal reasoning across domains, but then the failure of the universality prediction is not mitigated, since the evidence for nonformal reasoning is substantial. Even at the 11th-grade level, 37% fail to show formal reasoning on the physical tasks, 67% fail to show it on the interpersonal dilemma, and 30% fail to show it on either. On the other hand, one may infer from Piaget's (1972) recasting of the theory a prediction of discriminability of formal reasoning in different domains and thus of differential development across subjects in two domains as different as impersonal and interpersonal reasoning. But our data do not support this prediction either.

One could raise the objection that the written versions deviate significantly enough from the standard assessment procedures that they are invalid measures of the domains and hence do not provide an appropriate test of the prediction. Recall, however, that there is strong evidence for convergent validity, which should be drastically affected by the invalidity of alternate measures within the domain. This demonstrates only that the written versions are as valid as the standard interview versions, the validity of which have also been challenged (Keating, 1979a, 1979b).

Yet another objection is that the social domain does not offer a good alternative domain for investigating formal reasoning because such reasoning is likely to lag behind physical–mathematical reasoning, given the ambiguity and complexity of social information. While granting this possibility, we wonder what other domains would be more appropriate. The two investigated here seem to represent the extremes, from explicit rules with simple information (physics) to implicit rules with complex information (interpersonal relations). In any case, we cannot claim and have not claimed proof of the null hypothesis of no difference in formal reasoning in different domains but only that one quite reasonable test failed to disconfirm it.

The normative data provide evidence that whatever formal reasoning is required for good performance on these tasks, it is far more readily available to middle adolescents than to early adolescents. An important area of future research is the discovery and verification of the underlying sources of this robust developmental variance (Keating, 1979b).

It is worth questioning why physical, or impersonal, reasoning and interpersonal, or social, reasoning are not, against most reasonable expectations, empirically distinguishable. Two likely possibilities come to mind. First, the domain of social cognition is not yet well charted, and there is some evidence from the extremes of the preschool and the college years that its empirical coherence remains to be demonstrated (Ford, 1979; Keating, 1978). If we have not comprehended one of the two domains coherently or comprehensively, then the discriminability evidence is necessarily weakened.

Second, and perhaps more central, is the possibility that the basic approach to cognitive activity in the social domain has borrowed so heavily from existing cognitive approaches that there is little that is truly "social" about it. Consider the fact that the interpersonal assessment used here, which is similar in style to most such current assessment, asks the subjects to provide, upon reflection and analysis, their best response to the situation. Consider also that in most social or interpersonal situations, particularly those involving on-line social interchange, the opportunity for reflection and analysis typically is severely limited. Not only are there time constraints, but the individual must also allocate a significant proportion of available processing capacity to the social exchange itself (e.g., monitoring others' verbal and nonverbal behavior). Contemporary assessment in social cognition appears to capture little of this processing, and it is reasonable to suppose that there is variance in development of and among individuals in those skills. By failing to employ this conception of social cognition and by substituting for it tasks that have a large intellectual/analytic/reflective component, we may have inadvertently assured our inability to distinguish between impersonal and interpersonal thinking.

Reference Note

1. Selman, R. L. *The development of conceptions of interpersonal relations: A structural analysis and procedures for the assessment of levels of interpersonal reasoning based on levels of social perspective taking* (Scoring Manual, Judge Baker Social Reasoning Project). Unpublished manuscript, Harvard University, 1974.

References

Campbell, D. T., & Fiske, D. W. Convergent and discriminant validity by the multitrait-multimethod matrix. *Psychological Bulletin*, 1959, 56, 81–105.

Dye, N. W., & Very, P. S. Growth changes in factorial structure by age and sex. *Genetic Psychology Monographs*, 1968, 78, 55–88.

Ford, M. E. The construct validity of egocentrism. *Psychological Bulletin*, 1979, 86, 1169–1188.

Garfinkel, R., & Thorndike, R. L. Binet item difficulty then and now. *Child Development*, 1976, 47, 959–965.

Horn, J. L. Human abilities: A review of research and theory in the early 1970's. *Annual Review of Psychology*, 1976, 27, 437–485.

Inhelder, B., & Piaget, J. *The growth of logical thinking from childhood to adolescence.* New York: Basic Books, 1958.

Keating, D. P. A search for social intelligence. *Journal of Educational Psychology,* 1978, *70,* 218–223.

Keating, D. P. Thinking processes in adolescence. In J. Adelson (Ed.), *Handbook of adolescent psychology.* New York: Wiley, 1979. (a)

Keating, D. P. Toward a multivariate life-span theory of intelligence. In D. Kuhn (Ed.), *Intellectual development beyond childhood.* San Francisco: Jossey-Bass, 1979. (b)

Neimark, E. D. Intellectual development during adolescence. In F. D. Horowitz (Ed.), *Review of child development research* (Vol. 4). Chicago: University of Chicago Press, 1975.

Piaget, J. Intellectual evolution from adolescence to adulthood. *Human Development,* 1972, *15,* 1–12.

Raven, J. C. *Guide to the Standard Progressive Matrices.* London: Lewis, 1960.

Selman, R. L. Toward a structural analysis of developing interpersonal relations concepts: Research with normal and disturbed preadolescent boys. In A. D. Pick (Ed.), *Minnesota Symposia on Child Psychology* (Vol. 10). Minneapolis: University of Minnesota Press, 1976.

Shantz, C. U. The development of social cognition. In E. M. Hetherington (Ed.), *Review of child development research* (Vol. 5). Chicago: University of Chicago Press, 1975.

Stanley, J. C. Reliability. In R. L. Thorndike (Ed.), *Educational measurement* (2nd ed.). Washington, D.C.: American Council on Education, 1971.

Received June 28, 1979 ■

A questioning of old beliefs that moral stages can provide the
sole basis for moral education and that moral indoctrination
is necessarily invalid, as well as new views of the moral role
of the community and the status of stage 6.

revisions in the theory
and practice of
moral development

lawrence kohlberg

The two articles which follow represent reports of the methods and findings of
two major three-year projects of the Harvard Center for Moral Education.
One common thrust to the two projects is a practical one, the desire to
develop a coherent approach to assessing the effects of our deliberate efforts
at moral education in the schools. Colby's chapter reports the development of
an instrument useful for assessing stage change through deliberate moral education. Power and Reimer report pilot efforts to assess the stage and phase of
the moral atmosphere of a school. These efforts at assessment reflect a shift in
our aims and methods of moral education, as well as some modification in our
theory from a decade ago (Kohlberg, 1969, 1970, 1971; Kohlberg and Turiel,
1971).

My earlier statements on moral education arose in the context of
Blatt's replicated finding (Blatt and Kohlberg, 1975) that Socratic classroom

Anne Colby reports the thinking of a group involved in a National Institute of
Child Health and Development project on the measurement of moral judgment (the
group includes John Gibbs, Dan Candee, Betsey Speicher-Dubin, Marcus Lieberman,
and myself). Clark Power and Joseph Reimer report the thinking of a group involved in
a study funded by the Ford and Danforth Foundations assessing the effects of democratic school governance on students' moral development (the group includes Marvin
Berkowitz, Ann Higgins-Trenk, and myself).

New Directions for Child Development, 2, 1978   **83** discussions of hypothetical moral dilemmas lead to upward movement (typically one third of a stage) that is significantly greater than that demonstrated by control classrooms without such discussions. Building on these findings, I suggested an approach to moral education based on the idea of moral stages. The claim that stimulating the advance of moral reasoning stages through discussions should be the basis of moral education arose not only from the Blatt findings but also from findings supporting the cultural universality of the moral stages, as well as the necessity of moral judgment for certain types of moral action. In addition, this educational claim was based in turn on a philosophic stance, which was a restatement of Dewey's view that "development is the aim of education" (Kohlberg and Mayer, 1972) and of the Platonic view of education for justice (Kohlberg, 1970). My argument was that education for development through moral stages was education for justice in a culturally universal sense and that a developmentally later stage was a morally better stage (Kohlberg, 1971). Education for moral stage development, I argued, was nonindoctrinative, since it consists of the stimulation through a culturally universal sequence of *structures* of valuing rather than the transmission of some fixed, arbitrary cultural *content* of values.

Some years of active involvement with the practice of moral education have led me to realize that my notion that moral stages were *the* basis for moral education, rather than a partial guide to the moral educator, was mistaken. As I have reported elsewhere (Kohlberg, 1978), this recognition of the limits of moral stages does not invalidate the idea of education for moral development, in the sense of Dewey, or the idea of moral education for justice, in the sense of Socrates. It is rather a recognition that the psychologist's abstract concept "moral stage" is not a sufficient basis for moral education. Abstracting moral "cognition" (judgment and reasoning) from moral action and abstracting structure in moral cognition and judgment from content are necessary for certain psychological research purposes. Although the moral stage concept is valuable for research purposes, however, it is not a sufficient guide to the moral educator, who deals with concrete morality in a school world in which value content as well as structure, behavior as well as reasoning, must be dealt with. In this context the educator must be a socializer, teaching value content and behavior, not merely a Socratic facilitator of development. In becoming a socializer and advocate, the teacher moves into "indoctrination," a step that I originally believed to be invalid both philosophically and psychologically. I thought indoctrination invalid philosophically because the value content taught was culturally and personally relative and because teaching value content was a violation of the child's rights. I thought indoctrination invalid psychologically because it could not lead to meaningful structural change.

I no longer hold these negative views of indoctrinative moral education, and I now believe that the concepts guiding moral education must be partly "indoctrinative." This is true by necessity in a world in which children engage in stealing, cheating, and aggression and in which one cannot wait until children reach the fifth stage in order to deal directly with their moral behavior. It is also true in an even more basic sense in that education for moral action, as distinct from reasoning, always presupposes a concern about moral content for its own sake. I now believe that moral education can be in the form of advocacy or "indoctrination" without violating the child's rights, as long as teacher advocacy is democratic (or subject to the constraints of recognizing student participation in the rule-making and value-upholding process), recognizing the shared rights of teachers and students.

This revision in our conception of moral education led us to recast our intervention research and assessment efforts in moral education. As the Power and Reimer chapter suggests, our efforts focused on an attempt to integrate stage theory and method with theories of content and content learning (or "socialization"). We chose to integrate our analysis of socialization content with our analysis of structural development by moving in a sociological rather than a psychological direction. The theory of moral socialization that we chose to come to terms with was Durkheim's theory of moral education (1961). This was chosen partly because it was the theory that best rationalized what appeared to us (after research observation) to be a valid and effective practice of moral education: kibbutz collective education (Reimer, 1977). In this practice, adult educators advocate and facilitate the functioning of moral peer-group collective norms that are based on a strong sense of community (or group cohesion).

The way in which moral stages are integrated with Durkheimian collective norms guides our educational practice in the Cambridge Cluster School (where I have consulted for four years), as discussed in the Reimer and Power chapter. As a research project, as distinct from a document of an educational approach, the endeavor described in this chapter departs from previous moral development research in two ways. First, we have moved from the study of *individual development* to the study of *group development* (the stages and phases in the norms of the group *qua* group). And second, we have passed from a study of the internal mental structure of moral reasoning to an analysis of something which is neither internal consciousness nor external behavior, but something in between: group norms and expectations, ethnographically defined. We believe the behavioristic approach to studying individual moral conduct first taken by Hartshorne and May (1928–1930) to have failed, and we have chosen instead the group approach. Thus we examine behavior not in terms of individual moral character but in terms of the character or "moral atmosphere" of a group or community.

The Anne Colby chapter represents not a departure from earlier interests and assumptions but, as she elaborates, a bootstrapping process entailing a revision of conceptual definitions and methods in the study of moral stages. The project that she reports started four years ago and arose from an awareness of the defects in our previous methods of assessing moral stages. These defects had been critiqued by Kurtines and Greif (1974), but their analysis had a number of errors in scholarship and in understanding of the stage paradigm, as pointed out by Broughton (1978). In particular, Kurtines and Greif were in error in believing that defects in methodology can lead to a disconfirmation of a stage construct and in believing that the usual personality-test concepts of external validity (for example, predicting behavior) are appropriate for assessing the validity of a stage methodology. The misunderstanding of critics like Kurtines and Greif, however, does not justify the unsatisfactory reliability and validity that we found in our clinical method of assessing stage. Still, the high effort and expense it took to overcome these defects could best be justified by the practical importance of developing a standard and reliable method of assessing the effects of moral education programs. The major obvious theoretical payoff of this development in methodology is that it leads to "confirmation" of the invariance-of-stage-sequence expectation of the theory in longitudinal data from America and Turkey (by blind, intersubjectively reliable scoring methods). As Colby points out, such confirmation of our sequence expectation is not theory demonstration, in the sense of prediction from a prior theory, but rather the result of a circular process involving a revision of the theory in light of previous data. Nevertheless, it does mean that the sequence exists in the samples studied, though replication or other samples are needed. The confirming side of these research results is pointed out by some disconfirming results: the failure to find a sixth stage in American and Turkish longitudinal data. This result indicated that my sixth stage was mainly a theoretical construction suggested by the writings of "elite" figures like Martin Luther King, not an empirically confirmed developmental construct. In light of Colby's analysis of substages, we now think the safest interpretation would be to view the construct of a sixth stage as representing an elaboration of the B (or advanced) substage of Stage 5.

Colby suggests that the progress of the methodology project is progress in successive differentiation of stage structure from normative content in moral judgment. Colby stresses the increased reliability and validity of the stage-structure concept and method which has resulted from the differentiation. Of equal importance, however, is the development of our knowledge of content which has resulted. The method now makes it possible to analyze the development of content as well as of reasoning structure in terms of culturally universal (and culturally unique) norms and elements of moral values—the "atoms" of moral value content. This analysis of content immediately finds its use in the research described by Power and Reimer. The development over time of the content of the Cluster School moral atmosphere can now be described as the formation of new norms and new elements; and the idea of an "element" finds its use in our analysis of a child's sense of community.

It is my hope that these chapters will illustrate, as well as encourage, the movement of moral development research beyond either a cultist focus on moral judgment stages or a countercultist critique of them to an examination of the enduring problems of moral development and moral education.

references

Blatt, M., and Kohlberg, L. "The Effects of Classroom Moral Discussion upon Children's Level of Moral Judgment." *Journal of Moral Education*, 1975, *4*, 129-161.

Broughton, J. "Dialectics and Moral Development Ideology." In P. Scharf (Ed.), *Readings in Moral Education*. Minneapolis: Winston Press, 1978.

Durkheim, E. *Moral Education: A Study in the Theory and Application of the Sociology of Education*. New York: Free Press, 1961.

Hartshorne, H., and May, M. S. *Studies in the Nature of Character.* 2 vols. New York: Macmillan, 1928-1930.

Kohlberg, L. "Stage and Sequence: The Cognitive-Developmental Approach to Socialization." In D. Goslin (Ed.), *Handbook of Socialization Theory and Research.* Chicago: Rand McNally, 1969.

Kohlberg, L. "Education for Justice: A Modern Statement of the Platonic View." In T. Sizer (Ed.), *Moral Education.* Cambridge, Mass.: Harvard University Press, 1970.

Kohlberg, L. "From Is to Ought: How to Commit the Naturalistic Fallacy and Get Away with It in the Study of Moral Development." In T. Mischel (Ed.), *Cognitive Development and Epistemology.* New York: Academic Press, 1971.

Kohlberg, L. Introduction to P. Scharf (Ed.), *Readings in Moral Education.* Minneapolis: Winston Press, 1978.

Kohlberg, L., and Mayer, R. "Development as the Aim of Education." *Harvard Education Review,* 1972, *42,* 4.

Kohlberg, L., and Turiel, E. "Moral Development and Moral Education." In C. Beck and E. Sullivan (Eds.), *Psychology and Educational Practice.* Glenview, Ill.: Scott, Foresman, 1971.

Kurtines, W., and Greif, E. "The Development of Moral Thought: Review and Evaluation of Kohlberg's Approach." *Psychological Bulletin,* 1974, *81* (8), 453-470.

Reimer, J. "A Study in the Moral Development of Kibbutz Adolescents." Unpublished doctoral dissertation, Harvard University, 1977.

Lawrence Kohlberg is professor of education and social psychology at Harvard University.

57

Children's Reasoning about Interpersonal and Moral Conflicts

Judith G. Smetana

University of Rochester

Melanie Killen

Wesleyan University

Elliot Turiel

University of California, Berkeley

SMETANA, JUDITH G.; KILLEN, MELANIE; and TURIEL, ELLIOT. *Children's Reasoning about Interpersonal and Moral Conflicts.* CHILD DEVELOPMENT, 1991, **62,** 629–644. 2 studies were conducted to determine if children make judgments about both justice and interpersonal relations in conflictful situations. In Study 1, 48 subjects (24 males and 24 females) in the third, sixth, and ninth grades (mean ages = 8.40, 11.38, 14.38 years) were administered 2 stories entailing conflicts between justice and interpersonal concerns. Children judged and justified acts in 4 conditions systematically varying interpersonal and justice concerns. Children generally gave priority to justice and rights over friendship, based primarily on considerations of welfare or rights. In Study 2, 76 subjects (39 males and 37 females) in the third, sixth, and ninth grades (mean ages = 9.08, 12.10, 14.92 years) were presented with 3 stories entailing conflicts between justice and interpersonal relations. Subjects gave greater priority to interpersonal considerations in Study 2 than in Study 1, and their evaluations varied according to the salience of the different concerns. In both studies, few gender differences were obtained. The results demonstrate that across development, concerns with justice and interpersonal relationships coexist in judgments of male and female children, and that the ways they are applied depend on the situation.

A complex and vexing problem for moral theory and research on social development is the connection between interpersonal relationships and particularistic or generalized moral obligations. Interpersonal and moral considerations are important aspects of social interactions that can be in conflict. On the one hand, it is recognized that persons in close relationships (e.g., friends, family) have special obligations to each other. On the other hand, concerns with issues like justice, rights, and welfare are thought to entail obligations that often transcend particular interpersonal ties. For example, from the moral point of view, there are problems with favoritism in the distribution of goods, or with granting certain rights to and ensuring the welfare of only some people (such as friends, family, or members of one's racial and ethnic group) and not others. At the same time, subordinating the interests of close relations in favor of abstract moral claims of strangers is problematic, certainly from a subjective perspective, and perhaps from an ethical one (Scheffler, 1988; Williams, 1981).

The link between interpersonal relationships and considerations of justice, rights, or welfare has been considered in several approaches to social and moral development (e.g., Damon, 1977; Selman, 1980). In particular, there is an ongoing debate regarding how to best characterize the development of justice and interpersonal concerns. Gilligan (1982) has argued that Kohlberg's (1969, 1971) formulation of stages of moral development fails to adequately distinguish a morality of justice from a morality of care in interpersonal concerns and that, in Kohlberg's sequence, the latter is relegated to lower stages. Gilligan and her colleagues (e.g., Gilligan & Attanucci, 1988) propose that interpersonal concerns and jus-

We thank Patricia Barasch, Jennifer Lewis, Kathleen McBrien, Toni Saunders, Loree Vaillancour, and Jenny Yau for their assistance with the research. Reprint requests should be sent to Judith G. Smetana, Graduate School of Education and Human Development, University of Rochester, Rochester, NY 14627.

59

tice constitute two distinct types of moral orientation linked to gender, and that each type can take a different developmental trajectory in different individuals. For the most part, morality in males is dominated by concerns with justice and rights; for females it is dominated by concerns with care in interpersonal relationships.[1]

In the present research, we explored the proposition that concerns with interpersonal relationships and justice coexist within individuals (males and females) across development, and that the ways they are applied or coordinated may partially depend on parameters of the situation in which judgments are made. This perspective is adopted from research demonstrating that children form domains of social knowledge, including morality (justice, rights, welfare), social convention, and psychological issues (Nucci, 1981; Smetana, 1985; Turiel, 1983; Turiel, Smetana, & Killen, 1991). The research indicates that individuals hold heterogeneous social orientations and coordinate and weigh different situational features when evaluating situations that entail social conflicts.

For most people, maintaining and fostering interpersonal relationships is a central social consideration. However, judgments about justice or welfare can apply to persons in close relationships and to those with lesser or no interpersonal ties. Therefore, concerns with interpersonal relations can be in conflict with justice, rights, or welfare considerations in at least two ways. Justice or welfare considerations can conflict with an interpersonal concern that is morally neutral or even negative (e.g., giving priority to a friend in distributing resources when a stranger has a more just claim). There also

can be a conflict in the application of justice or welfare considerations in interpersonal and impersonal relationships (e.g., choosing between helping a sibling or a stranger when both are in need). If interpersonal and justice considerations do coexist in males and females, then we would expect that the ways these considerations are applied by them will, at least in part, depend on the situation (e.g., the nature of the relationship, the salience of an injustice). For instance, in situations in which the justice considerations are not in strong conflict with interpersonal considerations, females and males might give priority to justice and rights over interpersonal concerns, whereas in other situations, they might give priority to maintaining interpersonal relationships over justice. Our proposition, therefore, differs from the proposition that features of the situations (for instance, the type of dilemma) interact with subjects' gender in influencing responses of justice or care (Miller & Luthar, 1989; Pratt et al., 1988; Rothbart et al., 1986; Walker et al., 1987), as well as the proposition that the moral status of each type of orientation is culturally determined (Miller, Bersoff, & Harwood, 1990).

Two studies were undertaken in the present research. One aim was to ascertain if females and males differentiate justice concerns from concerns with maintaining and fostering interpersonal relationships, and if their judgments are influenced by situational features. In this regard, we distinguished among maintenance of relationships, concerns with welfare (avoiding harm to others), and justice or rights. It should be noted, therefore, that this research was not designed as a direct test of Gilligan's

---

[1] Gilligan's (1977, 1982) propositions have led to a number of investigations and reanalyses of existing data. Lyons (1983) reports data supporting Gilligan's propositions, although her scoring system has been criticized by Walker, de Vries, and Trevethan (1987); other studies using Lyons's scoring system on small samples (Gilligan & Attanucci, 1988) suggest that most adults use both orientations, but that females are more likely to focus on care, and males are more likely to focus on justice. Based on an extensive review and meta-analysis of studies using Kohlberg's assessments, Walker (1984) concludes that the overall pattern of studies provides no evidence for the sex differences suggested by Gilligan. (Walker's conclusions have been questioned by Baumrind [1986]; also see Walker's [1986a] rebuttal.) Several studies (Pratt, Golding, & Hunter, 1984; Walker, 1986b, 1989; Walker et al., 1987) examining the justice versus care orientation as scored within Kohlberg's system failed to find support for the predicted pattern of sex differences. Gibbs, Arnold, and Burkhart (1984) found no overall stage differences between males and females, but they interpret significant differences in the types of reasons males and females at Stage 3 endorse as consistent with Gilligan's thesis. Finally, several studies have found that type of dilemma (e.g., hypothetical vs. real-life), rather than gender, influences justice and care responses (Pratt, Golding, Hunter, & Sampson, 1988; Rothbart, Hanley, & Albert, 1986), although other studies found more equivocal support for such differences (Ford & Lowery, 1986; Walker, 1989; Walker et al., 1987). These two sets of studies, however, found no sex differences within orientations.

hypotheses since our definition of interpersonal concerns differs somewhat from hers. Gilligan's care orientation focuses primarily on positive responsiveness to others (though her definition does include a concern with maintaining relationships). Study 1 examined interpersonal concerns in the context of avoiding harm or unfairness to others. This was done in order to assess whether children differentiate justice and concerns with maintaining relationships.

In Study 1, the situations initially presented to children posed justice or rights considerations in conflict with interpersonal expectations (from a close friend) serving motives of self-interest. Therefore, in these situations justice and rights considerations were in conflict with interpersonal expectations which did not have compelling welfare, justice, or rights components. In addition, the salience of each type of consideration was systematically varied either by changing the interpersonal relationship (from close friend to sibling to acquaintance) or by changing the magnitude of the violation of justice or rights. It was expected that females and males would give priority to the justice or rights considerations in the initially presented situations, and that their judgments would change in accord with shifts in the salience of the situational components.

Study 2 included stronger conflicts between justice and claims of an interpersonal nature by presenting situations in which the interpersonal expectations were positive in their intent and goals (not motivated by self-interest). Study 2 more directly pertains to Gilligan's care orientation than Study 1, since concerns with welfare, justice, and rights could be applied to interpersonal relations and impersonally. Our expectation was that situational features would be more important than gender in children's justice or interpersonal considerations.

Study 1

One aim of Study 1 was to ascertain whether, in certain situations, both males and females make judgments based primarily on justice and rights, even in interpersonal contexts. Toward this end, children were presented with hypothetical situations which posed the possibility of committing a transgression to maintain a friendship by furthering the self-interest of the friend. For each of two types of transgression, unequal distribution (fairness) and stealing (property

rights), children were presented with a conflict (referred to as the Initial Situation), and their evaluations and reasoning were assessed. A further aim of Study 1 was to determine whether judgments are influenced by changes in the salience of the interpersonal or fairness/rights components. The salience of the components in each situation were systematically varied by presenting children with different information.

The interpersonal components of the situations were varied by altering only the type of relationship depicted. In one variation, the interpersonal relationship was described as between acquaintances (thus decreasing the salience), and in the other, the relationship was described as involving siblings (thus increasing the salience). The salience of the fairness or rights components was varied by changing the magnitude of the transgression. In the situation pertaining to unequal distribution, the salience of the fairness component was increased by depicting the transgression as more severe than in the Initial Situation, whereas in the stealing situation, the transgression was depicted as less severe. As previous research has shown that stealing is evaluated as more wrong than unequal distribution (Smetana, 1981; Smetana, Kelly, & Twentyman, 1984), this was done to counterbalance differences between the two situations in the magnitude of the transgression depicted. Second, the type of transgression was varied to assess additional fairness or rights transgressions. Thus, in one variation, physical harm was pitted against maintaining a friendship, whereas in the other variation a trust violation was pitted against maintaining a friendship.

Subjects evaluated what the story protagonist should do and provided justifications for their choices. In addition, the ways that children weighed the different alternatives were also examined by coding whether children discussed both fairness/rights and the interpersonal choices in making their judgments or whether they considered only one alternative. This was done as a further test of the hypothesis that children separate and distinguish between fairness/rights and interpersonal issues.

It was expected that in the Initial Situations, children would generally judge that fairness or rights considerations should have priority over friendship expectations. However, in situations in which the interpersonal considerations were more salient (e.g., the sibling condition) and/or the fairness/rights components were less salient, it was expected that children would give priority to maintaining the interpersonal relationship. Finally, it was expected that children would give priority to justice/rights when these considerations were made more salient.

METHOD

Subjects

Subjects in this study were 48 children evenly divided into eight males and eight females at the third, sixth, and ninth grades (mean ages = 8.40, 11.38, 14.38 years, respectively). Subjects, who were middle class and from different ethnic groups, came from one elementary school and one junior high school in the San Francisco Bay area.

Procedure

Each subject was individually administered questions pertaining to two hypothetical situations by a female interviewer who was blind to the hypotheses of the study. The interviews took approximately 35 min and were tape-recorded and transcribed. Each situation began with an initial description of a conflict between a fairness or rights precept and an expectation from a friend (the Initial Situation). The story descriptions, questions, and salience variations are summarized in Table 1. Story 1 depicts a child who is requested by a friend to distribute candy unequally. Story 2 depicts a child who is asked by a friend to steal for her. For the Initial Situations, subjects were asked to

make judgments as to what the protagonist should do and why. Then, subjects were asked about two interpersonal variations of the Initial Situation: whether the transgression should be done (*a*) for an acquaintance and (*b*) for a sibling (referred to as the Acquaintance and Sibling conditions, respectively). Finally, subjects were presented with two variations in fairness and rights that increased the magnitude of the transgressions. First, the amount of need was varied. In the distributive justice story, a situation of greater need of distribution (increased salience of fairness) was described, and the stealing story, a situation of less need for the goods (increased salience of property rights) was described (Greater Need and Less Need conditions, respectively). In another variation, the type of act was changed to depict physical harm (instead of distributive justice) and violating a trust (instead of stealing). These changes in the type of act were made to include more than one stimulus item for each story (Physical Harm and Trust Violation conditions, respectively). For each story, five sets of judgments and justifications were obtained (Table 1).

Coding and Reliability

Responses were coded using three systems developed for this study but based on previous work (Davidson, Turiel, & Black, 1983; Killen, 1990). Twelve protocols, four from subjects at each grade level, were randomly selected to refine the coding systems.

TABLE 1

STORY THEMES AND CONDITIONS FOR STUDY 1

Sharing Story
Initial Situation: Bob brings candy to share with everyone. His close friend George does not want Bob to give candy to Tim. George and Tim do not get along and Tim has been picking on George.
Interpersonal condition—Acquaintance: Bob is asked by an acquaintance (who does not get along with Tim) to not share with Tim.
Interpersonal condition—Sibling: Bob is asked by his brother (who does not get along with Tim) to not share with Tim.
Greater Need condition: Bob, who is in charge of distributing lunches, does not give one to Tim because he had picked on George.
Physical Harm condition: Bob inflicts physical harm on Tim to please George.

Stealing Story
Initial Situation: Pat asks her close friend Diane to steal a set of pens accessible to Diane and needed by Pat.
Interpersonal condition—Acquaintance: Diane is asked by an acquaintance to take pens.
Interpersonal condition—Sibling: Diane is asked by her sister to take pens.
Less Need condition: Diane is asked to take a pack of gum for her friend.
Trust condition: Diane is asked to break a promise in order to engage in an activity with her friend.

The coders, all of whom were females, were unaware of the study's hypotheses and subjects' gender. First, *judgments* as to what the protagonist should do were coded dichotomously as (1) affirming the choice of fairness (sharing) or rights (not stealing), or (2) affirming the interpersonal choice. The second coding, referred to as *coordination of components,* assessed the extent to which children integrated different choices when evaluating the conflicts. Responses were coded into two categories: a focus on both considerations and a focus on only one element. Third, *justifications* for choices were coded into five categories: (a) *fairness-welfare:* fairness ("it's not fair"), physical welfare ("she'll get hurt"), and psychological welfare ("he'll feel bad"); (b) *interpersonal:* maintain friendship/familial relationships or establish friendship ("it's the best thing to do so that they can stay friends"); (c) *psychological:* dispositional or personality characteristics of an actor as basis for evaluating an act ("if he doesn't give the candy to George he would become a greedy person and grow up to be mean"); (d) *conventional:* violation of a social norm ("he would be breaking the school rule"); and (e) *personal:* act within individual jurisdiction ("he can do whatever he wants; it's up to him to decide"). In coding justifications, we followed the procedure used in previous research (Davidson et al., 1983) of combining fairness and welfare responses (welfare is defined as acts that negatively affect another's physical or psychological well-being). There were no differences on the major study variables (age, sex, or condition) between fairness and welfare responses. In Story 1, fairness and welfare responses occurred in equal frequencies. Story 2 resulted in greater use of fairness (79%) than welfare (21%) responses.

Interrater reliability between two coders using 12 protocols in coding judgments, coordination of components, and justifications (using Cohen's kappa) was .80, .83, and .82, respectively.

RESULTS

Judgments
Table 2 displays the percentage of children at each age who give priority to sharing equally (Story 1) and not stealing (Story 2) for each condition. Responses for each story were analyzed by a 3 (grade) × 2 (sex) × 5 (salience condition) repeated-measures analysis of variance (ANOVA) with condition as the repeated measure. Responses

were arcsine-transformed to correct for nonnormality, which may sometimes occur with the use of percentages (Winer, 1971). In these and other analyses, Duncan multiple-range tests and Bonferroni t tests were performed to test for significant between-subjects and within-subjects effects, respectively.

Story 1: Sharing.—As can be seen in Table 2, for the most part the majority of subjects gave priority to the act of sharing in the Initial Situation; 87% overall). However, responses did vary by salience condition, $F(4,164) = 13.98$, $p < .0001$. As expected, Bonferroni t tests showed that greater priority was given to avoiding the transgression in the Physical Harm condition (98%) than in the Initial Situation (83%) or in the Sibling condition (74%; p's < .005). In addition, greater priority was given to sharing in the Greater Need condition (94%) than in the Sibling condition ($p < .005$). There were no significant main effects for sex (females = 93%; males = 84%) or grade (91%, 88%, and 87% for third, sixth, and ninth grades, respectively), and sex did not interact significantly with condition or grade.

Story 2: Stealing.—As with sharing, there was a main effect for salience condition, $F(4,164) = 15.16$, $p < .0001$. As expected, Bonferroni t tests indicated that children more frequently gave priority to the prescription against stealing in the Acquaintance condition (89%) or in the Less Need condition (81%) than when asked to steal by a friend as described in the Initial Situation (51%; p's < .005). In addition, children more frequently judged it wrong to steal in the Acquaintance condition than in the Sibling condition (60%), or to break a promise in the Trust Violation condition (43%; p's < .005). Children also judged it more wrong to steal in the Less Need condition than to break a promise in the Trust Violation condition ($p < .005$). There was no significant main effect for sex (males = 58%, females = 70% giving priority to not stealing). However, responses varied by grade, $F(2,41) = 17.80$; $p < .0001$. Third graders gave greater priority to not stealing than did sixth and ninth graders (90%, 59%, 44%, respectively).

There was a significant grade × condition interaction, $F(8,164) = 2.21$, $p < .05$. In the Initial Situation, third graders gave greater priority to not stealing than did sixth or ninth graders, $F(2,41) = 6.68$, $p < .01$. In the Trust Violation condition, third graders

TABLE 2

RESPONSES (in %) AFFIRMING SHARING AND NOT STEALING

STORY AND CONDITION	GRADE 3		GRADE 6		GRADE 9		
	Males	Females	Males	Females	Males	Females	TOTAL
Sharing story:							
Initial Situation	100	88	63	88	86	75	83
Interpersonal—Acquaintance	75	100	88	100	100	100	94
Interpersonal—Sibling	88	75	63	100	43	75	74
Greater Need	100	88	88	100	86	100	94
Physical Harm[a]	100	100	88	100	100	100	98
Stealing Story:							
Initial Situation	88	75	13	75	14	38	51
Interpersonal—Acquaintance	100	100	75	100	71	88	89
Interpersonal—Sibling	88	75	13	88	43	50	60
Less Need	100	100	63	88	71	63	81
Trust Violation[b]	88	88	50	25	0	0	43

[a] The Physical Harm condition was in place of Sharing.
[b] The Trust Violation condition was in place of Not Stealing.

more frequently judged it wrong to break a promise than did sixth or ninth graders, and sixth graders more frequently judged it wrong to break a promise than did ninth graders, $F(2,41) = 23.39, p < .0001$. Furthermore, in the Less Need condition, third graders gave greater priority to not stealing than did ninth graders, $F(2,41) = 3.19, p < .05$. A similar finding was obtained for the Sibling condition, which approached significance, $F(2,41) = 3.00, p < .06$.

Coordination of Components

In order to assess whether subjects considered the two components in arriving at their choices, analyses were performed on the percentage of responses entailing a consideration of both fairness/rights and interpersonal components. A 3 (grade) × 2 (sex) × 5 (salience condition) repeated-measures ANOVA with condition as the repeated measure was performed separately upon arcsine-transformed responses for each story.

Story 1: Sharing.—The majority of responses (72% overall) indicated a consideration of the two components in making judgments, although this varied by salience condition, as indicated by a significant main effect, $F(4,164) = 8.15, p < .0001$. Subjects more frequently considered both fairness and interpersonal components in the Initial Situation (92%) and the Sibling condition (81%) than in the Greater Need condition (50%).

Sex was not significant in this analysis. However, age differences were obtained. Sixth and ninth graders considered both components to a greater extent than did third

graders, $F(2,41) = 10.30, p < .001$ (79%, 84%, 52%, respectively). A grade × condition interaction, $F(8,164) = 3.24, p < .05$, indicated that differences occurred in the Acquaintance condition, $F(2,41) = 8.89, p < .001$, the Greater Need condition, $F(2,41) = 6.87, p < .01$, and the Physical Harm condition, $F(2,41) = 5.54, p < .01$. In the Acquaintance and Physical Harm conditions, sixth and ninth graders considered both elements to a greater extent than did third graders (82%, 94%, 37% in the Acquaintance condition; 88%, 72%, 37% in the Physical Harm condition); in the Greater Need condition, ninth graders considered both elements to a greater extent than did third graders (80%, 19%).

Story 2: Stealing.—In this story, too, the majority of responses (63%) indicated a consideration of both components. A main effect for salience condition, $F(4,164) = 7.77, p < .0001$, revealed that subjects considered both components to a greater extent in the Initial Situation (91%) than in the Acquaintance, Sibling, Less Need, and Trust Violation conditions (55%, 66%, 51%, 51%, respectively; p's $< .0001$). A main effect for grade, $F(2,41) = 6.23, p < .01$, indicated that, as with the previous story, sixth and ninth graders considered both components to a greater extent than did third graders (72%, 72%, 45%, respectively).

Justifications

The justifications were separated by subjects' choices in the stories. Table 3 presents the percentage of justification categories used by subjects at each grade and for

TABLE 3

JUSTIFICATIONS (in %) AFFIRMING SHARING AND NOT STEALING

	SHARING STORY			STEALING STORY		
Grade:	3	6	9	3	6	9
Initial Situation:						
Fairness-Welfare	60	33	40	69	44	23
Interpersonal	18	12	13	12	0	3
Psychological	18	33	30	0	0	3
Other	0	0	0	0	0	3
Interpersonal—Acquaintance:						
Fairness-Welfare	57	72	43	75	66	53
Interpersonal	14	9	50	9	6	23
Psychological	11	9	0	16	16	6
Other	0	3	7	0	0	0
Interpersonal-Sibling:						
Fairness-Welfare	47	41	26	59	25	37
Interpersonal	25	16	10	0	6	3
Psychological	9	22	23	22	19	3
Other	0	9	0	0	0	0
Need:[a]						
Fairness-Welfare	92	69	73	91	69	80
Interpersonal	2	3	3	0	0	0
Psychological	3	19	7	3	6	0
Other	0	0	10	6	0	0
Physical Harm/Trust Violation:[b]						
Fairness-Welfare	71	49	76	75	31	0
Interpersonal	15	9	10	6	0	0
Psychological	15	34	12	3	6	0
Other	0	0	0	3	0	0

[a] This condition depicted greater need for the Sharing story and Lesser Need for the Not Stealing story.
[b] The Physical Harm condition was in place of Sharing and the Trust Violation condition was in place of Not stealing.

each condition for the choice to share and not steal. (Because there were so few sex differences, responses for boys and girls are combined.) Since conventional and personal justifications were used infrequently, they were combined into an Other category and dropped from further analysis. Each justification could have been used with either choice in the story (e.g., the interpersonal justification for a sharing choice or a fairness-welfare justification for an interpersonal choice). The table shows that three categories (fairness-welfare, interpersonal, and psychological) were primarily used for the sharing and not stealing choices. For each story, separate 3 (grade) × 2 (sex) × 5 (salience condition) repeated-measures multivariate analyses of variance (MANOVAs) were performed on the arcsine-transformed proportions of responses in the fairness-welfare, interpersonal, and psychological categories.[2]

Three categories (fairness-welfare, interpersonal, and personal choice) were used in explaining the interpersonal choices of not sharing and not stealing. Given their low frequency, however, these data were not statistically analyzed.

Story 1: Sharing.—The MANOVA revealed differences in the choice of sharing, $F(2,38) = 43.96$, $p < .0001$; overall, fairness-welfare justifications (54%) were used more frequently than interpersonal (12%) or psychological (20%) justifications (p's $< .0001$). There was a significant main effect for salience condition in justifications on the MANOVA, $F(8,32) = 10.03$, $p < .0001$. Bonferroni t tests revealed that children more frequently used welfare-fairness justifications in the conditions with increased salience of the fairness component: they were used more in the Greater Need and Physical Harm conditions than in

[2] Analyses of covariance indicated that all significant effects remained statistically significant with story choice controlled.

the Initial Situation (p's $< .0001$) and in the Greater Need condition than in the Sibling condition ($p < .0001$). Children more frequently used interpersonal justifications in the Initial Situation and the Acquaintance condition than in the Greater Need condition (p's $< .005$). Psychological justifications were used more frequently in the Initial Situation than in the Acquaintance or Greater Need conditions (p's $< .005$). Finally, the MANOVA also revealed a significant salience condition $\times$ grade interaction in justifications, $F(16,64) = 3.04$, $p < .001$. There were grade $\times$ condition interactions for fairness-welfare justifications, $F(8,168) = 2.93$, $p < .01$, and interpersonal justifications, $F(8,168) = 2.97$, $p < .01$. In the Initial Situation, third graders gave more fairness-welfare justifications than did sixth or ninth graders, $F(2,44) = 6.62$, $p < .01$, whereas in the Physical Harm condition, third and ninth graders gave more fairness-welfare justifications than did sixth graders, $F(2,44) = 4.08$, $p < .05$. In the Acquaintance condition, ninth graders gave more interpersonal justifications than did third or sixth graders, $F(2,42) = 5.33$, $p < .01$. No sex differences in justifications were obtained.

Story 2: Stealing.—The justifications for the choice of not stealing paralleled the sharing choice in that the fairness-welfare justification was used more often than the others, as indicated by significant differences among justifications, $F(2,40) = 124.73$, $p < .0001$ (fairness-welfare = 50%; interpersonal = 3%; psychological = 5%). The MANOVA also revealed a main effect for grade, $F(4,80) = 6.26$, $p < .001$. Third graders more frequently justified the wrongness of stealing on the basis of fairness-welfare concerns than did sixth or ninth graders, $F(2,44) = 8.51$, $p < .0001$. Finally, the MANOVA revealed a significant main effect for salience condition, $F(8,34) = 5.63$, $p < .0001$. Children more frequently used welfare-fairness justifications in the Less Need condition than in the Initial Situation or the Acquaintance condition, p's $< .005$. Children more frequently used interpersonal justifications in the Acquaintance condition than in the Greater Need condition, p's $< .005$.

DISCUSSION

Study 1 demonstrates that children of both genders make judgments about justice and rights both in situations in which justice or rights considerations were in minimal conflict with interpersonal considerations

(e.g., the Initial Situations) and in situations in which the salience of the fairness-rights and interpersonal considerations were varied (to shift the balance between the two components). For most conditions, the majority of children gave priority to the fairness and rights choices over meeting the expectations of a friend, and their fairness and welfare justifications were consonant with their evaluations. There were no gender differences in the use of either fairness or welfare justifications.

The study also demonstrated that females and males take into consideration interpersonal concerns, and that they are attuned to situational features. With regard to stealing, children gave greater priority to interpersonal relationships and judged it more acceptable to violate rights for a friend or a sibling than for an acquaintance. In turn, the salience of the fairness and rights components influenced children's judgments and reasoning. For instance, when the need to share was increased (Greater Need condition in Story 1) or when the transgressions would result in physical harm, most children subordinated the interpersonal consideration. Similarly, when a child was asked by a friend to steal something of lesser need (Story 2), most subjects did not give priority to the interpersonal consideration. Reasoning in these situations was consistent with evaluations since children used fairness-welfare justifications to an even greater extent in the conditions with increased salience of the justice or rights components.

Based on previous research (Davidson et al., 1983; Smetana, 1985; Turiel, 1983), justifications pertaining to welfare and rights were combined in these analyses and compared to interpersonal justifications, which pertained primarily to maintaining friendships. This differs from previous research more directly testing Gilligan's hypotheses, where reasoning regarding care and interpersonal relations has been combined (e.g., Gilligan & Attanucci, 1988; Lyons, 1983; Miller & Luthar, 1989; Rothbart et al., 1986; Walker et al., 1987). It is possible that this procedure underestimated the prevalence of "care" responses in our sample. However, our conclusions are based on the findings for judgments as well as justifications, and it is important to note the congruence between them.

Analyses of the coordination of components represent a more fine-grained assessment of whether children are cognizant of each component than assessments of judgments. In some conditions, children of all the ages and both genders considered both components in their judgments. However, the finding that with age children become more consistent in considering both components when the two are placed in greater conflict must be interpreted cautiously. These findings may reflect an increased cognitive capacity to coordinate components in situations with greater conflicts, or they may simply reflect an increased ability to express judgments about the two components. In any event, the findings are consistent with Walker et al. (1987), who found that individuals at higher levels of moral development evidenced substantial amounts of both response and rights orientations in their reasoning. If our results were to reflect changes in cognitive capacities, it would indicate that, with age, children take more aspects of the situation into account in making judgments. More generally, the extent to which children evaluated both components varied according to the different salience conditions. Considered in conjunction with the results from the analysis of judgments, Study 1 suggests that children focused solely on justice and rights only in situations where those claims were most compelling (e.g., in situations of greater need) and in situations where the interpersonal claims were less convincing (e.g., the Acquaintance condition).

Study 1 primarily ascertained that female and male children reason on the basis of justice, rights, and welfare when those considerations are in conflict with self-interested interpersonal expectations from friends or siblings. The study did not address how children make judgments and reason about conflicts in which the interpersonal expectations have legitimacy and in which acts are performed to be helpful, kind, or considerate to another (rather than to avoid losing a friendship). Furthermore, since the order of conditions was not varied in Study 1, it is possible that the effects found for salience conditions were due to repeatedly asking children the same questions. Finally, the results may be unreliable due to the small sample size. Study 2 was designed to address these issues.

Study 2

Study 1 established that the availability of either interpersonal or justice concepts does not differ by gender and provided a context for additional research on judgments

about compelling conflicts between the two types of considerations. It is possible that females are more oriented than males to interpersonal considerations with positive intent and goals, as others (Rothbart et al., 1986) have claimed. There is no indication of this, however, from Study 1. Our hypothesis, instead, as noted earlier, is that the application of both justice and interpersonal concerns depends on elements of the situation.

The stimulus situations in Study 2 posed conflicts between justice or rights and interpersonal relationships calling for helpful or kind acts. Subjects were posed with situations in which an interpersonal act that benefits a friend or sibling entails unfairness or violation of rights toward an acquaintance or stranger. It is important to note that these stimulus situations (unlike Study 1) involve conflicts between welfare in interpersonal contexts, on the one hand, and impartial justice and rights considerations on the other. This comparison should be kept in mind when interpreting our terminology (for simplicity's sake we continue to refer to the components as interpersonal and justice/rights).

Three stories were used in Study 2. One depicted a brother's attempt to care for his vulnerable younger sister; by helping his sister the boy's action would result in unfair treatment of another female. In the second story, a girl chooses between (a) meeting a sick friend's request to help her complete a task to win a science fair contest, and (b) a boy's claim that doing so would violate the fairness of the competition. The third story was a conflict between welfare and property rights modeled after situations used by Kohlberg (1969) and Gilligan (1982), but adjusted to be more comprehensible to children. The conflict revolved around the choice to steal in order to protect the physical welfare of a sibling. We hypothesized that judgments and justifications would vary by the situation and that there would be no gender differences.

The methods of this study were similar to those of Study 1. Subjects were asked to judge and provide justifications about an Initial Situation. Then they were presented with conditions varying the salience of justice/rights and interpersonal components. Because Study 2 had three stories instead of two, the moral and interpersonal components were each varied in one condition (rather than two) to reduce the demands on the subjects. Since Study 1 indicated that nearly all children gave priority to justice/ rights in the Acquaintance condition, this condition was dropped in Study 2. The interpersonal conditions thus either depicted a friend or a sibling, depending on the relationship described in the Initial Situation. This, in turn, was varied to control for order effects in each story. The justice/rights conditions in the three stories varied in depicting situations of greater need, a different act (lying), and a rule violation.

METHOD

Subjects

A different sample of subjects from those in Study 1, consisting of 76 children (39 males and 37 females), was used in Study 2. There were 13 males and 11 females at the third grade, 14 males and 12 females at the sixth grade, and 12 males and 14 females at the ninth grade (mean ages = 9.08, 12.10, 14.92 years, respectively). As in Study 1, they were of mixed ethnicity and middle class. They were recruited from two elementary schools and two junior high schools in the San Francisco Bay area.

Procedure

Subjects were individually administered questions about three hypothetical situations, presented in counterbalanced order, by two females who were blind to the hypotheses of the study. The interview took

about 40 min and was tape-recorded and transcribed. The story descriptions, question, and variations in the components are summarized in Table 4. The first two stories (referred to as the music club and science club stories) depict conflicts between fairness and welfare in interpersonal relationships, and the third (the hurt brother story) depicts a conflict between protecting the physical welfare of a sibling and theft (the violation of property rights served interpersonal and welfare ends).

The situations were presented in the same way as in the previous study. To prevent fatigue because of an additional story, only one interpersonal and one justice/rights condition were presented for each story (see Table 4). Since the Initial Situations in two stories depicted sibling relationships, the relationship was varied to depict a friendship. The Initial Situation of the other story described a friendship relationship, and therefore in the interpersonal condition, a sibling relationship was described. Each story also had a different variation in the magnitude of the fairness or rights component. In the music club story, the salience of the fairness component was increased by describing a situation of greater need on the part of the girl than the sister. In the science project story, the fairness condition included the existence of an explicit rule prohibiting help for the contestants. In the hurt brother story,

TABLE 4

STORY THEMES AND CONDITIONS FOR STUDY 2

Music Club Story

Initial Situation: Sam, the leader of an afterschool club, lets his younger sister join the club to stop other children from teasing her. There is only space for one new member, and another girl is more deserving.

Interpersonal condition: Sam lets a friend into the club instead of another more deserving person.

Greater Need condition: The other girl would lose all her friends and be very unhappy if she were not in the club.

Science Project Story

Initial Situation: Amy is too sick to work on her science fair project and asks her best friend Sally to help her finish it. John, who is also competing in the science fair, thinks it would be unfair to have someone else help Amy on her project.

Interpersonal condition—Friend: Sally is asked by her younger sister to finish the work.

Rule Violation condition: The contest has an explicit rule prohibiting obtaining help.

Hurt Brother Story

Initial Situation: Walking home with his brother Jimmy, Marvin trips and cuts his leg. Very worried about his brother and not having enough money to call their mother, Jimmy goes to a store, but the storeowner won't let him use his phone. Jimmy takes $10 lying on the register to make a phone call to their mother.

Interpersonal condition—Friend: It is Jimmy's friend who is hurt rather than his brother.

Lying condition: Jimmy lies to the storeowner, telling him the $10 belongs to him.

TABLE 5

RESPONSES (in %) ENDORSING THE NONINTERPERSONAL CHOICE (Not Admitting Sister/
Not Taking Money/Not Helping Friend)

STORY AND CONDITION	GRADE 3		GRADE 6		GRADE 9		
	Males	Females	Males	Females	Males	Females	TOTAL
Music Club Story:							
Initial Situation	23	55	57	25	75	71	51
Interpersonal—Friend	85	100	93	92	100	100	95
Greater Need	23	55	64	33	75	71	54
Hurt Brother Story:							
Initial Situation	62	73	50	33	58	64	57
Interpersonal—Friend	77	73	29	42	50	64	55
Lying	85	100	86	83	92	100	91
Science Project Story:							
Initial Situation	15	18	36	8	17	36	22
Interpersonal Sibling	15	9	21	8	17	29	17
Rule Violation	92	91	79	75	92	86	84

the type of act was varied to depict a lie in conjunction with theft. As in Study 1, for each condition the child was asked to judge what the protagonist should do and why. Thus, for each of three stories, three sets of judgments and justifications were obtained.

Coding and Reliability

The three coding schemes from Study 1 were used. The first was a dichotomous assessment of *judgments* as to what the protagonist should do. The second was an assessment of the extent to which children integrated different choices when evaluating the conflicts (the *coordination of components* coding), with responses coded into two categories (focus on both components and focus on only one component). *Justifications* were coded using the same categories as in Study 1, with the addition of a *pragmatic* category (retribution or fear of punishment) that had not been given by subjects in Study 1. There were no age, sex, or condition effects in the comparisons of fairness and welfare justifications. Fairness and welfare justifications were used in each of the stories; they were mainly divided in accordance with choices in the stories. Interrater reliability, calculated as kappa coefficients between two coders scoring 20 protocols, was .86, .80, and .85 for judgments, coordination of components, and justifications, respectively.

RESULTS

Judgments

Table 5 displays the percentage of children at each age who gave priority to the fairness or rights choices (i.e., not admitting

the sister in the music club story, not helping the friend in the science project story, and not taking the money in the hurt brother story). The analyses were conducted on the percentage of children at each age who gave priority to the fairness or rights choices (i.e., not admitting the sister in the music club story, not helping the friend in the science project story, and not taking the money in the hurt brother story). Arcsine-transformed responses for each story were analyzed by 3 (grade) × 2 (sex) × 3 (salience condition) repeated-measures ANOVAs with condition as the repeated measure. Again, Duncan multiple-range tests and Bonferroni t tests were used to test significant effects.

Story 1: The music club story.—As seen in Table 5, subjects were evenly split in their choices for the Initial Situation (51% and 49%) and the Greater Need condition (54% and 46%). However, responses did vary by salience condition, $F(2,140) = 42.26, p < .0001$. The Interpersonal condition (friend rather than sibling) resulted in more frequent affirmation of the fairness choice (95%). There was also an age shift in the affirmation of the fairness choice. A main effect for grade, $F(2,70) = 4.92, p < .01$, indicated that ninth graders were more likely to give priority to fairness than third or sixth graders (82%, 57%, 61%, respectively). The main effect for sex was not significant, but there was a significant grade × sex interaction, $F(2,70) = 3.66, p < .05$. Third-grade males gave less priority to the fairness choice than did sixth- or ninth-grade males, $F(2,36) = 5.43, p < .01$ (44%, 71%, 83%, respectively), whereas the sixth-grade females gave less priority to the fairness choice than did ninth-grade females, $F(2,34) = 3.27$, $p < .05$.

Story 2: The science project story.—Table 5 shows that for the science project story only a minority of subjects gave priority to the fairness choice in the Initial Situation (22%) and the Interpersonal condition (17%), but this varied by condition, $F(2,140) = 105.59$, $p < .0001$. When helping the friend involved violating a rule, subjects more frequently judged it wrong to help (84%) than in the other conditions (p's $< .005$). These findings held for males and females across ages; there were no other significant main effects or interactions.

Story 3: Hurt brother story.—In this situation, too, there was a main effect for salience condition, $F(2,140) = 3.09$, $p < .05$. A greater proportion of children judged it wrong to steal in the Lying condition (91%) than in the Initial Situation (57%) or the Interpersonal condition (55%). There was a main effect for grade, $F(2,70) = 3.29$, $p < .05$. Duncan multiple-range tests indicated that third graders more frequently gave priority to not stealing than did sixth graders. No significant differences for gender were obtained.

Coordination of Components

Three (grade) × 2 (sex) × 3 (salience condition) repeated-measures ANOVAS with condition as the repeated measure were performed separately on the arcsine-transformed responses for each story. There were differences in consideration of components among the stories and between conditions within stories. In the music club story the majority of children at all ages (91%) considered both components. There were no main effects or interactions for sex, grade, or salience condition.

The science project story produced an increased use of two components with grade, as it interacted with condition. A main effect for salience condition, $F(2,140) = 11.28$, $p < .0001$, indicated that subjects considered both components more in the Initial Situation (65%), which depicted a friendship relationship, than in the Interpersonal (Sibling) condition (43%) or in the Rule Violation condition (31%). There was a significant grade × salience condition interaction, $F(2,70) = 4.06$, $p < .01$. Sixth and ninth graders more frequently considered both components of the Initial Situation than did third graders, $F(2,70) = 4.83$, $p < .01$ (77%, 77%, 42%, respectively).

In the hurt brother story, no grade or sex differences were obtained. A main effect for salience condition, $F(2,140) = 30.95$, $p < .0001$, indicated that subjects were less likely to consider two components in the Lying condition (13%) than in the Initial Situation (58%) or the Interpersonal (Friend) condition (58%).

Justifications

The percentages of use of justification categories are presented in Tables 6 and 7 as separated by subjects' choices in the stories. Since the conventional, personal, psychological, and pragmatic justification categories were used infrequently for the fairness choice, they were combined into an Other category (as discussed below, in a few conditions these were a substantial amount). In addition, the interpersonal category for the fairness or rights choices was used infrequently (see Table 6). Therefore, only the fairness-welfare justifications for the fairness choice were analyzed, using a 3 (grade) × 2 (sex) × 3 (salience condition) repeated-measure ANOVA. Since the frequency of interpersonal justifications was substantial in some conditions in Study 2, separate 3 (grade) × 2 (sex) × 3 (salience condition) repeated-measures MANOVAs were performed on the arcsine-transformed proportions of fairness-welfare and interpersonal justifications given for the interpersonal choice in each story. Few pragmatic justifications were given for the interpersonal choice, and thus they were not included in these analyses.

As we did in reporting justification category analyses in Study 1, we only highlight the major findings. For the music club story there were no sex differences in the use fairness-welfare justifications for the fairness choice. There were main effects for grade, $F(2,64) = 7.61$, $p < .001$, and salience condition, $F(2,128) = 40.00$, $p < .001$, as well as a grade × salience condition interaction, $F(4,128) = 2.64$, $p < .05$. Bonferroni t tests indicated that children used the fairness-welfare category more in the condition where the interpersonal component was less salient (Interpersonal condition with a friend; 91%) than in the Initial Situation (53%) and the Greater Need condition (44%). Second, across conditions, ninth graders used the fairness-welfare category more than did the younger subjects. The interaction reflects that in the Initial Situation ninth graders used the fairness-welfare category more than did sixth graders, $F(2,67) = 3.34$, $p < .05$, whereas in the Greater Need condi-

TABLE 6

JUSTIFICATIONS (in %) AFFIRMING THE NONINTERPERSONAL CHOICE

	MUSIC CLUB STORY			HURT BROTHER			SCIENCE PROJECT		
Grade:	3	6	9	3	6	9	3	6	9
Initial Situation:									
Fairness-Welfare	45	42	73	45	33	53	14	27	16
Interpersonal	2	0	0	0	0	0	0	0	0
Other	1	1	0	24	29	9	4	4	5
Interpersonal:[a]									
Fairness-Welfare	93	83	96	28	11	40	9	16	23
Interpersonal	2	12	0	0	9	4	0	0	0
Other	0	0	0	42	19	19	0	2	9
Moral:[b]									
Fairness-Welfare	24	34	73	26	37	42	31	46	46
Interpersonal	4	20	2	0	0	2	0	0	0
Other	12	0	8	68	49	45	56	38	44

[a] The Interpersonal condition pertained to friends in the Music Club Story and Hurt Brother Story, and to siblings in the Science Project Story.
[b] The Moral condition pertained to Greater Need in the Music Club Story, to Lying in the Hurt Brother Story, and to Rule Violation in the Science Project Story.

tion ninth graders used it more than did all the younger subjects, $F(2,69) = 9.79$, $p < .001$.

The MANOVA performed on justifications given for the interpersonal choice revealed a significant effect for type of justification, $F(1,64) = 9.42$, $p < .01$. Children used fairness-welfare justifications (20%) more than interpersonal justifications (4%) for the interpersonal choice. The MANOVA also revealed a salience condition × sex interaction in justifications, $F(2,64) = 5.36$, $p < .01$. The fairness-welfare category was used more by females than males for the in-

terpersonal choice in the Greater Need condition, $F(1,68) = 4.19$, $p < .05$.

For the science project story, there were no sex or grade effects in use of the fairness-welfare category for the fairness choice, as shown in Table 6. The only differences obtained were a main effect for salience condition on the MANOVA, $F(2,116) = 11.44$, $p < .0001$. The fairness-welfare category was used more in the Rule Violation condition (41%) than in the Initial Situation (19%) or the Interpersonal (Sibling) condition (16%), p's $< .001$. Children justified the interpersonal choices (as shown in Table 7) on the

TABLE 7

JUSTIFICATIONS (in %) AFFIRMING THE INTERPERSONAL CHOICES

	MUSIC CLUB STORY			HURT BROTHER			SCIENCE PROJECT		
Grade:	3	6	9	3	6	9	3	6	9
Initial Situation:									
Fairness-Welfare	29	35	19	26	37	38	74	46	72
Interpersonal	21	22	8	4	2	0	8	17	7
Interpersonal:[a]									
Fairness-Welfare	4	4	4	14	43	37	34	27	39
Interpersonal	0	0	0	11	14	0	34	50	20
Pragmatic	0	0	0	6	5	0	5	5	5
Moral:[b]									
Fairness-Welfare	36	32	13	0	13	2	10	13	8
Interpersonal	23	13	4	0	0	0	2	2	2

[a] The Interpersonal condition pertained to friends in the Music Club Story and Hurt Brother Story, and to siblings in the Science Project Story.
[b] The Moral condition pertained to Greater Need in the Music Club Story, to Lying in the Hurt Brother story, and to Rule Violation in the Science Project Story.

basis of fairness-welfare (36%) more than interpersonal concerns (16%), as indicated by a main effect for type of justification on the MANOVA, $F(1,58) = 17.74$, $p < .0001$. There were no sex or age effects.

In the hurt brother story, there was a somewhat different pattern of justifications than in the other stories. As shown in Table 6, there was substantial use of the pragmatic, conventional, and psychological categories (grouped as Other) in justifying the fairness choice. Furthermore, there were no main effects or interactions in the use of fairness-welfare justifications for the fairness choice. As shown in Table 7, however, there were differences between justifications for the interpersonal choice, $F(1,51) = 26.45$, $p < .0001$. Fairness-welfare (25%) was used more than interpersonal (3%) justifications ($p < .001$). There was also a main effect for salience condition in justifications, $F(2,50) = 14.20$, $p < .0001$. There was more use of the fairness-welfare category in the Initial Situation (34%) and in the Interpersonal condition (32%) than in the Lying condition (7%; p's $< .001$).

DISCUSSION

It appears that when children are faced with conflicts between fairness and positive interpersonal expectations, they make interpersonal choices to a greater extent than when the expectations are motivated by self-interest. Overall, children gave greater priority to interpersonal choices in Study 2 than in Study 1. Moreover, no gender differences were found in Study 2.

As in Study 1, a main finding of this study is that both females and males made judgments that accounted for situational features of the stories. There were differences between stories, as well as differences in accord with shifts in the salience of the interpersonal or fairness/rights considerations. In the science project story, children clearly gave priority to the interpersonal considerations. In the other two stories, children were nearly equally divided in their choices of whether to care for a sibling or meet other fairness or rights considerations.

It also appears that each of the stories tapped somewhat different judgments. In the music club story, both males and females (and especially the younger ones) were responsive to the need to care for a vulnerable younger sister. However, children gave greater priority to helping a sister than helping a friend in similar circumstances. Chil-

dren of both genders were especially responsive to the interpersonal expectations in the competitive context of the science project story since most of them, unlike in the music club story, judged it acceptable to help either a sibling or a friend. Perhaps lower priority was placed on impersonal fairness in this situation because the context of competition was not seen as including equal rights. Another difference between these two stories was that shifts in salience of the fairness or rights components resulted in children giving it greater priority only in the science project story (the Rule Violation condition).

The purpose of the hurt brother story was to assess judgments and justifications in the type of conflict used in previous discussions of gender differences. Again, no gender differences were found. Children were evenly divided in their choices regarding a sibling and a friend. There was the expected difference in salience condition; children were less likely to give priority to the interpersonal expectation when the protagonist lied as a means to help the sibling. The types of justifications used in this story indicate that it was perceived as more complex than the other stories. This story implicated additional considerations, such as the violation of laws and the possibility of punishment, and produced substantial use of pragmatic, conventional, and psychological justifications (grouped as Other). Children's perceptions of complexity in this story may account for the disparate and conflicting results obtained by other researchers using stories of this type (e.g., Baumrind, 1986; Gilligan, 1982; Walker, 1984, 1986a). That is, our results indicate that in these stories children perceive components from different domains (e.g., legal issues, sanctions), in addition to, for example, justice and care components. In the absence of systematic delineation of such components, it is possible that their salience varied from one study to another and, if so, might account for conflicting results.

The absence of gender differences in the story choices was paralleled by an absence of gender differences in justifications. Children primarily used fairness-welfare justifications to support their choices, especially in conditions with an increased salience of fairness or rights (as was also found in Study 1). It was also found that children reasoned about their interpersonal choices with fairness-welfare justifications more than interpersonal justifications. This indicates that, for both genders, interpersonal expectations are perceived to include fairness and welfare components. It should be stressed that, as in Study 1, males and females used fairness justifications to an equal extent as welfare justifications (the two were grouped in the analyses into one general category).

Finally, the main age-related findings in this study were consistent with those of Study 1. Although children of all ages were able to consider both components in some of their judgments, older children did so with greater consistency than the younger ones in the Science Project story. However, there were no significant age differences in the coordination of components in the other stories.

General Discussion

The findings of the two studies are complementary. Together, they demonstrate that children of both genders consider interpersonal relationships and justice, welfare, and rights. Moreover, in both studies children's judgments and reasoning shifted in accordance with situational variations. In Study 1, females and males generally favored the obligations of justice and rights over self-interested interpersonal expectations. It appears, therefore, that at least by middle childhood children have formed concepts of justice and rights that they apply to a range of social situations. At the same time, the concepts of justice and rights are not rigidly applied. Study 1 demonstrated that children also take interpersonal components into account, and that changes in the salience of one or the other component lead to changes in the ways they are applied.

The findings of Study 2 showed that children are responsive to more positive interpersonal expectations than those depicted in Study 1. In the context of interpersonal concerns with positive intent and goals, males and females make similar judgments and use similar reasoning categories. It must be stressed that we are not claiming that these studies demonstrate that no gender differences exist in moral orientations. More studies would be needed to even consider the possibility. Rather, we have obtained evidence that both males and females make judgments of justice, rights, and welfare, judge the necessity of maintaining interpersonal relationships, and apply concepts of justice, rights, and welfare to interpersonal relations and recognize potential conflicts

between the two. The features of a situation have a bearing on how it is approached and resolved.

It also should be noted that our studies had a different focus from most recent studies of gender differences (Baumrind, 1986; Gilligan, 1982; Walker, 1984, 1986a). We examined whether and how children use interpersonal and justice considerations in a series of situational contexts. The other studies have focused on general age-related shifts in "moral" reasoning through analyses of judgments about situations in which the interpersonal and justice components are not clearly specified or manipulated (e.g., through story comparisons or salience variations).

Therefore, the exact implications of our results for formulations (Damon, 1977; Kohlberg, 1969; Selman, 1980) of stages or levels of moral judgment about particular conflicts or dilemmas are uncertain. The findings of our studies, however, do suggest that there are not clear-cut individual or group differences regarding concerns with justice, welfare, and rights, on the one hand, and concerns with interpersonal relations, on the other hand. Each type of concern coexists in individuals' social judgments and reasoning.

References

Baumrind, D. (1986). Sex differences in moral reasoning: Response to Walker's (1984) conclusions that there are none. *Child Development*, 57, 511–521.

Damon, W. (1977). *The social world of the child*. San Francisco: Jossey-Bass.

Davidson, P., Turiel, E., & Black, A. (1983). The effects of stimulus familiarity on the use of criteria and justifications in children's social reasoning. *British Journal of Developmental Psychology*, 1, 49–65.

Ford, M. R., & Lowery, C. R. (1986). Gender differences in moral reasoning: A comparison of the use of justice and care orientations. *Journal of Personality and Social Psychology*, 50, 777–783.

Gibbs, J. C., Arnold, K. D., & Burkhart, J. E. (1984). Sex differences in the expression of moral judgment. *Child Development*, 55, 1040–1043.

Gilligan, C. (1977). In a different voice: Women's conceptions of self and of morality. *Harvard Educational Review*, 47, 481–517.

Gilligan, C. (1982). *In a different voice: Psychological theory and women's development*. Cambridge, MA: Harvard University Press.

Gilligan, C., & Attanucci, J. (1988). Two moral orientations: Gender differences and similarities. *Merrill-Palmer Quarterly*, 34, 223–237.

Killen, M. (1990). Children's evaluations of morality in the context of peer, teacher-child, and familial relations. *Journal of Genetic Psychology*, 151, 395–410.

Kohlberg, L. (1969). Stage and sequence: The cognitive-developmental approach to socialization. In D. A. Goslin (Ed.), *Handbook of socialization theory and research* (pp. 347–480). Chicago: Rand McNally.

Kohlberg, L. (1971). From is to ought: How to commit the naturalistic fallacy and get away with it in the study of moral development. In T. Mischel (Ed.), *Cognitive development and epistemology* (pp. 151–235). New York: Academic Press.

Lyons, N. (1983). Two perspectives: On self, relationships, and morality. *Harvard Educational Review*, 53, 125–145.

Miller, J. G., Bersoff, D. M., & Harwood, R. L. (1990). Perceptions of social responsibilities in India and in the United States: Moral imperatives or personal decisions? *Journal of Personality and Social Psychology*, 58, 33–47.

Miller, J. G., & Luthar, S. (1989). Issues of interpersonal responsibility and accountability: A comparison of Indians' and Americans' moral judgments. *Social Cognition*, 7, 237–261.

Nucci, L. P. (1981). The development of personal concepts: A domain distinct from moral or societal concepts. *Child Development*, 52, 114–121.

Pratt, M. W., Golding, G., & Hunter, W. J. (1984). Does morality have a gender? Sex, sex role, and moral judgment relationships across the adult lifespan. *Merrill-Palmer Quarterly*, 30, 321–340.

Pratt, M. W., Golding, G., Hunter, W., & Sampson, R. (1988). Sex differences in adult moral orientations. *Journal of Personality*, 56, 373–391.

Rothbart, M. K., Hanley, J., & Albert, M. (1986). Gender differences in moral reasoning. *Sex Roles*, 15, 645–653.

Scheffler, S. (1988). Agent-centered restrictions, rationality, and the virtues. In S. Scheffler (Ed.), *Consequentialism and its critics* (pp. 243–260). New York: Oxford University Press.

Selman, R. L. (1980). *The growth of interpersonal understanding: Developmental and clinical analyses*. New York: Academic Press.

Smetana, J. G. (1981). Preschool children's conceptions of moral and social rules. *Child Development*, 52, 1333–1336.

Smetana, J. G. (1985). Preschool children's conceptions of transgressions: The effects of varying moral and conventional domain-related attributes. *Developmental Psychology*, 21, 18–29.

Smetana, J. G., Kelly, M., & Twentyman, C. T. (1984). Abused, neglected, and nonmaltreated children's conceptions of moral and social-conventional rules. *Child Development*, 55, 277–287.

Turiel, E. (1983). *The development of social knowledge: Morality and convention*. Cambridge: Cambridge University Press.

Turiel, E., Smetana, J. G., & Killen, M. (1991). Social contexts in social cognitive development. In W. M. Kurtines & J. L. Gewirtz (Eds.), *Handbook of moral behavior and development* (Vol. 2, pp. 307–332). Hillsdale, NJ: Erlbaum.

Walker, L. J. (1984). Sex differences in the development of moral reasoning. *Child Development*, 55, 677–691.

Walker, L. J. (1986a). Sex differences in the development of moral reasoning: A rejoinder to Baumrind. *Child Development*, 57, 522–526.

Walker, L. J. (1986b). Experiential and cognitive sources of moral development in adulthood. *Human Development*, 29, 113–124.

Walker, L. J. (1989). A longitudinal study of moral reasoning. *Child Development*, 60, 157–166.

Walker, L. J., de Vries, B., & Trevethan, S. D. (1987). Moral stages and moral orientation in real-life and hypothetical dilemmas. *Child Development*, 58, 842–858.

Williams, B. (1981). *Moral luck*. Cambridge: Cambridge University Press.

Winer, B. J. (1971). *Statistical principles in experimental design*. New York: McGraw-Hill.

Prosocial Development in Late Adolescence: A Longitudinal Study

Nancy Eisenberg, Gustavo Carlo, Bridget Murphy, and Patricia Van Court

Arizona State University

EISENBERG, NANCY; CARLO, GUSTAVO; MURPHY, BRIDGET; and VAN COURT, PATRICIA. *Prosocial Development in Late Adolescence: A Longitudinal Study.* CHILD DEVELOPMENT, 1995, 66, 1179–1197. Change in prosocial moral reasoning over 15 years, gender differences in prosocial reasoning, and the interrelations of moral reasoning, prosocial behavior, and empathy-related emotional responses were examined with longitudinal data from 17–18- and 19–20-year-olds and data from adolescents interviewed for the first time. Hedonistic reasoning declined in use until adolescence, and then increased somewhat in early adulthood. Needs-oriented and stereotypic reasoning increased until mid-childhood or early adolescence and then declined in use. Direct reciprocity and approval reasoning, which appeared to be on the decline in mid-adolescence in previous follow-ups, showed no decline into early adulthood. Several modes of higher-level reasoning increased in use across adolescence and early adulthood. Females' overall reasoning was higher than males'. Scores on interview and objective measures of prosocial moral reasoning were positively correlated. Consistent with expectations, there was some evidence of relations among prosocial reasoning, prosocial behavior, sympathy, and perspective taking.

Most research on moral judgment has concerned reasoning about moral dilemmas in which rules, laws, authorities' dictates, and formal obligations are central (Kohlberg, 1969, 1981; Rest, 1979). There has been much less research on positive morality (Eisenberg, 1986; Gilligan & Attanucci, 1988). To eliminate this gap in the research, Eisenberg and her colleagues have studied age changes in, and correlates of, prosocial moral reasoning (reasoning about moral dilemmas in which one person's needs or desires conflict with those of others in a context in which the role of prohibitions, authorities' dictates, and formal obligations is minimal; Eisenberg, 1986). The primary purpose of the present study was to extend the existing longitudinal study on this topic into late adolescence/early adulthood—that is, to age 17 to 18 years and age 19 to 20 years—and to examine the relations of prosocial moral reasoning to prosocial behavior and empathy-related characteristics. A secondary goal was to examine the relations among empathy-related characteristics and prosocial behavior.

The age-related changes in prosocial moral reasoning found in childhood and early to mid-adolescence generally have been consistent with Kohlberg's (1981) view that the capacities for complex perspective taking and for understanding abstract concepts are associated with advances in moral reasoning. Specifically, researchers have found that young children tend to use primarily hedonistic reasoning or needs-oriented (primitive empathic) prosocial reasoning. In elementary school, children's reasoning begins to reflect concern with approval and enhancing interpersonal relationships as well as the desire to behave in stereotypically "good" ways, although such reasoning appears to decrease in use somewhat in high school (Eisenberg, 1986). Direct reciprocity reasoning, which reflects an orientation to self-gain, has been found to increase in the elementary school years, perhaps because of the cognitive sophistication involved in thinking about reciprocity over time (Eisenberg et al., 1987). However, according to longitudinal data, such reasoning drops off in use somewhat in mid-

This research was supported by grants from the National Science Foundation (BNS8807784 and DBS-9208375), a Career Development Award from the National Institute of Child Health and Development (K04 HD00717), and a Research Scientist Development Award from the National Institute of Health (K02 MH00903) to Nancy Eisenberg. The authors thank the mothers and students in our longitudinal samples, and the principals, students, and teachers at McClintock High School for their participation. We also appreciated the assistance of Nicole Cordova, Susan Quezada, and My-Chau Tran with data entry. Requests for reprints should be addressed to Nancy Eisenberg, Psychology, Arizona State University, Tempe, AZ 85287.

adolescence (Eisenberg, Miller, Shell, McNalley, & Shea, 1991). Beginning in late elementary school or thereafter, children begin to express reasoning reflecting abstract principles, internalized affective reactions (e.g., guilt), and self-reflective sympathy and perspective taking. Nonetheless, at all ages individuals sometimes verbalize less mature modes of reasoning, although hedonistic reasoning decreases with age in childhood (Eisenberg, 1986). Of particular interest is the finding that in mid-adolescence (particularly at age 15 to 16 years), hedonistic reasoning, which dropped off sharply until age 11 to 12, increased somewhat, particularly for boys (Eisenberg et al., 1991). The latter finding is consistent with Eisenberg's (1986) view that levels of prosocial moral reasoning are not hierarchical, integrated structures (so an individual's reasoning is not necessarily primarily at one stage) or invariant in sequence and universal.

At this time, to our knowledge there are no data on prosocial moral reasoning beyond high school. Longitudinal data on prosocial moral reasoning have been collected from children from 4 to 5 years of age to 15 to 16 years of age (Eisenberg et al., 1991). Because moral development in regard to justice-related issues continues into adulthood (Colby, Kohlberg, Gibbs, & Lieberman, 1983), and advances in logical and sociocognitive capabilities occur during adolescence and early adulthood (Kuhn, Amsel, & O'Loughlin, 1988; Selman, 1980), there are theoretical reasons to expect further development of prosocial moral reasoning in late adolescence and beyond. Moreover, changes in the complexity of the social environment as individuals move into late adolescence and college might be expected to stimulate perspective taking and, consequently, the development of higher-level moral reasoning (see Mason & Gibbs, 1993; Rest & Narvaez, 1991). Thus, we expected greater use of higher-level, internalized modes of reasoning with age. In contrast, stereotypic and approval/interpersonal-oriented reasoning, mid-level modes of prosocial moral reasoning, were expected to continue to decrease slightly with age (as they do in justice-oriented reasoning during late adolescence and adulthood; Colby et al., 1983).

It was more difficult to make predictions regarding changes in hedonistic (and, to some degree, direct reciprocity) reasoning. Although hedonistic reasoning reflects lower-level concerns and is most common in young children, some investigators have noted relative increases in such lower-level reasoning in late adolescence/early adulthood (Kohlberg & Kramer, 1969). Whether or not one finds evidence of an increase in lower-level reasoning at this age appears to depend on the method of coding of factors such as relativity in moral reasoning and structure of reasoning (see Candee & Kohlberg, 1987; Murphy & Gilligan, 1980). In the older coding system used with justice-oriented moral reasoning data—a system that tapped content of reasoning and structure of reasoning—regression in reasoning was noted in early adulthood (Kohlberg & Kramer, 1969). When the coding system was modified to assess primarily structure of justice-oriented moral reasoning and moral competence (rather than actual use of all types of moral reasoning), little evidence of moral regression was found (Colby et al., 1983). However, the more recently developed coding system involves several procedures that result in the discarding of lower-level reasoning (e.g., if such reasoning occurs infrequently or if a higher-level reason is stated for the same issue; see Colby & Kohlberg, 1987; Eisenberg, 1986). In the scoring of prosocial moral reasoning, content (e.g., an emphasis on egoistic issues) as well as structure, and performance rather than competence, are assessed; thus, a decrease in level of reasoning in late adolescence similar to that found with the older Kohlberg coding system might be expected. Such a "regression" might be due to the relativism, accompanied by seemingly egoistic reasoning due to an emphasis on individualism and individual rights. According to some theorists, relativistic reasoning and a seemingly individualistic focus are part of the process of rejecting conventional moral reasoning (moral reasoning oriented toward the arbitrary maintenance of social order, authority, and societal rules) and shifting to principled, internalized moral reasoning that emphasizes individual rights (Kohlberg & Gilligan, 1971; Turiel, 1974).

From another perspective, Gilligan (1977) noted a shift in early adulthood from a focus on goodness as self-sacrifice to an emphasis on responsibility for the self as well as others. In prosocial moral dilemmas, the conflict is between one's own and another's needs, wants, and desires; story protagonists can assist another, but at a cost. Thus, some older adolescents and young adults may express more self-oriented reasoning in response to prosocial moral dilemmas as they realistically weigh the relative costs, and their responsibilities, to self and other in moral dilemmas. Given all the aforementioned factors, it was difficult to predict age-related changes in hedonistic moral reasoning in late adolescence.

As in prior follow-ups of the longitudinal study, prosocial moral reasoning was assessed with Eisenberg's interview procedures. However, at the 15-year follow-up (at age 19 to 20 years), an objective pencil-and-paper measure of prosocial moral judgment (the PROM) also was used (Carlo, Eisenberg, & Knight, 1992). This relatively new instrument had never been used with individuals past tenth grade; thus, we wanted to examine its relation to empathy, perspective taking, prosocial behavior, and moral reasoning as assessed in interviews for this age group.

As noted previously, a goal of this study was to examine the relations among prosocial moral reasoning, prosocial behavior, and empathy-related reactions in late adolescence/early adulthood. Few researchers have studied adolescents' empathy-related reactions, and even studies of adolescents' prosocial behavior are rare (Eisenberg, 1990).

Theorists such as Candee and Kohlberg (1987) and Rest (1979) have argued that moral reasoning influences individuals' moral decisions and behavior. In fact, moral reasoning, including prosocial moral judgment, in general is modestly correlated with the performance of prosocial behaviors (Eisenberg, 1986; Underwood & Moore, 1982). Children's and early- to mid-adolescents' prosocial behavior generally has been positively related to needs-oriented reasoning, negatively related to hedonistic reasoning (Eisenberg, 1986; Eisenberg et al., 1987), and occasionally positively correlated with a composite measure of adolescents' prosocial moral reasoning (e.g., at age 15 to 16, but not 13 to 14, in the longitudinal study; Eisenberg et al., 1991). Researchers have hypothesized that the relation between moral reasoning and behavior increases with age because higher-level reasoning is associated with the "progressive stripping away of bases for justifying behavior that are extrinsic to principle" (p. 104, Rholes & Bailey, 1983), resulting in stronger motivation to maintain consistency between attitudes and behaviors at higher stages of development (Kohlberg & Candee, 1984). Thus, measures of the

longitudinal subjects' prosocial behavior and inhibition of aggression in late adolescence/early adulthood were expected to be positively correlated with other-oriented and perhaps higher-level modes of reasoning, and negatively correlated with hedonistic reasoning.

Some types of prosocial moral reasoning explicitly reflect cognitive perspective taking and sympathetic tendencies; further, perspective taking is viewed as underlying advances in moral judgment (Colby et al., 1983; Eisenberg, 1986) and some types of prosocial behavior (Underwood & Moore, 1982). Nonetheless, there are very few studies of the relations of empathy-related dispositional characteristics to moral reasoning or adolescents' prosocial behavior, particularly studies in which researchers have differentiated among various empathy-related responses. Investigators have argued that sympathy (concern for others based on the apprehension of another's state) and empathy (an emotional reaction elicited by and congruent with another's state) stimulate the development of internalized moral reasoning reflecting concern for others' welfare (Hoffman, 1987) and prime the use of pre-existing other-oriented moral cognitions (Eisenberg, 1986). Further, sympathy, which frequently may stem from empathy and perspective taking (Hoffman, 1987), is viewed as resulting in other-oriented, altruistic motivation and has been associated with higher levels of prosocial behavior (Eisenberg & Fabes, 1991). In contrast, personal distress (a self-focused, aversive reaction to cues regarding another's negative state or emotion; Davis, 1983) has been theoretically linked to egoistic motives and empirically associated with low levels of prosocial behavior (Batson, 1991; Eisenberg & Fabes, 1991). Thus, cognitive perspective taking and sympathy would be expected to be positively correlated with higher-level, other-oriented modes of prosocial moral reasoning and altruism, whereas an inverse pattern of relations would be expected for personal distress.

Consistent with these expectations, at age 15 to 16, cognitive perspective taking was positively related to higher-level reasoning (on the moral reasoning composite score) and negatively related to hedonistic reasoning, whereas dispositional sympathy was positively correlated with primitive empathic (i.e., needs-oriented) reasoning and negatively correlated with hedonistic reasoning (Eisenberg et al., 1991). Similarly,

Carlo et al. (1992) found a positive relation between seventh and tenth graders' internalized prosocial moral reasoning on the PROM and their sympathy and perspective taking. Findings in regard to personal distress are less consistent. Personal distress was unrelated to adolescents' prosocial moral reasoning in the longitudinal study (Eisenberg et al., 1991); in contrast, it was negatively related to internalized and stereotypic reasoning, and positively related to approval-oriented reasoning, on the PROM (Carlo et al., 1992). In the present study, we further examined the relations of prosocial moral reasoning with various empathy-related dispositional characteristics.

Consistent with theory (Hoffman, 1987), some evidence of relations between prosocial behavior and empathy-related characteristics also has been found, primarily in studies involving younger children and global measures of empathy (see Eisenberg & Fabes, 1991; Eisenberg & Miller, 1987; Underwood & Moore, 1982). In a prior follow-up of the longitudinal study, measures of helping behavior and mothers' reports of children's prosocial behavior at age 15 to 16 were unrelated to adolescents' sympathy, perspective taking, or personal distress, whereas adolescents' self-reported prosocial behavior was positively correlated with both sympathy and perspective taking (Eisenberg et al., 1991). Thus, findings in regard to the relations of specific empathy-related characteristics to adolescents' prosocial behavior are inconsistent. Consequently, another goal of this study was to examine the relations between empathy-related characteristics and prosocial behavior during late adolescence/early adulthood.

Also of interest was the consistency of measures of both empathy-related responding and prosocial behavior across time. Although relevant research is quite limited, there is evidence of some consistency in prosocial behavior across 2 or more years in childhood (Eisenberg et al., 1987; Radke-Yarrow & Zahn-Waxler, 1984) and across 2 years (Eisenberg et al., 1991) or several weeks (Small, Zeldin, & Savin-Williams, 1983) in early to mid-adolescence. To our knowledge, consistency of prosocial behavior across longer periods of time in adolescence, and into adulthood, has not been examined. The research on consistency of empathy-related reactions is even more sparse, although sympathy, personal distress, and perspective taking appear to be fairly consistent across 2 or 3 years' time in the junior high and high school years (Eisenberg et al., 1991). Davis and Franzoi (1991) noted that the magnitude of these correlations increased somewhat (albeit nonsignificantly) with age; thus, we expected the consistency of empathy-related characteristics to be fairly high from age 17–18 to 19–20.

Finally, it is possible that self-report measures of moral reasoning and behavior are contaminated by self-presentational concerns. Thus, in the present study we examined the relation of social desirability to other moral indexes. However, because measures of social desirability may partially tap characteristics associated with moral functioning, such as the ability to inhibit oneself (King, Emmons, & Woodley, 1992), as well as the desire to present oneself in a positive light, controlling for social desirability may be a conservative analytic strategy.

Method

Subjects

Two groups of middle-class children participated in this study. The primary longitudinal cohort (C1) consisted of 16 girls and 16 boys (all Caucasian except two) who had been interviewed seven times previously, at ages 4–5, 5½–6½, 7–8, 9–10, 11–12, 13–14, and 15–16 years (at 156, 138, 120, 96, 72, 48, and 24 months prior to the first assessment in this study); the nine testing sessions henceforth will be referred to as T1 to T9. The mean ages of the children at T8 and T9 were 211 months (range = 202–219 months; approximately age 17–18 years) and 235 months (approximately age 19–20 years). No children were lost since T3 (in 12 years); five have been lost over the 15-year period (three boys, two girls). Mean years of maternal and paternal education for this sample (as reported at T8) were 16.0 and 17.0, respectively (range = 12 to 20 years for both). At T8, all subjects except one were living at home; at T9, all but five were attending college, and only 11 were living with their parents.

The second sample (C2) consisted of 34 twelfth graders from middle-class, predominantly (85%) Caucasian families (20 girls, 14 boys; M age = 213 months). These children attended a public school in the suburban city in which the longitudinal subjects lived at the beginning of the study. They were interviewed only at T8. Means years of education for subjects' mothers and fathers were 14.6 and 15.6 years, respectively.

Instruments

Moral reasoning.—Children's prosocial moral reasoning was assessed in two ways. First, at both T8 and T9, students were interviewed with the same four moral reasoning stories used in prior follow-ups (see Eisenberg, Lennon, & Roth, 1983; Eisenberg et al., 1987, 1991), although a few words were changed at adolescent follow-ups to make the stories sound less childlike (e.g., "birthday party" was changed to "birthday celebration"). An additional story previously used with adolescents in another study (concerning going into the hospital to donate blood at a cost to the self; Eisenberg-Berg, 1979) also was used at T6 to T9. This story was added because the costs of helping in the giving blood story likely would be substantial for adolescents (losing time at work and school). Story protagonists (if specified) were the same sex as the subject. At T8, the moral reasoning interview for a C2 male was lost due to experimenter error. At T9, four C1 participants did not complete the interview portion of the study because they had moved from the state (2), could not be reached (1), or refused (1).

Second, at T9 only (and, consequently, for only C1), participants were administered the PROM (Carlo et al., 1992). Participants were mailed a version of the PROM containing six stories, five of which were very similar in content to the vignettes used in the moral reasoning interview. The PROM is modeled after Rest's (1979) Defining Issues Test (DIT); subjects are presented with moral dilemmas and then rate the importance of six reasons why the protagonist should or should not help the needy other in a given story on a 5-point scale (1 = not at all to 5 = greatly). Each of the stories included a hedonistic item, which pertained to simple hedonistic or direct reciprocity reasoning (e.g., "It depends how much fun Mary expects the party to be, and what sorts of things are happening at the party), one needs-oriented item (e.g., "It depends whether the girl really needs help or not"), an approval-oriented item (e.g., "It depends whether Mary's parents and friends will think she did the right or she did the wrong thing"), a stereotypic item (e.g., "It depends if Mary thinks it's the decent thing to do or not), and an item reflecting higher-level reasoning (i.e., sympathetic, perspective taking, internalized affect, or abstract internalized reasoning, e.g., "It depends how Mary would feel about herself if she helped or not"). The sixth reasoning choice was a lie/nonsense item that sounded abstract but did not make sense (e.g., "It depends whether Mary believes in people's values of metacognition or not"); these items were used merely to eliminate subjects who scored high on this subscale (none were eliminated). In a prior study, test-retest reliabilities for the reasoning subscales ranged from .70 to .79.

As done previously (as Carlo et al., 1992), scores on each of the PROM subscales were averaged across stories and then transformed to proportion scores by dividing each of the PROM composite scores (for the five types of reasoning) by the sum of the five PROM composite scores. The hedonistic response for one story (the only one involving direct reciprocity) was dropped because it lowered the alpha for this subscale substantially. Alphas for the hedonistic, needs-oriented, approval, stereotypic, internalized, and nonsense scales for C1 at T9 were .61 .64, .85, .86, .87, and .64, which is fairly high given that there were only five items per scale (Nunnally, 1967) and subjects were all approximately the same age, so there was limited variation in responding.

Social desirability.—To assess social desirability (SD), participants in C1 and C2 completed 25 items from the Marlowe-Crowne (Crowne & Marlowe, 1964) social desirability scale (alphas = .84 and .89 for C1 at T8 and T9, respectively, and .74 for C2 at T8). Items were averaged to compute a composite score. SD was missing for one subject at T9.

Empathy-related responding.—At T8 and T9, three subscales of Davis's (1983) Interpersonal Reactivity Scale were administered (definitions and alphas for C1 at T8 and T9, and C2 at T8, are in parentheses): sympathy (the tendency to experience feelings of warmth and concern for others; alphas = .71, .83, and .72, respectively; one item was dropped at T8), perspective taking (the tendency to adopt the point of view of others; .79, .91, and .84), and personal distress (the tendency to feel unease and discomfort in tense interpersonal settings involving others' needs or emotions; .71, .76, and .76). Items on each scale were averaged (after reversing items if appropriate). Scores for these scales were missing for one C1 subject at T8.

Moral behavior.—At T8, students filled out a 23-item adapted version of Rushton, Chrisjohn, and Fekken's (1981) self-report altruism scale (alphas = .87 for both C1 and

C2). This measure (henceforth called reported prosocial behavior) also was used at T6 and T7. Students indicated on a five-point scale (from "never" to "very often") how frequently they engaged in 23 behaviors, such as giving money to charity or volunteer work.

At T8, mothers of children in C1 reported on their children's prosocial behavior using the same measure (with the wording slightly modified). Because they were given the additional option of "Don't know," alphas could not be computed (items with this response were coded as missing, so few mothers had scores for all items). One mother did not complete this measure. For both child and mother versions of the scale, scores on the items were averaged.

Students at T8 in both C1 and C2 also were given an opportunity to assist the experimenter by filling out some additional questionnaires and returning them in a stamped, addressed envelope (henceforth called the measure of helping). Students were given a score indicating whether they returned the measures (1 = not returned; 2 = returned).

An additional donating task was administered only to C2 participants at T8. At the end of the interview session, C2 students were paid $5 (4 $1 bills and 4 quarters) for their time, and were told that the experimenter belonged to an organization at the university that was collecting money for a widely publicized child that needed a liver transplant (a newspaper article was presented to them alongside a covered donation box with money in it). Students also were told that they could donate money if they wished to do so and were left alone for 1 min. The amount of money donated was the measure of donating. The donating task was not used for C1 because subjects remembered similar tasks used when they were younger.

At T9, self-reported moral behavior was assessed for C1 with portions of Weinberger's Adjustment Inventory (WAI; Weinberger, 1991; also see Feldman & Weinberger, 1994). Items from the longer version of two restraint subscales that concerned moral behavior were used (rated 1 = false to 5 = true). The subscales used were as follows (sample items, numbers of items, and alphas for this sample are in parentheses): consideration of others ("I often go out of my way to do things for other people," seven items, .79) and suppression of aggres-

sion ("I lose my temper and 'let people have it' when I'm angry" [reversed], seven items, .87). Items within each subscale were averaged.

Friends' reports.—At T9, subjects were asked to provide the names of one or two friends to fill out a questionnaire about the subject. Reports from at least one friend were obtained for 25 subjects; reports from two friends were obtained for 11 participants. Mean length of time that friends reported knowing the subjects was 66.42 months. The friends' questionnaire packet included the seven-item sympathy and perspective-taking subscales (modified slightly for an other-report format). In addition, friends responded to items from Weinberger's WAI Rating Items, which contains three items per scale. Items on these subscales were similar to those used in the subject report measures. If reports from two friends were obtained, they were averaged (correlations between reports for the two friends for sympathy, perspective taking, consideration for others, and suppression of aggression were .85, .18, .59, .21). Alpha coefficients for the three-item scales were .77 and .62 for consideration of others and aggression.

Procedures

C1 at T8.—Interviews for C1 at T8 usually took place at the university. Mother and child were interviewed individually in different rooms, the mother by a woman and the children by a man who had not been involved in any previous follow-ups. For the adolescents, the prosocial dilemmas were presented in random order; they were read to the adolescents while the adolescents read along (responses were taped). Participants repeated dilemmas to check for comprehension, and a standard sequence of questioning was followed (Eisenberg et al., 1987).

Either subsequent or prior to the moral interview (sequence was counterbalanced across subjects), the children completed measures of empathy-related constructs, social desirability, and self-reported prosocial behavior (presented in random order). The students were told that their responses were confidential. Next the children were paid for their participation ($20) and the experimenter told the students that he would appreciate them filling out a few more forms at home, but that they need not do so. If the student agreed to take the questionnaires (all did), they were given the forms and a stamped, addressed envelope.

C2 at T8.—Adolescents in C2 were administered the same interview and questionnaires as C1 at their schools by either a male or female experimenter (the male experimenter was the same as used for C1 at T8; approximately half the subjects of each sex were interviewed by each experimenter). Subjects' mothers were not involved. At the end of the session, the helping and donating tasks described previously were administered.

C1 at T9.—At T9, the subjects in C1 were first sent a packet including the PROM and the sympathy, personal distress, perspective taking, and WAI questionnaires (order of the PROM and questionnaires was counterbalanced). Subjects were also asked to supply names and addresses of friends if they were willing to do so (all but three did so). Completed questionnaires were returned by mail, and subjects were sent $25 for participation. After completing the questionnaires, subjects were asked if they would be willing to complete the prosocial moral reasoning interview. Twenty-eight subjects were available for the interview, and they were individually interviewed approximately 1 to 4 months after completing the questionnaires (depending on their availability). Participants were paid an additional $20 for the interview.

Scoring of the Prosocial Reasoning Stories (Interviews)

Reasoning was coded into the categories of reasoning outlined by Eisenberg et al. (1983, 1987, 1991; Eisenberg-Berg, 1979). Those used with any frequency were as follows:

Hedonistic reasoning: (a) *hedonistic gain to the self* (orientation to gain for oneself), (b) *direct reciprocity* (orientation to personal gain because of direct reciprocity or lack of reciprocity from the recipient of an act), (c) *affectional relationship* (orientation to the individual's identification or relationship with another or liking for the other);

Pragmatic (orientation to practical concerns that are unrelated to selfish considerations);

Needs-oriented (orientation to the physical, material, or psychological needs of the other person, e.g., "He needs blood," or "He's sad");

Stereotypes of a good or bad person (orientation to stereotyped images of a good or bad person);

Approval and interpersonal orientation (orientation to others' approval and acceptance in deciding what is the correct behavior);

Self-reflective empathic orientation: (a) *sympathetic orientation* (expression of sympathetic concern and caring for others), (b) *role taking* (the individual explicitly takes the perspective of the other or has the story protagonist do so), (c) *internalized positive affect related to consequences* (orientation to internal positive affect as a result of a particular course of action because of the consequences of one's act for the other person, (d) *internalized negative affect related to consequences* (the same as [c] but for negative affect);

Internalized affect because of loss of self-respect and not living up to one's values: (a) *positive* (orientation to feeling good as a consequence of living up to internalized values), (b) *negative* (concern with feeling bad as a consequence of not living up to internalized values);

Internalized law, norm, and value orientation (orientation to an internalized responsibility, duty, or need to uphold the laws and accepted norms or values);

Other abstract and/or internalized types of reasoning: (a) *generalized reciprocity* (orientation to indirect reciprocity in a society, that is, exchange that is not one-to-one but eventually benefits all or a larger group), (b) *concern with the condition of society* (orientation to improving the society or community as a whole), (c) *concern with individual rights and justice* (orientation to protecting individual rights and preventing injustices that violate another's rights), (d) *equality of people* (orientation to the principle of the equal value of all people).

Subjects were assigned scores indicating the frequency with which they used each of the various types of reasoning when discussing both the pros and cons of helping the needy other in the story dilemma (1 = no use of category; 2 = vague, questionable use; 3 = clear use of a mode of reasoning; 4 = a major type of reasoning used). Next, the scores for each category were summed across the stories. At T8, a second scorer coded half the data for reliability; at T9, two additional people co-scored the data for reliability. Interrater reliabilities for T1 to T7 are presented in previous papers (e.g., Eisenberg et al., 1983, 1987, 1991). For all time periods, the primary coder was the same person, whereas seven persons have served as reliability coders over the nine time periods. To prevent bias in scoring, the primary coder (as well as the secondary coder at T8 and one secondary coder at T9) was blind to the identity of the children. The coders also were blind to any information regarding the subjects' scores on other measures. Interrater reliabilities (Pearson correlations) computed for each reasoning category at T8 and T9 (using data for all subjects at T9, and for half the subjects at T8) ranged from .70 to 1.00 at T8, with most being above .85, and from .77 to 1.00 at T9 (with all but two being above .83). (These reliabilities are for five stories; those for four stories were very similar.)

To determine if there was change in the primary coder's scoring over the years (and to prevent the primary coder from knowing the age of subjects being coded), four protocols from each of the previous follow-ups were mixed together with the various protocols from T8 and T9 and rescored by the primary coder to determine if there was any change in her scoring over the years (the coder was blind to which protocol was from which follow-up). Scoring of the data from earlier sessions was highly similar to the original scores for the same data (agreement on codings within 1 point was 90% or higher on all categories).

The categories of reasoning are viewed as representing components of developmental levels of prosocial moral reasoning; these levels were derived from the results of cross-sectional research (Eisenberg-Berg, 1979; see Eisenberg, 1986). Briefly, the levels are as follows: Level 1, hedonistic, self-focused orientation; Level 2, needs-of-others orientation; Level 3, approval and interpersonal orientation and stereotyped orientation; Level 4, self-reflective, empathic orientation; and Level 5, strongly internalized orientation. Based on these levels, a score representing level of moral judgment was computed for each child. The level score was constructed in a manner similar to that used to score Kohlbergian moral reasoning; subjects were assigned composite scores by weighing the proportion of the child's reasoning at each level (see Eisenberg et al., 1983, for more detail). Because it is debatable whether Level 5 is more moral than Level 4, and because they were weighted equally in previous follow-ups, they were weighted equally in the analyses presented in this article (although the data changed little if Level 5 was weighted higher).

Results

Age Changes in Moral Judgment

To examine age changes in moral reasoning for C1 over the 15 years, multivariate and univariate trend analyses of variance were computed with one within-subjects factor (time; adjusted for unequal time gaps when appropriate) and one between-subjects factor (sex). Only the 28 subjects interviewed at T9 were included in the trend analyses (recall that four C1 subjects were not interviewed at T9). Different multivariate analyses had to be computed for groups of reasoning that emerged at different ages because linear dependencies in the data occur if a particular mode of reasoning is not used at more than one time period (and because quadratic trends could occur if a type of reasoning was not used in childhood and then emerged in adolescence). Only categories of reasoning used with some frequency during at least one time period were included in the analyses. Because types of reasoning that were used infrequently tended to be positively skewed, a logarithmic transformation was performed on the data (although the means presented in Table 1 and in the text are nontransformed means). Linear, quadratic, and cubic trends were examined for early emerging modes of reasoning because from early childhood through late adolescence, some categories of reasoning were expected to show both increases and decreases in usage, sometimes with a period of relative stability in use (which could result in a cubic trend analysis).

In the first analysis, the categories of reasoning were those that had been used with some frequency (by at least one sex) at eight or more time periods (i.e., hedonistic, needs-oriented, pragmatic, direct reciprocity, approval-oriented, and stereotypic; see Eisenberg et al., 1987). Scores were computed from the four stories used at all seven follow-ups. The multivariate Fs for the linear, quadratic, and cubic effects of time were highly significant, $F(7, 20) = 36.47, 13.55,$ and 3.34, $ps < .001, .001,$ and $.016$. For hedonistic reasoning, the univariate Fs for the linear and quadratic trends were highly significant; the cubic trend was somewhat lower in significance. Hedonistic reasoning decreased sharply with age until 11–12 years, and then increased somewhat in adolescence and early adulthood (with a slight drop at age 17 to 18; see Table 1 for means and Table 2 for Fs). Interestingly, perusal of the means indicated that scores on hedonistic reasoning for girls changed little in adolescence until age 19 to 20 years (Ms for T5,

TABLE 1

MORAL REASONING CATEGORIES: MEANS FOR COHORT 1

REASONING CATEGORY	TIME OF ASSESSMENT								
	1	2	3	4	5	6	7	8	9
Hedonistic	12.11	8.89	6.46	5.39	4.57	4.86	5.32	4.75	5.43
Direct reciprocity	4.00	4.07	4.11	4.25	5.32	5.71	4.89	5.29	5.50
Affectional relationship	4.04	4.43	4.00	4.18	4.21	4.11	4.61	4.36	4.18
Pragmatic	4.07	4.11	4.18	4.86	5.36	6.00	6.46	5.75	6.50
Needs-oriented	8.46	11.39	13.64	13.32	13.61	12.14	11.89	12.00	10.57
Stereotypic	4.57	4.36	4.68	5.14	5.71	6.79	6.46	6.43	6.25
Approval/interpersonal	4.00	4.07	4.21	4.36	4.82	4.96	5.00	4.61	5.00
Sympathetic	4.00	4.03	4.00	4.21	4.39	4.07	4.14	4.04	4.32
Role taking	4.00	4.00	4.07	4.68	4.68	5.14	6.00	5.57	6.07
Positive affect/simple or related to consequences	4.00	4.00	4.11	4.57	4.79	5.21	5.39	4.79	6.04
Negative affect/simple or related to consequences	4.00	4.00	4.00	4.18	4.21	4.11	4.29	4.61	4.68
Positive affect/values and self-respect	4.00	4.00	4.11	4.04	4.00	4.14	4.25	4.68	4.39
Negative affect/values and self-respect	4.00	4.00	4.00	4.07	4.00	4.07	4.07	4.07	4.29
Internalized law, norm, or value orientation	4.00	4.00	4.04	4.00	4.00	4.18	4.39	4.46	4.86
Generalized reciprocity	4.00	4.00	4.00	4.00	4.00	4.04	4.29	4.18	4.25
Condition of society	4.00	4.00	4.00	4.00	4.00	4.04	4.18	4.14	4.14
Individual rights	4.00	4.00	4.00	4.00	4.14	4.14	4.04	4.11	4.14
Equality of individuals	4.00	4.00	4.00	4.00	4.04	4.00	4.07	4.00	4.00

NOTE.—Means presented are for the nontransformed data for the 28 subjects with interviews at all time periods.

TABLE 2

TREND ANALYSES FOR THE INDIVIDUAL MORAL REASONING CATEGORIES:
UNIVARIATE EFFECTS

MORAL CATEGORY	TREND		
	Linear	Quadratic	Cubic
Hedonistic	63.13****	85.03****	10.72**
Direct reciprocity	49.84****	2.60	1.75
Affectional relationship	8.98**	.40	2.61
Pragmatic	64.36****	4.12+	3.30+
Needs-oriented	1.69	51.97****	17.76***
Stereotypic	35.96****	3.52+	7.17*
Approval	22.21****	2.71	.31
Sympathetic	.48	.01	. . .ᵃ
Role taking	17.26**	.57	. . .
Positive affect/simple or related to consequences	41.20****	.12	. . .
Negative affect/simple or related to consequences	8.98**	1.35	. . .
Positive affect/values and self-respect	10.59**	.88	. . .
Negative affect/values and self-respect	2.08	.51	. . .
Internalized law, norm, or value orientation	19.36	2.68	. . .
Generalized reciprocity	3.82+	. . .	. . .
Condition of society	2.66	. . .	. . .
Individual rights	.01	. . .	. . .
Equality of individuals	.86	. . .	. . .

ᵃ Indicate that an analysis was not computed (see text).
+ p < .10.
* p < .05.
** p < .01.
*** p < .001.
**** p < .0001.

83

T6, T7, T8, and T9 were 4.60, 4.60, 4.67, 4.27, and 5.00), whereas such reasoning started to increase in frequency at age 13 to 14 (T6) for boys (Ms = 4.54, 5.15, 6.08, 5.31, and 5.92). According to an additional analysis, the increase in hedonistic reasoning from T8 to T9 was significant, F(1, 26) = 4.46, p < .045. For needs-oriented reasoning, there was a highly significant quadratic trend and a weaker (but highly significant) cubic trend. Needs-oriented reasoning increased with age until 7–8 years, was relatively stable from 7–8 to 11–12 years, and declined considerably in adolescence, particularly at age 19 to 20 years (see Table 1). According to a highly significant linear trend, direct reciprocity reasoning increased in use with age; specifically, it was used with little frequency until age 9–10, increased in use until early adolescence (13–14 years), started to decline slightly in mid-adolescence, and then shot up in usage in late adolescence. For stereotypic reasoning, there was a highly significant linear trend and a cubic trend. Stereotypic reasoning was used infrequently until mid- to late elementary school, increased in use until age 13–14, and then decreased slightly in use in mid- to late adolescence. For approval-oriented reasoning, only the linear trend was significant; such reasoning increased until age 15 to 16, dropped slightly at age 17 to 18, and then rose slightly again at age 19 to 20. Finally, pragmatic reasoning increased in a linear fashion with age.

A second 2 (sex) × 5 (time) trend analysis was computed for those higher-level categories of reasoning used with any frequency at T3 or T4 (sympathetic, role taking, internalized positive affect about consequences, internalized negative affect about consequences, internalized positive affect about values, internalized negative affect about values, and internalized law, norm, or value orientation reasoning). The multivariate Fs for sex and the linear trend for time were significant, Fs(7, 20) = 2.60 and 16.38, p < .044 and .001. Females scored higher than males (at p < .059 or better) on role taking, positive affect/values, and negative affect/consequences reasoning, Fs(1, 26) =

3.91, 5.73, and 4.20, ps < .059, .024, and .051 (Ms = 5.47, 4.35, and 4.43 for females; 4.84, 4.09, and 4.14 for males). Role taking, positive affect/consequences, positive affect/values, negative affect/consequences, and internalized norm, rule, and law reasoning increased with age (see Table 2).

In a third 2 (sex) × 3 (time) analysis, we examined linear and quadratic age changes in the use of categories of reasoning that emerged only in adolescence (generalized reciprocity, concern with society, rights and justice, and equality of people reasoning). These categories of reasoning were used quite infrequently (see Table 1). The multivariate effect for the sex × quadratic interaction was significant, p < .041; however, follow-up analyses were not. The multivariate linear trend was only marginally significant, p < .10.

In a summary analysis, we examined change in C1 adolescents' moral reasoning composite scores from late childhood (T5) through late adolescence. According to a 2 (sex) × 5 (time) trend analysis, there were main effects of sex and a strong linear trend, Fs(1, 26) = 18.84 and 30.09, ps < .001. Females scored higher than males, and scores increased with age (Ms = 231, 241, 251, 252, and 270 for T5, T6, T7, T8, and T9, respectively).[1]

Correlations also were computed to examine the relations between moral reasoning at earlier periods of adolescence (T6 and T7) and moral reasoning at T8 and T9. Reasoning at T6 was at least marginally positively related to reasoning at T7 and T8, rs(30) = .37 and .32, ps < .035 and .078. Reasoning at T7 was significantly correlated with reasoning at T8, r(30) = .46, p < .001. In contrast, there was a discontinuity in reasoning at T9; T9 composite scores were not significantly related to analogous scores at T6, T7, or T8, rs(26) = .20, .22, and .07, N.S.

If the age trends in the children's reasoning were primarily the result of repeated testing, one would not expect the reasoning for C1 to be similar to that of children of the same age interviewed for the first time at T8 (C2). At T8, the only difference in reasoning

---

[1] For the entire sample of longitudinal and cross-sectional subjects, there was not a significant sex difference in the moral reasoning composite scores at T8, whereas at T9 females scored higher than males on the composite scores composed of both five stories and marginally higher on that for the primary four stories, ps < .016 and .08. In regard to individual moral reasoning categories, for C1 and C2 at T8, males scored higher on affectional relationship reasoning, ps < .044, whereas females scored higher on pragmatic reasoning at T9, p < .007 (ps are for four stories; those for five stories were similar).

between C1 and C2 was that C1 used more approval and needs-oriented reasoning, $Fs(1, 62) = 5.33$ and 7.11, $ps < .024$ and $.011$. Neither of these types of reasoning is higher level; thus, if there was any effect of repeated testing, it was to encourage greater expression of relatively low-level reasoning.

Correlation of Interview Moral Reasoning with Scores on the PROM

Mean scores for adolescents' PROM subscales are presented in Table 3; according to an analysis of variance for repeated measures, the means differed significantly, $F(4, 124) = 24.14$, $p < .001$. Internalized reasoning was most preferred; scores on stereotyped and needs-oriented reasoning were moderately high; hedonistic reasoning was the second least preferred category; and approval-oriented reasons were least preferred. All categories differed significantly from one another at $p < .01$, except needs-oriented reasoning did not differ from either internalized or stereotypic reasoning, and hedonistic and stereotypic reasoning differed at $p < .05$ (Tukey's tests). This pattern is highly consistent with that obtained by Carlo et al. (1992).

To compare reasoning on the PROM with the composite index of interview proso-cial moral reasoning, a composite score for the PROM was computed. Based on the means in this study and the findings in Carlo et al. (1992), a weighted score was computed in which percent of internalized reasoning was multiplied by 3, percent of needs-oriented and stereotypic reasoning was multiplied by 2, and percents of hedonistic and approval-oriented reasoning were multiplied by 1. These weighted values were then summed. Although approval-oriented reasoning is considered of moderate level in studies of spontaneously elicited moral reasoning (e.g., Eisenberg et al., 1991), it is clear that the approval-oriented items on the PROM, a preference measure of moral judgment requiring merely the endorsement or rejection of options, reflected relatively low-level moral reasoning. Students tended to reject the blatantly worded approval-oriented items, and use of these items decreased with age (Carlo et al., 1992). When the composite PROM and interview moral reasoning composites (computed for all five vignettes at T9) were correlated, the relation was moderate and comparable to findings for the DIT, $r(26) = .57$, $p < .002$. Moreover, adolescents' interview moral reasoning composite scores at T8 were positively correlated with their PROM composite score at

TABLE 3

MEANS AND STANDARD DEVIATIONS FOR MEASURES OF SOCIAL DESIRABILITY, PROSOCIAL BEHAVIOR, EMPATHY-RELATED CHARACTERISTICS, AND SCORES ON THE PROM[a]

MEASURE	T8		T9	
	M	SD	M	SD
Social desirability[b]	1.42	.18	1.39	.24
Helping[b]	1.45	.50	. . .	. . .
Donating[c]	1.82	1.86	. . .	. . .
Self-reported moral behavior[de]	3.17	.52	.00	1.80
Mothers' reports of prosocial behavior[d]	3.13	.53	. . .	. . .
Sympathy[f]	3.95	.64	5.51	.99
Perspective taking[f]	3.37	.76	4.64	1.29
Personal distress[f]	3.17	.52	3.00	.94
Scores on PROM:[g]				
Hedonistic	. . .	. . .	.17	.06
Approval	. . .	. . .	.13	.03
Needs-oriented	. . .	. . .	.23	.06
Stereotypic	. . .	. . .	.21	.05
Internalized	. . .	. . .	.25	.05
Composite score	. . .	. . .	1.95	.10

[a] T8, data are from C1 and C2 combined when possible.
[b] Scores could range from 1 to 2.
[c] Scores were in dollars and available only for C2.
[d] Scores could range from 1 to 5.
[e] Modified Rushton et al. (1981) scale at T8; standardized WAI subscales at T9.
[f] Scores could range from 1 to 5 at T8 and 1 to 7 at T9.
[g] The scores presented are the proportional scores.

1190 Child Development

T9, $r(30) = .38$, $p < .03$. Note that two-tailed correlations are reported here and throughout, even though specific hypotheses frequently were formulated.

Consistency of Social Desirability, Prosocial Behavior, and Empathy-Related Responding across Time

Similar scales of social desirability, prosocial behavior, and empathy-related responding were administered at more than one time period. In general, there was consistency across time for these measures. The Marlowe-Crowne Social Desirability Scale (administered at T7, T8, and T9) was highly correlated from T7 to T8 and T9, $rs(30$ and $29) = .86$ and $.76$, $ps < .001$, and also between T8 and T9, $r(29) = .69$, $p < .001$. Children's reported prosocial behavior (on the modified Rushton et al., 1981, scale) at T8 was positively correlated with their reports on the same measure at T6 and T7, both $rs(30) = .43$ and $.50$, $ps < .013$ and $.004$. Mothers' reports of children's prosocial behavior at T8 also were significantly correlated with their reports at T6 and T7, $rs(27) = .54$ and $.65$, $ps < .003$ and $.001$. Helping by returning questionnaires at T8 was positively correlated with similar helping at T6 and T7, $rs(30) = .35$ and $.45$, $ps < .049$ and $.011$.

In regard to empathy-related constructs, reports of sympathy at T8 were positively related to scores on Bryant's (1982) empathy scale at T5 and T6, both $rs(29) = .55$, $p < .001$, as well as scores on the same sympathy scale at T7, $r(29) = .53$, $p < .002$. Sympathy at T9 also was positively correlated with empathy at T5 and T6, $rs(30) = .45$ and $.49$, $ps < .011$ and $.005$, as well as sympathy at T7, $r(30) = .56$, $p < .001$, and T8, $r(29) = .77$, $p < .001$. Similarly, perspective taking (PT) scores at T8 and T9 were highly related, $r(29) = .74$, $p < .001$, and were positively correlated with PT at T7, $rs(29$ and $30) = .62$ and $.62$, $ps < .001$, respectively. Finally, personal distress (PD) was positively correlated from T8 to T9, $r(29) = .58$, $p < .001$, and PD at T7 was positively correlated with PD at both T8 and T9, $rs(29$ and $30) = .49$ and $.45$, $ps < .005$ and $.01$.

Relations of Friends' Reports at T9 to Subjects' Reports

Recall that for 25 subjects, friends reported (often with shortened scales) on friends' perspective taking, sympathy, consideration for others, and aggression. Correlations between subjects' and friends' reports on these measures were as follows

(degrees of freedom generally were 22 or 23): perspective taking, .05, N.S.; sympathy, .59, $p < .002$; consideration for others, .43, $p < .032$; suppression of aggression, .39, $p < .057$. These correlations provided some evidence of the validity of subjects' self-reports of sympathy, consideration for others, and suppression of aggression. Perspective taking is an internal process that is not easily observed by others; thus, scores on this variable were retained in the analyses even though friends' and subjects' reports were not related. Because of the small sample size for friend data (the degrees of freedom would be only 20 for some analyses), the friend data were not used in the primary analyses.

Interrelations of Measures of Morally Relevant Behavior

The measures of prosocial behavior were helping at T8 (C1 and C2), mothers' reports of offsprings' prosocial behavior at T8 (C1), adolescents' reports of prosocial behavior at T8 (C1 and C2), donating at T8 (C2), and adolescents' reports of consideration for others and aggression at T9. Relations among prosocial behaviors at each time period were examined with correlations. In these and all subsequent analyses, data from C2 as well as C1 were used at T8 when possible.

At T8, there were no significant relations among the prosocial behavior measures, although $r(29) = .35$, $p < .057$ between mother and child report measures and $r(31) = .31$, $p < .076$ between C2 donating and reported prosocial behavior.

At T9, consideration for others ($M = 3.82$, $SD = .64$) and suppression of aggression ($M = 3.60$, $SD = .90$) were highly correlated, $r(30) = .63$, $p < .001$. Thus, these two measures were standardized and aggregated for further analyses (henceforth called the moral behavior aggregate). This aggregate score was moderately positively related to the same composite score computed from the data from friends, $r(23) = .52$, $p < .026$. This composite score was not significantly correlated with helping at T8, although it was positively correlated with self-reported prosocial behavior at T8, $r(30) = .46$, $p < .008$, and with mothers' reports of prosocial behavior at T8, $r(29) = .44$, $p < .013$.

Relation of Social Desirability to Moral Judgment, Moral Behavior, and Empathy

In these and subsequent analyses involving moral judgment, results for the composite scores from all five stories are re-

86

ported because composite scores based on more items generally are assumed to be more reliable (Rushton, Brainerd, & Pressley, 1983), and the extra story was considered to be more age-appropriate than some of the other four stories. However, the findings based on these composite scores generally were very similar to those based on data from four stories.

There were numerous relations between adolescents' scores on social desirability (SD) and other measures obtained from the adolescents. At T8, SD was positively correlated with sympathy, perspective taking, $rs(63) = .37$ and $.54$, $ps < .002$ and $.001$, and reported prosocial behavior, $r(64) = .35$, $p < .004$, and negatively correlated with personal distress, $r(63) = -.27$, $p < .027$. At T9, SD was not significantly correlated with any measure of reasoning (including PROM scores) except stereotypic reasoning during the interview, $r(25) = .45$, $p < .02$. However, SD was positively correlated at T9 with perspective taking, sympathy, and the moral behavior aggregate, $rs(29) = .54$, $.69$, and $.63$, $ps < .002$, $.001$, and $.001$.

Because of the aforementioned relations between SD and some of our measures and the socially desirable nature of both empathy-related and prosocial responding, auxiliary partial correlations controlling for SD were computed in addition to zero-order correlations in subsequent analyses. In most cases, the partial correlations were similar to the zero-order correlations. Thus, zero-order correlations are reported in all subsequent analyses, although partial correlations are also mentioned in text if they differ considerably from the zero-order correlations.

The Relation of Moral Reasoning to Prosocial Behavior

The relations of measures of prosocial/moral behavior to moral reasoning were examined with correlational analyses. Data are presented for the interview composite score, as well as the two types of interview reasoning that most frequently have been associated with moral behavior (i.e., hedonistic and needs-oriented reasoning; Eisenberg, 1986; Eisenberg et al., 1991). Correlations for other individual categories that were used with some regularity (i.e., Ms of at least 4.45) were less frequent, and were always consistent with the findings for the composite scores and/or theoretical expectations. For the PROM, correlations for the five level scores and the composite score are presented.

At T8, adolescents' reports of their prosocial behavior were unrelated to their composite moral interview scores, but were positively correlated with needs-oriented moral reasoning. Similarly, mothers' reports of greater prosocial responding at T8 were positively correlated with adolescents' needs-oriented reasoning, and negatively correlated with hedonistic reasoning (see Table 4). Helping was unrelated to any of the three measures of reasoning. C2's donating at T8 was significantly positively correlated with higher-level prosocial moral reasoning as assessed by the interview composite score and negatively correlated with hedonistic reasoning.

At T9, scores on the moral behavior aggregate were positively correlated with the interview moral reasoning composite score and needs-oriented reasoning, and negatively correlated with hedonistic reasoning (see Table 4). In addition, they were positively related to the PROM composite score and internalized PROM reasoning, and negatively correlated with PROM hedonistic reasoning (see Table 5).

Relations of Moral Reasoning to Empathy-Related Constructs

To examine the relation of empathy-related constructs to moral reasoning, scores on sympathy, personal distress, and perspective taking at both T8 and T9 were correlated with moral reasoning as assessed contemporaneously (with interviews and, at T9, with the PROM). In general, sympathy and perspective taking were related to moral reasoning, whereas personal distress was not.

Specifically, at T8 and T9, sympathy was negatively correlated with hedonistic reasoning during the interview (Table 4). However, the significant correlation for hedonistic reasoning was not even marginally significant at T9 when social desirability was partialed. At T9, sympathy was also positively correlated with the PROM composite score, as well as internalized and stereotypic PROM reasoning, and negatively correlated with hedonistic reasoning on the PROM (see Table 5).

Perspective taking at T8 was negatively correlated with hedonistic reasoning and positively related to needs-oriented reasoning (see Table 4); the correlation for hedonistic reasoning dropped considerably (to $-.15$) when social desirability was controlled. At T9, PT was positively correlated with the composite interview measure of

TABLE 4

RELATIONS OF INTERVIEW MEASURES OF PROSOCIAL MORAL REASONING TO
CONTEMPORANEOUS PROSOCIAL BEHAVIOR AND EMPATHY-RELATED CHARACTERISTICS

	MEASURE OF MORAL REASONING		
	Hedonistic	Needs-Oriented	Composite Score
Prosocial index:			
T8 self-report	−.24$^+$	.30*	.17
T8 maternal report	−.35	.50**	.12
T8 helping	−.07	.06	.15
T8 donating	−.38*	.11	.51**
T9 composite score	−.52*	.33$^+$	.37*
Empathy-related			
characteristics:			
T8 sympathy	−.33**	.17	.21$^+$
T8 perspective taking	−.28*	.28*	.14
T8 personal distress	−.04	.09	−.03
T9 sympathy	−.40*	.21	.34$^+$
T9 perspective taking	−.31	.15	.44*
T9 personal distress	−.14	.17	.00

NOTE.—Correlations for the T8 helping, self-report prosocial measure, and empathy-related
measures were for Cohorts 1 and 2 combined; donating was assessed only for C2 at T8; and
maternal reports of prosocial behavior at T8 were assessed for C1. At T9, data were available
for only C1.
$^+$ $p < .10$.
* $p < .05$.
** $p < .01$.

moral reasoning.[2] In addition, at T9, PT was positively related to the PROM composite score and negatively correlated with approval-oriented moral reasoning on the PROM (see Table 5).

Because role-taking moral reasoning (during the interview) was conceptually related to perspective taking, its relation to perspective taking also was examined. Such reasoning was significantly correlated with perspective taking at both T8 and T9, $rs(62$ and $26) = .27$ and $.37$, $ps < .032$ and $.05$. Personal distress was not significantly related to any measures of moral reasoning.

Relation of Prosocial Behavior to Empathy-Related Constructs

At T8, adolescents' reported prosocial behavior was positively correlated with both sympathy and perspective taking, but not personal distress (see Table 6). Similarly, mothers' reports of adolescents' prosocial behavior were positively correlated with children's perspective taking. In contrast, neither donating nor helping at T8 were significantly correlated with empathy-related characteristics. At T9, the moral behavior aggregate was highly positively correlated with sympathy and perspective taking, but not personal distress.[3]

Discussion

The age-related trends identified in this study are similar to those presented in previous reports on this longitudinal study because only the last two follow-ups in the trend analyses are new to the study. None-

[2] Because direct reciprocity is considered a type of hedonistic reasoning, it is also interesting to note the strong negative correlations between direct reciprocity reasoning and both sympathy and perspective taking at T9, $rs(26) = −.50$ and $−.56$, $ps < .007$ and $.002$.
[3] At T8, females scored higher than males on reported prosocial behavior, $t(64) = 2.86$, $p < .006$ ($Ms = 3.33$ and 2.98, respectively), sympathy, $t(63) = 5.76$, $p < .001$ ($Ms = 4.29$ and 3.55, respectively), and personal distress, $t(63) = 2.86$, $p < .006$ ($Ms = 2.72$ and 2.23). At T9, females scored higher on perspective taking, sympathy, and the moral behavior composite ($Ms = 5.21, 5.96, .75$) than did males ($Ms = 4.07, 5.07,$ and $−.75$, respectively), $ts(30) = 2.72, 2.79,$ 2.54, $ps < .011, .009,$ and $.016$. In addition, females at T9 scored higher than males on the PROM composite score ($Ms = 1.99$ and 1.88) and internalized reasoning on the PROM ($Ms = .28$ and $.22$) and lower on hedonistic reasoning ($Ms = .14$ and $.20$), $ts(30) = 4.02, 3.67,$ and $−2.97$, $ps < .001, .001,$ and $.006$.

TABLE 5

RELATIONS OF MORAL REASONING ON THE PROM TO PROSOCIAL BEHAVIOR AND EMPATHY-RELATED CHARACTERISTICS AT T9

PROSOCIAL/EMPATHY MEASURES	PROM INDEX					
	Composite Index	Hedonistic Reasoning	Needs-Oriented Reasoning	Approval Reasoning	Stereotypic Reasoning	Internalized Reasoning
Prosocial aggregrate	.51**	−.47**	−.05	−.17	.32+	.35*
T9 sympathy	.49**	−.49**	−.11	−.24	.42**	.37*
T9 perspective taking	.44*	−.30+	.03	−.38*	.21	.31+
T9 personal distress	−.03	−.02	.06	−.16	.16	−.08

+ $p < .10$.
* $p < .05$.
** $p < .01$.

TABLE 6

CORRELATIONS OF PROSOCIAL BEHAVIOR MEASURES TO CONTEMPORANEOUS
EMPATHY-RELATED CHARACTERISTICS

| | EMPATHY-RELATED CHARACTERISTIC | | |
PROSOCIAL INDEX	Sympathy	Perspective Taking	Personal Distress
T8 self-report	.49***	.46***	.05
T8 maternal report	.27	.45**	.23
T8 helping	.11	−.15	.03
T8 donating	.04	.11	.17
T9 prosocial aggregate	.80***	.65***	−.16

NOTE.—Correlations for the T8 helping, self-report prosocial measure, and empathy-related measures were for Cohorts 1 and 2 combined; donating was assessed only for C2 at T8; and maternal reports of prosocial behavior at T8 were assessed for C1. At T9, data were available for only C1.
** $p < .01$.
*** $p < .001$.

theless, the results of the last two follow-ups provide interesting information on a variety of aspects of prosocial functioning in late adolescence and early adulthood. As predicted, some self-reflective and internalized modes of moral reasoning (role taking, positive affect/consequences, positive affect/values, negative affect/consequences, internalized norm, rule, and law reasoning) increased in use, whereas stereotypic reasoning continued to decrease in use into adulthood. The linear increases in positive affect/values and negative affect/consequences had not been found by mid-adolescence. However, hedonistic reasoning, which had decreased into early mid-adolescence and then started to increase slightly in mid-adolescence, continued to increase in use at age 19–20 (although there was a small drop in its use from age 15 to 16 to age 17 to 18). Moreover, direct reciprocity and approval-oriented reasoning, which had begun to decline in mid-adolescence at the T7 follow-up (when 32 rather than 28 subjects were included), showed little evidence of declining in early adulthood (and even increased somewhat). Although there was a linear increase in overall reasoning throughout adolescence, moral reasoning at age 19 to 20 was not predicted from moral reasoning at earlier points in adolescence, apparently due to substantial declines in reasoning (due to increases in direct reciprocity and hedonistic reasoning) for some people and substantial increases in reasoning due to the use of higher level categories of reasoning for some others. In contrast, there was some continuity in reasoning across age 13–14 to 17–18.

As just noted, there were increases in some modes of high-level, internalized moral reasoning that were not found in prior follow-ups. It is likely that such advances are due not only to increases in formal operational reasoning in late adolescence and early adulthood, but also to increased opportunities for role-taking experiences (Mason & Gibbs, 1993). Further, college experience has been associated with increases in moral reasoning, perhaps due to the general level of intellectual stimulation in college courses and the extracurricular college milieu (Rest & Narvaez, 1991). However, entry into college did not seem to enhance moral reasoning in regard to some modes of internalized reasoning in this study; for example, the increase in positive affect/values and negative affect/consequences reasoning seemed to occur between ages 15 to 16 years and 17 to 18 years. Most of our subjects were only second semester freshmen, however, so it may have been too early to find any effects of the college experience.

The aforementioned rise in subjects' use of hedonistic and direct reciprocity moral reasoning during adolescence/early adulthood is reminiscent of Kohlberg and Kramer's (1969) finding of a regression in moral judgment in early adulthood, and similar to Gilligan's (1977) data in regard to an increase in focus on responsibility to self rather than merely to others at a late stage of development. However, it is important to note that hedonistic reasoning was relatively infrequent in early adulthood, and was used primarily in response to dilemmas in which the costs of helping were high. Further, subjects' moral composite scores continued to rise into early adulthood due to increased use of numerous higher-level modes of reasoning. Most of the 19- and 20-year-olds did not verbalize principles such as responsibility to the self and did not use reasoning that could be viewed as relativistic (Murphy & Gilligan, 1980); rather, they simply seemed to have weighed long-term and substantial costs to self versus other (e.g., money for college, class time, possible injury or poor health) more carefully and realistically than when in high school and, perhaps, were relatively self-focused in their perspective. This explanation is consistent with prior work indicating that subjects' reasoning sometimes plummets in high-cost situations and is not always consistent in terms of level (Eisenberg-Berg, 1979; Rest, 1979). Perhaps young adults are cognitively able and inclined to evaluate the long-term costs for helping in some of our dilemmas (e.g., in terms of getting behind in school or losing money needed for college), whereas younger adolescents, who are less likely to use formal operational reasoning, are less likely to do so. In addition, late adulthood and early adulthood may be a time of life in which concerns about achieving success and independence are heightened, so potential costs in these domains are viewed as substantial. In brief, we suggest that the rise in egoistic modes of reasoning was not due to structural or competence-based factors. However, we have no definitive evidence regarding the reason for this increase. Indeed, whether the increase in egoistic modes of reasoning is interpreted as relativism or merely greater use of lower-level reasoning likely pivots on whether one views moral development as involving invariant, irreversible stages in which higher-level reasoning restructures lower-level reasoning (see Turiel, 1974) or as involving the emergence of new levels of reasoning that do not eliminate or restructure lower-level reasoning (Eisenberg, 1986; Rest, 1979).

In general, the pattern of findings regarding the PROM suggests that the PROM has adequate psychometric properties to use with young adults. Young adults' scores on their moral reasoning interviews were moderately correlated with their scores on the PROM, even though the two measures usually were administered at least a month apart in time. Further, the alphas for the PROM subscales were adequate. The pattern of correlations between the PROM scores and perspective taking, sympathy, and reported moral behavior also was similar to the pattern between interview scores and these constructs. These findings provide further evidence of the validity of the PROM for use with young adults.

At T9, some interview as well as PROM measures of prosocial moral judgment were significantly correlated with contemporaneous self-reported prosocial behavior and, to some degree, with individual differences in sympathy and perspective taking in early adulthood. Similarly, at T8, moral interview scores were significantly correlated with the more costly mode of prosocial behavior (donating), with subjects' and mothers' reports of prosocial behavior, and, to some degree, with sympathy and perspective taking. This pattern of findings is consistent with theoretical assertions and findings in prior follow-ups linking moral judgment with individual differences in perspective taking, sympathy, and moral behavior. However, these links have seldom been demonstrated in adolescence or adulthood.

Of interest is the fact that moral reasoning was more often significantly related to subjects' and mothers' reports of prosocial behavior and donating behavior than to helping behavior. The helping task—filling out a few forms and mailing them in a stamped envelope—was relatively low cost and not anonymous. In contrast, donating, which was relatively high cost and anonymous, was significantly correlated with higher-level reasoning and negatively related to hedonistic reasoning. Taken together, these findings are consistent with previous data demonstrating a relation between moral reasoning and costly behaviors such as donating but not low-cost helping behaviors (e.g., Eisenberg et al., 1987; Eisenberg & Shell, 1986). In addition, in the present study, subjects' and mothers' reports of prosocial behavior included a variety of prosocial actions; thus, the links between these measures of prosocial behavior and moral reasoning may have occurred because aggregate measures of a construct generally are more reliable than a single index.

The self- and mother-report measures of prosocial behavior, but not donating or helping, were positively related to subjects' sympathy (for child report only) and perspective taking. This pattern is similar to that found at T7 in mid-adolescence (except mothers' reports of prosocial behavior were unrelated at T7; Eisenberg et al., 1991). Perhaps this pattern of findings was obtained because the recipient of donating was not vividly depicted, and the benefits of helping for the experimenter (the recipient) may not have seemed high. Thus, sympathy and perspective taking may not have been relevant to helping or donating (particularly the former).

Measures of prosocial behavior, empathy-related constructs, and social desirability were relatively stable over periods of 4 years and longer. Thus, individual differences in these behaviors and reactions appear to have an enduring quality in adolescence and early adulthood. Moreover, judging from the findings in previous follow-ups, in general the patterns of relations among moral judgment, prosocial behavior, and empathy-related characteristics were fairly similar across adolescence and early adulthood (although, for example, different measures of prosocial behavior may relate to moral reasoning or empathy-related responding at different ages). Further, interrelations, when significant, generally have been consistent with theoretical expectations. Consequently, it appears that at least some of the processes involved in prosocial development are relatively stable across adolescence and into early adulthood. However, research on people other than middle-class Caucasians is needed because it is unclear whether our findings from a small, middle-class, primarily Caucasian sample can be generalized to other groups.

References

Batson, C. D. (1991). *The altruism question.* Hillsdale, NJ: Erlbaum.

Bryant, B. K. (1982). An index of empathy for children and adolescents. *Child Development,* 53, 413–425.

Candee, D., & Kohlberg, L. (1987). Moral judgment and moral action: A reanalysis of Haan, Smith, and Block's (1968) Free Speech Movement data. *Journal of Personality and Social Psychology,* 52, 554–564.

Carlo, G., Eisenberg, N., & Knight, G. P. (1992). An objective measure of adolescents' prosocial moral reasoning. *Journal of Research on Adolescence,* 2, 331–349.

Colby, A., & Kohlberg, L. (1987). *The measurement of moral judgment.* Cambridge: Cambridge University Press.

Colby, A., Kohlberg, L., Gibbs, J., & Lieberman, M. (1983). A longitudinal study of moral judgment. *Monographs of the Society for Research in Child Development,* 48(1–2, Serial No. 200).

Crowne, D. P., & Marlowe, D. (1964). *The approval motive.* New York: Wiley.

Davis, M. H. (1983). Measuring individual differences in empathy: Evidence for a multidimensional approach. *Journal of Personality and Social Psychology,* 44, 113–126.

Davis, M. H., & Franzoi, S. (1991). Stability and change in adolescent self-consciousness and empathy. *Journal of Research in Personality,* 25, 70–87.

Eisenberg, N. (1986). *Altruistic emotion, cognition and behavior.* Hillsdale, NJ: Erlbaum.

Eisenberg, N. (1990). Prosocial development in early and mid adolescence. In R. Montemayor, G. R. Adams, & T. P. Gullotta (Eds.), *Advances in adolescence: Vol. 2. From childhood to adolescence: A transitional period?* (pp. 240–269). Newbury Park, CA: Sage.

Eisenberg, N., & Fabes, R. A. (1991). Prosocial behavior and empathy: A multimethod, developmental perspective. In P. Clark (Ed.), *Review of personality and social psychology* (Vol. 12, pp. 34–61). Newbury Park, CA: Sage.

Eisenberg, N., Lennon, R., & Roth, K. (1983). Prosocial development: A longitudinal study. *Developmental Psychology,* 19, 846–855.

Eisenberg, N., & Miller, P. A. (1987). The relation of empathy to prosocial and related behavior. *Psychological Bulletin,* 101, 91–119.

Eisenberg, N., Miller, P. A., Shell, R., McNalley, S., & Shea, C. (1991). Prosocial development in adolescence: A longitudinal study. *Developmental Psychology,* 27, 849–857.

Eisenberg, N., & Shell, R. (1986). The relation of prosocial moral judgment and behavior in children: The mediating role of cost. *Personality and Social Psychology Bulletin,* 12, 426–433.

Eisenberg, N., Shell, R., Pasternack, J., Lennon, R., Beller, R., & Mathy, R. M. (1987). Prosocial development in middle childhood: A longitudinal study. *Developmental Psychology,* 23, 712–718.

Eisenberg-Berg, N. (1979). Development of children's prosocial moral judgment. *Developmental Psychology,* 15, 128–137.

Feldman, S. S., & Weinberger, D. A. (1994). Self-restraint as a mediator of family influences on boys' delinquent behavior: A longitudinal study. *Child Development,* 65, 195–211.

Gilligan, C. (1977). In a different voice: Women's conceptions of self and morality. *Harvard Educational Review,* 47, 481–517.

Gilligan, C., & Attanucci, J. (1988). Two moral orientations: Gender differences and similarities. *Merrill Palmer Quarterly,* 34, 223–238.

Hoffman, M. L. (1987). The contribution of empathy to justice and moral judgment. In N. Eisenberg & J. Strayer (Eds.), *Empathy and its development.* Cambridge: Cambridge University Press.

King, L. A., Emmons, R. A., & Woodley, S. (1992). The structure of inhibition. *Journal of Research in Personality, 26,* 85–102.

Kohlberg, L. (1969). Stage and sequence: The cognitive-developmental approach to socialization. In D. A. Goslin (Ed.), *Handbook of socialization theory and research* (pp. 325–480). New York: Rand McNally.

Kohlberg, L. (1981). *The philosophy of moral development: Moral stages and the idea of justice.* San Francisco: Harper & Row.

Kohlberg, L., & Candee, D. (1984). The relationship of moral judgment to moral action. In W. M. Kurtines & J. L. Gewirtz (Eds.), *Morality, moral behavior, and moral development* (pp. 52–73). New York: Wiley.

Kohlberg, L., & Gilligan, C. (1971). The adolescent as a philosopher: The discovery of the self in a postconventional world. *Daedalus, 100,* 1051–1086.

Kohlberg, L., & Kramer, R. (1969). Continuities and discontinuities in childhood and adult moral development. *Human Development, 12,* 93–120.

Kuhn, D., Amsel, E., & O'Loughlin, M. (1988). *The development of scientific thinking skills.* Orlando, FL: Academic Press.

Mason, M. G., & Gibbs, J. C. (1993). Social perspective taking and moral judgment among college students. *Journal of Adolescent Research, 8,* 109–123.

Murphy, J. M., & Gilligan, C. (1980). Moral development in late adolescence and adulthood: A critique and reconstruction of Kohlberg's theory. *Human Development, 23,* 77–104.

Nunnally, J. C. (1967). *Psychometric theory.* New York: McGraw-Hill.

Radke-Yarrow, M., & Zahn-Waxler, C. (1984). Roots, motives, and patterns in children's prosocial behavior. In E. Staub, D. Bar-Tal, J. Karylowski, & J. Reykowski (Eds.), *Develop-*

ment and maintenance of prosocial behavior: International perspectives on positive behavior (pp. 81–99). New York: Plenum.

Rest, J. R. (1979). *Development in judging moral issues.* Minneapolis: University of Minnesota Press.

Rest, J., & Narvaez, D. (1991). The college experience and moral development. In W. M. Kurtines & J. L. Gewirtz (Eds.), *Handbook of moral behavior and development: Vol. 2. Research* (pp. 229–245). Hillsdale: NJ: Erlbaum.

Rholes, W. S., & Bailey, S. (1983). The effects of level of moral reasoning in consistency between moral attitudes and related behaviors. *Social Cognition, 2,* 32–48.

Rushton, J. P., Brainerd, C. J., & Pressley, M. (1983). Behavioral development and construct validity: The principle of aggregation. *Psychological Bulletin, 94,* 18–38.

Rushton, J. P., Chrisjohn, R. D., & Fekken, G. C. (1981). The altruistic personality and the self-report altruism scale. *Personality and Individual Differences, 2,* 1–11.

Selman, R. L. (1980). *The growth of interpersonal understanding: Developmental and clinical analysis.* New York: Academic Press.

Small, S. A., Zeldin, R. S., & Savin-Williams, R. C. (1983). In search of personality traits: A multimethod analysis of naturally occurring prosocial and dominance behavior. *Journal of Personality, 51,* 1–16.

Turiel, E. (1974). Conflict and transition in adolescent moral development. *Child Development, 45,* 14–29.

Underwood, B., & Moore, B. (1982). Perspective-taking and altruism. *Psychological Bulletin, 91,* 143–173.

Weinberger, D. A. (1991). *Social-emotional adjustment in older children and adults: I. Psychometric properties of the Weinberger Adjustment Inventory.* Unpublished manuscript, Case Western Reserve University.

JOURNAL OF RESEARCH ON ADOLESCENCE, 3(2), 171-191

Socialization and Mothers' and Adolescents' Empathy-Related Characteristics

Nancy Eisenberg and Sandra McNally

Arizona State University

The primary purpose of this study was to examine the relations of maternal childrearing practices over an 8-year period to adolescents' sympathy, personal distress, and cognitive perspective-taking. In addition, the relations of maternal empathy-related characteristics to children's empathy-related characteristics and to their own childrearing practices were assessed. Maternal practices were assessed with a Q-sort on five occasions, each 2 years apart; mothers' and adolescents' empathy-related characteristics were assessed when the adolescents were 15 to 16 years old. Mothers' positive emotional communication and rational independence training were positively correlated with adolescents' perspective taking, as well as with mothers' perspective taking. Mothers' reluctance to discipline was associated with low levels of adolescents' (particularly girls') personal distress. In addition, maternal positive emotional communication was associated with high sympathy in girls and low personal distress in boys.

In the past decade there has been increasing interest in the topic of *empathy* (i.e., an affective reaction that is based on the apprehension of another's emotional state or condition and similar to that other person's emotion or condition; Eisenberg & Miller, 1987) and its socialization. This interest is probably due to the theoretical and empirical association between empathy or related emotional responses and both children's prosocial behavior (Eisenberg & Fabes, 1990; Eisenberg & Miller, 1987; Hoffman, 1982; Staub, 1979) and social competence (Eisenberg & Miller, 1987; Saarni, 1990). However, there is relatively little research con-

Requests for reprints should be sent to Nancy Eisenberg, Department of Psychology, Arizona State University, Tempe, AZ 85287.

cerning the socialization of vicarious emotional responding, particularly research in which adolescents were participants and parental practices were assessed over a period of time (see Barnett, 1987).

Moreover, investigators examining the socialization of empathy infrequently have differentiated between two emotional reactions that may often stem from empathy: *sympathy* (i.e., other-oriented sorrow or concern for another which frequently stems from sympathy) and *personal distress* (i.e., a self-focused aversive emotional response resulting from the apprehension of another's state or condition). Both sympathy and personal distress are viewed as frequently stemming from empathy, whereas empathy often results from *cognitive perspective-taking* (i.e., understanding others' cognitions and emotions by taking their role) or related cognitive processes (see Batson, 1987; Eisenberg, Shea, Carlo, & Knight, 1991). Recently, researchers have suggested that empathic overarousal results in a self-focused response due to the aversive nature of high levels of vicarious arousal (i.e., results in personal distress) whereas sympathy is more likely to predominate if the empathic arousal is moderate in intensity (see Eisenberg & Fabes, 1992; Hoffman, 1982). Given that personal distress tends to be negatively related or unrelated to children's prosocial behavior whereas sympathy generally is positively related (see Batson, 1987; Eisenberg & Fabes, 1990), the distinction between sympathy and personal distress is very important.

Because of the importance of empathy-related emotions in social development and prosocial behavior (e.g., Batson, 1987; Eisenberg & Fabes, 1990, 1992), the primary purpose of the present study was to examine the relation between adolescents' empathy-related characteristics and maternal childrearing attitudes and behaviors over an 8-year period. Parental practices and children's empathy-related characteristics are related in childhood; thus, one would expect some association between the two in adolescence, particularly given the considerable consistency in parental practices over time (see Hock & Lindamood, 1981; McNally, Eisenberg, & Harris, 1991; Roberts, J. H. Block, & J. Block, 1984). Nonetheless, because of the increasing separation between parent and child in adolescence, it is possible that the association between maternal practices and offspring's empathy decreases with the age of the child.

Specifically, researchers have found that supportive, empathic parenting during childhood is associated with the development of empathy and sympathy (e.g., Kestenbaum, Farber, & Sroufe, 1989; see Barnett, 1987). However, maternal warmth by itself has not always been associated with offsprings' empathy (Janssens & Gerris, 1992; Koestner, Franz, & Weinberger, 1990), perhaps because sympathy and personal distress were not differentiated in some relevant studies (e.g., Janssens & Gerris, 1992). In general, parental sympathy appears to be associated with the development of sympathy in same-sex children (Eisenberg et al., 1992; Eisenberg, Fabes, Schaller, Carlo, & Miller, 1991; Fabes, Eisenberg, & Miller, 1990) whereas parental abuse has been associated with low levels of empathy in children (Miller & Eisenberg, 1988). In addition, the open expression of positive and/or negative submissive emotion (e.g., noncontrolling negative emotions such as sadness over someone leaving, apologizing; see Halberstadt, 1986) has been associated with offspring's sympathy (Eisenberg et al., 1992; Eisenberg, Fabes, Schaller, Carlo, & Miller, 1991) whereas dominant (hostile, controlling) negative familial emotion such as anger has been negatively related to boys' sympathy and positively related to girls' personal distress (Eisenberg et al., 1992). Thus, it is reasonable to predict that a positive rather than a negative affective tone in the parent–child relationship is positively related to adolescents' sympathy and perhaps negatively related to their tendency to respond with personal distress to others in need or distress. Moreover, based on the previous association between maternal sympathy and school-age daughters' sympathy, mothers' sympathy (which probably is reflected in maternal warmth; Feshbach, 1978) would be expected to be associated with daughters' sympathy.

Parental directiveness has also been positively related to children's empathy (Janssens & Gerris, 1992) and social responsibility (Baumrind, 1971). Thus, parental reluctance to direct their children and punish when necessary and appropriate (e.g., parental overindulgence) would be expected to be negatively related to children's sympathy and perspective taking. However, it is likely that directiveness is linked with positive attributes in children only if it is authoritative in style (i.e., combined with rational discipline, support, and respect for the child's autonomy) rather than authoritarian in tone (Baumrind, 1971). Indeed, parents who are very controlling may not allow their children the opportunity to be exposed to others' emotional states, an experience that is believed to foster the development of empathy (Hoffman, 1970). Thus, it is likely that parents who encourage their children to act independently while providing rational punishments for transgressions facilitate the development of children's empathy. In contrast, children who are overprotected and overly controlled may not have opportunities to learn how to cope with others' negative emotions and may be prone to experience personal distress.

One way that maternal encouragement of autonomy may foster the development of children's sympathy is through encouraging the development of cognitive perspective-taking (the ability or tendency to cognitively comprehend another's perspective), which itself is viewed as either a component of empathy (Davis, 1983b; Feshbach, 1978; Hoffman, 1982) or a process that facilitates sympathetic responding (Batson, 1987; Eisenberg, Shea, Carlo, & Knight, 1991). Cooper and Grotevant found that adolescents who experienced individuated patterns of familial interactions, involving the expression of separateness as well as *permeability* (e.g., responsiveness or openness of an individual to the ideas of others), were relatively advanced in their perspective taking (see Cooper, Grotevant, & Condon, 1983; Grotevant & Cooper, 1986). Consistent with these findings, McDevitt, Lennon, and Kopriva (1991) found that parental practices that acknowledge the child's perspective and encourage perspective taking were associated with higher levels of adolescents' moral reasoning about others in need or distress (and moral reasoning is expected to reflect perspective taking; Kohlberg, 1984). Thus, it was hypothesized that parental emphasis on autonomy, combined with the use of authoritative, rational discipline, would be associated with adolescents' perspective taking and sympathy.

In summary, we hypothesized that:

1. Mothers who are themselves sympathetic will have sympathetic daughters.
2. A positively toned affective relationship between mother and child will be associated with children's sympathy and low personal distress.
3. Maternal encouragement of autonomy and use of rational discipline will be associated with children's sympathy and perspective taking and perhaps low levels of personal distress.
4. Maternal reluctance to discipline (i.e., indulgence and reluctance to use any discipline) will correlate with low levels of offsprings' sympathy and perspective taking.

In addition, mothers' childrearing practices may be associated with their own empathy and sympathy. Feshbach (1987) and Dix (in press) have argued that parental empathy is an important component of parental childrearing practices, and that empathic parents are sensitive, emotionally involved, and supportive in interactions with their children. Consistent with this assumption, empathic mothers are more involved, more positive, and less negative with their children than are less empathic mothers (Feshbach, 1987); furthermore, low levels of maternal empathy have been associated with child abuse (Miller & Eisenberg, 1988). Thus, a second goal of this study was to examine the relations between maternal childrearing practices and maternal sympathy, personal distress, and cognitive perspective-taking (i.e., cognitively taking the role of others). It was hypothesized that maternal practices reflecting positive rather than negative affect and maternal granting of autonomy combined with rational discipline would be positively associated with maternal sympathy and perspective taking, whereas the reverse relations would hold for maternal personal distress.

The distinctions among sympathy, personal distress, and cognitive perspective-taking are relatively recent and have seldom been examined in adolescence (see, however, Eisenberg, Miller, Shell, McNally, & Shea, 1991). One problem in studying these different vicarious emotional responses is the lack of questionnaire measures of sympathy and personal distress suitable for children. However, Davis (1983b) developed a questionnaire measure for use with adults that operationalizes these critical distinctions, and recent research suggests that Davis's scale can be used with adolescents (Eisenberg, Miller, et al., 1991). Although self-report measures of vicarious emotional responding may be influenced by individuals' willingness to acknowledge and report their emotional responses (and, in fact, self-reports of sympathy and personal distress tend to be positively correlated; Batson, 1987), such measures appear to be reliable and at least reasonably valid (see Davis, 1983a, 1983b; Eisenberg et al., 1992; Eisenberg, Fabes, Schaller, Carlo, & Miller, 1991; Eisenberg, Fabes, Schaller, Miller, et al., 1991; Eisenberg & Miller, 1987; Eisenberg, Miller, Shell, McNally, & Shea, 1991). Nonetheless, because of the relation between self-report measures of sympathy and personal distress and social desirability in some studies (see, e.g., Eisenberg, Shell, McNally, & Shea, 1991; Eisenberg et al., 1987), in this study we also assessed social desirability so that it could be controlled in the statistical analyses.

METHOD

Subjects

The participants were 32 mothers and their children (16 girls, 16 boys). The mothers were first interviewed about their childrearing practices when their children were 7 to 8 years of age ($M = 91$ months; Time 1) and were reinterviewed when their children were ages 9 to 10 years ($M = 115$ months; Time 2), 11 to 12 years ($M = 139$ months; Time 3), 13 to 14 years ($M = 163$ months; Time 4), and 15 to 16 years ($M = 187$ months; Time 5). Most of the children were in Grades 2, 4, 6, 8, and 10 at the respective interview sessions (several were in one grade lower). The measures of the children's and mothers' sympathy, perspective taking, and personal distress were obtained at Time 5. The mothers and their children are part of an ongoing longitudinal study on prosocial development (see Eisenberg, Miller, Shell, McNally, & Shea, 1991); 5 of the original 37 families have been lost over an 11-year period, but only 1 was lost during the 8-year period relevant to this article. The children were initially recruited at ages 4 to 5 from their preschool. The families were from middle-class suburban neighborhoods, including two Mexican-American families and 30 non-Hispanic, White families. Nearly all the children attended public schools in suburban neighborhoods of the greater Phoenix area (a number had moved over the years but stayed in the same metropolitan area). Most of the mothers had some college education. Because maternal data were missing for 2 mothers at one interview each, only 30 mothers were included in some analyses, although (as is described later) aggregate childrearing data from all 32 mothers were used in the primary analyses.

Procedure

The Child Rearing Practices Report (CRPR; J. H. Block, 1965) was individually administered to each mother to assess childrearing practices at each of the five interview sessions. The experimenter was a different person at each interview. Although the mothers in this study had been administered the CRPR five times, it does not seem that they remembered their previous responses and became more consistent (in regard to test–retest reliabilities) over time. Indeed, maternal responses were not notably more consistent from the first to third administration than from the third to fifth administration (see McNally et al., 1991).

The CRPR is a Q-sort procedure consisting of 91 items, all phrased in the first-person form, that describe childrearing attitudes, behaviors, and values (see Roberts et al., 1984). Mothers were instructed to respond to items in relation to the particular target child who was a participant in the longitudinal study. Based on mothers' sorting of the items into piles varying in their descriptiveness of the mother, each item received a score ranging from *least descriptive of the mother* (1) to *most descriptive* (7). Evidence of the reliability and validity of the CRPR has been reported (J. Block, 1969; J. H. Block, 1965; Kochanska, 1990; Kochanska, Kuczynski, & Radke-Yarrow, 1989; McNally et al., 1991).

At Time 5, the mothers and children were individually administered the seven-item Perspective Taking (PT; e.g., "I try to look at everybody's side of a disagreement before I make a decision"), Empathic Concern (EC; i.e., sympathy; e.g., "I am often quite touched by things that I see happen"), and Personal Distress (PD; e.g., "In emergency situations, I feel anxious and ill-at-ease") scales of Davis's (1983b) Interpersonal Reactivity Scale. Alphas for the PT, EC, and PD were, respectively, .72,

.86, and .72 for the children and .79, .77, and .84 for the mothers.[1] Data for these scales were lost for one mother. Scores on this measure have been associated with facial measures of concerned attention and personal distress (Eisenberg et al., 1988). Moreover, scores on the sympathy or perspective-taking subscales frequently have been positively associated with measures of prosocial behavior (e.g., Carlo, Eisenberg, Troyer, Switzer, & Speer, 1991; Davis, 1983a; Eisenberg et al., 1989), as well as with adolecsents' prosocial moral reasoning (Carlo, Eisenberg, & Knight, 1992; Eisenberg, Miller, Shell, McNally, & Shea, 1991), whereas personal distress has been negatively related to higher level reasoning (Carlo, Eisenberg, & Knight, 1992). Thus, Davis's scale appears to be reliable and valid.

Finally, the children also responded to 25 items from the Marlowe-Crowne Social Desirability Scale (Crowne & Marlowe, 1964). The alpha coefficient for this measure was .87.

Development of Childrearing Composites

With the sample used in this study, McNally et al. (1991) refined the composites that Roberts et al. (1984) developed for the Q-sort. Items that substantially lowered the alpha coefficients for a given cluster (i.e., reduced it by 3 or more points for 3 or more time periods) were dropped from the cluster. Items that we judged to be conceptually related to a particular cluster were added if the items improved the internal reliabilities of the item clusters. Clusters with low mean alphas (less than .45 for scales with few items and a four-item scale with an alpha of .50) were eliminated, as were clusters dealing with narrow aspects of childrearing (especially if they included small numbers of items). The relatively high test–retest consistencies reported in McNally et al. for most composites over 4 or even 8 years (they ranged from .31 to .83; the majority were above .60) were also evidence of the reliability of the composites. The results of these analyses were eight scales: Independence, Control, Enjoyment of Child, Negative Affect, Expression of Affect, Emphasis on Achievement, Rational Guidance, and Nonphysical Punishment. The alphas for these initial scales are presented in McNally et al. (1991). In addition, we included one other composite that we developed but did not present in McNally et al. (1991): Investment in

---

[1]At Time 4, children were given the same sympathy, personal distress, and perspective-taking scales to take home, complete, and return by mail. Nineteen children returned the scales. Children's reports of sympathy, personal distress, and perspective-taking were relatively consistent over the 2-year period, $rs(17) = .72, .67$, and $.46, p < .001, .002$, and $.055$, respectively.

Child. The latter reflects overindulgence (the four items in this scale are listed in Table 1; alphas for the five time periods ranged from .34 to .60, with mean alpha = .50; McNally, 1990).

In this study, we selected maternal childrearing composites of conceptual relevance to empathy-related emotion (those pertaining to the quality of the mother–child relationship, the expression of emotion, punishment, control, and the encouragement of independence; i.e., all those just listed except Emphasis on Achievement) and intercorrelated them at each time period. Based on the intercorrelations among the composites, we formed three superordinate composites by standardizing and averaging two or three conceptually similar composites. The first was a combination of Independence, Control (reverse coded), and Rational Guidance; this new composite henceforth is called *Rational Independence Training*. Independence was negatively and significantly correlated with Control at all time periods (rs ranged from $-.41$ to $-.62$, $M = -.50$), Independence was positively related to Rational Guidance at four time periods (rs ranged from .14 to .46, $M = .38$), and Control was negatively related to Rational Guidance at four time periods and marginally related ($p < .08$) at the fifth (rs ranged from $-.32$ to $-.60$, $M = -.46$). The items from these three composites that were combined are listed in Table 1; alphas for this new composite ranged from .73 to .80 for the five time periods ($M = .76$).[2]

The second composite (henceforth called *Positive Emotional Communication*) was formed by combining Expression of Affect (primarily positive affect), Negative Affect (reverse coded), and Enjoyment of Child at each time period. Expression of Affect was significantly negatively related to Negative Affect at all time periods (rs ranged from $-.48$ to $-.70$; $M = -.58$) and significantly positively related to Enjoyment of Child at four time periods (rs ranged from .28 to .55; $M = .42$). Negative Affect was significantly and highly negatively related to Enjoyment of Child at the three later time periods (rs ranged from $-.07$ to $-.48$, $M = -.31$, with rs for Times 3 to 5 all being $-.42$ or higher). The alphas for the five time periods for the new Positive Emotional Communication composite ranged from .64 to .84 ($M = .76$).

The third composite (henceforth called *Reluctance to Discipline*) was formed by combining Nonphysical Punishment (items were reverse coded) with Investment in Child at all time periods. These two composites were at least marginally significantly correlated ($p < .10$) for three time periods (rs ranged from $-.06$ to $-.40$, $M = -.31$). The alphas for

---

[2]Item 76 was in both the Independence and Control composites (albeit reverse coded in the former; see McNally et al., 1991). However, it was used only once in forming the new composite score.

TABLE 1

Maternal Composites: Items, Alphas, and Reliabilities Over Time

Items Grouped by Composite	Range of Alphas for Five Time Periods	Mean Alpha	Range of Test–Retest Correlations[a]	Mean Test–Retest Over a 2-Year Period
Rational Independence Training				
Independence	.73 to .80	.76	.66 to .90	.77
1. I respect my child's opinions and encourage him/her to express them.				
6. If my child gets into trouble, I expect him/her to handle the problem mostly by himself/herself.				
24. I feel a child should have time to think, daydream, and even loaf sometimes.				
26. I let my child make many decisions for himself/herself.				
54. I believe children should not have secrets from their parents.[b]				
67. I teach my child that he/she is responsible for what happens to him/her.				
75. I want my child to be independent of me.				
76. I make sure I know where my child is and what he/she is doing.[b]				
Control				
14. I believe physical punishment to be the best way of disciplining.				
21. I encourage my child to wonder and think about life.[b]				
31. I do not allow my child to wonder and think about life.				
43. I have strict, well-established rules for my child.				
45. I encourage my child to be curious, to explore and question things.[b]				

(continued)

103

TABLE 1 (continued)

Items Grouped by Composite	Range of Alphas for Five Time Periods	Mean Alpha	Range of Test–Retest Correlations[a]	Mean Test–Retest Over a 2-Year Period
47. I expect my child to be grateful and appreciate all the advantages he/she has.				
70. I do not allow my child to question my decisions.				
76. I make sure I know where my child is and what he/she is doing.				
Rational Guidance				
38. I talk it over and reason with my child when he/she misbehaves.				
51. I believe in praising a child when he/she is good and think it gets better results than punishing him/her when he/she is bad.				
52. I make sure my child knows that I appreciate when he/she tries or accomplishes.				
73. I let my child know how ashamed and disappointed I am when he/she misbehaves.[b]				
Positive Emotional Communication	.64 to .68	.76	.62 to .82	.77
Negative Affect				
5. I often feel angry with my child.				
69. There is a good deal of conflict between my child and me.				
Expression of Affect				
18. I express affection by hugging, kissing, and holding my child.				
34. I am easygoing and relaxed with my child.				
40. I joke and play with my child.				
42. My child and I have warm, intimate times together.				

104

Enjoyment of Child

19. I find some of my greatest satisfactions in my child.
66. I sometimes tease and make fun of my child.
77. I find it interesting and educational to be with my child for long periods.

Reluctance to Discipline .49 to .63 .56 .26 to .78 .66

Nonphysical Punishment

7. I punish my child by putting him/her off somewhere by himself/herself.
60. I punish my child by taking away a privilege he/she otherwise would have had.

Investment in Child

25. I find it difficult to punish my child.
35. I give up some of my own interests because of my child.
36. I tend to spoil my child.
48. I sometimes feel that I am too involved with my child.

[a]These include correlations over 2-, 4-, 6-, and 8-year periods.
[b]Indicates items reverse coded in the original composites. In addition, as discussed in the text, items on some composites were reversed when aggregated into superordinate composites.

105

the new Reluctance to Discipline composite for the five time periods ranged from .49 to .63, mean alpha = .56. Items incorporated into this composite reflect the reluctance to punish the child by "putting him/her off by himself/herself" (Item 7) or by "taking away a privilege he/she otherwise would have had" (Item 60) and a general tendency to indulge the child (e.g., "I find it difficult to punish my child," Item 25; "I tend to spoil my child," Item 36). An alpha of .50 is considered adequate for a new or short scale (because the alpha varies in part as a function of the number of items in a scale; see Nunnally, 1967), particularly if there is other evidence of reliability (e.g., test–retest reliability).

Finally, each of the three new composite scores was highly consistent over time (see McNally et al., 1991, for consistencies over time of the component composites), a finding that provides further evidence of the reliability of the composites. When Rational Independence Training was correlated across the five time periods (i.e., composites for all five time periods were intercorrelated), the correlations ranged from .66 to .90. The range for Positive Emotional Communication was .62 to .82; that for Reluctance to Discipline was .48 to .78 (with most above .60) for all time periods except the first. Correlations of Time 1 Reluctance to Discipline with this composite at the other time periods ranged from .26 to .66. Mean correlations over the various 2-year periods were .77, .77, and .66 for Rational Independence Training, Positive Emotional Communication, and Reluctance to Discipline, respectively. Because of the generally high intercorrelations of the composites across time and the fact that aggregate measures generally are more reliable than single measures of a construct (Rushton, Brainerd, & Pressley, 1983), the composite indices at each time period were standardized and then each composite was averaged across all time periods for which a given mother had a score (recall that 2 mothers were missing data at one time period). Thus, our final three composite childrearing indices reflected maternal practices across an 8-year period.

RESULTS

Descriptive Statistics

The relations among children's empathy-related measures were examined with partial correlations in which the effect of sex of the child was partialed out. Children's sympathy ($M = 3.97$, $SD = 0.75$), was significantly correlated with their perspective-taking ($M = 3.37$, $SD = .68$), but not personal distress ($M = 2.61$, $SD = 0.70$). For mothers, the only significant correlation among empathy-related measures was between maternal perspective-taking (M = 4.09, SD = 0.63) and sympathy (M = 4.20, SD = 0.59), Pearson $r(29)$ = .38, p < .035 (for mothers' personal distress, M = 2.48, SD = 0.75).

The only significant correlation among the three maternal childrearing composites was between Positive Emotional Communication and Rational Independence Training, $r(30)$ = .55, p < .002. Children's social desirability scores were significantly related to their perspective taking and sympathy, $rs(30)$ = .58 and .47, ps < .001 and .007, but not their personal distress.

Relations Between Maternal Childrearing Practices and Adolescents' Perspective-Taking, Sympathy, and Personal Distress

In the analyses pertaining to the relation of maternal practices to adolescents' perspective-taking, sympathy, and personal distress, partial correlations were computed for the combined sample (controlling sex) whereas Spearman correlations were computed when males and females were examined separately. The partial correlations between maternal childrearing composites and children's empathy-related measures for the total sample are presented in Table 2. Maternal Positive Emotional Communication was positively related to children's (particularly girls') cognitive perspective-taking and girls' sympathy, and negatively related to boys' personal distress. Reluctance to Discipline was negatively related to children's (particularly girls') personal distress. Maternal Rational Independence Training was significantly positively related to children's perspective-taking when the effect of social desirability as well as sex was partialed out, partial $r(28)$ = .47, p < .01; this finding probably emerged when social desirability was controlled because partialing minimizes the effect of the high correlation between social desirability and children's reported perspective-taking. None of the other correlations changed substantially when children's social desirability was partialed out.

In supplementary analyses, we correlated the maternal childrearing composites for each of the five time periods with children's scores at Time 5 for perspective taking, sympathy, and personal distress. There were no clear patterns of linear change in the magnitude of the correlations; indeed, the correlations were quite similar at the five time periods. Moreover, there were no instances of significant correlations between one of the three child variables and a maternal childrearing practice when the same correlation involving the composite measure was not at least marginally significant. Thus, the relations between

TABLE 2
Correlations Between Maternal Childrearing Composites and Mothers' and Children's
Empathy-Related Characteristics

Empathy-Related Variables	Positive Emotional Communication	Rational Independence Training	Reluctance to Discipline
Child			
Sympathy			
Girls	.64**	.14	−.18
Boys	−.06	−.25	−.29
Both	.21	.01	−.24
Personal distress			
Girls	.12	−.23	−.84***
Boys	−.58*	.28	−.12
Both	−.10	−.12	−.43*
Perspective taking			
Girls	.53**	.39	−.26
Boys	.42	.13	.20
Both	.37*	.24	−.07
Mother			
Sympathy	−.02	−.20	.12
Personal Distress	−.28	.01	.13
Perspective Taking	.63***	.47*	.00

Note. Sex of child is partialed in all correlations except those done separately by sex.
Spearman correlations were used for computation of correlations within each sex.
*p < .05. **p < .01. ***p < .001.

maternal practices and adolescents' empathy-related characteristics did
not appear to markedly strengthen or weaken with age of the mother
and the child.

Correlations Between Maternal
and Child Empathy-Related Measures

There were no significant relations between children's and mothers'
sympathy, personal distress, and perspective taking for the total sample. However, among younger children, it appears that mothers'
empathy-related characteristics are related to the analogous characteristics primarily for their daughters (e.g., Eisenberg et al., 1992; Eisenberg,
Fabes, Schaller, Carlo, & Miller, 1991; Fabes et al., 1990). Thus, although
our samples of girls and boys are rather small if considered separately,
we correlated the mothers' and children's empathy-related characteristics within each sex. Modest support for our prediction was obtained;
mothers' perspective-taking was marginally positively related to girls'
sympathy, Spearman $r(13) = .51$, $p = .051$ (Spearman $r = .04$ for boys).

Relations Between Maternal Childrearing Practices and Maternal Perspective-Taking, Sympathy, and Personal Distress

The correlations between the mothers' empathy-related measures and their childrearing practices are presented in Table 2. Mothers' Positive Emotional Communication was positively related to maternal perspective-taking and negatively related to maternal personal distress. In addition, maternal Rational Independence Training was positively related to maternal perspective-taking. Mothers' reported Reluctance to Discipline was unrelated to their empathy-related characteristics.

DISCUSSION

In this study, mothers' reported socialization practices, aggregated over an 8-year period, were related to adolescents' vicarious emotional responding and cognitive perspective-taking. For example, mothers who reported expressing positive emotions toward their child and relatively low levels of negative affect had children who scored relatively high in perspective taking, daughters who scored high in sympathy, and sons who scored low in personal distress. In addition, maternal Reluctance to Discipline was associated with low levels of personal distress, whereas maternal Rational Independence Training was correlated with children's perspective taking when social desirability, which was highly related to children's reported perspective-taking, was controlled. In general, these findings were consistent with what has been found with younger children, suggesting some continuity in the socialization of vicarious emotional responding and perspective taking.

The finding of a relation between positive maternal communication and children's perspective-taking is consistent with theorizing (e.g., Dix, in press; Feshbach, 1987) and some prior research (see Barnett, 1987; Grotevant & Cooper, 1986) indicating that mothers who are supportive and warm have children who are prone to take the perspective of others. Supportive, sensitive mothers are likely to be adept at perspective taking themselves and may model such behavior for their children.

In addition, the finding that maternal independence training combined with rational, supportive guidance was positively related to children's perspective taking (when controlling social desirability) is consistent with Grotevant and Cooper's (1986) finding that parental practices that foster adolescents' individuation are associated with adolescents' perspective-taking. Parents who encourage their children

109

to think and act for themselves and who use rational discipline model perspective taking and may encourage their children to take others' perspectives. Because perspective-taking skills appear to develop well into adolescence (e.g., Selman, 1980), adolescence may be an important period for fostering offsprings' understanding and concern about others.

As noted previously, mothers who were reluctant to discipline their children, even with nonphysical methods of punishment such as deprivation of privileges or time out, and who tended to indulge their children, had offspring who scored relatively low in personal distress (and were not particularly high in sympathy). Thus, maternal permissiveness was associated with low distress or anxiety when dealing with others' emotional states. These data are consistent with the finding that parental emphasis on children's constructive instrumental coping with problems is associated with high levels of boys' sympathy/empathy (Eisenberg et al., 1991). Permissiveness may communicate to children that they can do whatever they wish and that they need not be concerned with the feelings and expectations of others (Moore & Eisenberg, 1984). Moreover, permissive mothers may not provide children with cues and information regarding others' emotions and needs, with the consequence that their children are relatively insensitive to others.

Not surprisingly, mothers' perspective-taking also was associated with their reported childrearing practices. Mothers who were high in perspective taking were high in positive (rather than negative) affect in relation to their children and were likely to encourage independence while using rational discipline. Such findings are consistent with Dix's (1991, in press) argument that empathic parenting goals are associated with responsive, sensitive parenting behaviors.

It is somewhat surprising that maternal sympathy was unrelated to children's sympathy (although maternal perspective-taking was marginally positively related to daughters' sympathy) or their own childrearing practices. Mothers' dispositional empathy has been significantly correlated with children's self-reported empathy (Strayer, 1983), and maternal sympathy has been positively correlated with elementary school children's sympathy and negatively related to their personal distress (Eisenberg et al., 1992; Eisenberg, Fabes, Schaller, Carlo, & Miller, 1991; Fabes et al., 1990). Maternal sympathy or empathy has also been associated with the expression of positive emotion (Dix, in press; Feshbach, 1987).

Perhaps the relation of maternal sympathy to children's sympathy simply no longer holds in adolescence. The fact that the correlations were small suggests that the failure to find a relation was not due merely to sample size. By the time children are adolescents, other models of sympathy (e.g., peers, the media) may be more important or socializers of sympathetic responding. Mothers' sympathy also may not be related to the same childrearing practices when their children are adolescents as when they were younger. With age, sympathetic mothers, who probably are also sensitive mothers, may find that they must use different practices to control adolescents than younger children, and a shift in their practices could weaken the relation between maternal sympathy and children's sympathy. Consistent with this possibility, maternal emphasis on achievement (see McNally et al., 1991) was negatively correlated with maternal sympathy at $p < .09$ or better (partial rs ranged from $-.32$ to $-.38$) for the data from Time 1 to Time 4, but was unrelated in midadolescence, partial $r(28) = -.10$. Alternatively, highly sympathetic mothers may have some difficulty imposing even constructive discipline on their adolescents, which could weaken the relation between maternal sympathy and adolescents' sympathy. Additional research is needed to determine whether these findings replicate for other samples of adolescents.

Although the sample sizes for girls and boys were small, some intriguing gender differences emerged. Consistent with prior findings (e.g., Eisenberg, Fabes, Schaller, Carlo, & Miller, 1991; Fabes et al., 1990), maternal perspective-taking was marginally significantly related to girls', but not boys', sympathy. Moreover, the relations between maternal Positive Emotional Communication and children's perspective taking and between maternal Reluctance to Discipline and personal distress appeared to be due primarily to the data for girls; in addition, maternal emotional communication was positively related to girls' (and not boys') sympathy and negatively related to boys', but not girls', personal distress. In general, the pattern of findings is consistent with Eisenberg, Fabes, Schaller, Carlo, and Miller's (1991) finding of stronger correlations in regard to the socialization of vicarious emotional responding with same-sex than with other-sex children (i.e., stronger between mothers and daughters than between mothers and sons).

An interesting finding was the correlation between children's social desirability and their perspective-taking and sympathy. Similar findings have been obtained in studies with adults (e.g., Eisenberg et al., 1989). Perhaps people concerned with impression management want to be perceived as high in perspective taking and sympathy. Alternatively, children who are aware of societal expectations may be better perspective takers or more motivated to engage in perspective taking (and perspective taking is conceptually and empirically linked to sympathy; see Batson, 1987; Hoffman, 1982).

Finally, it should be noted that a limitation of this study is that the measures were self-report indices and the sample was homogeneous and relatively small (particularly for the separate analyses by sex). However, the fact that the mothers' childrearing practices were relatively reliable over 4 (and sometimes 8) years (McNally et al., 1991) suggests that these indices are reliable. Moreover, the findings generally were consistent with theory. Nonetheless, it is possible that findings would differ somewhat if the sample were larger and if non-self-report measures of vicarious emotional responding (e.g., facial expressions, physiological measures; Eisenberg & Fabes, 1990) or observational measures of maternal practices were used. Further, the pattern of findings might be different if fathers rather than mothers were subjects; fathers' sympathy and emotion-related childrearing practices may play a unique and important role in the development of boys' sympathy (Eisenberg, Fabes, Schaller, Carlo, & Miller, 1991).

ACKNOWLEDGMENTS

This research was supported by National Science Foundation Grants BNS-8807784 and DBS-9208375, Career Development Award KO4 HD00717 from the National Institute of Child Health and Development, and Career Development Award KO2 MH00903-01 from the National Institute of Mental Health to Nancy Eisenberg.
The authors thank Jerry Harris, Randy Lennon, Paul Miller, Jeanette Pasternack, Cindy Shea, and Rita Shell for their assistance in earlier phases of this work. We also express our gratitude to the students and mothers who have been so helpful over many years.

REFERENCES

Barnett, M. A. (1987). Empathy and related responses in children. In N. Eisenberg & J. Strayer (Eds.), *Empathy and its development* (pp. 46–162). Cambridge, England: Cambridge University Press.

Batson, C. D. (1987). Prosocial motivation: Is it ever truly altruistic? In L. Berkowitz (Ed.), *Advances in experimental social psychology* (Vol. 20, pp. 65–122). New York: Academic.

Baumrind, D. (1971). Current patterns of parental authority. *Developmental Psychology Monographs, 4*, 1–103.

Block, J. (1969). *Retrospective reports revisited: Evidence for validity.* Unpublished manuscript, University of California, Berkeley.

Block, J. H. (1965). *The child-rearing practices report.* Unpublished manuscript, University of California, Berkeley.

Carlo, G., Eisenberg, N., & Knight, G. P. (1992). An objective measure of adolescents' prosocial moral reasoning. *Journal of Research on Adolescence, 2*, 331–349.

Carlo, G., Eisenberg, N., Troyer, D., Switzer, G., & Speer, A. L. (1991). The altruistic personality: In what contexts is it apparent? *Journal of Personality and Social Psychology, 61,* 450–458.

Cooper, C. R., Grotevant, H. D., & Condon, S. M. (1983). Individuality and connectedness in the family as a context for adolescent identity formation and role-taking skill. In H. D. Grotevant & C. R. Cooper (Eds.), *Adolescent development in the family* (pp. 43–59). San Francisco: Jossey-Bass.

Crowne, D. P., & Marlowe, D. (1964). *The approval motive.* New York: Wiley.

Davis, M. H. (1983a). Empathic concern and the muscular dystrophy telethon: Empathy as a multidimensional construct. *Personality and Social Psychology Bulletin, 9,* 223–229.

Davis, M. H. (1983b). Measuring individual differences in empathy: Evidence for a multidimensional approach. *Journal of Personality and Social Psychology, 44,* 113–126.

Dix, T. (1991). The affective organization of parenting: Adaptive and maladaptive processes. *Psychological Bulletin, 110,* 3–25.

Dix, T. (in press). Parenting on behalf of the child: Empathic goals in the regulation of responsive parenting. In I. E. Sigel, A. V. McGillicuddy-DeLisi, & J. J. Goodnow (Eds.), *Parental belief systems: The psychological consequences for children* (Vol. 2). Hillsdale, NJ: Lawrence Erlbaum Associates, Inc.

Eisenberg, N., & Fabes, R. A. (1990). Empathy: Conceptualization, assessment, and relation to prosocial behavior. *Motivation and Emotion, 14,* 131–149.

Eisenberg, N., & Fabes, R. A. (1992). Emotion, self-regulation, and social competence. In M. S. Clark (Ed.), *Review of personality and social psychology: Vol. 14. Emotion and social behavior* (pp. 119–150). Newbury Park, CA: Sage.

Eisenberg, N., Fabes, R. A., Carlo, G., Troyer, D., Speer, A. L., Karbon, M., & Switzer, G. (1992). The relations of maternal practices and characteristics to children's vicarious emotional responsiveness. *Child Development, 63,* 583–602.

Eisenberg, N., Fabes, R. A., Schaller, M., Carlo, G., & Miller, P. A. (1991). The relations of parental characteristics and practices to children's vicarious emotional responding. *Child Development, 62,* 1393–1408.

Eisenberg, N., Fabes, R. A., Schaller, M., Miller, P. A., Carlo, G., Poulin, R., Shea, C., & Shell, R. (1991). Personality and socialization correlates of vicarious emotional responding. *Journal of Personality and Social Psychology, 61,* 459–471.

Eisenberg, N., & Miller, P. (1987). The relation of empathy to prosocial and related behaviors. *Psychological Bulletin, 101,* 91–119.

Eisenberg, N., Miller, P. A., Schaller, M., Fabes, R. A., Fultz, J., Shell, R., & Shea, C. (1989). The role of sympathy and altruistic personality traits in helping: A reexamination. *Journal of Personality, 57,* 41–67.

Eisenberg, N., Miller, P. A., Shell, R., McNally, S., & Shea, C. (1991). Prosocial development in adolescence: A longitudinal study. *Developmental Psychology, 27,* 849–857.

Eisenberg, N., Schaller, M., Fabes, R. A., Bustamante, D., Mathy, R., Shell, R., & Rhodes, K. (1988). The differentiation of personal distress and sympathy in children and adults. *Developmental Psychology, 24,* 766–775.

Eisenberg, N., Shea, C. L., Carlo, G., & Knight, G. (1991). Empathy-related responding and cognition: A "chicken and the egg" dilemma. In W. Kurtines & J. Gewirtz (Eds.), *Handbook of moral behavior and development: Vol. 2. Research* (pp. 63–88). Hillsdale, NJ: Lawrence Erlbaum Associates, Inc.

Eisenberg, N., Shell, R., Pasternack, J., Lennon, R., Beller, R., & Mathy, R. M. (1987). Prosocial development in middle childhood: A longitudinal study. *Developmental Psychology, 24,* 712–718.

Fabes, R. A., Eisenberg, N., & Miller, P. (1990). Maternal correlates of children's vicarious emotional responsiveness. *Developmental Psychology, 26,* 639–648.

Feshbach, N. D. (1978). Studies of empathic behavior in children. In B. A. Maher (Ed.), *Progress in experimental personality research* (Vol. 8, pp. 1–47). New York: Academic.

Feshbach, N. D. (1987). Parental empathy and child adjustment/maladjustment. In N. Eisenberg & J. Strayer (Eds.), *Empathy and its development* (pp. 271–291). New York: Cambridge University Press.

Grotevant, H. D., & Cooper, C. R. (1986). Individuation in family relationships. *Human Development, 29,* 82–100.

Halberstadt, A. G. (1986). Family socialization of emotional expression and nonverbal communication styles and skills. *Journal of Personality and Social Psychology, 51,* 827–836.

Hock, E., & Lindamood, J. (1981). Continuity of child-rearing attitudes in mothers of young children. *Journal of Genetic Psychology, 138,* 305–306.

Hoffman, M. L. (1970). Moral development. In P. H. Mussen (Ed.), *Carmichael's manual of child development* (Vol. 2, pp. 261–359). New York: Wiley.

Hoffman, M. L. (1982). Development of prosocial motivation: Empathy and guilt. In N. Eisenberg (Ed.), *The development of prosocial behavior* (pp. 281–313). New York: Academic.

Janssens, J. M. A. M., & Gerris, J. R. M. (1992). Childrearing, empathy and prosocial behavior. In J. M. A. M. Janssens & J. R. M. Gerris (Eds.), *Child rearing: Influence on prosocial and moral development* (pp. 31–55). Amsterdam: Swets.

Kestenbaum, R., Farber, E. A., & Sroufe, L. A. (1989). Individual differences in empathy among preschoolers: Relation to attachment history. In N. Eisenberg (Ed.), *New directions for child development: Vol. 44. Empathy and related emotional responses* (pp. 51–64). San Francisco: Jossey-Bass.

Kochanska, G. (1990). Maternal beliefs as long-term predictors of mother–child interaction and report. *Child Development, 61,* 1934–1943.

Kochanska, G., Kuczynski, L., & Radke-Yarrow, M. (1989). Correspondence between mothers' self-reported and observed child-rearing practices. *Child Development, 60,* 56–63.

Koestner, R., Franz, C., & Weinberger, J. (1990). The family origins of empathic concern: A 26-year longitudinal study. *Journal of Personality and Social Psychology, 58,* 709–717.

Kohlberg, L. (1984). *Essays on moral development: Vol. 2. The psychology of moral development.* San Francisco: Harper & Row.

McDevitt, T. M., Lennon, R., & Kopriva, R. J. (1991). Adolescents' perceptions of mothers' and fathers' prosocial actions and empathic responses. *Youth & Society, 22,* 387–409.

McNally, S. (1990). *Shifts in maternal child-rearing practices as a function of the age of the child.* Unpublished master's thesis, Arizona State University, Tempe.

McNally, S., Eisenberg, N., & Harris, J. D. (1991). Consistency and change in maternal child-rearing practices and values: A longitudinal study. *Child Development, 62,* 190–198.

Miller, P., & Eisenberg, N. (1988). The relation of empathy to aggression and externalizing/antisocial behavior. *Psychological Bulletin, 103,* 324–344.

Moore, B. S., & Eisenberg, N. (1984). The development of altruism. In G. Whitehurst (Ed.), *Annals of child development* (pp. 107–174). Greenwich, CT: JAI.

Nunnally, J. C. (1967). *Psychometric theory.* New York: McGraw-Hill.

Roberts, G. C., Block, J. H., & Block, J. (1984). Continuity and change in parents' child-rearing practices. *Child Development, 55,* 586–597.

Rushton, J. P., Brainerd, C. J., & Pressley, M. (1983). Behavioral development and construct validity: The principle of aggregation. *Psychological Bulletin, 94,* 18–38.

Saarni, C. (1990). Emotional competence: How emotions and relationships become integrated. In R. A. Thompson (Ed.), *Socioemotional development* (pp. 115–182). Lincoln: University of Nebraska Press.

Selman, R. L. (1980). *The growth of interpersonal understanding: Developmental and clinical analysis.* New York: Academic.

Staub, E. (1979). *Positive social behavior and morality: Vol. 2. Socialization and development.* New York: Academic.
Strayer, J. (1983, April). *Emotional and cognitive components of children's empathy.* Paper presented at the meeting of the Society for Research in Child Development, Toronto.

Received October 24, 1991
Revision received October 30, 1992
Accepted December 7, 1992

The Youth Charter: towards the formation of adolescent moral identity

WILLIAM DAMON & ANNE GREGORY
Brown University, USA

ABSTRACT   *Studies of adolescent conduct have found that both exemplary and antisocial behaviour can be predicted by the manner in which adolescents integrate moral concerns into their theories and descriptions of self. These findings have led many developmentalists to conclude that moral identity—in contrast to moral judgement or reflection alone—plays a powerful role in mediating social conduct. Moreover, developmental theory and research have shown that identity formation during adolescence is a process of forging a coherent and systematic sense of self. Despite these well-founded conclusions, many moral education programmes fail to engage a young person's sense of self, focus exclusively on judgement and reflection and make little or no attempt to establish coherence with other formative influences in a young person's life. The authors propose a new method, called "the youth charter", for promoting adolescent self-identification with a coherent set of moral standards.*

A number of theoretical and empirical studies have concluded that the importance of a person's moral concerns to the person's sense of self—a person's "moral identity"—is the best predictor of the person's commitment to moral action. Blasi (1984), for example, argues that moral identity provides a powerful incentive for conduct, because identity engenders a sense of responsibility to act in accord with one's conception of self. Moral judgement alone does not provide this sense of personal responsibility: it is only when people conceive of themselves, and their life goals, in moral terms that they acquire a strong propensity to act according to their moral judgements. As Nisan writes, "if a person sees a value or a way of life as essential to their identity, then they feel that they ought to act accordingly" (Nisan, 1996, p. 78).

In a study of 23 adult moral exemplars, Colby and Damon (1992) found high levels of integration between self and moral concerns; although they found no signs of elevated levels of moral reasoning on the Kohlberg moral judgement measure. Colby and Damon concluded that sustained moral commitment requires a "uniting

This is the text of The 9th Annual Kohlberg Memorial Lecture which was delivered at The 22nd Annual Conference of the Association for Moral Education, Ottawa, Canada. 15 November, 1996, by William Damon.

0305-7240/97/020117-14 © 1997 The Norham Foundation

117

of self and morality". "People who define themselves in terms of their moral goals are likely to see moral problems in everyday events, and they are also likely to see themselves as necessarily implicated in these problems. From there it is a small step to taking responsibility for the solution" (Colby and Damon, 1992, p. 307).

People differ in the degree to which they define themselves in terms of moral concerns and aims. In an interview study with 80 males and females ranging in age from 16 to 84 years, Walker et al. found that "morality had differing degrees of centrality in people's identities: For some, moral considerations and issues were pervasive in their experience because morality was rooted in the heart of their being; for others, moral issues seemed remote and the maintenance of moral values and standards was not basic to their self-concept and self-esteem" (Walker et al. 1995, p. 398).

During adolescence, the development of self-understanding is often marked by a small gradual increase in the use of moral concepts (Damon and Hart, 1988, 1992). When asked to describe themselves, most adolescents used a modest sampling of morally tinged adjectives such as "kind", fair-minded and "honest". Some adolescents even go so far as to describe themselves *primarily* in terms of systematic moral beliefs and goals (Damon and Hart, 1988, 1992; Hart & Fegley, 1995; Hart et al. 1995). Among the adolescents who do so, there is evidence of sustained moral commitment similar to that observed in the Colby and Damon (1992) study of adult moral exemplars. For example, Hart and Fegley (1995) found that an unusually high proportion of adolescent "care exemplars" (boys and girls who were nominated by community members as exceptionally committed to voluntary service) had an understanding of self based upon systematic moral belief systems; yet these "care exemplars" scored no higher than matched peers on the Kohlberg moral judgement measure. The Hart and Fegley study is noteworthy because it was conducted in an economically deprived urban setting, among an adolescent population often stereotyped as high-risk and criminally inclined.

The other end of the moral spectrum from extraordinary altruism is antisocial behaviour. Here, too, there is evidence that moral identity plays a mediating role. Damon and Hart (1988) reported data from a study that found developmental delays in futuristic self-conceptions of delinquent youth. Oyserman and Markus (1990) found that delinquent adolescents were less able to articulate both positively and negatively valued possibilities for themselves than were a matched sample of non-delinquents. A case illustration of such findings is provided in a study of youth crime in Brooklyn, New York (Sullivan, 1989). The following quote is from a response by a 17-year-old juvenile offender to an ethnographic request for a self-description. The boy's confusion about future conceptions of self, the lack of social—relational or occupational prospects to anchor his identity, the lack of agency over the direction that his life has taken, and the persistent choice of material over moral goals, are all painfully apparent in the boy's overall sense of dissatisfaction with himself:

> "Let's say it was right before the burglary with a serious armed robbery charge on me and pending. How was I thinking then? If I was to write my

thinking about myself in a scale of 1 to 10, it was a 2 if I was lucky. 1. Didn't care if I got caught by police, prepared to do any crime. Down to shoot, stab, not fatal thoughts though, mug, rob anybody, burglarize any property. 2. No job at all. 3. No girlfriend or person to count on. 4. School, I gave up on that. 5. Family, let down. 6. Real tight dirty relationships. 7. Try to get over on cheap shit (crime in general). 8. Thinking to do a job for some money. 9. Wasting time on absolutely nothing but to think of nasty and dirty things to do. 10. Damaging myself physically on a day-to-day basis without doing any positive thinking for myself. 11. Almost every penny to get high or find dumb pleasures. 12. Didn't handle boredom the right way. 13. Being in the neighborhood 90% of the time. 14. Hanging out with the wrong people 85% of the time I hang out. 15. Thinking that I had authority to rob and steal. 16. Not think about the future at all, or serious thing not to do especially at such a young age. 17. Just falling into hell. 18. Not using nothing at all as lessons. 19. Not knowing all I was doing was wrong and later going to be punished for it. 20. Letting money problems get to me thinking I was slick, having a let's do it attitude. 21. Nothing to be happy about" (Sullivan, 1989, pp. 42–43).

Identity formation during adolescence is a process of forging a coherent, systematic sense of self. *Moral* identity formation is a process of constructing deeply held moral beliefs that serve as the ideational core for a cohesive sense of identity (Erikson, 1968; Blasi, 1993). Given the importance of moral identity for moral action and moral commitment, it would seem essential for moral education programmes to promote this sense of coherence—that is, a moral identity founded upon a deeply held set of beliefs. Yet, as we shall discuss below, many moral education programmes fail to engage the student's sense of self, focus almost exclusively on moral judgement and reflection, and make little or no attempt to establish coherence with other formative influences and social relationships in a young person's life.

Moral Education in the Present Epoch

During the past decade there has been a worldwide surge of interest in moral education. It is not difficult to speculate why this has occurred. Over the same period of time, practically all indicators of antisocial behaviour among young people have shown alarming trends. Rates of gang-related violence, sexual assault, suicide, robbery, drug use, vandalism, gambling, cheating in school, absenteeism from school and disorderly conduct have risen dramatically year by year (cites from Damon, 1995). In contrast to popular impressions, these trends have accelerated at about the same rate in affluent as in disadvantaged neighbourhoods. (The base rate of incidents, however, remains higher among the disadvantaged). Perhaps most troubling, the indicators look worst for the youngest among the cohort. Such trends have been well publicized, both in the aggregate and by a barrage of anecdotal news stories that appear daily in print and electronic media. It is little wonder that the public has turned to the field of moral education with some urgency for solutions to this problem.

The response from the field of moral education has been energetic and innovative. New methods have been developed and classic theories have been adapted and revised for today's youth. Moral development curricula have made their way into literally thousands of schools and teacher training programmes throughout North America, Europe and Israel. By 1996, there were over 150 separate centres for "character education" operating in the United States alone.

Many of the approaches draw upon research and writing conducted in the field of moral education during the past three decades. The approaches reflect the entire diversity of the field. Values clarification, pro-social skill and negotiation training, Aristotelian ethics, Deweyesque participation in democratic governance, Durkheimian efforts to create orderly school climates, Kohlbergian moral dilemmas and "just community" procedures, feminist and critical-theory reflection sessions, narrative exemplifications of public virtue through literature and history and *in vivo* demonstrations of personal virtue through teacher action are all part of the rich mix of moral edification available to today's students.

Very few of these efforts has been studied by collecting either process or outcome data, so we know little about their effectiveness (see Emler, 1996). Among the few exceptions to this are, at the primary school level, the prosocial methods of the Developmental Studies Centre (Solomon *et al.*, 1988) and, at the secondary school level, the "Equip" programme (Gibbs, Potter & Goldstein, 1995). Both programmes have shown promising results in careful, though limited, assessments. By and large, however, the most that we know about most attempts is that, although they seem benign and well-intentioned, there is little evidence that they are actually having effects on youth conduct. We do know, of course, that they have not attenuated the disturbing trends in youthful antisocial behaviour that continue unabated throughout the world.

In the absence of compelling statistical indicators to the contrary, it seems safe to conclude that moral education programmes touch the lives of some young people in occasional and unpredictable ways. A youngster may be inspired to charitable action by the story of a moral leader or dissuaded from cruel behaviour by an exercise in empathy; yet many of the youngster's classmates may have brought little or nothing away from the same lessons. Even the best data from well-documented "success stories" (Solomon *et al.*, 1988; Gibbs, *et al.*, 1995) show this kind of variability. Programmes that are less carefully implemented and assessed are likely to be more irregular in their effect.

It is no accident that we have witnessed only sparse outcomes from moral education programmes thus far. Nor is it necessary to accept limited success. It is possible to reach multitudes of young people who have never been personally affected by moral education, but this will require a more expansive strategy than we have been pursuing at present. Most importantly, the new strategy must be based on a different sort of implicit message from that emphasized by many of today's moral and character education programmes.

Limitations of Present-day Approaches

For all their innovative methods and uses of philosophical and developmental theories, today's moral education programmes typically suffer from three limitations that prevent them from promoting the development of moral identity during the adolescent years. The first is that they are disconnected with one another and other key experiences in young people's lives. The second is a failure to provide clear, specific, action-orientated directives for core elements of young people's behaviour. The third is a neglect (or, in some cases, repudiation) of human qualities that enable young people to develop a commitment to moral goals and an enduring sense of moral purpose. We elaborate on each limitation below.

In most schools, youth problems are addressed through a string of disconnected programmes that may include alcohol counselling, conflict-resolution training, community service activities, AIDS awareness days, citizenship education, "drug-free schools" advocacy, teenage sexuality or pregnancy prevention workshops, self-esteem exercises, safe driving clinics, and so on. All these issues focus on values—in many cases, important moral values such as concern for human welfare, non-violence, honesty, respect for others and personal responsibility. Alongside such programmes, schools often devote time to moral education. Usually this is done as part of the curriculum; but the effort may also include speeches, rallies and, in the character education movement, symbolic gestures such as prizes, songs or uniforms.

There is a striking lack of coordination among such programmes, despite their obvious overlap in substance and their implicit attention to common values. Each of these programmes uses its own instructional materials, and seldom does any programme makes explicit reference to the concepts, ideas, examples and concerns introduced by the other programmes. The common concerns are there, but they are left implicit and usually unnoticed. When a student learns about the hazards of risky sex or unsafe driving in programmes devoted to such problems, there is rarely an allusion to a moral education lesson that may have stressed respect for the lives and welfare of others. A character education lecture may discuss tensions between honesty and loyalty, or between fairness and instrumental gain, while discussing the immediate problem of school cheating; but there is little chance that anyone will point out that the same human tensions play a pivotal role in the political drama conveyed by the student's citizenship education course. Conflict-resolution exercises help students deal with the contradiction between self-expression and harmony, but this is a contradiction that shows up in many venues of the modern world; and we have never heard the connection made for students, either while resolving their own conflicts or while studying conflicts of others. There is rarely, if ever, cross-referencing of similar problems. Nor is there any highlighting of similar values, any linkage among the various behavioural solutions that are being prescribed, or any continuity among the scattered messages.

The aim of all the programmes is to promote good behaviour in the student's life within and beyond school (including, of course, the student's future life). The lack of coordination among the programmes makes this goal difficult to achieve. As noted above, building a bridge to moral action requires developing an overall moral perspective that integrates moral values into one's personal identity. This requires a systematic sense of why one should make particular moral choices—that is, how these choices relate to one another and to one's own sense of self. If a school fails to draw meaningful connections among the moral messages that it attempts to convey, it risks failing to convey anything at all that students can take seriously. What comes across instead is a cacophony of discord and confusion.

To make matters worse, in some schools, instructors in charge of various programmes fight turf battles with one another (Wynne & Ryan, 1992). They see themselves as rivals in the struggle to win over the hearts and minds of the young. A pregnancy counsellor may dispute the school's teenage sexuality programme on the grounds that it promotes "loose morals". Guest speakers during an AIDS awareness day may openly criticise school administrators who are in charge of the school character education initiative, on the grounds that they are intolerant. From the perspective of the student, the result of such conflicting messages is an attitude of indifference at best and cynicism at worst (Damon, 1995). Far from motivating students toward proper action, such discord often leaves them emotionally cold and behaviourally demobilised.

The second major limitation, partly but not wholly linked to the first, is that programmes vary greatly in the specificity of their instruction. Programmes about driving, safe sex and conflict resolution teach particular skills and solutions. In contrast, moral education (at least of the Kohlberg and values clarification varieties) emphasises general cognitive procedures of reflection and reasoning (Power et al., 1989). Character education also tends towards abstractions, promoting values such as respect, honesty, caring, fairness, orderliness, etc. (Wynne & Ryan, 1992). The varying levels of abstraction prevent programmes from reinforcing one another's messages. In fact, it adds to the confusion that we have noted above. Unless students are provided with contexts where they can reconcile the general principles of moral education with the specific demands of life's moral tasks, their moral lessons will remain too vague, bland and disengaged from their own lives to provide any enduring influence on the formation of their personal identities.

The third major limitation is a negative bias in the overall message conveyed by many of today's moral and character education programmes. Most often, the focus is exclusively on bad behaviour and how to deter, defuse or repair it (Lickona, 1996; Oser, 1996). The solutions are preventive in nature. If people follow society's rules, abide by proper values, develop virtues, respect traditional codes, understand principles of right and wrong and rely on fair negotiation procedures, they will avoid conflict, resist temptation and stay out of trouble. The overwhelming thrust of moral and character education is to show children how to stay within societal bounds by regulating their anti-social impulses.

Behavioural regulation is certainly important for every young person to learn, but it is not the sum total of a moral life. In fact, preventative proscriptions cannot provide young people with the motivation that they need to form moral goals, construct a moral identity and build enduring moral commitments. The key motivational element is a belief system that transcends everyday behavioural regulation. As

Nisan has written, "Identity-based motivation ... includes expressing and affirming one's identity—performing positive acts" (Nisan, 1996).

If young people are to dedicate themselves to moral goals, they need to acquire beliefs that provide them with a sense of higher purpose for the creation of their moral identities. They must encounter moral ideas that they find inspiring, not merely constraining. In the Colby and Damon (1992) study, virtually every one of the moral exemplars identified an early discovery of an inspiring moral purpose— charity, justice, peace, human rights, global protection—as the source of their enduring moral commitments. The exemplars reported that their beliefs in a higher moral purpose not only inspired their dedication to sustained moral action through- out life but also defined the essence of their self-identities (Colby & Damon, 1992).

The three shortcomings that we have noted have a common, indeed a cumulat- ive, effect: they conspire to demoralise young people who are subject to them (see Damon, 1995). In this context, demoralisation has two meanings. First, it means a debilitating loss of purpose (as in the familiar military usage of the term). Secondly, and closer to the word's original root, it means a cynical attitude towards moral values. Young people become demoralised by conflicts and confusion among those to whom they look for direction; they become demoralised by vague, empty assertions that fail to connect meaningfully to their own life choices; and they become demoralised by messages that are overwhelmingly negative and discouraging in tone. These, of course, are precisely the three moral education shortcomings that we have identified above. The co-occurrence of the three makes for an unholy combination, because they reinforce one another's demoralising influences.

The Youth Charter Approach

One solution to the shortcomings of present-day approaches is to use the com- munity rather than the school as the primary point of entry. In this approach a community determines the methods and substance of moral education, and the school is one of many sites where the action takes place. This creates the necessary condition for coordination among the sites, thus avoiding many of the problems cited above. With proper communication and a general sense of agreement, conflicts can be avoided, confusions can be clarified and young people can be offered many contexts in which they can turn abstract ideas into moral acts. Moreover, in a whole community it is possible to find many people who can introduce young people into the positive, inspirational possibilities of moral commitment. Similarly, an entire community affords many opportunities for authentic service activities, such as helping those in need, that can provide young people with a chance to experience the psychological rewards of moral commitment.

The notion of basing moral education in communities instead of schools is hardly new. The classic Aristotelian view, for example, was that all citizens—chil- dren and adults alike—were educated into a life of virtue through their active participation in the laws and mores of their communities. During pre-modern times in western societies, moral education of the young was shared between the home, the neighbourhood, the workplace (for the many children who either laboured or did apprenticeships) and the church. Of these contexts, the church was the ultimate authority, with the sacred texts of Jews and Christians providing the sources of moral instruction and guidance. In many non-western societies, religious traditions retain their authoritative role in moral education (see, for example, Jessor, 1996). In America, when formal schooling first became available to multitudes of children, there was a tight connection between the community's values and those of the teaching staff—a staff that was largely composed of parents and local adults (Cremin, 1964). Only with the increased professionalisation of teaching during the latter part of the twentieth century did the school become a separate, and in many ways primary, source of instruction for the young.

Such separation makes little sense in the moral domain; and it especially makes no sense to think of school as a privileged context in this regard. As we have argued in the first part of this paper, when sources of moral guidance become separated from one another, they often fall into conflict. They then can provide only confusion and disillusionment for the young, rather than coherent moral guidance. It is essential to locate moral education in the entire community rather than in a collection of separate contexts.

However, this is not easy in modern times, since so many communities have become polarised around matters of belief. In order to accomplish moral education in times of society-wide discord, communities must make special efforts to identify their common values, at least with respect to their hopes and expectations for their young. What Durkheim (1961) assumed comes naturally to societies—an almost transcendental sense of unifying belief—now must be worked at. Otherwise, as Etzioni has written, we shall live in aggregations rather than true communities (Etzioni, 1993).

Is it possible consciously to create—or at least to discover—the kinds of shared beliefs that are essential for community and for the moral identities of the young? We believe that it is possible, and that it is readily within our reach to do so. The fractiousness of public discourse has created a widespread yearning for common values. In this sense, we believe that Durkheim was right about the inevitable ideational foundation of any society (Durkheim, 1961). One sign of the widespread yearning, in fact, has been the avid receptiveness of many people to such fundamentalist doctrines that have rushed to fill the contemporary void; but such approaches are too authoritarian and too exclusionary to be sustainable. They mesh poorly with the pluralism and egalitarianism inherent in democratic societies, creating yet further conflict. In order to build common community values in modern times, we need procedures that draw upon the unique qualities and virtues of a democratic society rather than reacting against them.

One such procedure is a "youth charter". A youth charter is a consensus of clear expectations shared among the important people in a young person's life and communicated to the young person in multiple ways. In times and places where there is a strong sense of community, a youth charter is implicit. It may be given voice by an educational leader or emphasized in a religious sermon; but by and large the consensus of expectations is widely accepted without much articulation. In seventeenth century New England, for example, it was taken for granted that children would be raised to respect their elders, perform household duties, study the Bible, obey the Ten Commandments, acquire proper manners, learn skills, find a calling, work hard and establish a family (Miller, 1954). Achieving consensus around such standards was not considered to be a problem worth discussing. The standards permeated every setting where children spent time, were internalised as children grew up, and were passed along to the next generation without hesitation.

Some communities have implicit youth charters, some have partial or uneven ones and some have none that can be detected. Those that have implicit youth charters arrive at them spontaneously, through frequent communication among people who are in a position to influence the young. Francis Ianni, the sociologist who originally coined the term "youth charter", found evidence of cohesive youth charters in a range of American settings, including large cities, suburbs, towns and rural areas (Ianni, 1989). But Ianni also found a significant number of American settings where there was little or no sign of a youth charter.

Not surprisingly, young people growing up in communities with youth charters show stronger signs of moral identity than young people who grow up in places without them. After a 12-year study of American youth, Ianni concluded that the best predictor of an adolescent's social conduct—better than economic background or other social indicators—was the extent to which the people and institutions in the child's life shared a set of common standards for the youngster's behaviour. Ianni wrote: "We soon discovered that the harmony and accord among the institutions and what their adolescent members heard from them *in concert* was what scored the adolescent experience" (Ianni, 1989, p. 20).

Yet Ianni found that harmony and accord were the exception rather than the rule in most of American society. Ianni looked at how schools, families, peer groups, local institutions, the media and the job market send messages to youth. He found that most often these messages clashed rather than harmonised. Ianni noted that this lack of coherence had created a fragmented and confusing context for youth development.

Ianni concluded that, for positive identity formation, every young person needs coherent structure, "... a set of believable and attainable expectations and standards from the community to guide movement from child to adult status" (Ianni, 1989, p. 267). When disparate institutions such as the family, school, and other public and private agencies offer young people coherent guidance, the young person's identity is not a "a collection of isolated experiences", but rather as an "organization of experiences and exposures in the various social worlds of the community" (Ianni, 1989, p. 279).

In places that operate like true communities there are many ways in which families, schools, workplaces, agencies and peer groups connect with one another through their contact with youth. For example, schools are influenced by the values and attitudes that students pick up in their families. Students' family lives are in turn influenced by their quest for academic achievement, which fills their afterschool time with homework—and which in turn is supported on the home front. A young person's identity formation, rooted initially in the family, is shaped by a sense of belonging in the community, including sports teams, media, clubs, religious institutions and jobs. In such communities, there also is concordance between the norms of the peer culture and those of adults.

In places where the sense of community has waned, young people are often faced with conflicting demands and messages from each of these sources. The problem, as Ianni wrote, is that many communities have lost the traditional social networks which once guided youth into adulthood. Without these networks, role models are lacking, intergenerational guidance is rare and isolation prevails. The institutions within the community blame one another for all the problems of its youth. Ianni concluded that such fragmentation is injurious to adolescent development.

To provide a clear, firm and consistent set of behavioural and social standards and expectations for adolescents, Ianni advocates development of a network of social institutions by a community. He writes, "A well-integrated and consciously developed pattern of relationships can provide a stabilizing transformational structure that produces equally integrated identities as workers and citizens and parents; no single institution has the resources to develop all of these roles alone" (Ianni, 1989, p. 279). Ianni's name for this stabilizing structure was a "youth charter", a term that we borrow here. Ianni proposed several suggestions for developing a successful youth charter in communities that do not already have them. First, the community must work towards a consensus of values and standards in order to coordinate expectations. Secondly, all members of the community must be invited to participate; outside imposition of a charter will not be successful. Thirdly, young people must be involved in the process of developing the charter. Finally, the charter must be open and able to adapt to change.

The Development and Implementation of Youth Charters

We have expanded upon Ianni's notion of a youth charter in order to develop a process through which a community can build their own consensus of shared understandings concerning their expectations for youth development. A youth charter is usually not formalized in a written document; rather, evolving sets of records are kept about areas of agreement and resolutions for action. To build a youth charter, community members go through a process of discussion, a movement towards agreement and the development and implementation of action plans. Elements of the process may include special meetings sponsored by local institutions; constructive media coverage on a periodic basis; and the formation of standing committees that open new lines of communication among parents, teachers and neighbours.

In our procedure (see Appendix), we begin with discussion among the adult members of the community and then, after a common language and agenda are established, young members of the community may be invited to participate. A youth charter may be revised as circumstances dictate, and it can vary from community to community. The essential requirements of a youth charter are that (1) it must address the core matters of morality and achievement necessary for becoming a responsible citizen; and (2) it must focus on areas of common agreement rather than on doctrinaire squabbles or polarising issues of controversy. A youth charter guides the younger generation towards fundamental moral virtues such as honesty, civility, decency and the pursuit of benevolent purposes beyond the self. A youth charter is a moral and spiritual, rather than a political, document.

In our early pilot work with the youth charter procedure, we have conducted meetings in a small number of towns and schools. The focus of the discussions has varied widely among the different settings. In one setting, community members were mainly concerned about a rash of cheating incidents at the local academy. In another setting, a recent pair of teenage suicides and some widespread (and perhaps related) drug use among the town's young people dominated the conversations. In a third, parents were upset about an epidemic of binge drinking, especially at teenage parties. Other preliminary pilot meetings have traversed a wider range of issues, from racial and ethnic conflict to disrespect of authority in academic and work settings.

In some of these settings, the large and small-group discussions have identified core values that provide a basis of response to the problem or crisis. For example, after an afternoon of intense discussion, adults and students in an academy community with a cheating problem agreed that cheating was wrong because (1) it violates trust between teacher and student;(2) it gives students who cheat an unfair advantage over those who do not;(3) it encourages dishonest behaviour; and (4) it undermines the integrity of a school. This agreement was apparently a change from prior sentiments, which were reportedly ambivalent about cheating. (For example, some teachers were quoted as saying that it was hard for them to hold students to a non-cheating standard in a society where people cheat on taxes, spouses and so on). Based on the new-found agreement, it became possible to create more widely supported codes and sanctions in the school. It also became possible for teachers and staff to explain clearly, in unambiguous terms, why they expected young people not to cheat. From the adolescents' perspectives, their new understanding of the moral purposes of anti-cheating codes may prepare them to accept this societal standard as part of their own moral identities. They may become more likely to assert, as one student phrased it, that "I don't want to become the kind of person who cheats all the time".

In another community, a coalition of local institutions and people, originally formed to reduce the use of drugs and alcohol among youth, invited us in to help them develop a youth charter. The coalition was made up of representatives from private and public schools, the police force, parents, an interfaith council, local colleges, the business community, human service agencies, the town council and other concerned citizens. A subcommittee of the larger coalition organised a town-wide forum. With the hopes of gathering a substantial cross-section of the community, the organizers launched large-scale publicity of the forum. The publicity efforts included articles to the local newspaper, posted flyers, notices to the parents of students and presentations to community groups, such as the Rotary club, the police department and senior centres. The forum was scheduled on a weekend afternoon for three-and-a-half hours in the local high school auditorium. Large and small-group discussions, as described in the Appendix below, covered a series of topics that related to how young people were spending their time after school. From the forum arose a number of resolutions, action plans and task forces, mostly dedicated to resolving the following issues: (1) the need for alternative town settings that provide young people with more opportunities to participate in constructive, safe and purposeful activities. (More specifically, they are working to bring a movie theatre back to the town and to build a coffee house where young people can congregate); (2) youth sports in the community—the scheduling conflicts between sports and religious services, the pressures of competitive sports on young people, and the standards and expectations held by coaches, players and referees; (3) the development of a community service programme; and (4) the unhealthy use of drugs and alcohol by young people from all parts of town.

It is likely that this community will need to continue their work of building networks of communication, of opening up dialogue across different constituencies about issues affecting young people, and of developing and implementing action plans. Moreover, as the task forces proceed and more community members join in, a process of reflection will also be needed. Any youth charter should be renewed periodically, perhaps yearly, to adapt to the changing needs of the community.

Youth charters are communications devices. They can help young people anticipate and understand the reactions of others to their behaviour. When a teacher is disappointed in a student's performance, or when a neighbour calls the local police about a miscreant teenager, a youth charter can turn the youngster's shame or outrage into a constructive developmental experience. A youth charter can define high moral standards for adolescent conduct throughout the entire community. It can provide a conduit for regular feedback between young people, their friends and the adult world. It is the multifaceted and yet *coherent* nature of this feedback that enables it to facilitate the formation of a young person's moral identity.

Correspondence: Dr William Damon, Professor of Education, Center for The Study of Human Development, Brown University, Providence, Rl, 02912, USA. Fax: 001-401-863-1276.

REFERENCES

BLASI, A. (1993) The development of identity: some implications for moral functioning, in: G. NOAM & T. WREN (Eds) *The Moral Self* (Cambridge, MA, MIT Press).
BLASI, A. (1984) Moral identity: its role in moral functioning, in: W. KURTINES & J. GEWIRTZ (Eds) *Morality, Moral Behavior, and Moral Development*, (New York, Wiley).
COLBY, A. & DAMON, W. (1992) *Some Do Care: contemporary lives of moral commitment*, (New York, Free Press).
COLBY, A. & DAMON, W. (1993) The uniting of self and morality in the development of extraordinary moral commitment, in: G. NOAM & T. WREN (Eds) *The Moral Self*, (Cambridge, MA, MIT Press).
CREMIN, L. (1964) *The Transformation of the School: progressivism in American education*, (New York, Knopf).
DAMON, W. (1995) *Greater Expectations*, (New York, The Free Press).
DAMON, W. (1977) *The Social World of the Child*, (San Francisco, Jossey-Bass).

DAMON, W. & HART, D. (1988) *Self-Understanding in Childhood and Adolescence*, (New York, Cambridge University Press).

DAMON, W. & HART, D. (1992) Self-understanding and its role in social and moral development, in: M. BORNSTEIN & M.E. LAMB (Eds) *Developmental Psychology: an advanced textbook*, 3rd edn, pp. 421–464 (Hillsdale, NJ, Erlbaum).

DURKHEIM, E. (1961) *Moral Education: a study in the theory and application of the sociology of education*, (New York, The Free Press).

EMLER, N. (1996) How can we decide whether moral education works? *Journal of Moral Education*, 25, pp. 117–126.

ERIKSON, E. (1968) *Identity: youth and crisis*, (New York, Norton).

ETZIONI, A. (1993) *The Spirit of Community; rights, responsibilities and the communitarian agenda*, (New York, Crown Publishers).

GIBBS, J., POTTER, G. & GOLDSTEIN, A. (1995) *The Equip Program*, (Illinois, Research Press).

HART, D. & FEGLEY, S. (1995) Prosocial behavior and caring in adolescence: relations to self-understanding and social judgment, *Child Development*, 66, pp. 1346–1359.

HART, D., YATES, M., FEGLEY, S. & WILSON, G. (1995) Moral commitment in inner-city adolescents, in: M. KILLEN & D. HART (Eds) *Morality in Everyday Life: developmental perspectives*, (New York, Cambridge University Press).

IANNI, F. (1989) *The Search for Structure: a report on American youth today*, (New York, Free Press).

JESSOR, R., COLBY A. & SHWEDER, R. (Eds) (1996) *Ethnography and Human Development: context and meaning in social inquiry*, (Chicago, University of Chicago Press).

LICKONA, T. (1996) Eleven principles of effective character education, *Journal of Moral Education*, 25, pp. 93–100.

MILLER, P. (1954) *The New England Mind: the seventeenth century*, (Cambridge, Harvard University Press).

NISAN, M. (1996) Personal identity and education for the desirable, *Journal of Moral Education*, 25, pp. 75–83.

OSER, F. (1996) Learning from negative morality, *Journal of Moral Education*, 25, pp. 67–74.

OYSERMAN, D. & MARKUS, H. (1990) Possible selves and delinquency, *Journal of Personality and Social Psychology*, 59, pp. 112–125.

POWER, F.C., HIGGINS, A. & KOHLBERG, L. (1989) *Lawrence Kohlberg's Approach to Moral Education*, (New York, Columbia University Press).

SOLOMON, D., WATSON, M., DELUCCHI, K., SCHAPS, E. & BATTISTICH, V. (1988) Enhancing children's prosocial behavior in the classroom, *American Educational Research Journal*, 25, pp. 527–554.

SULLIVAN, M. (1989) *"Getting Paid": youth crime and work in the inner city*, (Ithaca, Cornell University Press).

WALKER, L., PITTS, R., HENNIG, K. & MATSUBA, M. (1995) Reasoning about morality and real-life moral problems, in: M. KILLEN & D. HART (Eds) *Morality in Everyday Life*, pp. 371–407 (New York, Cambridge University Press).

WYNNE, E. & RYAN, K. (1992) *Reclaiming Our Schools: teaching character, academics and discipline*, (Upper Saddle River, NJ, Merrill).

Appendix

Guidelines for Implementation of a Youth Charter

A youth charter begins with an initial meeting in a community centre, a school auditorium or any other accessible location which can accommodate a large group. The meeting is sponsored by a local organisation that also takes responsibility for widespread publicity of the meeting. An effort should be made to draw out as many people as possible from different sectors of the community. It is important that the initial investment in the process be as widespread as possible to guard against the dangers of mis-representation or exclusion. Publicity efforts can include flyers sent home with students, announcements in the local press and radio and a banner hung in a visible location.

An initial meeting is the first step of opening up dialogue among community members about their concerns regarding youth development. This meeting requires at least 3 or 4 hours. After a brief introduction of the goals of the meeting, the participants break into small groups. The small groups should be made up of individuals representing different organisations and interests in order to encourage the opening of new lines of communication.

Facilitators, who are volunteers from the community, are designated in advance and meet with each other before the meeting to discuss the goals of the small group discussions. With the guidance of the facilitators, the small group discussions cover a series of topics. First, the groups list their collective concerns for young people and the community. Next, the groups clarify and identify the expectations and standards that are currently being held for young people. They then list the standards and expectations for young people which can be agreed upon and implemented by the community as a whole. Finally, the groups address their first list of concerns by devising possible solutions, forming future task forces and recognising community strengths which had been under-utilised thus far. Overall, the small group discussion should end with a concrete list of identified needs for youth and the community, and ways to resourcefully address those needs.

All the participants then reconvene to hear summaries of the small group discussions as presented by the facilitators. Out of all the small group summaries comes a clear list of areas which need to be addressed by future task forces. In the final hour, these task forces hold their first meeting with participants who have decided to volunteer themselves for a more sustained involvement. The task forces discuss their goals and determine future meeting times.

At this point it is important to involve young people in the development of the youth charter. Each task force must recruit several youth to be active members of a task force. The young people should be integral members of each task force whereby they contribute their own ideas and concerns to the development and implementation of action plans.

A youth charter should be renewed periodically, at least yearly, to adapt to the changing needs of the community. Large community town meetings can occur annually to encourage reflection on the achieved progress and the future challenges.

In the Mind of the Actor:
The Structure of Adolescents' Achievement
Task Values and Expectancy-Related Beliefs

Jacquelynne S. Eccles
Allan Wigfield
University of Michigan

The authors assessed the dimensionality of and relations between adolescents' achievement-related beliefs and self-perceptions, focusing on subjective valuing of achievement. Beliefs derived from expectancy-value theory (adolescents' valuing of achievement activities, expectancies for success and ability perceptions, and perceptions of task difficulty) were assessed. Adolescents completed questionnaires once a year for 2 years. Confirmatory factor analyses indicated that achievement-related beliefs separate into three task values factors (interest, perceived importance, and perceived utility), one expectancy/ability factor (comprising beliefs about one's competence, expectancies for success, and performance perceptions), and two task difficulty factors (perceptions of difficulty and perceptions of effort required to do well). Task values and ability perceptions factors were positively related to each other and negatively correlated to perceptions of task difficulty.

Individual differences in achievement-related behaviors have been a central concern of social and personality theory for at least the last 40 years. Because most achievement theories derive from classic expectancy/value models of behavior (e.g., Atkinson, 1957), they typically include constructs linked to both expectancies and task value. However, most theorists have focused on the expectancy component of the expectancy/value dichotomy, and so constructs related to this component have proliferated in the literature. In contrast, until recently, very little attention has been given to either defining and measuring the value component or empirically assessing its relationship to the expectancy component. In this article, we undertake these tasks, focusing in particular on the values construct. We begin by reviewing existing work on expectancies and values.

Expectancies

Expectations for success, and related constructs, have been assigned a central role in almost all cognitive theories of motivation, such as attribution theory (e.g., Weiner et al., 1971), self-efficacy theory (Bandura, 1986), the self-worth perspective (Covington, 1984), and classic expectancy/value theory (Atkinson, 1957). Theorists have differed, however, in their operational definitions of expectations for success and in how broadly they conceptualize the construct. Atkinson (1957) defined subjective expectancy and objective task difficulty as synonymous, and he operationally defined expectancy in terms of the proportion of individuals who have succeeded at the task in the past. He labeled this construct P_s (probability of success) and gave it a prominent role in his classic theory of achievement motivation.

In contrast, other theorists have argued for a more explicit operational distinction between subjective expectancy and task difficulty, arguing that task difficulty, defined as the proportion of individuals in the population who succeed in the task, is just one of several influences on subjective expectancy (e.g., Bandura, 1986; Crandall, 1969; Eccles, 1987; Eccles [Parsons] et al., 1983; Feather, 1982; Heckhausen, 1977; Kukla, 1972, 1978; Weiner et al., 1971). For example, in their

Authors' Note: Allan Wigfield is now at the University of Maryland. The writing of this article was supported in part by a grant from the National Science Foundation (BNS-8510504) to Jacquelynne S. Eccles and Allan Wigfield. Data collection was supported by a grant from the National Institute of Child Health and Human Development (G78-0022) to Jacquelynne S. Eccles. Address correspondence to Jacquelynne S. Eccles, 5271 ISR, University of Michigan, Ann Arbor, MI 48106-1248.

PSPB, Vol. 21 No. 3, March 1995 215-225
© 1995 by the Society for Personality and Social Psychology, Inc.

model of motivated task choice and performance, Eccles (Parsons) et al. (1983) distinguished between self-concept of one's domain-specific abilities and perceived task difficulty, and predicted that these two beliefs would interact in predicting expectations for success in particular school subjects. Self-concept of domain-specific ability was predicted to relate positively to expectancies, whereas task difficulty perceptions were predicted to relate negatively to expectancies.

The importance of distinguishing between constructs associated with confidence in one's ability and task-specific expectancy has become very salient in the past 15 years, as more and more theorists have emphasized domain-specific self-concept of ability and domain-specific self-efficacy beliefs as prime psychological mediators of behavior (e.g., Bandura, 1986; Covington, 1984; Harter, 1982; Kukla, 1972; Nicholls, 1984). Generally, then, although the theorists discussed have all endorsed the important role of expectancies in motivating behavior, the conceptualization of this construct and its causal antecedents have become much more refined, and the role of domain-specific ability perceptions has gained prominence.

Task Value

Atkinson (1957) defined task value in terms of the incentive value of anticipated success (the anticipated pride one would feel in accomplishment). He operationally defined it in terms of P_s, arguing that the incentive value of success at any particular task is inversely related to its objective difficulty (i.e., incentive value = $1 - P_s$). This definition effectively eliminated task value from his equation for achievement behavior, which may account for the relative sparsity of either theoretical or empirical work on task value within the achievement literature (see Eccles, 1987; Eccles [Parsons] et al., 1983; Parsons & Goff, 1980; Wigfield & Eccles, 1992).

A variety of other theorists have offered less mathematically precise but broader definitions of task value. Both Battle (1966) and Crandall (1969) defined task value in terms of the subjective attainment value (the importance of attaining a goal) and objective task difficulty. Rotter (1982) defined task value as the anticipated reward the individual will receive from engaging in the activity. Rewards may derive either directly from the activity itself or indirectly through the activity's instrumental role in acquiring other desired consequences.

Building on Rokeach's (1980) work on broader human values, Feather (1982) discussed task value in terms of systems that

capture the focal, abstracted qualities of past encounters, that have a normative or oughtness quality about them, and that function as criteria or frameworks against which present experience can be tested. They are tied to our feelings and can function as general motives. (p. 275)

In terms of motivational consequences of these value systems, he assumed that values affect the valence of specific activities or situations for the individual and, therefore, are linked to action (e.g., approaching or avoiding the activity).

Building on a similar conception of values, value systems, and activity valence, Eccles and her colleagues (Eccles [Parsons] et al., 1983; Parsons & Goff, 1980) offered a broad definition of subjective task value and specified several subcomponents. In general, these investigators assumed that task value is determined by characteristics of the task itself; by the broader needs, goals, values, and motivational orientations of the individual; and by affective memories associated with similar tasks in the past. The degree to which a particular task is able to fulfill needs, confirm central aspects of one's self-schema, facilitate reaching goals, affirm personal values, and/or elicit positive versus negative affective associations and anticipated states is assumed to influence the value a person attaches to engaging in that task. In turn, Eccles (Parsons) et al. predicted that individuals will be more likely to engage in valued tasks; thus individuals' values are posited to have both motivational and behavioral consequences. Finally, Eccles and her colleagues (1987; Parsons & Goff, 1980) argued that gender differences in task value may underlie many of the gender differences in role-choice behaviors, such as occupational and leisure activity choice.

Eccles and her colleagues (1987; Parsons & Goff, 1980) further argued that task value be conceptualized in terms of four major components: attainment value, intrinsic value or interest, utility value, and cost. Like Crandall (1969), they defined attainment value as representing the importance of doing well on a task in terms of one's self-schema and core personal values. Intrinsic or interest value is the inherent enjoyment or pleasure one gets from engaging in an activity (see also Deci & Ryan, 1985). Utility value is the value a task acquires because it is instrumental in reaching a variety of long- and short-range goals. Finally, cost is what is lost, given up, or suffered as a consequence of engaging in a particular activity (see Eccles, 1984; Eccles [Parsons] et al., 1983). The first three components are best thought of as attracting characteristics that affect the positive valence of the task. Cost, in contrast, is best thought of as those factors (such as anticipated anxiety and anticipated cost of failure) that affect the negative valence of the activity.

Relations Between Expectancy and Task Value Constructs

As discussed earlier, Atkinson (1957) proposed that expectancies for success and incentive values are inversely related. Unlike Atkinson, few other investigators have made explicit predictions concerning the relationship between subjective task value and expectancies for success, and those who have make discrepant predictions. For example, decision theorists typically assume that expectancies and values are independent of one another (e.g., Fischoff, Goitein, & Shapira, 1982). In contrast, Feather (1982) hypothesized a positive relationship because of people's tendency toward wishful thinking: People will overestimate their probability of success on activities they value highly. One also would expect a positive association based on principles of classical conditioning: To the extent that affective memories influence task value, it seems likely that the constructs linked to task value will be positively, rather than negatively, associated with self-perceptions linked to expectancy. This should be especially true for those activities that are inherently challenging or at least moderately difficult, such as most activities in academic achievement contexts.

Summary and Specific Analytic Goals

Thus, over time, there has been an evolution in the conceptualization of constructs linked to expectancy for success and task value, as well as a refinement in the components of each construct. In this study, we addressed these issues by examining the dimensionality of a set of items measuring the components of task value, expectancies for success, and perceptions of task difficulty, and by looking at the relations between constructs. We assessed domain-specific beliefs (in this case beliefs about math) because recent work in the self-beliefs literature suggests that individuals' beliefs are domain specific and the strongest links between beliefs and behavior occur at this level (Fishbein & Ajzen, 1975; Marsh & Shavelson, 1985). Previous work using exploratory factor analytic procedures with this set of variables from a different sample of adolescents (see Parsons, 1980) yielded a fairly simple three-factor solution: Self-Concept of Ability (which included the perceived competence, perceived performance, and expectancy indicators), Perceived Task Difficulty (which included the required and actual effort and task difficulty indicators), and Subjective Task Value (which included the items assessing all four of the task value components). Although these results suggest that many of the distinctions being made in the theoretical literature do not obtain in the minds of lay individuals, they also suggest that expectancy-ability measures are distinct from perceptions of task difficulty and task value. In this study, we used confirmatory factor analysis to obtain a more sensitive test of the factor structure underlying this set of variables and to test more explicitly our model of the dimensionality of these different constructs.

Based on the literature reviewed earlier, the model proposed by Eccles (Parsons) et al. (1983) and the empirical work (on a different sample of adolescents) re-

ported in Eccles, Adler, and Meece (1984) and Parsons (1980), we predicted a three-factor structure for the Subjective Task Value items reflecting the latent variables of intrinsic interest value, attainment value (importance of being competent in the domain), and extrinsic utility value of engaging in the activity. We predicted two separate factors for expectancy/ability beliefs, with the expectancy items factoring separately from the ability and performance perception items. For the Perceived Task Difficulty items, we predicted that two factors will be distinguished, one tapping perceptions of the difficulty of the subject area, and the other the amount of effort required to do well in the subject.

In previous work, a measure of subjective task value that combined attainment value, intrinsic value, and extrinsic utility value of an activity related positively to the subjects' ability perceptions (Parsons, 1980). In this study, we assessed how each of these constructs relates to adolescents' ability/expectancy perceptions. We hypothesized that individuals should come to like or enjoy (intrinsically value) those activities at which they have done well at in the past and are reasonably confident of being able to succeed. Conversely, individuals should come to dislike those tasks that they have done poorly at in the past, especially if they have attributed previous poor performance to lack of a culturally valued ability. Thus liking and expectancy/ability perceptions should be positively related (for similar arguments, see Fishbein & Ajzen, 1975). A similar positive association between expectancy-related constructs and attainment value (perceived importance) seems likely to the extent that individuals are interested in maintaining a positive self-image. One effective way to maintain one's self-esteem is to rate as very important those activities that one is most confident about succeeding at and to rate relatively less important those activities one is least confident about succeeding at (for related arguments, see Eccles, Wigfield, Blumenfeld, & Harold, 1984; Epstein, 1973; Harter, 1985).

Predictions regarding perceived utility are more tentative. Because the perceived utility value of any particular task is determined by its links to goals and activities that are extrinsic to the task, utility value can be influenced by a wide range of things, such as the gender role-appropriateness of the goals or activities the task is seen as instrumental in achieving. Given these other influences on utility value, we predicted that the positive links between expectancy-related constructs and the utility value of math will be weaker than the links between expectancy-related constructs and attainment value and interest.

We also tested how expectancy-related constructs and task value relate to task difficulty perceptions. Based on the literature reviewed previously, we predicted negative relations between perceptions of expectancy/ability and perceptions of task difficulty. Because of the predicted positive association between the expectancy/ability constructs and the value constructs, there should be negative associations between the components of task value and the components of perceived task difficulty. However, because we viewed this negative association as mediated by the impact of perceived task difficulty on the expectancy/ability constructs, we expected that these latter negative associations should be weaker. It is important to note that this prediction is counter to the association hypothesized by Atkinson (1957). He predicted that the value of success on a task would increase with increasing perceived task difficulty. Although this prediction may be true for broad ranges of task difficulty (e.g., very easy to moderately difficult) and for more mature reasoners, we predicted that it will not be true for adolescents' beliefs about academic subject areas that they perceive as rather difficult. In that situation, we believe the self-esteem maintenance motives outlined above will dominate adolescents' judgments of task value.

METHOD

Participants

The Year 1 sample consisted of 742 predominantly White, middle-class adolescents in Grades 5 through 12, with approximately 90 adolescents at each grade. Adolescents comprised the sample because they have differentiated self-beliefs (Marsh & Shavelson, 1985) and extensive experience with mathematics. There were 366 females and 376 males in the sample. Data from the Year 1 sample were used to develop the various models. The Year 2 sample consisted of 575 adolescents in Grades 6 through 12 (88% of the 5th through 11th graders of Year 1). The Year 2 data were used to test the models developed with the Year 1 data. The sample was drawn using the mathematics classroom as an intermediate sampling unit. Classrooms at each grade level were chosen randomly from among classrooms whose teachers volunteered to participate in the study. Within each classroom, all adolescents were asked to participate. Project staff members administered questionnaires to adolescents who had returned permission slips (about 85% of the adolescents) indicating their willingness to participate. All questionnaires were administered during the spring of each year of the study. In the analyses reported in this article, only adolescents with complete data on all measures are included (n for Year 1 = 707, n for Year 2 = 545).

Self- and Task-Perception Questionnaire

The Self- and Task-Perception Questionnaire contained items assessing many different constructs related to adolescents' beliefs, attitudes, and values about particular achievement domains as well as items assessing

more general characteristics such as gender-role orientation and locus of control. The psychometric properties of the items and scales are quite good and have been reported elsewhere (see Eccles, Adler, & Meece, 1984; Eccles [Parsons] et al., 1983; Parsons, 1980). The items used in the analyses in the present study included 29 items comprising the following theoretically generated domain-specific constructs: enjoyment in doing task, perceived importance of the task, perceptions of the extrinsic utility value of the subject area, ability perceptions, performance perceptions, expectations for success, perceived task difficulty, amount of effort required to do well, and actual amount of effort exerted. All items focused on the domain of mathematics. Responses for all of these items were made on 7-point Likert-type scales anchored only at the end points.

ANALYSIS

In the present study, the factor structure of these constructs was explored through exploratory and confirmatory factor analyses of the 29 items. The data were collapsed across age and gender, based on analyses of the invariance of the covariance structure of the data (see below), and also because developmental studies suggest that by the fifth grade, children have acquired these belief structures (Marsh & Shavelson, 1985; Nicholls, 1978; Parsons & Ruble, 1977). The exploratory factor analyses were used to eliminate items in order to define the constructs more precisely. The confirmatory analyses were used to test predictions concerning the factor structure of the general constructs (task value, task difficulty perceptions, and ability perceptions) and assessed relations between the various constructs (Long, 1983).

RESULTS

Covariance Invariance Analyses

To determine whether we could test the models on the whole sample, we assessed the invariance of the covariance matrices of the items for boys and girls, and younger (5th through 7th grade) and older (8th through 12th grade) adolescents, following procedures described by Jöreskog and Sörbom (1984). Results of the covariance invariance analyses showed that the matrices were reasonably invariant across groups. For the boys and girls, the chi-square with 190 degrees of freedom 280.98, and Jöreskog and Sörbom's goodness-of-fit index (GFI) was .96, indicating invariance across the two groups. For the younger and older groups, the chi-square with 190 degrees of freedom was 535.86, with a GFI of .95, again indicating reasonable invariance across groups. The fit was somewhat poorer in the analysis of the younger and older adolescents, primarily because one of the covariance terms (between two of the values items) was smaller in the older group than in the younger group. Based on these results, we tested our models on the full sample.

Exploratory Factor Analyses

Separate exploratory factor analyses using an oblique rotation were conducted on the item sets measuring task values, task difficulty perceptions, and ability perceptions. Factors with eigenvalues equal to or greater than 1.0 were retained. For the nine task value items, the exploratory analyses suggested that a two- or three-factor solution best fit the data, based on an examination of the eigenvalues (the first three were 3.58, 1.16, and .99). Two of the nine items did not load highly in any of the exploratory analyses and so were dropped from the subsequent analyses reported in this article. The three-factor solution was consistent with the theoretical framework used to generate the items; the first factor of this three-factor set represented intrinsic value, the second represented attainment value, and the third represented extrinsic utility value (see appendix). Because the third eigenvalue was slightly less than 1.0, in the confirmatory analyses we assessed both two- and three-factor models of adolescents' task values.

For the 10 ability perceptions items, a one-factor solution appeared to best fit the data (the first three eigenvalues were 5.67, .83, and .66). All the items had loadings on this factor exceeding .50. A two-factor solution produced many double loadings and a weak second factor. Because only one factor appeared to be needed to describe the interrelations between the 10 variables, the five items loading greater than .70 were retained in the analyses reported below. These items are listed in the apendix.

For the 10 task difficulty perception items, a two-factor solution appeared to best describe the data (the first three eigenvalues were 4.58, 1.23, and .84). Three items assessing adolescents' perceptions of the actual effort they exert in math did not load highly on any of the factors in the exploratory analyses, and so they were dropped from subsequent analyses, leaving seven items (see appendix).

The retained 19 items tapping task values, task difficulty perceptions, and one's own ability perceptions are presented in the appendix. A principal components analysis of this set of items indicated that a three-factor solution best described the data (the first three eigenvalues were 7.27, 2.71, and 1.38). Inspection of the loadings from an oblique factor rotation indicated that the seven math items assessing perceptions of task difficulty loaded on the first factor, the seven math task value items on the second factor, and the five math ability perception items on the third factor. Few double loadings occurred. The items comprising each factor, and models proposing

relations between the factors, were explored further using confirmatory factor analyses.

Confirmatory Factor Analyses

Confirmatory factor analysis (CFA) allows the researcher to test more precisely theoretically derived hypotheses about the structure of a set of variables, and it allows for the explicit comparison of different alternative models. It also provides statistical information about the models that help the researcher choose the best fitting model. In these ways (and others), CFA is an important advance over exploratory factor analytic techniques (see Long, 1983). CFA is best used when models are derived from explicit theories; because the models tested in the present study were derived from the theoretical model of Eccles (Parsons) et al. (1983) of children's achievement beliefs, CFA was very appropriate to use in this study. We used CFA to assess the factor structure of individuals' self-perceptions and to compare the structures in different groups. The particular program used was LISREL VI (Jöreskog & Sörbom, 1984).

Various goodness-of-fit indexes are used in CFA to assess how well a given model fits the data; unfortunately, there still is no one generally accepted index (see Marsh, Balla, & McDonald, 1988). We report two frequently used overall fit indexes—chi-square and Jöreskog and Sörbom's (1984) GFI. Marsh et al. (1988) showed that with increasingly large samples, the chi-square value for the same model increases, making it more likely that the model will be rejected. In their comparison of different goodness-of-fit indexes for the same model assessed with different sample sizes, they concluded that the GFI was one of the least affected overall indexes, and so we focus on that index.

For the comparisons of different factor models, we report the Tucker-Lewis (1973) index (TLI), which compares the fit of a theoretically derived model to a "null" model positing no relations between the variables. Marsh et al. (1988) showed that this index is less affected by sample size than are some other comparative indexes. We also used chi-square difference tests (see Long, 1983) to compare different target models. Finally, for the comparisons across groups, we examined whether the covariance matrices were invariant across groups (see Jöreskog & Sörbom, 1984; Marsh & Hocevar, 1985). This test has been described as the most rigorous way to examine invariance in the pattern of relations in a set of variables across different groups.

We first present separate CFAs of the items measuring each individual construct (five items tapping ability perceptions, seven items assessing task difficulty perceptions, and seven items assessing task value perceptions). These analyses assessed our predictions concerning the dimensionality of each of these sets of constructs. By comparing the fit of different alternative models, we were able to assess the usefulness of adding additional dimensions to explain the structure underlying superordinate constructs. Then we present a factor model based on all 19 items that assessed the dimensionality of all the general constructs and the relations between the different constructs. We developed the models using the data from Year 1, and then used the Year 2 data as an independent test of final models generated on the Year 1 data. We also assessed whether the covariance matrices were invariant across Year 1 and Year 2.

For these models, we assumed that the items would load on only one factor (the theoretical factor they were designed to measure), and we estimated all the factor loadings. The variances of the latent variables were set to 1, and the relations between the latent variables and the measurement error variances for each variable were estimated. We also allowed measurement error for items with similar wording or content to covary.

Task value. GFIs for a series of CFAs assessing the null, one-factor, two-factor (generated by combining in all possible ways the three theoretically defined components), and the three-factor models of task value are presented in Table 1. The null model fit very poorly, and each of the other models represented a highly significant improvement in fit over the null model. Inspection of the various GFIs indicated that in line with our predictions, the three-factor model fit the data quite well and represented a highly significant improvement in fit over all the one- and two-factor models. Thus the three-factor model was preferred for this set of items. The standardized confirmatory factor loadings and relations between factors in each year's sample are presented in Table 2. As predicted, adolescents' task value perceptions consisted of three components: an intrinsic interest component, an attainment value component, and an extrinsic utility value component. Also as predicted, these components were all positively related. In the Year 2 model, the three-factor model also provided very good fit. The pattern of factor loadings and relations between factors were very similar to those in the Year 1 analyses (see Table 2). The covariance invariance test presented in Table 1 shows that the matrices of these five items were invariant across years.

Expectancy/ability-related perceptions. The exploratory analyses indicated that a one-factor solution best described the data. Because we had predicted that there would be two factors, we generated both a two-factor model and a one-factor model in the confirmatory analyses. The GFIs for the null, one-, and two-factor models for ability perceptions are presented in Table 1. As can be seen, the null model fit quite poorly, and the one-factor model showed highly significant improvement in fit over

the null model. In the one-factor model, we allowed for correlated error between Items 2 and 5, because the wording on those items was similar. The two-factor model actually fit more poorly because the constraint that items could only load on one factor was not tenable. Also, the correlation between the two factors was .95. Thus the one-factor model best described the interrelations in this set of items. The items loading on this factor in both years assessed adolescents' perceptions of their math ability, expectancies for success in math, and perceived performance in math (see appendix). This one-factor model also provided excellent fit in the Year 2 data (see Table 1), and the factor loadings were very similar. The covariance invariance test presented in Table 1 shows that the matrices of these five items were invariant across years.

Task difficulty perceptions. GFIs for null, one-, and two-factor models of task difficulty are presented in Table 1. The one- and two-factor models each provided significant improvements in fit over the null model. In terms of the various GFI criteria, the two-factor model fit better than the one-factor model and fit well in an absolute sense. We allowed for a correlated error term between Items 8 and 12 in this model, because the wording of those items was similar. Loadings for this model from each year are presented in Table 3. One factor in this model represented adolescents' perceptions of the difficulty of the subject area, and the other represented their perceptions of how much effort they thought was required to do well in the subject area (see appendix). The relationship between the two factors (.88) was strong and positive. In the Year 2 model, the two-factor model also provided excellent fit. The pattern of factor loadings and relation between the two factors were quite similar to the Year 1 model (see Table 3). The covariance invariance test presented in Table 1 shows that the matrices of these seven items were relatively invariant across years, although the GFIs indicated less invariance than for either the ability perceptions or the task values items.

Based on the results of both the exploratory and confirmatory factor analyses, we constructed scales for each of these different constructs. The reliabilities are presented in the appendix. The reliabilities were quite good, especially given the minimal number of items comprising some of the scales.

Six-factor model. The separate CFAs done on the individual constructs suggested that there were three task value factors, two perception of task difficulty factors, and one self-ability perception factor. Thus we next specified a six-factor model of the relations between all 19 of the observed variables. As in the analyses of the individual constructs, in this larger model we assumed that the items would load on only one factor, and we estimated all factor loadings (19 loadings). The variances of the six

TABLE 1:   Goodness-of-Fit Indexes (GFI) for the Factor Models

	df	Chi-Square	GFI	Tucker-Lewis Coefficient
Task value perceptions				
Null model, Year 1	21	1409.55	.52	
Null model, Year 2	21	1355.01	.45	
One-factor model, Year 1	14	155.53	.94	.85
Two-factor A, Year 1	13	66.90	.97	.94
Two-factor B, Year 1	13	98.53	.91	.90
Two-factor C, Year 1	13	124.17	.95	.87
Three-factor model, Year 1	11	16.78	.99	.99
Three-factor model, Year 2	11	6.97	.99	.99
Invariance, Year 1—Year 2	28	40.56	.99	
Ability perceptions				
Null model, Year 1	10	2462.90	.34	
Null model, Year 2	10	2057.61	.34	
One-factor model, Year 1	4	13.52	.99	.99
One-factor model, Year 2	4	16.50	.99	.98
Two-factor model, Year 1	4	109.37	.93	.89
Invariance, Year 1—Year 2	15	41.68		.98
Task difficulty perceptions				
Null model, Year 1	21	2189.72	.40	
Null model, Year 2	21	2006.03	.36	
One-factor model, Year 1	13	126.12	.95	.92
Two-factor model, Year 1	12	63.60	.97	.96
Two-factor model, Year 2	12	25.43	.98	.99
Invariance, Year 1—Year 2	28	61.64	.98	
Task value, ability perceptions,				
and task difficulty perceptions				
Null model, Year 1	171	7247.16	.29	
Null model, Year 2	171	6260.73	.25	
Six-factor model, Year 1	135	435.03	.94	.95
Six-factor model, Year 2	135	356.04	.93	.95
Invariance, Year 1—Year 2	190	283.77	.97	

specified latent variables were set to 1, and the relations between the latent variables were estimated. Measurement error variances for each individual variable were also estimated. We also allowed measurement error for items with similar wording or content to covary. This model was compared to a null model postulating no relations between the constructs.

The GFIs for this model in the Year 1 and 2 data sets are presented in Table 4. As can be seen, the null model fit very poorly. The six-factor model provided a highly significant improvement in fit over the null model and fit quite well in an absolute sense. Table 4 presents the factor loadings and relations between factors in this model. Each of the items loaded highly on the appropriate factor. The relations between the different factors confirmed our predictions. As in the analysis of the individual constructs, relations between each of the values factors were positive, as were relations between the two task difficulty factors. The task value factors all related positively and moderately strongly to the ability perceptions factor, with the weakest of these relations occurring between utility value and ability perceptions, as predicted. The task difficulty perception factors re-

lated negatively to the ability perceptions and task value factors, with this negative relationship particularly strong for ability perceptions and task difficulty, as predicted. As with the other models, this six-factor model also fit very well in the Year 2 data. The factor loadings and relations between factors were quite similar to those at Year 1. The covariance invariance test showed that the matrices were quite similar each year.

DISCUSSION

Results of both the exploratory and confirmatory factor analytic findings suggest that adolescents' ability perceptions, task difficulty perceptions, and task value perceptions are clearly distinguishable from one another. Moreover, more fine-grained distinctions can be made within two of these general constructs. The fact that these distinctions emerged in both years of the study and were quite similar both years lends credence to their theoretical and substantive meaning.

Our results concerning achievement task values argue strongly for distinguishing task values from expectancies, and so we take a broader view of task value than that

TABLE 2:   Factor Loadings for the Task Value Perceptions Model and Relations Between Factors

Item Number	Factor 1. Intrinsic	Factor 2. Utility	Factor 3. Importance
Item 1	.74 (.72)		
Item 2	.84 (.88)		
Item 3		.75 (.82)	
Item 4		.60 (.57)	
Item 5			.75 (.81)
Item 6			.69 (.72)
Item 7			.54 (.64)

Factor	Intrinsic Interest	Importance
Intrinsic interest	1.00	
Importance	.78 (.78)	1.00
Utility	.55 (.67)	.72 (.78)

NOTE: Factor loadings and relations between factors are standardized estimates from the confirmatory factor analyses. Year 2 values are in parentheses.

TABLE 3:   Factor Loadings for Ability Perceptions and Task Difficulty Perceptions Models, and Relations Between Factors

Model/Item Number	Factor 1. Ability/Expectancy
Ability perceptions	
Item 8	.84 (.87)
Item 9	.83 (.78)
Item 10	.79 (.80)
Item 11	.87 (.87)
Item 12	.79 (.83)

	Factor 1. Difficulty	Factor 2. Effort Required
Task difficulty perceptions		
Item 13	.77 (.86)	
Item 14	.78 (.77)	
Item 15	.73 (.76)	
Item 16		.59 (.63)
Item 17		.65 (.64)
Item 18		.78 (.80)
Item 19		-.73 (-.78)
Relations between factors:	.88 (.93)	

NOTE: Factor loadings and relations between factors are standardized estimates from the confirmatory factor analyses. Year 2 values are in parentheses.

proposed by Atkinson (1957) in his initial formulation of the achievement motivation model. We find clear support for the theoretical components of task value that Eccles (Parsons) et al. (1983) proposed: attainment value, or the importance of doing well on a task; intrinsic value, or how much the individual is interested in and likes the task; and utility value, or the usefulness of the task for achieving future goals. Once again, these factors are positively correlated, but the correlations are not as strong as in the analyses of adolescents' ability perceptions or task difficulty perceptions. More important, the three-factor model provides such a good fit for these data that we are quite confident that the distinctions between these different aspects of task value are both theoretically and substantively meaningful.

Given the clarity of these factors, we believe that researchers should assess the development of perceived task values and how the components of task value become differentiated from one another. We also suggest that researchers study the differential prediction of various types of behavior from the different components of task value. For instance, which component of task value most strongly predicts adolescents' continuing participation in various activities once participation is optional? Is it their interest in the activity or domain, as one might argue from an intrinsic motivation perspective? Or would perceived utility value be a stronger predictor, such that adolescents continue to engage in those activities that they believe have the most relevance to their future goals? Developmental studies (Harter, 1981) suggest that children's motivation for academic achievement, in particular, becomes more extrinsic as they get older. If this is so, then older children's course selection, for example, might be more influenced by the perceived

utility value of a course, whereas younger children's enrollment plans might be more influenced by their interest in the subject matter. In support of this possibility, Wigfield and Eccles (1989) found age differences in how the components of task value predicted adolescents' intentions to keep taking math. For junior high school adolescents, only their intrinsic interest in math predicted their intentions. For the high school adolescents, both their intrinsic interest in the subject area and the perceived utility of the subject area predicted their future enrollment plans.

Regarding adolescents' expectancy-related beliefs, one factor emerges in the CFAs. This factor can best be characterized as an ability/expectancy/competence factor, because the items loading on the factor concern adolescents' perceptions of how good they are at the task and also how well they think they will do at the task. Although we could empirically distinguish these adolescents' ability/expectancy perceptions from their perceptions of task difficulty and task value, we find little evidence to justify distinguishing among their ratings of their ability, their current levels of performance, and their expectations regarding their future levels of performance, even using CFA.

Concerning task difficulty perceptions, we find that a two-factor model best fits the relations between the different items. The first factor can be characterized as the "objective" difficulty of math for adolescents (for themselves and in comparison to other adolescents and other

TABLE 4:   Factor Loadings for the Six-Factor Model and Relations Between Factors

Item Number	Interest	Import	Utility	Ability	Difficulty	Effort Required
Item 1	.73 (.70)					
Item 2	.85 (.88)					
Item 3		.75 (.81)				
Item 4		.67 (.71)				
Item 5		.57 (.66)				
Item 6			.75 (.81)			
Item 7			.59 (.57)			
Item 8				.83 (.85)		
Item 9				.84 (.78)		
Item 10				.80 (.82)		
Item 11				.86 (.86)		
Item 12				.80 (.83)		
Item 13					.74 (.84)	
Item 14					.80 (.80)	
Item 15					.74 (.76)	
Item 16						.57 (.62)
Item 17						.63 (.63)
Item 18						.79 (.80)
Item 19						−.73 (−.78))

Factor	Interest	Import	Utility	Ability	Difficulty
Interest	1.00				
Importance	.77 (.77)	1.00			
Utility	.56 (.69)	.71 (.79)	1.00		
Ability	.53 (.51)	.53 (.51)	.37 (.40)	1.00	
Difficulty	−.44 (−.44)	−.30 (−.35)	−.27 (−.30)	1.00	
Effort Required	−.24 (−.32)	−.14(−.23)	−.13 (−.22)	−.13 (−.22)	−.63

NOTE: Factor loadings and relations between factors are standardized estimates from the confirmatory factor analyses. Year 2 values are in parentheses.

subjects), and the second can be characterized as the amount of effort required to do well in math. The correlation between these two factors is quite high, which suggests that adolescents see a close correspondence between how hard a task is and how much effort they need to exert to do well on it. Most lay individuals likely use both these dimensions in arriving at judgments of task difficulty. Given the relation between required effort and task difficulty, it is intriguing that the actual effort adolescents report exerting in math (included in the exploratory analyses) does not relate to either of these two sets of items. This finding suggests that task difficulty is not a major determinant of the amount of effort adolescents actually do put into a task; other influences must be more important.

Turning to the relations between these factors, the ability perception and task value factors are positively related, and both of these belief systems relate negatively to adolescents' task difficulty perceptions. Hence adolescents tend to value an activity when they think they are good at it. Adolescents are less likely to believe they are good at something if they think it is difficult, and they devalue the activity if they think it is difficult. These relations do not support Atkinson's (1957) contention

that expectancies/ability perceptions and values are inversely related; rather, we find support for the views of Eccles (Parsons) et al. (1983), Battle (1966), Crandall (1969), and Harter (1985) that people value those activities in which they excel. We believe that this positive relation will help individuals maintain their self-esteem, because it shows that values and ability perceptions are in congruence rather than inversely related. If individuals placed the most value on tasks that they thought they had the least likelihood of completing successfully, their behavioral strivings would often be frustrated, which could lead to declines in self-esteem.

As predicted, we also find that adolescents' perceptions of ability relate more strongly to the attainment value and intrinsic interest in the task than to its perceived utility value. The perceived utility value of a task or activity may be more influenced by other factors, such as broader cultural values, gender-role stereotyping, and so on, rather than by individual's perceptions of their own abilities.

Results of this study cannot tell us the direction of causality in these relations. Do adolescents first decide what they are good at and then attach values accordingly, or does the opposite pattern occur? Or do both constructs have quite different but correlated antecedents? Many current achievement theories (e.g., Covington, 1984; Nicholls, 1984) posit ability perceptions as taking causal precedence over other achievement self-perceptions. We believe this issue needs scrutiny, particularly in studies with younger children whose achievement self-perceptions are becoming established. We predict that task values have other antecedents, such as the needs and goals of the individuals in addition to their ability perceptions.

It is also critical that future research assesses the extent to which these three different types of perceptions relate to various types of behaviors. Our previous work suggests that performance on a task (e.g., course grades) is most highly related to self-concept of ability, whereas task choices (e.g., course enrollment decisions) are more highly related to the perceived task value constructs. In contrast, neither course grades nor enrollment patterns have related very strongly to perceived task difficulty in our previous work (Eccles, 1984; Eccles, Adler, & Meece, 1984; Eccles [Parsons] et al., 1983; Meece, Wigfield, & Eccles, 1990). Because few studies include measures of the various self- and task perceptions as well as multiple types of behaviors, we know relatively little about the generalizability of these findings to nonacademic activity domains.

APPENDIX
Items Assessing Children's Self- and Task Perceptions in the Domain of Mathematics

PERCEIVED TASK VALUE ITEMS
Intrinsic Interest Value
   Item 1. In general, I find working on math assignments (very boring, very interesting)
   Item 2. How much do you like doing math? (not very much, very much)
      Alpha coefficient = .76
Attainment Value/Importance
   Item 3. Is the amount of effort it will take to do well in advanced high school math courses worthwhile to you? (not very worthwhile, very worthwhile)
   Item 4. I feel that, to me, being good at solving problems which involve math or reasoning mathematically is (not at all important, very important)
   Item 5. How important is it to you to get good grades in math? (not at all important, very important)
      Alpha coefficient = .70
Extrinsic Utility Value
   Item 6. How useful is learning advanced high school math for what you want to do after you graduate and go to work? (not very useful, very useful)
   Item 7. How useful is what you learn in advanced high school math for your daily life outside school? (not at all useful, very useful)
   Alpha coefficient = .62
ABILITY/EXPECTANCY-RELATED ITEMS
   Item 8. Compared to other students, how well do you expect to do in math this year? (much worse than other students, much better than other students)
   Item 9. How well do you think you will do in your math course this year? (very poorly, very well)
   Item 10. How good at math are you? (not at all good, very good)
   Item 11. If you were to order all the students in your math class from the worst to the best in math, where would you put yourself? (the worst, the best)
   Item 12. How have you been doing in math this year? (very poorly, very well)
      Alpha coefficient = .92
PERCEIVED TASK DIFFICULTY ITEMS
Task Difficulty
   Item 13. In general, how hard is math for you? (very easy, very hard)
   Item 14. Compared to most other students in your class, how hard is math for you? (much easier, much harder)
   Item 15. Compared to most other school subjects that you take, how hard is math for you? (my easiest course, my hardest course)
      Alpha coefficient = .80
Required Effort
   Item 16. How hard would you have to try to do well in an advanced high school math course? (not very hard, very hard)
   Item 17. How hard do you have to try to get good grades in math? (a little, a lot)
   Item 18. How hard do you have to study for math tests to get a good grade? (a little, a lot)
   Item 19. To do well in math I to work (much harder in math than in other subjects, much harder in other subjects than in math)
      Alpha coefficient = .78

NOTE: All items were answered on Likert-type scales ranging from 1 to 7.

REFERENCES

Atkinson, J. W. (1957). Motivational determinants of risk-taking behavior. *Psychological Review, 64*, 359-372.

Bandura, A. (1986). *Social foundations of thought and action: A social cognitive theory.* Englewood Cliffs, NJ: Prentice-Hall.

Battle, E. (1966). Motivational determinants of academic competence. *Journal of Personality and Social Psychology, 4*, 534-642.

Covington, M. V. (1984). The motive for self-worth. In R. Ames & C. Ames (Eds.), *Research on motivation in education* (Vol. 1, pp. 77-113). New York: Academic Press.

Crandall, V. C. (1969). Sex differences in expectancy of intellectual and academic reinforcement. In C. P. Smith (Ed.), *Achievement-related motives in children* (pp. 11-45). New York: Russell Sage.

Deci, E. L., & Ryan, R. M. (1985). *Intrinsic motivation and self-determination in human behavior.* New York: Plenum.

Eccles, J. S. (1984). Sex differences in achievement patterns. In T. Sonderegger (Ed.), *Nebraska Symposium on Motivation* (Vol. 32, pp. 97-132). Lincoln: University of Nebraska Press.

Eccles, J. S. (1987). Gender roles and women's achievement. *Psychology of Women Quarterly, 9*, 15-19.

Eccles, J. S., Adler, T. F., & Meece, J. L. (1984). Sex differences in achievement: A test of alternate theories. *Journal of Personality and Social Psychology, 46*, 26-43.

Eccles, J., Wigfield, A., Blumenfeld, P., & Harold, R. (1984). *Psychological predictors of competence development.* Unpublished grant proposal to the National Institute for Child Health and Human Development.

Eccles (Parsons), J., Adler, T. F., Futterman, R., Goff, S. B., Kaczala, C. M., Meece, J. L., & Midgley, C. (1983). Expectancies, values, and academic behaviors. In J. T. Spence (Ed.), *Achievement and achievement motivation* (pp. 75-146). San Francisco: W. H. Freeman.

Epstein, S. (1973). The self-concept revisited or a theory of a theory. *American Psychologist, 28*, 405-416.

Feather, N. T. (1982). Human values and the prediction of action: An expectancy-value analysis. In N. T. Feather (Ed.), *Expectations and actions: Expectancy-value models in psychology* (pp. 263-289). Hillsdale, NJ: Lawrence Erlbaum.

Fischoff, B., Goitein, B., & Shapira, Z. (1982). The experienced utility of expected utility approaches. In N. T. Feather (Ed.), *Expectations and actions: Expectancy-value models in psychology* (pp. 315-339). Hillsdale, NJ: Lawrence Erlbaum.

Fishbein, M., & Ajzen, I. (1975). *Belief, attitude, intention, and behavior: An introduction to theory and research.* Reading, MA: Addison-Wesley.

Harter, S. (1981). A new self-report scale of intrinsic versus extrinsic orientation in the classroom: Motivational and informational components. *Developmental Psychology, 17*, 300-312.

Harter, S. (1982). The Perceived Competence Scale for Children. *Child Development, 53*, 87-97.

Harter, S. (1985). Competence as a dimension of self-evaluation: Toward a comprehensive model of self-worth. In R. L. Leahy (Ed.), *The development of the self* (pp. 55-121). New York: Academic Press.

Heckhausen, H. (1977). Achievement motivation and its constructs: A cognitive model. *Motivation and Emotion, 1*, 283-329.

Jöreskog, K. G., & Sörbom, K. (1984). *LISREL VI: Analysis of linear structural relationships by maximum likelihood and least squares methods.* Chicago: National Educational Resources.

Kukla, A. (1972). Foundations of an attributional theory of performance. *Psychological Review, 79*, 454-470.

Kukla, A. (1978). An attributional theory of choice. In L. Berkowitz (Ed.), *Advances in experimental social psychology* (Vol. 11, pp. 113-144). New York: Academic Press.

Long, J. S. (1983). *Confirmatory factor analysis.* Beverly Hills, CA: Sage.

Marsh, H. W., Balla, J. R., & McDonald, R. P. (1988). Goodness-of-fit indexes in confirmatory factor analysis: The effect of sample size. *Psychological Bulletin, 103*, 391-410.

Marsh, H. W., & Hocevar, D. (1985). Application of confirmatory factor analysis to the study of self-concept: First- and higher-order factor models and their invariance across groups. *Psychological Bulletin, 97*, 562-582.

Marsh, H. W., & Shavelson, R. (1985). Self-concept: Its multifaceted hierarchical structure. *Educational Psychologist, 20*, 107-123.

Meece, J. L., Wigfield, A., & Eccles, J. S. (1990). Predictors of math anxiety and its consequences for young adolescents' course enrollment intentions and performances in mathematics. *Journal of Educational Psychology, 82*, 60-70.

Nicholls, J. G. (1978). The development of the concepts of effort and ability, perceptions of academic attainment, and the understanding that difficult tasks require more ability. *Child Development, 49*, 800-814.

Nicholls, J. G. (1984). Achievement motivation: Conceptions of ability, subjective experience, task choice, and performance. *Psychological Review, 91*, 328-346.

Parsons, J. E. (1980). *Self-perceptions, task perceptions and academic choice: Origins and change.* Unpublished final technical report to the National Institute of Education, Washington, DC. (ERIC Document Reproduction Service No. ED 186 477)

Parsons, J. E., & Goff, S. B. (1980). Achievement motivation and values: An alternative perspective. In L. J. Fyans (Ed.), *Achievement motivation* (pp. 349-373). New York: Plenum.

Parsons, J. E., & Ruble, D. N. (1977). The development of achievement-related expectancies. *Child Development, 48*, 1075-1079.

Rokeach, M. (1980). Some unresolved issues in theories of beliefs, attitudes, and values. In M. M. Page (Ed.), *Nebraska Symposium on Motivation* (pp. 261-304). Lincoln: University of Nebraska Press.

Rotter, J. B. (1982). Social learning theory. In N. T. Feather (Ed.), *Expectations and actions: Expectancy-value models in psychology* (pp. 241-260). Hillsdale, NJ: Lawrence Erlbaum.

Tucker, L. R., & Lewis, C. (1973). The reliability coefficient for maximum likelihood factor analysis. *Psychometrika, 38*, 1-10.

Weiner, B., Frieze, I., Kukla, A., Reed, L., Rest, S., & Rosenbaum, R. M. (1971). *Perceiving the causes of success and failure.* Morristown, NJ: General Learning.

Wigfield, A., & Eccles, J. S. (1989, March). *Relations of expectancies and values to students' math grades and intentions.* Paper presented at the meeting of the American Educational Research Association, San Francisco.

Wigfield, A., & Eccles, J. S. (1992). The development of achievement task values: A theoretical analysis. *Developmental Review, 12*, 1-41.

Received January 13, 1992
Revision received June 30, 1993
Accepted June 30, 1993

Individual-Contextual Relationships and Mathematics Performance:
Comparing American and Serbian Young Adolescents

Jasna Jovanovic
University of Illinois, Champaign-Urbana
Richard M. Lerner
Michigan State University

This study examined whether the system of relationships between individual-psychological characteristics (i.e., spatial ability, scholastic ability perception, mathematics stereotype), social contextual levels of family and culture, and mathematics performance differs for young adolescent girls and boys. Subjects included 160 American (i.e., from the United States) sixth graders and 242 Serbian fifth and sixth graders. Findings indicated that in both cultures scholastic ability perception was associated with the mathematics performance of boys and girls. In addition, both among American and Serbian boys and among Serbian girls, spatial ability was linked to their mathematics performance. Interestingly, among American girls but not among Serbian girls, holding a less traditional mathematics stereotype related negatively to mathematics performance. Finally, the family appeared to be a particularly salient context for Serbian young adolescents, especially for girls. These findings underscore the notion that at different levels of the social context young adolescents' individual-psychological characteristics can vary, leading to different academic outcomes.

Young adolescents' academic development occurs within a multilevel social context. Given this context, one must consider as important to the academic development process not only the proximal family and school levels but also the community, society, and culture levels (Bronfenbrenner, 1979; Lerner, 1984, 1986, 1991). Furthermore, at each level of the social context, individual-

---

This research was supported in part by a grant to Richard M. Lerner, Jacqueline V. Lerner, and Alexander von Eye from the National Institute of Child Health and Human Development (HD23229). In addition, this research was supported in part by dissertation fellowships to Jasna Jovanovic from the International Research and Exchanges Board and the Department of Education Fulbright-Hays. This research was conducted while both authors were at the Pennsylvania State University. The authors thank Dr. Lidija Vucic and Dragica Pavlovic of the University of Belgrade for their assistance with the Yugoslav data collection.

Journal of Early Adolescence, Vol. 14 No. 4, November 1994 449-470
© 1994 Sage Publications, Inc.

psychological characteristics relevant to young adolescents' academic development (e.g., cognitive ability, ability appraisals, and attitudes) may have a different impact (Lerner, 1987; Lerner & Busch-Rossnagel, 1981). The implication of this view, then, is that there is potential for great individual variation both in the system of individual-context relationships associated with academic development and also in the outcomes the system effects (Lerner, Delaney, Hess, Jovanovic, & von Eye, 1990).

This view of young adolescents' academic development becomes particularly relevant in discussions of young adolescents' mathematics performance. In the United States, there are disparate outcomes in the mathematics performance of boys and girls. For example, on standardized tests of achievement, junior high and high school boys outperform girls in critical areas of mathematical ability (e.g., problem solving and mathematical reasoning) (Dossey, Mullis, Lindquist, & Chambers, 1988; Friedman, 1989; Hyde, Fennema, & Lamon, 1990). In addition, more boys than girls enroll in advanced mathematics courses and aspire to mathematics-related careers (Dossey et al., 1988; National Science Foundation, 1988). Therefore, the question that arises is this: Is the system of individual-contextual relationships that is associated with mathematics performance different for girls and boys?

Gender differences in mathematics performance have been attributed to several individual-psychological characteristics. For example, spatial ability is often associated with the gender differences found in mathematics achievement scores (Benbow & Stanley, 1980; Maccoby & Jacklin, 1974). The argument is that mathematics ability is related to spatial ability and that boys have higher spatial ability than girls. However, this link is questionable given recent evidence that the gender gap in spatial ability has essentially closed (Linn & Hyde, 1989; Linn & Petersen, 1985). Children's scholastic ability perceptions, on the other hand, appear to be more clearly gender differentiated. It has been reported, for example, that girls perceive themselves as less competent in mathematics than do boys (e.g., Fennema, 1974; Levine, 1976) even though girls, in general, tend to get better grades in mathematics than do boys (Benbow & Stanley, 1982; Noble & McNabb, 1989). This gender difference in scholastic ability perceptions is consistent with a stereotype in American culture that defines mathematics as a male domain (Armstrong & Kahl, 1979; Ernest, 1976; Fennema & Sherman, 1977); that is, mathematics is better suited for and more useful to males than to females (Boswell, 1985; Linn, 1991). Moreover, this mathematics stereotype is formed before girls and boys enter high school, where they are faced with decisions regarding course choices (Hill & Lynch, 1983; Kaminski, Erickson, Ross, & Bradfield, 1976).

The social context, in turn, plays an important role in determining the ability perceptions and stereotype attitudes that young adolescents hold (Fox,

1980). For example, family members, particularly parents, give young adolescents the support and encouragement to succeed academically (Kurdek & Sinclair, 1988; Smith, 1989). However, parental support is often predicated on the stereotypes to which parents subscribe (Yee & Eccles, 1988). Therefore, it has been found that parents who believe mathematics to be a male domain are less likely to support their daughters' pursuits in mathematics than parents who view mathematics as a neutral domain (Boswell, 1985; Stallings, 1985). In the same respect, the interactions young adolescents have with the school level are influenced by the gender biases their teachers and classmates each hold. In general, teachers call on boys far more often than girls and give positive feedback to boys more frequently than to girls (Brophy & Good, 1974; Kelly, 1988). In addition, there is evidence that male classmates behave negatively toward female classmates who demonstrate high levels of mathematics proficiency (Skolnick, Langbort, & Day, 1982).

At the outermost level of the social context, the culture can influence the beliefs and attitudes held by parents, teachers, or classmates. For example, differing cultures may endorse different social models concerning women and men (Block, 1973; Chandler, Shama, & Wolf, 1983). Block (1973) noted, for example, that in capitalistic societies, as compared to socialistic societies, personality characteristics such as assertiveness, dominance, independence, and achievement are associated more with men than they are with women. In addition, the culture can determine the degree of importance that is attached to academic achievement. For example, Uttal, Lummis, and Stevenson (1988) contend that the large differences in mathematics achievement scores found among children from the United States, China, and Japan are in part due to a higher level of satisfaction among American mothers in comparison to Chinese and Japanese mothers regarding their children's abilities and accomplishments. This material high satisfaction, they believe, decreases the level of motivation among children in the United States to strive harder in their studies (Uttal et al., 1988).

Clearly, boys' and girls' mathematics performance involves a complex system of relationships both between their individual-psychological characteristics and the multiple levels—from the family to the culture—of their social context. Moreover, this system of relationships that affects young adolescents' mathematics performance is formed well before children reach the junior high and high school age levels, when the gender difference emerges. Therefore, the most comprehensive explanation for why there are gender differences in mathematics performance would involve identifying the entire system of relationships, and doing so before young adolescents enter seventh grade when, the literature suggests, gender differences in mathematics performance typically emerge. Although examining the entire

145

system of relationships would be optimal, this is difficult. Therefore, this study is an initial attempt at identifying components of this system. Specifically, this study examined the relationships between several individual-psychological characteristics that commonly are associated with the gender differences in mathematics (i.e., spatial ability, scholastic ability perception, mathematics stereotype), the social contextual levels of the family and culture, and mathematics performance among the young adolescents. Very few studies to date have considered the influence of culture in identifying the reasons for the gender differences in mathematics performance.

One way to examine the influence of the culture is to make assessments within cultures that vary (Kohn, 1987). In this study, the relationships between the individual-psychological characteristics, the family context, and mathematics performance were examined within the United States and within Yugoslavia, specifically Serbia. The Serbian culture presents an important context within which to examine girls' and boys' mathematics outcomes. Given Serbia's socialist ideology, there has been an expectation for Serbian men and women to receive equal education and to pursue occupations of equitable status (Denich, 1977; Woodward, 1985). This expectation is put forth both in the school (Organization for Economic Co-Operation and Development, 1981) and at home, where parents have equal hopes for daughters and sons regarding future career goals (Denich, 1977). In fact, Serbian parents play a particularly intensive role in their children's lives, including their educational and social development (Simic, 1983), especially when compared to parents in the United States (Joksimovic, 1986). Regarding the mathematics achievement of Serbian youth, demographic data indicate that among the university graduates in Yugoslavia who received degrees in 1988 in mathematics and the natural sciences (e.g., biology, chemistry, and physics), 40% were male and 60% were female (*Statistical Yearbook*, 1989). These percentages are in direct contrast to those found in the United States. In 1987, among university graduates who received bachelor's degrees in mathematics, 46% were female, and among those receiving degrees in the physical sciences, 28% were female (U.S. Bureau of the Census, 1990).

Whether this affinity for mathematics and science among Serbian females is a result of better spatial abilities, higher self-appraisals of scholastic ability, and/or less traditional gender-role stereotypes regarding mathematics is not known. It may be that the closeness or support from family, specifically parents, instills in Serbian females the confidence to succeed. The identification of such relationships not only may provide insights into which variables operate to discriminate the mathematics performance of young individuals across cultures but also may expose those variables that are universal in promoting the successful mathematics performance of boys and girls more generally. Therefore, this study explored the relations between individual-psychological characteristics (i.e., spatial ability, scholastic ability perceptions, and mathematics stereotypes), the family context, and mathematics performance within samples of girls and boys in the United States and Serbia.

METHOD

Subjects

The sample from the United States (from here on referred to as the American sample) was composed of subjects from the Replication and Extension of the Pennsylvania Early Adolescent Transitions Study (RE-PEATS) (Lerner, Lerner, & von Eye, 1988). The REPEATS sample consists of two cohorts (1989-1990 and 1990-1991) of sixth graders from three middle schools within a central Pennsylvania semirural school district. The RE-PEATS is a cohort comparative longitudinal study that was designed to follow the two cohorts of sixth graders across their middle school years. Data were initially collected on the first cohort of sixth graders in October 1989 (Wave 1). These data were used in the present study. The REPEATS sample for Wave 1 consisted of 160 students who voluntarily agreed to participate. This resulted in a 35% rate of participation. School records of those students who did not agree to participate were not available. The mean age of the REPEATS subjects (44% male; 99% White) at the time of the first wave of testing was 11.8 years ($SD = .45$).

The Serbian sample consisted of 242 fifth and sixth graders (49% male; 99% Serbian ethnicity) from two elementary schools (first through eighth grade) in a semirural area of Serbia. As with the American sample, the Serbian sample participated voluntarily. The resulting participation rate was 100%. Both fifth and sixth graders were sampled in Serbia because, unlike children in the United States who begin first grade at the age of 6 years, Serbian children begin first grade at the age of 7 years. However, because no effect for grade level was found among the individual-psychological and the social contextual variables, the samples for fifth and sixth grade were pooled. Data collection was conducted in April 1990 in collaboration with the University of Belgrade in Yugoslavia. The mean age of these Serbian subjects at that time of testing was 12.3 years ($SD = .59$).

Measurement Model

As previously discussed, it is difficult to measure all the variables that represent the system of relationships between young adolescents' individual-psychological characteristics and the multiple levels of their social context relevant to mathematics performance. However, samples can be taken from the array of qualitative and quantitative variables to begin to understand this complex system of relationships. In this study, American and Serbian young adolescents' spatial ability, scholastic ability perception, mathematics stereotype, family context, and mathematics performance were sampled. Furthermore, this was done using a preexisting data set, one that was set up to examine the psychosocial development of young adolescents as they move through their middle school years.[1]

Individual-Psychological Variables

The variables sampled in this study to index relevant individual-psychological characteristics of each young adolescent were spatial ability, scholastic ability perception, and mathematics stereotype. Although, as previously indicated, there is little evidence to support a link between spatial ability and gender differences in mathematics achievement scores, it was of interest in this study to examine whether, as early as sixth grade, those girls and boys who are good at mathematics are those young adolescents with a high spatial ability. In the same respect, it was of interest to assess whether the relationships between young adolescents' scholastic ability perceptions, mathematics stereotype, and mathematics performance are different among boys and girls as early as the sixth grade. Such an investigation of these relationships within two varying cultural contexts has never before been done.

Spatial ability. Spatial ability was assessed using the Piaget and Inhelder (1956) spatial perception water-level task. Spatial perception is a domain of spatial ability in which gender differences in samples of young individuals from the Unites States has been demonstrated (Linn & Petersen, 1985).

The water-level task consists of six drawings of bottles tipped at various angles. Subjects are asked to show the way water would look in each of the six bottles if each were half full. A response is scored as correct if the water is drawn within 5 degrees of the horizontal, yielding a total score of 0 to 6 bottles correct.

Piaget and Inhelder (1956) did not report psychometric information regarding the water-level task. Internal consistency coefficients among the REPEATS and Serbian samples were .89 and .80, respectively.

148

Scholastic ability perception. To index subjects' views of their own ability in school, the Scholastic Competence subscale of the Harter (1983) Self-Perception Profile for Children (SPP) was administered. The Harter (1983) SPP was developed to assess children's perceptions of their competency in several domains, including scholastic ability. An example item from the Scholastic Competence subscale reads, "Some kids feel that they are very good at their school work, BUT, other kids worry about whether they can do the school work assigned to them." The children respond by deciding which kind of child is most like them and to which degree this is true. Each item is scored on a scale from 1 through 4, with 1 indicating a low self-perceived competence or adequacy and 4 reflecting a high self-perceived competence or adequacy.

Harter (1983) reported a .80 reliability (internal consistency) coefficient among sixth graders for the Scholastic Competence subscale. For Wave 1 of the REPEATS sample, the internal consistency coefficient was .75. The corresponding coefficient within the Serbian sample was .79. The measurement equivalency of the SPP was validated in a previous assessment of Serbian fifth and sixth graders (Jovanovic, Lerner, Vucic, & Pavlovic, 1989).

Mathematics stereotype. To assess young adolescents' stereotypes regarding mathematics or mathematics-related activities, four items assessing attitudes toward mathematics and science from the Occupations, Activities, and Traits Attitude Measure (OAT-AM; Bigler, Liben, & Yekel, 1991) were used. An example item reads, "Who should be good at math?" Subjects are asked to select among response alternatives labeled *only boys, only girls, both boys and girls,* or *neither boys nor girls.* Each item is scored by assigning a score of 1 to the "both" responses. Subjects then receive a total mathematics stereotype score based on the number of items they assign to the "both" category. Therefore, among the present sample of young adolescents, a high total score of 4 reflected the presence of a less traditional gender role stereotype toward mathematics.

For Wave 1 of the REPEATS sample, the internal consistency coefficient for the mathematics stereotype variable was .87. The corresponding coefficient within the Serbian sample was .70.

Family Context Variables

To index the family context, young adolescents' self-perceptions of the cohesion, or closeness, in their families and the quality of their relationships with their parents were measured. It was believed that a measure of young adolescents' perceptions of their family relationships is an indicator of the support given by the family context. Furthermore, given that there is evidence that family closeness or intensity is different in the United State and Serbia (Joksimovic, 1986), the relationship between the family context and mathematics performance also may vary across these cultures.

Family cohesion. As an index of the cohesion, or closeness, young adolescents feel within the family, the Family Cohesion subscale of the Family Adaptability and Cohesion Evaluation Scale (FACES III; Olson, Portner, & Lavee, 1985) was used. The FACES III is a 20-item self-report inventory that indexes two factors: family cohesion and family adaptability, or flexibility. For each item, young adolescents are asked to indicate how often each statement is true for their family, using a response format that ranges from 1 = *almost never* through 5 = *almost always*. Representative items include "Family members ask each other for help," and "Family togetherness is very important." The family cohesion score is calculated by summing across the 10 cohesion items.

Olson et al. (1985) reported an internal consistency coefficient of .77 for the Family Cohesion subscale. Within the REPEATS sample and Serbian samples, the reliability estimates for Family Cohesion were .86 and .61, respectively. In addition, factor analysis of the Serbian data resulted in an identical factor-loading pattern as reported by Olson et al. (1985), thereby increasing confidence in the validity of the FACES III within the Serbian sample.

Parent-child relationships. To index the subjects' perceptions of the quality of their relationship with their mothers and fathers, a modified version of the Parental Acceptance and Rejection Questionnaire (PARQ; Rohner, 1980) was used. The PARQ indexes the amount of warmth that young adolescents perceive to be receiving from their mother or father through the bipolar dimensions of parental affection and rejection. A 35-item modified PARQ, constructed and validated by McHale, Bartko, Crouter, and Perry-Jenkins (1990), was used in the present study. In addition, an item that reflected physical punishment to the child was omitted due to potential liability in regard to knowledge of child abuse. Examples of the 34 remaining items are "Says nice things about me," "Treats me harshly," and "Treats me gently and with kindness." Subjects complete separate questionnaires for mothers and fathers. In the response format, young adolescents are asked to indicate the degree to which an item is true or untrue of the way their mother or father treats them. Each item is scored from 1 through 4, with 1 indicating a high perceived level of rejection and 4 reflecting a high perception of acceptance. In this way, a maximum total score of 136 indicates a high level of warmth in the parent-child relationship.

Rohner, Saavedra, and Granum (1978) reported reliability estimates ranging from .72 through .90. Within the REPEATS sample, internal consistency coefficients at Wave 1 were .88 for the mother version of the PARQ and .97 for the father version of the PARQ. The corresponding coefficients for the Serbian sample were .90 and .96, respectively.

Mathematics Performance

As previously described, young adolescents' mathematics performance involves an array of outcomes, from their scores on standardized achievement tests to their career aspirations. In this study, subjects' grades at the middle of the school year in the mathematics class were used as an index of mathematics performance. The primary focus of this study was to identify the system of relationships between individual-psychological characteristics and the social context that relate to mathematics performance before gender differences in mathematics emerge. The focus was not to assess gender differences in mathematics performance in sixth grade per se. In fact, based on previous research, it was anticipated that at least in the American sample either no difference or a gender difference in favor of girls would be found. Grades in the American sample were calculated on a 0 through 4 scale, with 4 indicating a grade of A and 0 indicating a grade of F. In the Serbian sample, grades were calculated on a 1 through 5 scale, with 5 being equivalent to an American A grade and 1 being equivalent to a failing grade.[2]

Procedure

All the measures were back-translated into Serbo-Croatian for use with the Serbian sample. In addition, researchers at the University of Belgrade confirmed the appropriateness of each of the scales' formats for use with Serbian young adolescents.

Data collection at Wave 1 (October 1989) of the REPEATS involved group testing in each of the three middle schools. Each school was visited across 2 consecutive days within a span of 10 days. All of the participants were tested, within their respective schools. Testing occurred in small groups of approximately 10 young adolescents accompanied by one or two group leaders. Across the 2 days of testing, participants completed several self-report questionnaires including the questionnaires used in the present study. Data collection in Yugoslavia (April 1990) was conducted in each of the two elementary schools across 2 consecutive days within a span of 10 days. All participants, under the direction of Serbo-Croatian-speaking research assistants, completed the questionnaires within their respective classrooms during a specific time of the school day.

RESULTS

To explore the system of relationships between the individual-psychological variables, the family context variables, and mathematics performance within the American and Serbian samples, analyses proceeded in three steps. In the first step, univariate analyses of variances (ANOVAs) were conducted for each of the individual-psychological variables (i.e., spatial ability, scholastic ability perception, mathematics stereotype) and the variables indexing the family context (i.e., family cohesion, mother-child relationship, father-child relationship) to identify cultural and/or gender differences. The use of separate ANOVAs with a Bonferroni adjustment of the alpha level is considered to be a viable alternative to using multivariate analyses of variances when an investigation, like the present study, is specifically interested in examining differences for each variable individually (Bray & Maxwell, 1985). Therefore, if a Bonferroni correction was to have been made, a minimum acceptable alpha level of .008 would have resulted. However, given the exploratory nature of the present study, the less conservative alpha level of .05 was used for these analyses and the remaining analyses in the study. In addition to the ANOVAs, t-test procedures were used to assess the mean difference in mathematics performance (i.e., mathematics grade point average [GPA]) between boys and girls within each culture. The second step examined the intercorrelations between the individual-psychological variables, the family context variables, and mathematics performance within the American and Serbian samples. In the third step, simple multiple regression analyses assessed the relative influences of the individual-psychological variables and family context variables on mathematics performance for the American and Serbian girls and boys.

Gender and Culture Comparisons of the
Individual-Psychological and Family Context Variables

Table 1 presents the means, standard deviations, and fixed effects, between-between, 2 × 2 (Gender × Culture) ANOVA results for the three individual-psychological variables and the three family context variables. The results indicated that there were no significant interaction effects between Gender and Culture; therefore, only main effects are reported.

As indicated in Table 1, a gender difference occurred among two of the individual-psychological variables and one of the family context variables. Both American and Serbian boys outperformed American and Serbian girls on the spatial ability task, although effect sizes were moderate to small in each culture. On the other hand, girls in both cultures held less traditional stereotypes regarding mathematics and reported warmer relationships with their mothers than did the boys in the two cultural groups.

Regarding cultural differences, Serbian young adolescents overall perceived mathematics as a more neutral domain than did the American young adolescents. In addition, the cultural main effects found among all three family context variables indicated that Serbian girls and boys consistently reported more positive family interactions than did their American counterparts.

Gender Differences in Mathematics Performance

As previously described, school grades in mathematics were collected as an index of mathematics performance. Due to the potential differences in the content of school subjects and procedures for grading, cross-cultural comparisons of the actual grades were not made. However, it was assumed that within both cultures mathematics GPA represented an equivalent marker of boys' and girls' academic performance in this subject area. Therefore, within the American sample, the mean mathematics midyear GPA was 2.92 ($SD = 0.87$) for girls and 2.79 ($SD = 1.00$) for boys. Within the Serbian sample, the mean mathematics midyear GPA was 2.98 ($SD = 1.10$) for girls and 2.37 ($SD = 1.10$) for boys; this difference in the Serbian sample was found to be statistically significant, $t(242) = 4.33, p < .01$.

Intercorrelations Between the Individual-Psychological Variables, Family Context Variables, and Mathematics Performance

To examine the relationships between the individual-psychological variables (i.e., spatial ability, scholastic ability perception, and mathematics stereotype), the family context variables (i.e., family cohesion, mother-child relationship, and father-child relationship), and mathematics performance (mathematics GPA) among girls and boys within and across cultures, Pearson product-moment correlations were computed among these variables. Tables 2 and 3 present the intercorrelations for boys and girls within each culture.

TABLE 1: Gender and Culture Main Effects for the Individual-Psychological and Family Context Variables

| | Americans | | | | Serbians | | | | | | |
| | Boys (n = 72) | | Girls (n = 88) | | Boys (n = 119) | | Girls (n = 123) | | | | |
Variable	X̄	SD	X̄	SD	X̄	SD	X̄	SD	Gender F	Culture F	df
Individual psychological											
Spatial ability	2.13	2.10	1.34	1.51	2.36	2.02	1.82	1.68	12.44*	3.66	396
Scholastic ability perception	2.85	0.56	2.85	0.63	2.93	0.62	2.86	0.61	0.29	0.66	398
Mathematics stereotype	2.69	1.68	3.13	1.34	3.20	1.21	3.62	0.83	10.96*	15.29*	398
Family context											
Family cohesion	32.71	9.26	34.39	7.80	41.71	5.10	42.20	6.05	2.36	142.18*	398
Mother-child relationship	107.99	13.69	110.91	15.98	113.97	15.29	120.33	11.26	10.43*	28.74*	398
Father-child relationship	102.09	32.37	106.02	26.21	114.31	18.84	117.80	24.27	2.09	21.76*	392

*$p < .05$.

154

TABLE 2: Intercorrelations Between the Individual-Psychological Variables, Family Context Variables, and Mathematics Performance for American Boys (Below Diagonal) and Girls (Above Diagonal)

Variable	1	2	3	4	5	6	7
Individual-psychological							
1. Spatial ability	1.00	.03	.08	−.14	−.11	−.07	.01
2. Scholastic ability perception	−.19	1.00	.14	.13	.23*	.17	.44*
3. Mathematics stereotype	.16	.17	1.00	.06	.03	−.01	−.16
Family context							
4. Family cohesion	−.11	.26*	.32*	1.00	.60*	.56*	.05
5. Mother-child relationship	.03	.36*	.28*	.48*	1.00	.40*	.16
6. Father-child relationship	.06	.32*	.24*	.27*	.23*	1.00	.07
Mathematics performance							
7. Math grade point average	.18	.33*	.12	.28*	.33*	.12	1.00

*p < .05.

Relationships between the variables were more similar than different, both across gender and culture. In both cultures, scholastic ability perception was positively related to mathematics GPA. In addition, a high scholastic ability perception was related to positive reports on all three family context variables. However, in the Serbian sample, scholastic ability perception correlated higher with the mother-child relationship for girls than it did for boys, $z = 2.44, p < .05$.

In the American sample, the relationship between spatial ability and mathematics GPA was not significant, although for boys there was a low positive trend, $r = .18, p < .10$. In the Serbian sample, this was not the case. Both for Serbian girls and boys, spatial ability was significantly related to mathematics GPA.

In both cultures, boys' and girls' mathematics stereotypes did not relate to their scholastic ability perceptions or to their mathematics performance. However, holding a less traditional mathematics stereotype did relate to reports of strong family cohesion among boys in both cultures and also to reports of boys' warm relationships with mothers in the Serbian sample. In turn, among Serbian boys and girls and American boys, strong family cohesion and warm mother-child relationships related to high mathematics GPAs. In fact, the correlation between family cohesion and mathematics GPA was significantly higher for Serbian girls than it was for American girls, $z = 2.05, p < .05$.

TABLE 3:   Intercorrelations Between the Individual-Psychological Variables, Family Context Variables, and Mathematics Performance for Serbian Boys (Below Diagonal) and Girls (Above Diagonal)

Variable	1	2	3	4	5	6	7
Individual-psychological							
1. Spatial ability	1.00	.21*	.12	.28*	.16	.05	.26*
2. Scholastic ability perception	.03	1.00	.09	.23*	.42*	.11	.43*
3. Mathematics stereotype	.04	−.08	1.00	.11	.13	−.02	.04
Family context							
4. Family cohesion	−.01	.18*	.24*	1.00	.49*	.41*	.33*
5. Mother-child relationship	.01	.13	.17	.31*	1.00	.33*	.26*
6. Father-child relationship	.14	.24*	.06	.31*	.33*	1.00	.03
Mathematics performance							
7. Math grade point average	.37*	.38*	−.10	.20*	.19*	.17	1.00

*p < .05.

Finally, in the American sample, the relationship between family cohesion and the father-child relationship was stronger for girls than for boys, $z = 2.17$, $p < .05$. In contrast, in the Serbian sample, the relationship between family cohesion and the mother-child relationship was stronger for girls than for boys, $z = 2.14$, $p < .05$.

The Relative Influence of the Individual-Psychological and Family Context Variables on Boys' and Girls' Mathematics Performance

Table 4 presents results of the regression analyses involving the use of the individual-psychological variables and the family context variables as predictors of girls' and boys' mathematics performance in each culture. In both cultural groups, it appears that in the presence of all the other individual-psychological variables and the family context variables, spatial ability and scholastic ability perceptions were the best predictors of boys' mathematics GPAs.

In contrast to the similar influences on mathematics performance that emerged for American and Serbian boys, more discrepant influences were found for girls in the two cultural groups. Both for American and Serbian girls, the scholastic ability perception variable, relative to all other variables, was the best predictor of mathematics GPAs. In addition to ability perceptions, Serbian girls' feelings of family cohesion also predicted their mathematics performance. This predictor was not seen among American girls.

TABLE 4: Regression of the Individual-Psychological Variables and Family Context Variables Onto Mathematics Grade Point Averages (GPAs): Unstandardized (and Standardized) Beta Coefficients

Equation	Individual-Psychological Variables			Familial Variables			R^2
	Spatial Ability	Scholastic Ability Perception	Mathematics Stereotype	Family Cohesion	Mother-Child Relationship	Father-Child Relationship	
American							
Boys' math GPA	.14 (.30)*	.54 (.31)*	−.04 (−.07)	.02 (.21)	.01 (.13)	.00 (−.06)	.25
Girls' math GPA	.01 (.02)	.62 (.45)*	−.15 (−.23)*	.00 (−.02)	.01 (.09)	.00 (.03)	.25
Serbian							
Boys' math GPA	.20 (.37)*	.58 (.32)*	−.13 (−.14)	.03 (.14)	.01 (.14)	.00 (−.05)	.32
Girls' math GPA	.09 (.14)	.63 (.35)*	−.06 (−.04)	.05 (.24)*	.00 (.00)	.00 (−.11)	.25

NOTE: Tolerance levels indicated threat of multicollinearity absent in each equation. No significant differences were found among the R^2s.
*$p < .05$.

Instead, for American girls, mathematics stereotype was an additional predictor of their mathematics performance. It appears that within the American sample those girls who perceived mathematics to be a neutral domain were performing poorly in their mathematics classes.[3]

DISCUSSION

The purpose of this study was to explore whether the system of individual-contextual relationships associated with mathematics performance differs for young adolescent girls and boys. Although boys and girls share many similarities, the results indicated that as early as sixth grade there are indeed certain differences in the system of relationships.

As was expected, scholastic ability perception was associated with the mathematics performance of girls and boys. That is, both American and Serbian young adolescents who were self-confident in their overall scholastic abilities were those who performed well in mathematics. Furthermore, boys and girls did not differ in their ability perceptions. Although this finding is consistent with that of Harter (1985), it appears somewhat contrary to other investigations that have noted that girls hold lower self-perceptions in mathematics than do boys. The present study implies that girls who reported high scholastic ability perceptions either perceived themselves as doing well in all subjects, including mathematics, or compensated for their low self-perceptions in mathematics by their successes in other subjects. The higher mathematics GPA found among girls in both samples (which was numerically, but not significantly, higher in the American sample) lends support to the former interpretation. Yet, if this interpretation is extended to boys, the expectation would be that boys' perceptions of their scholastic abilities would be lower than girls' perceptions. It appears, at least in these samples, that boys have the ability to preserve an academic self-confidence level equal to girls' level of self-confidence despite their poorer performance in mathematics.

The regression analyses indicated that among boys in both cultures spatial ability (i.e., spatial perception) related to mathematics performance. In addition, an examination of the intercorrelations between the variables indicated that spatial ability was related to mathematics performance among Serbian girls. This consistent relationship between spatial ability and mathematics performance for the young adolescents in Serbia, as compared to the young adolescents in the United States, may be a reflection of the varying curricula in the two cultures. In Serbia, the mathematics curriculum in the fifth and sixth grade includes the recognition of geometric figures as sets of points, rotation and symmetry, triangles and quadrangles, and calculation of areas.

In the United States, such mathematical activities are typically not expected of students until the eighth grade. Nevertheless, the lack of a relationship between spatial ability and mathematics performance among American girls, and the fact that in the regression analysis spatial ability dropped out as a predictor for Serbian girls, indicated that spatial ability was not a necessary basis for these young adolescents' successful performance in mathematics.

In both cultures, boys' and girls' mathematics stereotypes did not relate to their scholastic ability perceptions. Mathematics stereotypes, however, did predict mathematics performance among the American girls. Apparently for these girls, thinking of mathematics as a neutral domain did not facilitate positive mathematics performance. Although counterintuitive, this result is consistent with that of Eccles et al. (1985) who found that the stereotyping of mathematics as a male domain had a positive effect both for boys and girls. They hypothesized that this relationship reflects young individuals' awareness of the high-status jobs that are predominantly male and mathematics related; therefore, these young individuals are willing to exert more effort in mathematics (Eccles et al., 1985). The absence of this relationship among the Serbian young adolescents only furthers this postulation. As previously indicated, mathematics and many mathematics-related fields are not male dominated in Serbia. Therefore, the type of status and the degree of desirability may not be attached to mathematics in Serbia in the same way that it is in the United States. This, then, leads to a different evaluation of mathematics among Serbian young adolescents. Indeed, both Serbian girls and boys in the present sample reported mathematics to be a more neutral domain than did their American counterparts.

Not surprisingly, the family context played a role in the mathematics performance of these middle school aged young adolescents in both cultures. Although directionality cannot be assumed, the significant correlation between mathematics stereotype and family cohesion found among boys implies that within the family context boys receive messages regarding what is or is not appropriate gender-specific behavior. In addition, both boys' and girls' perceptions regarding their scholastic ability were related to the quality of their relationships with their mothers and/or fathers. As Parsons, Adler, and Kaczala (1982) have demonstrated, children's beliefs about their achievement potential are related more often to their parents' beliefs than to their own past achievements.

The results also indicated, however, that elements of the family context can vary at the level of culture. As anticipated, Serbian young adolescents reported higher levels of family cohesion and warmer relationships with parents than did American young adolescents. Moreover, these positive family dynamics appeared to play a particularly significant role in the

mathematics performance of Serbian girls. It appears that a close and supportive family environment is associated with Serbian girls' successful performance in mathematics. This relationship was not found among the American
girls. It may be, however, that for American girls the family participates in
their mathematics performance in other ways not measured in the present
investigation. Perhaps for these girls, more practical support from parents—
such as making sure homework is completed or meeting with school teachers—is more important to their academic performance (Galambos & Maggs,
1991; Steinberg, 1986). It also may be that for these middle school aged
American girls other social contexts—such as the peer group (Hill & Lynch,
1983; Simmons, Carlton-Ford, & Blyth, 1987) or classroom environment
(Eccles, Midgley, & Adler, 1984)—play an important role in their academic
development.

Clearly, the present study is only an initial attempt at identifying the
complex system of relationships between the individual-psychological characteristics and the social context that determines and/or discriminates between the mathematics performance of boys and girls. However, the results
indicate that this system is put into place before young adolescents enter
seventh grade, when, as the literature suggests, gender differences typically
emerge. Furthermore, the differences found between the American and
Serbian young adolescents lend support to the notion that if young adolescents' academic development and the disparate outcomes that occur are to be
fully understood, not only the proximal levels of young adolescents' social
context must be considered but also the more distal level of culture must be
taken into account (Bronfenbrenner, 1979; Lerner, 1991). This does not mean
that only comparisons of young adolescents from different nations must be
made. Within the United States, the consideration of cultural diversity also
is quite relevant. This diversity should be studied with vigor to understand
better the role of the context in an individual's academic development.

NOTES

1. However, as is the case with all studies using an existing data archive, the efficiency and
cost effectiveness of the present investigation must be counterbalanced by the fact that measures
present in an archive may ceteris paribus not be chosen to index constructs of interest when an
investigator organizes his or her own data set (Livson & Peskin, 1980).

2. One problem that confronts researchers doing comparative studies involving classrooms,
especially when the classrooms vary culturally, is the issue of standardizing grades. This issue
was at least partially obviated in the present study by the fact that in each school, both in the
United States and in Serbia, there was only one mathematics teacher. In addition, in Serbia the
educational system is highly centralized. All teaching activities are outlined by a governmental

committee so that all fifth and sixth graders are taught an identical curriculum. In turn, the American sample represents children drawn from three schools in the same school district in a small Pennsylvania town, whose socioeconomic status was rather uniform. Therefore, there was no reason to believe that the curriculum or the students varied greatly across schools within each culture.

3. Response frequencies on the four mathematics stereotype scale items were examined for those American boys and girls who did not perceive mathematics or mathematics-related activities to be a neutral domain (i.e., who gave the "both boys and girls" response). Results of one-way chi-square tests indicated that for two of the four items there were unequal frequency distributions due to a large proportion of "only boys" responses, χ^2 = 18.16 and 12.66, respectively, $p < .05$ in both cases.

REFERENCES

Armstrong, J. M., & Kahl, S. (1979). A national assessment of participation and achievement of women in mathematics. In S.F. Chipman, L.R. Brush, & D. M. Wilson (Eds.), *Women and mathematics, Balancing the equation* (pp. 59-94) Hillsdale, NJ: Lawrence Erlbaum.

Benbow, C. P., & Stanley, J. C. (1980). Sex differences in mathematical ability: Fact or artifact? *Science, 210*, 1262-1264.

Benbow, C. P., & Stanley, J. C. (1982). Intellectually talented boys and girls: Educational profiles. *Gifted Child Quarterly, 26*, 82-88.

Bigler, R. S., Liben, L. S., & Yekel, C. A. (1991). *The Occupations, Activities, and Traits Attitude Measure (OAT-AM)*. Unpublished manuscript, Pennsylvania State University, University Park.

Block, J. H. (1973). Conceptions of sex roles: Some cross-cultural and longitudinal perspectives. *American Psychologist, 28*, 283-308.

Boswell, S. L. (1985). The influence of sex-role stereotyping on women's attitudes and achievement in mathematics. In S. F. Chipman, L. R. Brush, & D. M. Wilson (Eds.), *Women and mathematics: Balancing the equation* (pp. 175-198). Hillsdale, NJ: Lawrence Erlbaum.

Bray, J. H., & Maxwell, S. E. (1985) *Multivirate analysis of variance*. Beverly Hills, CA: Sage Publications.

Bronfenbrenner, U. (1979). *The ecology of human development*. Cambridge, MA: Harvard University Press.

Brophy, J., & Good, T. (1974). *Teacher-student relationships: Causes and consequences*. New York: Holt, Rinehart & Winston.

Chandler, T. A., Shama, D. D., & Wolf, F. M. (1983). Gender differences in achievement and affiliation attributions: A five-nation study. *Journal of Cross-Cultural Psychology, 14*, 241-256.

Denich, B. (1977). Women, work, and power in modern Yugoslavia. In A. Schlegel (Ed.), *Sexual stratification: A cross-cultural view* (pp. 215-244). New York: Columbia University Press.

Dossey, J. A., Mullis, I., Lindquist, M. M., & Chambers, D. L. (1988). *The mathematics report card: Are we measuring up?* Princeton, NJ: Educational Testing Service.

Eccles, J., Adler, T. E., Futterman, R., Goff, S. B., Kaczala, C. M., Meece, J. L., & Midgley, C. (1985). Self-perceptions, task perceptions, socializing influences, and decision to enroll in mathematics. In S. F. Chipman, L. R. Brush, & D. M. Wilson (Eds.), *Women and mathematics: Balancing the equation* (pp. 95-122). Hillsdale, NJ: Lawrence Erlbaum.

Eccles, J., Midgley, C., & Adler, T. E. (1984). Grade-related changes in the school environment: Effects on achievement motivation. In J. G. Nicholls (Ed.), *The development of achievement motivation* (pp. 283-331) Greenwich, CT: JAI Press.

Ernest, J. (1976). Mathematics and sex. *American Mathematical Monthly, 83*(8), 595-614.

Fennema, E. (1974). Mathematics learning and the sexes: A review. *Journal for Research in Mathematics Education, 5*, 126-139.

Fennema, E., & Sherman, J. (1977). Sexual stereotyping and mathematics learning. *The Arithmetic Teacher, 24*, 369-372.

Fox, L. H. (1980). *The problem of women and mathematics: A report to the Ford Foundation.* Washington, DC: Library of Congress Cataloging in Publication Data.

Friedman, L. (1989). Mathematics and the gender gap: A meta-analysis of recent studies on sex differences in mathematical tasks. *Review of Educational Research, 59*(2), 185-213.

Galambos, N. L., & Maggs, J. L. (1991). Children in self-care: Figures, facts, and fiction. In J. V. Lerner & N. L. Galambos (Eds.), *Employed mothers and their children* (pp. 131-158). New York: Garland.

Harter, S. (1983). *Supplementary description of the Self-Perception Profile for Children: Revision of the Perceived Competence Scale for Children.* Denver, CO: University of Denver.

Harter, S. (1985). *Manual for the Self-Perception Profile for Children.* Denver, CO: University of Denver.

Hill, J. P., & Lynch, M. E. (1983). The intensification of gender-related role expectation during early adolescence. In J. Brooks-Gunn & A. C. Petersen (Eds.), *Girls at puberty: Biological and psychosocial perspectives* (pp. 201-228). New York: Plenum.

Hyde, J. S., Fennema, E., & Lamon, S. J. (1990). Gender differences in mathematics performance: A meta-analysis. *Psychological Bulletin, 107*, 139-155.

Joksimovic, S. (1986). Mladi u drustvu vrsnjaka [Youth in the company of their peers]. Belgrade, Yugoslavia: The Institute for Pedagogical Research.

Jovanovic, J., Lerner, R. M., Vucic, L., & Pavlovic, D. (1989, April). *Self-perceived competence and adjustment in early adolescence: A cross-cultural comparison.* Paper presented at the 1989 biennial meeting of the Society for Research in Child Development, Kansas City, MO.

Kaminski, D. M., Erickson, E. L., Ross, M., & Bradfield, L. (1976, March). *Why females don't like mathematics: The effect of parental expectations.* Paper presented at the meeting of the American Sociological Association, New York.

Kelly, A. (1988). Gender differences in teacher-pupil interactions: A meta-analytic review. *Research in Education, 39*, 1-23.

Kohn, M. L. (1987). Cross-national research as an analytic strategy. *American Sociological Review, 52*, 713-731.

Kurdek, L. A., & Sinclair, R. J. (1988). Relation of eighth graders' family structure, gender, and family environment with academic performance and school behavior. *Journal of Educational Psychology, 80*, 90-94.

Lerner, R. M. (1984). *On the nature of human plasticity.* New York: Cambridge University Press.

Lerner, R. M. (1986). *Concepts and theories of human development.* New York: Random House.

Lerner, R. M. (1987). A life-span perspective for early adolescence. In R. M. Lerner & T. T. Foch (Eds.), *Biological-psychological interactions in early adolescence* (pp. 9-34). Hillsdale, NJ: Lawrence Erlbaum.

Lerner, R. M (1991). Changing organism-context relations as the basic process of development: A developmental contextual perspective. *Developmental Psychology, 27*, 27-32.

Lerner, R. M., & Busch-Rossnagel, N. A. (1981). Individuals as producers of their development: Conceptual and empirical bases. In R. M. Lerner & N. A. Busch-Rossnagel (Eds.), *Individuals as producers of their development: A life-span perspective* (pp. 1-36). New York: Academic Press.

Lerner, R. M., Delaney, M., Hess, L. E., Jovanovic, J., & von Eye, A. (1990). Early adolescent physical attractiveness and academic competence. *Journal of Early Adolescence, 10*, 4-20.

Lerner, R. M., Lerner, J. V., & von Eye, A. (1988). *Early adolescent school achievement: Organismic bases* (Grant no. HD23229). Washington, DC: National Institute of Child Health and Human Development.

Linn, M. C. (1991). Gender differences in educational achievement. *Proceedings of the 1991 Educational Testing Service Invitational Conference: Sex Equity in Educational Opportunity, Achievement, and Testing*. Princeton, NJ: Educational Testing Service.

Linn, M. C., & Hyde, J. S. (1989). Gender, mathematics, and science. *Educational Researcher, 18*(8), 17-27.

Linn, M. C., & Peterson, A. C. (1985). Emergence and characterization of sex differences in spatial ability: A meta-analysis. *Child Development, 56*, 1479-1498.

Livson, N., & Peskin, H. (1980). Perspectives on adolescence from longitudinal research. In J. Adelson (Ed.), *Handbook of adolescent psychology* (pp. 47-98). New York: Wiley.

Maccoby, E. E., & Jacklin, C. N. (1974). *The psychology of sex differences*. Stanford, CA: Stanford University Press.

McHale, S. M., Bartko, W. T., Crouter, A. C., Perry-Jenkins, M. (1990). Children's housework and psychosocial functioning: The mediating effects of parents' sex-role behaviors and attitudes. *Child Development, 61*, 1413-1426.

National Science Foundation. (1988). *Women and minorities in science and engineering*. Washington, DC: U.S. Government Printing Office.

Noble, J. P., & McNabb, T. (1989). *Differential coursework and grades in high school: Implications for performance on the ACT assessment*. Iowa City, IA: American College Testing Program.

Olson, D. H., Portner, J., & Lavee, Y. (1985). *FACES III*. St. Paul, MN: Family Social Science, University of Minnesota.

Organization for Economic Co-Operation and Development. (1981). *Review of national policies for education: Yugoslavia*. Paris: OECD Publications Office.

Parsons, J. E., Adler, T. F., & Kaczala, C. M. (1982). Socialization of achievement attitudes and beliefs: Parental influences. *Child Development, 53*, 310-321.

Piaget, J., & Inhelder, B. (1956). *The child's conception of space*. New York: Norton.

Rohner, R. P. (1980). *Handbook for the study of parental acceptance and rejection*. Unpublished manuscript, University of Connecticut.

Rohner, R. P., Saavedra, J. M., & Granum, E. O. (1978). Development and validation of the Parental Acceptance-Rejection Questionnaire. *Catalog of Selected Documents in Psychology, 8*, 7-8.

Simic, A. (1983). Machismo and cryptomatriarchy: Power, affect, and authority in the contemporary Yugoslav family. *Ethos, 11*(1-2), 66-86.

Simmons, R. B., Carlton-Ford, S., L., & Blyth, D. A. (1987). Predicting how a child will cope with the transition to junior high school. In R. M. Lerner & T. T. Foch (Eds.), *Biological-psychological interactions in early adolescence: A life-span perspective* (pp. 325-375). Hillsdale, NJ: Lawrence Erlbaum.

Skolnick, J., Langbort, C., & Day, L. (1982). *How to encourage girls in math and science*. Englewood Cliffs, NJ: Prentice-Hall.

Smith, T. E. (1989). Mother-father differences in parental influence on school grades and educational goals. *Sociological Inquiry, 59,* 88-98.

Stallings, J. (1985). School, classroom, and home influences on women's decisions to enroll in advanced mathematics courses. In S. F. Chipman, L. R. Brush, & D. M. Wilson (Eds.), *Women and mathematics: Balancing the equation* (pp. 199-224). Hillsdale, NJ: Lawrence Erlbaum.

Statistical Yearbook of the Socialist Federal Republic of Yugoslavia: Volume 36. (1989). Belgrade, Yugoslavia: ISKRO.

Steinberg, L. (1986). Latchkey children and susceptibility to peer pressure: An ecological analysis. *Developmental Psychology, 22,* 433-439.

U.S. Bureau of the Census. (1990). *Statistical abstract of the United States* (119th ed.). Washington, DC: Author.

Uttal, D. H., Lummis, M., & Stevenson, H. (1988). Low and high mathematics achievement in Japanese, Chinese, and American elementary-school children. *Developmental Psychology, 24,* 335-342.

Woodward, S. (1985). The rights of women: Ideology, policy, and social change in Yugoslavia. In S. L. Wolchik & A. G. Meyer (Eds.), *Women, state, and party in Eastern Europe* (pp. 234-256). Durham, NC: Duke University Press.

Yee, D. K., & Eccles, J. S. (1988). Parent perceptions and attributions for children's math achievement. *Sex Roles, 19,* 317-333.

Reprint requests should be addressed to Jasna Jovanovic, University of Illinois, Champaign-Urbana, Division of Human Development and Family Studies, 1105 W. Nevada, Urbana, IL 61801.

Ethnic Differences in Adolescent Achievement

An Ecological Perspective

Laurence Steinberg   *Temple University*
Sanford M. Dornbusch   *Stanford University*
B. Bradford Brown   *University of Wisconsin—Madison*

Using data collected from a large sample of high school students, the authors challenge three widely held explanations for the superior school performance of Asian-American adolescents, and the inferior performance of African- and Hispanic-American adolescents: group differences in (a) parenting practices, (b) familial values about education, and (c) youngsters' beliefs about the occupational rewards of academic success. They found that White youngsters benefit from the combination of authoritative parenting and peer support for achievement, whereas Hispanic youngsters suffer from a combination of parental authoritarianism and low peer support. Among Asian-American students, peer support for academic excellence offsets the negative consequences of authoritarian parenting. Among African-American youngsters, the absence of peer support for achievement undermines the positive influence of authoritative parenting.

One of the most consistent and disturbing findings in studies of adolescent achievement concerns ethnic differences in school performance. Many studies indicate that African-American students "generally earn lower grades, drop out more often, and attain less education than do whites" (Mickelson, 1990, p. 44). Although less research has focused on direct comparisons between other ethnic groups, recent reports on adolescent achievement in America suggest that the performance of Hispanic adolescents also lags behind that of their White counterparts, but that the performance of Asian-American students exceeds that of White, African-American, and Hispanic students (see Sue & Okazaki, 1990). Despite the widely held assumption that ethnic differences in achievement are accounted for by group differences on other variables, such as socioeconomic status and family structure, research indicates quite clearly that these patterns of ethnic differences in achievement persist even after important third variables are taken into account.

Although there is considerable agreement that these ethnic differences in school performance are genuine, there is little consensus about the causes of these differences, and a variety of explanations for the pattern have been offered. Among the most familiar are that (a) there are inherited differences between ethnic groups in intellectual abilities, which are reflected in differences in school performance (e.g., Lynn, 1977; Rushton, 1985); (b) that

ethnic differences in achievement-related socialization practices in the family lead youngsters from some ethnic groups to develop more positive achievement-related attitudes and behaviors (e.g., Mordkowitz & Ginsburg, 1987); (c) that there are ethnic differences in cultural values, and especially in the value placed on educational success (see Sue & Okazaki, 1990, for a discussion); and (d) that there are ethnic differences in perceived and actual discrimination within educational and occupational institutions (e.g., Mickelson, 1990; Ogbu, 1978).

This article focuses on ethnic differences in school achievement, a phenomenon that, as a recent article in this journal put it, is "in search of an explanation" (Sue & Okazaki, 1990, p. 913). Because the genetic hypothesis has received so little support in studies of school achievement (see Sue & Okazaki, 1990; Thompson, Detterman, & Plomin, 1991), we focus instead on the various environmental accounts of the phenomenon. To do so, we present and integrate several sets of findings from the first wave of data collected as part of a program of research on a large, multiethnic sample of high school students. The research is aimed at understanding how different contexts in youngsters' lives affect their behavior, schooling, and development.

Overview of the Research Program

During the 1987–1988 school year, we administered a 30-page, two-part questionnaire with a series of standardized psychological inventories, attitudinal indices, and demographic questions to approximately 15,000 stu-

Lewis P. Lipsitt served as action editor for this article.

This article is based on an invited address by Laurence Steinberg to Division 7 (Developmental Psychology) of the American Psychological Association, Boston, August 12, 1990. Work on this article was supported by a grant to the author from the Lilly Endowment. The research described herein was supported by a grant to Laurence Steinberg and B. Bradford Brown from the U.S. Department of Education, through the National Center on Effective Secondary Schools at the University of Wisconsin—Madison, and by a grant from the Spencer Foundation to Sanford M. Dornbusch and P. Herbert Leiderman at the Stanford University Center for the Study of Families, Children, and Youth. The contributions of Nancy Darling, Sue Lamborn, Mindy Landsman, Nina Mounts, Phil Ritter, and Lance Weinmann are gratefully acknowledged.

Correspondence concerning this article should be addressed to Laurence Steinberg, Department of Psychology, Temple University, Philadelphia, PA 19122.

dents at nine different high schools. The schools were selected to provide a window on the contrasting social ecologies of contemporary American adolescents. They included an inner-city school in Milwaukee, Wisconsin, serving a substantially Black population; a San Jose, California, school serving a large number of Hispanic students; a small rural Wisconsin school in a farming community; a semirural California school with youngsters from farm families, migrant workers, and recently arrived Asian refugees; and several suburban schools serving mixtures of working-class and middle-class adolescents from a variety of ethnic backgrounds. All told, our sample was approximately one third non-White, with nearly equal proportions of African-American, Hispanic, and Asian-American youngsters—much like the adolescent population in the United States today (Wetzel, 1987). The sample was quite diverse with respect to socioeconomic status and household composition.

The questionnaires, which were administered schoolwide, contained numerous measures of psychosocial development and functioning, as well as several measures of social relations in and outside of school. The outcome variables fell into four general categories: *psychosocial adjustment* (including measures of self-reliance, work orientation, self-esteem, and personal and social competence); *schooling* (including measures of school performance, school engagement, time spent on school activities, educational expectations and aspirations, and school-related attitudes and beliefs); *behavior problems* (including measures of drug and alcohol use, delinquency, susceptibility to antisocial peer pressure, and school misconduct); and *psychological distress* (including measures of anxiety, depression, and psychosomatic complaints).

This outcome battery is more or less standard fare in the field of adolescent social and personality development. What makes our database different, however, is that it is equally rich in measures of the contexts in which our adolescents live. We have tried to move beyond the simple "social address" models that are pervasive in survey research, in which measures of the environment do not go beyond checklists designed to register the number of persons present in the setting and their relationship to the respondent (see Bronfenbrenner, 1986, for a critique of such models). Accordingly, our measures of family relationships include a number of scales tapping such dimensions as parental warmth, control, communication style, decision making, monitoring, and autonomy granting. Our peer measures include affiliation patterns, peer crowd membership, perceptions of peer group norms, and time spent in various peer activities. Our measures of extracurricular and work settings provide information on the activities the adolescents engage in outside of school. Our measures of the school environment concern the classes the adolescents are taking and the classroom environments they encounter. For each student, we also have information on the family's ethnicity, composition, socioeconomic status, marital history, immigration history, and patterns of language use. For some of these variables, the questionnaire data was supplemented with in-

terviews with both students and parents from a cross section of the schools.

Our large and heterogeneous sample permits us to examine a number of questions about the importance of contextual variations in shaping and structuring youngsters' lives and behavior during the high school years. Because the youngsters in our sample are growing up under markedly different circumstances, we can ask whether and how patterns of development and adjustment differ across these social addresses. Because we have detailed information on processes of influence within these social addresses, we can look more specifically at mechanisms of influence, both across and within contexts. And because we have information on more than one context in youngsters' lives, we can look at the interactions between contexts and how variations in the way in which contexts are themselves linked affect youngsters' development. Indeed, as we shall argue, ethnic differences in school performance can be explained more persuasively by examining the interplay between the major contexts in which youngsters develop—the family, the peer group, and the school—than by examining any one of these contexts alone.

Socialization of Achievement in the Family

According to familial socialization explanations of ethnic group differences of achievement discussed above, we should be able to account for achievement differences among ethnic groups by taking into account the extent to which they use different sorts of parenting practices. Although psychologists have only recently begun examining ethnic differences in adolescent development (Spencer & Dornbusch, 1990), interest among developmentalists in the relation between parenting practices and youngsters' school performance has quite a lengthy history (see Maccoby & Martin, 1983). This literature indicates that adolescent competence, virtually however indexed, is higher among youngsters raised in *authoritative* homes—homes in which parents are responsive and demanding (see Baumrind, 1989)—than in other familial environments (Steinberg, 1990). Presumably, better performance in school is just one of many possible manifestations of psychosocial competence. Researchers writing in this tradition have hypothesized that parental authoritativeness contributes to the child's psychosocial development, which in turn facilitates his or her school success (e.g., Steinberg, Elmen, & Mounts, 1989).

Recently, it has been suggested that three specific components of authoritativeness contribute to healthy psychological development and school success during adolescence: parental acceptance or warmth, behavioral supervision and strictness, and psychological autonomy granting or democracy (Steinberg, 1990; Steinberg et al., 1989; Steinberg, Mounts, Lamborn, & Dornbusch, 1991). This trinity—warmth, control, and democracy—parallel the three central dimensions of parenting identified by Schaefer (1965) in his pioneering work on the assessment of parenting practices through children's reports. These components are also conceptually similar to dimensions of parental control proposed by Baumrind (1991a, 1991b) in her recent reports: supportive control (similar to warmth), assertive control (similar to behavioral supervision and strictness), and directive/conventional control (similar to the antithesis of psychological autonomy granting).

The parenting inventory embedded in our questionnaire contained scales designed to assess parental warmth, behavioral control, and psychological autonomy granting. In our model, authoritative parents were defined as those who scored high in acceptance, behavioral control, and psychological autonomy granting. Not surprisingly, these parenting dimensions are moderately intercorrelated with each other and with other aspects of the parent–child relationship. For example, authoritative parents not only are warmer, firmer, and more democratic than other parents, but they are also more involved in their children's schooling, are more likely to engage in joint decision making, and are more likely to maintain an organized household with predictable routines. In view of this, we have used a categorical approach to the study of parenting, in which we used scores on each of our three dimensions to assign families to one of several categories. Using this general model of authoritative parenting, we have documented in several different studies that adolescents who are raised in authoritative homes do indeed perform better in school than do their peers (Dornbusch, Ritter, Leiderman, Roberts, & Fraleigh, 1987; Lamborn, Mounts, Steinberg, & Dornbusch, 1991; Steinberg et al., 1989; Steinberg et al., 1991).

Can ethnic differences in school performance be explained by ethnic differences in the use of authoritative parenting? According to Dornbusch's earlier work (Dornbusch et al., 1987; Ritter & Dornbusch, 1989), the answer is no. For example, although Asian-American students have the highest school performance, their parents are among the least authoritative. Although African-American and Hispanic parents are considerably more authoritative than Asian-American parents, their children perform far worse in school on average. Given the strong support for the power of authoritative parenting in the socialization literature, these findings present somewhat of a paradox.

One explanation for this paradox is that the effects of authoritative parenting may differ as a function of the ecology in which the adolescent lives. Some writers have speculated that parental authoritarianism may be more beneficial than authoritativeness for poor minority youth (e.g., Baldwin & Baldwin, 1989; Baumrind, 1972). To examine this possibility, we used three demographic variables to partition our sample into 16 ecological niches, defined by ethnicity (four categories: African-American, Asian-American, Hispanic, and White), socioeconomic status (two categories: working class and below versus middle class and above), and family structure (two categories: biological two-parent and nonintact; for details, see Steinberg et al., 1991).

After ensuring that the reliability of each of our three parenting scales was adequate in every ecological niche, we categorized families as authoritative or nonauthoritative. Families who scored above the entire sample median on warmth, behavioral control, and psychological autonomy granting were categorized as authoritative. Families who had scored below the entire sample median on any of the three dimensions were categorized as nonauthoritative. Consistent with previous research (e.g., Dornbusch et al., 1987), we found that authoritativeness is more prevalent among White households than minority households. Also consistent with previous work, we found that Asian-American youngsters are least likely to come from authoritative homes. Again, in light of the superior performance of Asian-American students, this finding runs counter to the family socialization hypothesis.

We contrasted the adolescents from authoritative and nonauthoritative homes within each niche on several outcome variables, including our indices of school performance. Across the outcome variables that are not related to school (psychosocial development, psychological distress, and behavior problems), we found that youngsters from authoritative homes fared better than their counterparts from nonauthoritative homes, in all ethnic groups. When we looked at youngsters' school performance, however, we found that White and Hispanic youngsters were more likely to benefit from authoritative parenting than were African-American or Asian-American youngsters. Within the African-American and Asian-American groups, youngsters whose parents were authoritative did not perform better than youngsters whose parents were nonauthoritative. Virtually regardless of their parents' practices, the Asian-American students in our sample were receiving higher grades in school than other students, and the African-American students were receiving relatively lower grades than other students. Indeed, we found that African-American students' school performance was even unrelated to their parents' level of education (Dornbusch, Ritter, & Steinberg, in press)—a finding that is quite surprising, given the strong association between parental social class and scholastic success reported in the sociological literature on status attainment (e.g., Featherman, 1980).

Glass Ceiling Effect

Why would authoritativeness benefit Asian-American and African-American youngsters when it comes to psychological development and mental health, but not academic performance? One possibility we explored derives from the work of urban anthropologist John Ogbu and his colleagues (e.g., Fordham & Ogbu, 1986; Ogbu, 1978). Ogbu has argued that African-American and Hispanic youngsters perceive the opportunity structure differently than White and Asian-American youngsters do. Because adolescents from what he has called "caste-like" minorities believe that they will face a job ceiling that prohibits them from "receiving occupational rewards commensurate with their educational credentials" (Mickelson, 1990, p. 45), they put less effort into their schoolwork. According to this view, the lower school performance of African-American and Hispanic youngsters is a rational response to their belief that, for them, educational effort does not pay off.

Although Ogbu's (1978) thesis has received a great deal of popular attention, it has been subjected to very little empirical scrutiny. The main tests of his hypothesis have come from ethnographic studies focusing on single peer groups of Black adolescents. Although important in their own right, these studies have not permitted the crucial cross-ethnic comparisons that are at the heart of Ogbu's thesis, because it is impossible to determine from these studies whether the beliefs expressed by the students in these samples are unique to minority adolescents. As several commentators (e.g., Steinberg, 1987) have pointed out, the notion that it is admirable to work hard in school is not widespread among contemporary American adolescents, whatever their color.

On one of our questionnaires, students responded to two questions designed to tap their beliefs about the likelihood of school success: (a) "Suppose you *do* get a good education in high school. How likely is it that you will end up with the kind of job you hope to get?"; and (b), "Suppose you *don't* get a good education in high school. How likely is it that you will still end up with the kind of job you hope to get?" Interestingly, responses to these two questions were only modestly correlated.

When we examined the correlations between our two measures of beliefs about the value of school success and our indices of school performance and school engagement, we found results that are generally consistent with one of the central assumptions of Ogbu's (1978) theory—namely, that the more students believe that doing well in school pays off, the more effort they exert in school and the better they perform there. Of particular interest, however, is the finding that the extent to which students believe that there are *negative* consequences of school failure is a better predictor of their school performance and engagement than the extent to which they believe that there are positive consequences of school success. That is, across ethnic groups, the more youngsters believe that not getting a good education hurts their chances, they better they do in school.

We then looked at ethnic differences in the extent to which youngsters endorse these beliefs. The results were quite surprising. We found no ethnic differences in the extent to which youngsters believe that getting a good education pays off. From the point of view of educators, the news is good: Virtually all students in our sample, regardless of their ethnicity, endorsed the view that getting a good education would enhance their labor market success. However, on the second of these questions—concerning students' beliefs about the consequences of not getting a good education—we found significant variability and significant ethnic differences. Much more than other groups, Asian-American adolescents believe that it is unlikely that a good job can follow a bad education. Hispanic and African-American students are the most optimistic. In other words, what distinguishes Asian-American students from others is not so much their stronger belief that educational success pays off, but their stronger fear that

educational failure will have negative consequences. Conversely, unwarranted optimism, rather than excessive pessimism, may be limiting African-American and Hispanic students' school performance.

We noted earlier that academic success and school engagement are more strongly correlated with the belief that doing poorly in school will have negative repercussions than with the belief that doing well will have positive ones. The pattern of ethnic differences on our measures of school performance and engagement is generally consistent with this general principle. In general, Asian-American students, who in our sample were the most successful in school and were most likely to believe that doing poorly in school has negative repercussions, devote relatively more time to their studies, are more likely to attribute their success to hard work, and are more likely to report that their parents have high standards for school performance. Asian-American students spend twice as much time each week on homework as do other students and report that their parents would be angry if they came home with less than an A−. In contrast, African-American and Hispanic students, who do less well in school, are more cavalier about the consequences of poor school performance, devote less time to their studies, are less likely than others to attribute their success to hard work, and report that their parents have relatively lower standards.

In sum, we found that students' beliefs about the relation between education and life success influence their performance and engagement in school. However, it may be students' beliefs about the negative consequences of doing poorly in school, rather than their beliefs about the positive consequences of doing well, that matter. Youngsters who believe that they can succeed without doing well in school devote less energy to academic pursuits, whereas those who believe that academic failure will have negative repercussions are more engaged in their schooling. Although African-American and Hispanic youth earn lower grades in school than their Asian-American and White counterparts, they are just as likely as their peers to believe that doing well in school will benefit them occupationally.

In essence, our findings point to an important discrepancy between African-American and Hispanic students' values and their behavior. In contrast to the differential cultural values hypothesis outlined earlier—which suggests that ethnic differences in achievement can be explained in terms of ethnic differences in the value placed on education—we found that African-American and Hispanic students are just as likely as other students to value education. Their parents are just as likely as other parents to value education as well. Yet, on average, African-American and Hispanic youth devote less time to homework, perceive their parents as having lower performance standards, and are less likely to believe that academic success comes from working hard.

These ethnic differences in student behaviors have important implications for how students are perceived by their teachers and may help illuminate the relation between ethnicity and student performance. A recent paper by George Farkas and his colleagues (Farkas, Grobe, & Shuan, 1990) helps to make this link more understandable. In a large-scale study of Dallas students, they found that teachers assigned grades to students in part on the basis of such noncognitive factors as their work habits. The lower relative performance of African-American and Hispanic students and the higher relative performance of Asian-American students may be in large measure due to differences in these groups' work habits, which affect performance both directly, through their influence on mastery, and indirectly, through their effects on teachers' judgments.

We noted earlier that our analysis of the influence of authoritative parenting on psychosocial development, including youngsters' work orientation, indicated similar effects across all ethnic groups. Because earlier work had indicated that work orientation is a very strong predictor of school performance, and authoritative parenting a strong predictor of work orientation (Patterson, 1986; Steinberg et al. 1991), we were left with somewhat of a mystery. Why should youngsters who say they value school success, who believe in the occupational payoff of school success, and whose parents rear them in ways known to facilitate a positive work orientation, perform less well in school than we would expect? For African-American students in particular, where was the slippage in the processes linking authoritative parenting, work orientation, and school success? To understand this puzzle, we turned to yet another context—the peer group—and examined how it interacts with that of the family.

Peers and Parents as Influences on Achievement

Many of the items on our questionnaire asked students directly about the extent to which their friends and parents encouraged them to perform well in school. We used a number of these items to calculate the degree to which a student felt he or she received support for academic accomplishment from parents and, independently, from peers. We then used these indices of support to predict various aspects of students' attitudes and behaviors toward school.

We found, as have others (e.g., Brittain, 1963), that although parents are the most salient influence on youngsters' long-term educational plans, peers are the most potent influence on their day-to-day behaviors in school (e.g., how much time they spend on homework, whether they enjoy coming to school each day, and how they behave in the classroom). There are interesting ethnic differences in the relative influence of parents and peers on student achievement, however. These differences help to shed light on some of the inconsistencies and paradoxes in the school performance of minority youngsters.

For reasons that we do not yet understand, at least in the domain of schooling, parents are relatively more potent sources of influence on White and Hispanic youngsters than they are on Asian-American or African-American youngsters (Brown, Steinberg, Mounts, & Phi-

lipp, 1990). This is not to say that the mean levels of parental encouragement are necessarily lower in minority homes than in majority homes. Rather, the relative magnitude of the correlations between parental encouragement and academic success and between peer encouragement and academic success is different for minority than for majority youth. In comparison with White youngsters, minority youngsters are more influenced by their peers, and less by their parents, in matters of academic achievement.

Understanding the nature of peer group norms and peer influence processes among minority youth holds the key to unlocking the puzzle about the lack of relation between authoritative parenting and academic achievement among Asian-American and African-American youth. To fully understand the nature of peer crowds and peer influence for minority youth, it is essential to recognize the tremendous level of ethnic segregation that characterizes the social structure of most ethnically mixed high schools. We discovered this quite serendipitously. To map the social structure of each school, we interviewed students from each ethnic group in each grade level about the crowds characteristic of their school and their classmates' positions in the crowd structure (Schwendinger & Schwendinger, 1985).

For the most part, students from one ethnic group did not know their classmates from other ethnic groups. When presented with the name of a White classmate, for instance, a White student could usually assign that classmate to one of several differentiated peer crowds— "jocks," "populars," "brains," "nerds," and so forth. When presented with the name of an African-American classmate, however, a White student would typically not know the group that this student associated with, or might simply say that the student was a part of the "Black" crowd. The same was true for Hispanic and Asian-American students. In other words, within ethnic groups, youngsters have a very differentiated view of their classmates; across ethnic groups, however, they see their classmates as members of an ethnic group first, and members of a more differentiated crowd second, if at all.

The location of an adolescent within the school's social structure is very important, because peer crowd membership exerts an effect on school achievement above and beyond that of the family (Steinberg & Brown, 1989). Across all ethnic groups, youngsters whose friends and parents both support achievement perform better than those who receive support only from one source but not the other, who in turn perform better than those who receive no support from either. Thus, an important predictor of academic success for an adolescent is having support for academics from both parents and peers. This congruence of parent and peer support is greater for White and Asian-American youngsters than for African-American and Hispanic adolescents.

For White students, especially those in the middle class, the forces of parents and peers tend to converge around an ethic that supports success in school. Working with our data set, Durbin, Steinberg, Darling, and Brown

169

(1991) found that, among White youth, youngsters from authoritative homes are more likely to belong to peer crowds that encourage academic achievement and school engagement—the "jocks" and the "populars." For these youngsters, authoritative parenting is related to academic achievement not only because of the direct effect it has on the individual adolescent's work habits, but because of the effect it has on the adolescent's crowd affiliation. Among White youngsters, authoritatively raised adolescents are more likely to associate with other youngsters who value school and behave in ways that earn them good grades.

The situation is more complicated for youngsters from minority backgrounds, because the ethnic segregation characteristic of most high schools limits their choices for peer crowd membership. We recently replicated Durbin et al.'s (1991) analyses on the relation between parenting practices and peer crowd affiliation separately within each ethnic group. Surprisingly, among African-American and Asian-American students, we found no relation between parenting practices and peer crowd membership. In other words, authoritatively raised minority youngsters do not necessarily belong to peer groups that encourage academic success. Those whose peers and parents do push them in the same direction perform quite well in school, but among authoritatively reared minority youth who are not part of a peer crowd that emphasizes achievement, the influence of peers offsets the influence of their parents.

In ethnically mixed high schools, Asian-American, African-American, and, to a lesser extent, Hispanic students find their choices of peer groups more restricted than do White students. But the nature, and consequently, the outcome of the restriction vary across ethnic groups. More often than not, Asian-American students belong to a peer group that encourages and rewards academic excellence. We have found, through student interviews, that social supports for help with academics—studying together, explaining difficult assignments, and so on—are quite pervasive among Asian-American students. Consistent with this, on our surveys, Asian-American youngsters reported the highest level of peer support for academic achievement. Interestingly, and in contrast to popular belief, our survey data indicate that Asian-American parents are less involved in their children's schooling than any other group of parents.

African-American students face quite a different situation. Although their parents are supportive of academic success, these youngsters, we learned from our interviews, find it much more difficult to join a peer group that encourages the same goal. Our interviews with high-achieving African-American students indicated that peer support for academic success is so limited that many successful African-American students eschew contact with other African-American students and affiliate primarily with students from other ethnic groups (Liederman, Landsman, & Clark, 1990). As Fordham and Ogbu (1986) reported in their ethnographic studies of African-American teenagers, African-American students are more likely than others to be caught in a bind between performing well in school and being popular among their peers.

Understanding African-American and Asian-American students' experiences in their peer groups helps to account for the finding that authoritative parenting practices, although predictive of psychological adjustment, appear almost unrelated to school performance among these youngsters. For Asian-American students, the costs to schooling of nonauthoritative parenting practices are offset by the homogeneity of influence in favor of academic success that these youngsters encounter in their peer groups. For African-American youngsters, the benefits of authoritative parenting are offset by the lack of support for academic excellence that they enjoy among their peers. Faced with this conflict between academic achievement and peer popularity, and the cognitive dissonance it must surely produce, African-American youngsters diminish the implications of doing poorly in school and maintain the belief that their occupational futures will not be harmed by school failure. This, we believe, is one explanation for the apparent paradox between African-American students' espoused values and their actual school behavior.

The situation of Hispanic students is different still. Among these youngsters, as among White youngsters, the family exerts a very strong influence on school performance and the relative influence of the peer group is weaker. Yet Hispanic students report grades and school behaviors comparable with those of African-American students. This illustrates why the influence of the family must be evaluated in terms of the other contexts in which youngsters are expected to perform. Although Hispanic youngsters may be influenced strongly by what goes on at home (at least as much as White youngsters), what goes on in many Hispanic households may not be conducive to success in school, at least as schools are presently structured. As is the case in Asian-American homes, in Hispanic homes, the prevalence of authoritative parenting is relatively lower, and the prevalence of authoritarian parenting relatively higher. In a school system that emphasizes autonomy and self-direction, authoritarian parenting, with its emphasis on obedience and conformity and its adverse effects on self-reliance and self-confidence, may place youngsters at a disadvantage. Without the same degree of support for academics enjoyed by Asian-American students in their peer group, the level of parental authoritarianism experienced by Hispanic students may diminish their performance in school.

Conclusion

These findings illustrate the complex mechanisms through which the contexts in which adolescents live influence their lives and their achievement. We began by looking at one process occurring in one context: the relation between authoritative parenting and adolescent adjustment. We found, in general, that adolescents whose parents are warm, firm, and democratic achieve more in school than their peers. At the same time, however, our findings suggest that the effects of authoritative parenting must be examined without the broader context in which the family lives and in which youngsters develop. Our findings suggest that the effect of parenting practices on youngsters' academic performance and behavior is moderated to large extent by the social milieu they encounter among their peers at school.

The nature of this moderating effect depends on the nature of the peers' values and norms: Strong peer support or academics offsets what might otherwise be the ill effects of growing up in a nonauthoritative home, whereas the absence of peer support for academics may offset some of the benefits of authoritativeness. Whether such offsetting and compensatory effects operate in other outcome domains is a question we hope to investigate in further analyses of these data.

We do not believe that we have explained the phenomenon of ethnic differences in achievement in any final sense. We do believe that the ecological approach, with its focus on the multiple contexts in which youngsters live, offers promise as a foundation for future research on this important social issue. Any explanation of the phenomenon of ethnic differences in adolescent achievement must take into account multiple, interactive processes of influence that operate across multiple interrelated contexts.

REFERENCES

Baldwin, C., & Baldwin, A. (1989, April). The role of family interaction in the prediction of adolescent competence. Symposium presented at the meeting of the Society for Research in Child Development, Kansas City, MO.

Baumrind, D. (1972). An exploratory study of socialization effects on Black children: Some Black–White comparisons. Child Development. 43, 261–267.

Baumrind, D. (1989). Rearing competent children. In W. Damon (Ed.), Child development today and tomorrow (pp. 349–378). San Francisco: Jossey-Bass.

Baumrind, D. (1991a). Parenting styles and adolescent development. In J. Brooks-Gunn, R. Lerner, and A. C. Petersen (Eds.), The encyclopedia of adolescence (pp. 746–758). New York: Garland.

Baumrind, D. (1991b). Effective parenting during the early adolescent transition. In P. A. Cowan & E. M. Hetherington (Eds.), Advances in family research (Vol. 2, pp. 111–163). Hillsdale, NJ: Erlbaum.

Brittain, C. V. (1963). Adolescent choices and parent–peer cross-pressures. American Sociological Review, 28, 385–391.

Bronfenbrenner, U. (1986). Ecology of the family as a context for human development: Research perspectives. Developmental Psychology, 22, 723–742.

Brown, B., Steinberg, L., Mounts, N., & Philipp, M. (1990, March). The comparative influence of peers and parents on high school achievement: Ethnic differences. In S. Lamborn (Chair), Ethnic variations in adolescent experience. Symposium conducted at the biennial meetings of the Society for Research on Adolescence, Atlanta.

Dornbusch, S. M., Ritter, P. L., Liederman, P., Roberts, D., & Fraleigh, M. (1987). The relation of parenting style to adolescent school performance. Child Development, 58, 1244–1257.

Dornbusch, S., Ritter, P., & Steinberg, L. (in press). Differences between African Americans and non-Hispanic Whites in the relation of family statuses to adolescent school performance. American Journal of Education.

Durbin, D., Steinberg, L., Darling, N., & Brown, B. (1991). Parenting style and peer group membership in adolescence. Manuscript submitted for publication.

Farkas, G., Grobe, R., & Shuan, Y. (1990). Cultural differences and school success: Gender, ethnicity, and poverty groups within an urban school district. American Sociological Review, 55, 127–142.

Featherman, D. L. (1980). Schooling and occupational careers: Constancy and change in worldly success. In O. Brim, Jr., & J. Kagan (Eds.), Constancy and change in human development (pp. 675–738). Cambridge, MA: Harvard University Press.

Fordham, S., & Ogbu, J. U. (1986). Black students' school success: Coping with the burden of "acting White." Urban Review, 18, 176–206.

Lamborn, S. D., Mounts, N. S., Steinberg, L., & Dornbusch, S. M. (1991). Patterns of competence and adjustment among adolescents from authoritative, authoritarian, indulgent, and neglectful families. Child Development, 62, 1049–1065.

Liederman, P. H., Landsman, M., & Clark, C. (1990, March). Making it or blowing it: Coping strategies and academic performance in a multiethnic high school population. Paper presented at the biennial meetings of the Society for Research on Adolescence, Atlanta.

Lynn, R. (1977). The intelligence of the Japanese. Bulletin of the British Psychological Society, 40, 464–468.

Maccoby, E., & Martin, J. (1983). Socialization in the context of the family: Parent–child interaction. In E. M. Hetherington (Ed.), Handbook of child psychology: Vol. 4. Socialization, personality, and social development. (pp. 1–101). New York: Wiley.

Mickelson, R. (1990). The attitude–achievement paradox among Black adolescents. Sociology of Education, 63, 44–61.

Mordkowitz, E., & Ginsberg, H. (1987). Early academic socialization of successful Asian-American college students. Quarterly Newsletter of the Laboratory of Comparative Human Cognition, 9, 85–91.

Ogbu, J. (1978). Minority education and caste. San Diego, CA: Academic Press.

Patterson, G. (1986). Performance models for antisocial boys. American Psychologist, 41, 432–444.

Ritter, P., & Dornbusch, S. (1989, March). Ethnic variation in family influences on academic achievement. Paper presented at the American Education Research Association Meeting, San Francisco.

Rushton, J. (1985). Differential K theory: The sociobiology of individual and group differences. Personality and Individual Differences, 6, 441–452.

Schaefer, E. (1965). Children's reports of parental behavior: An inventory. Child Development, 36, 413–424.

Schwendinger, H., & Schwendinger, J. (1985). Adolescent subcultures and delinquency. New York: Prager.

Spencer, M., & Dornbusch, S. (1990). Challenges in studying minority youth. In S. Feldman & G. Elliot (Eds.), At the threshold: The developing adolescent (pp. 123–146). Cambridge, MA: Harvard University Press.

Steinberg, L. (1987, April 25). Why Japan's students outdo ours. The New York Times, p. 15.

Steinberg, L. (1990). Autonomy, conflict, and harmony in the family relationship. In S. Feldman & G. Elliot (Eds.), At the threshold: The developing adolescent. (pp. 255–276). Cambridge, MA: Harvard University Press.

Steinberg, L., & Brown, B. (1989, March). Beyond the classroom: Family and peer influences on high school achievement. Paper presented to the Families as Educators special interest group at the annual meetings of the American Educational Research Association. San Francisco.

Steinberg, L., Elmen, J., & Mounts, N. (1989). Authoritative parenting, psychosocial maturity, and academic success among adolescents. Child Development, 60, 1424–1436.

Steinberg, L., Mounts, N., Lamborn, S., & Dornbusch, S. (1991). Authoritative parenting and adolescent adjustment across various ecological niches. Journal of Research on Adolescence. 1, 19–36.

Sue, S., & Okazaki, S. (1990). Asian-American educational achievements: A Phenomenon in search of an explanation. American Psychologist, 45, 913–920.

Thompson, L., Detterman, D., & Plomin, R. (1991). Association between cognitive abilities and scholastic achievement: Genetic overlap but environmental differences. Psychological Science, 2, 158–165.

Wetzel, J. (1987). American youth: A statistical snapshot. New York: William T. Grant Foundation Commission on Work, Family, and Citizenship.

JOURNAL OF RESEARCH ON ADOLESCENCE, 4(1), 21–44
Copyright © 1994, Lawrence Erlbaum Associates, Inc.

Explaining the School Performance of African-American Adolescents

Ronald D. Taylor
Department of Psychology and
Center for Research in Human Development and Education
Temple University

Robin Casten, Susanne M. Flickinger, and Debra Roberts
Center for Research in Human Development and Education
Temple University

Cecil D. Fulmore
Howard University

This study examined the hypothesis that African-American adolescents' school achievement is detrimentally influenced by their perception of a discriminatory "job ceiling" affecting their employment opportunities. As a consequence of these perceptions, African-American adolescents allegedly: (a) devalue the importance of educational achievements, (b) perceive that they have low academic ability, and (c) develop a social or racial identity at odds with academic achievement. These predictions were examined in a sample of 344 African-American and White students attending public and Catholic high schools. Results consistent with the model revealed that the more aware of discrimination the African-American adolescents were, the less important they perceived academic achievement to be, and the less engaged they were in their school work. However, the adolescents' awareness of discrimination was unrelated to their self-perceptions of their own academic abilities and their ethnic identity. Indeed, adolescents' ethnic identity was positively associated with their school achievement and engagement. Overall, the findings offer mixed support for the model.

Requests for reprints should be sent to Ronald D. Taylor, Departent of Psychology, Temple University, Weiss Hall, Philadelphia, PA 19122.

One of the most pressing issues confronting educators, researchers, and policy makers is the underachievement of African-American children and adolescents. Humphreys (1988) summarized data from past and recent large-scale surveys and showed that achievement differences between African-American and White youngsters begin in elementary school and persist throughout all grade levels. Indeed, a survey of 28,000 students in Maryland has revealed that by 8th grade almost half of the African-American and Hispanic students were performing below grade level and were not likely to catch up (Norman, 1988). The discrepancy between African-American and White achievement is especially distressing in light of current and expected shifts in the labor market toward jobs requiring higher skills and higher levels of education. The issue of minority education has ramifications beyond the life chances and well-being of minority individuals. Because minority youngsters represent an increasing segment of the population (Wetzel, 1987), and thus the future work force, issues like the production of goods and services in the United States and the competitiveness of the United States in world markets will undoubtedly be affected by the skills and competence possessed by minority children and adolescents.

A promising and increasingly popular explanation for the academic problems of African-American students has been the work of Ogbu and his associates (Fordham, 1988; Fordham & Ogbu, 1986; Ogbu, 1986, 1987). They suggest that the persistent underachievement of African Americans is in fact an adaptive response "to their limited social and economic opportunities in adult life" (Fordham & Ogbu, 1986, p. 178). African Americans represent a "castelike minority" (p. 178) because they were not incorporated into the country voluntarily and, as a group over time, have not had the same access as Whites to employment, education, political power, and places of residence. Low school achievement according to the thesis represents an adaptive response to the "requirements of cultural imperatives" (p. 178) that exist within the social contexts or "ecological structure" (p. 178) facing African Americans.[1]

---

[1]It is important to note that this research focuses upon central aspects of Ogbu's theory that pertain to the school performance of African-American adolescents. A comprehensive examination of the model requires, among other things, comparisons of the attitudes, beliefs, and school adjustment and performance of noncastelike subgroups (e.g., autonomous and immigrant minorities). Extensive comparisons of this nature are beyond the intent and scope of this study.

ECOLOGICAL CONDITIONS ASSOCIATED
WITH CASTELIKE STATUS

In this study, we examined the impact of adolescents' perceptions of a discriminatory "job ceiling" on attitudes and values relevant to their school achievement and engagement. Specifically, central among the components of the ecological structure that affect African Americans' schooling is a job ceiling. According to the hypothesis, African Americans face a job ceiling that limits their access to jobs, wages, and benefits appropriate for their level of education. This job ceiling "tends to give rise to disillusionment about the real value of schooling, especially among older children, and thereby discourages them from working hard in school" (Fordham & Ogbu, 1986, p. 179). Also, the job ceiling and other "discriminatory treatment" have a negative impact on African Americans' self-confidence and perceptions that they can compete with White Americans in important areas. Specifically, according to Fordham and Ogbu (1986), the experience of discrimination and a job ceiling "engenders among black [sic] Americans a feeling of impotence and a lack of self-confidence that they can compete successfully with whites [sic] in matters considered traditionally as white [sic] people's domain, such as good jobs and academic tasks" (p. 179).

Fordham and Ogbu (1986) suggested that discrimination and experiences, such as a limited opportunity structure and a job ceiling, also lead African Americans to develop an oppositional collective or social identity. A sense of collective social identity is proposed to develop from the belief that White Americans have acted purposely to limit the access of African Americans as a group to full and equal status as citizens. The oppositional identity is relevant to the schooling of African-American children because academic achievement is viewed as consisting of behaviors, activities, and symbols associated with White-American frames of reference. Thus, school learning is viewed as having detrimental effects on the social identity of African Americans. School learning is viewed as a "subtractive process" in which individuals must sacrifice something of their collective sense of identity in favor of cultural frames of reference having negative implications for individuals' self-perceptions. In essence, African-American adolescents' social identity and their school achievement are conceived as inversely related.

In sum, in the theoretical propositions examined here, it is suggested that in the ecological structure facing African Americans, discrimination, and in particular a job ceiling: (a) leads individuals to question the value of school achievement; (b) leads individuals to perceive that they have limited academic ability; and (c) gives rise to a social identity that opposes the identity of White Americans, including behaviors and values associated with academic achievement. Each of these three factors has a negative influence on African-American adolescents' school achievement.

Despite the growing popularity of Ogbu's theoretical model as an explanation for students' underachievement, research assessing the formulation is needed for several reasons. First, findings regarding the theory are inconsistent. For example, recent work supporting the model has shown that, to the extent that African-American adolescents believe that due to discrimination, the returns of school achievement are low, they tend to perform less well in school (Mickelson, 1990). Also, Dornbusch and Steinberg (1990) and Steinberg, Dornbusch, and Brown (1992) have shown that across ethnic groups, youngsters' school performance varies as a function of their belief that school achievement enhances their occupational success. Finally, the link between castelike status and lower school achievement has been revealed in cultures outside the United States (see Ogbu, 1987 for a discussion).

In contrast, however, findings inconsistent with the model also have been found. In addition to the findings just discussed and contrary to the formulation, Dornbusch and Steinberg (1990) found no evidence that "castelike minorities" in their sample (i.e., African-American and Hispanic students) were more skeptical about the value of schooling for their future than were other students who were not members of caste groups. Also, findings inconsistent with the notion that an African-American social identity has a negative impact on students' achievement also have been revealed. Bowman and Howard (1985) obtained evidence showing that parental support for the development of an African-American identity was positively associated with students' grade reports. Brown (cited in Spencer, 1987) suggested that racial consciousness and identification may entail feelings of pride and self-respect concerning the features and accomplishments of one's racial group. Ethnic identity development may be related positively to African-American adolescents' well-being and psychosocial adjustment and, hence, may positively influence their school performance.

Second, research on the components of the model are needed because the generalizability of the model is not clear. Like Fordham and Ogbu (1986), a portion of the data collected here was obtained from African-American students attending a predominantly African-American public school in a low-income area of a large city. However, as Fordham (1988) noted, data are needed on the application of the model to both African-American students attending school in other settings and other racial or ethnic groups. Therefore, in this study, data were collected from African-American and White students attending an urban Catholic high school.

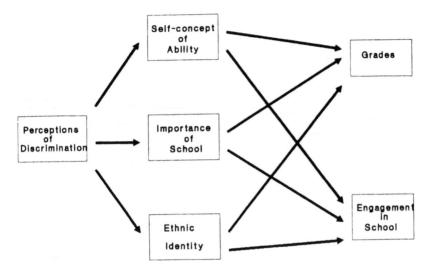

FIGURE 1   Conceptual model of the predictors of grades and school engagement examined.

Based on the components of the model discussed and examined here, we expected that (a) African-American adolescents' perceptions of the existence of a job ceiling would be negatively associated with their perceptions of the importance of school; (b) African-American adolescents' perceptions of a job ceiling would be negatively related to their perceptions of their academic abilities; (c) African-American adolescents' perceptions of a job ceiling would be positively associated with their ethnic identity development; and (d) African-American adolescents' perceptions of the importance of school, their perceptions of their academic abilities, and their ethnic identity would be significantly associated with their school performance and engagement. Data obtained from White students were collected to determine whether the components of the model operate similarly in groups other than African Americans. The components of the model discussed and examined here are illustrated in Figure 1.

METHOD

Sample

The students in our sample were from a public and a Catholic high school in a large northeastern city. The students from the public high school consisted of 69 male subjects and 95 female subjects, ranging in age from 14.5 to 19.7 years. According to school district data the total enrollment of the school was approximately 1,200 students, with the racial composition of the student population consisting of 2% White, 89% African American, 8% Hispanic American, and 1% Asian American. The actual racial composition of the public school sample, according to student self-reports, was Asian American = 3, Hispanic = 8, American Indian = 4, Mixed race = 14, and African American = 135. School district data also indicate that 60.1% of the students were from economically disadvantaged homes. The public school included in the sample was chosen because of the similarity of its population and neighborhood setting to the school included in the Fordham and Ogbu (1986) study. The sample, although not random, was appropriate for the research questions assessed in the study. Indeed, in many important criteria, (e.g., achievement test scores, socioeconomic make-up of the school), the school was highly similar to other public schools serving economically disadvantaged African-American communities in the city. All students in the school had as their first class a counseling and advisory period. School officials made available the identifying number of each advisory class. To ensure that all students were equally likely to be included in the sample, we selected students for participation by randomly selecting 6 of the possible 40 advisory classes. A comparison of the achievement test scores and grades of the participating students with the average scores for all students at the school on these measures revealed no differences.

We employed parents' education as a measure of respondents' socioeconomic status. Recent findings have shown that parental education is the most stable component of a family's social class (see Dornbusch & Steinberg, 1990, for a discussion). The public school students reported, on average, that their parents had completed high school. School district data revealed that parents' average educational level for the entire school was also the completion of high school.

The Catholic school students consisted of 89 male subjects and 91 female subjects, ranging in age from 12.91 to 19.08 years. According to school records the total enrollment of the school was approximately 1,500, with the racial composition of student population consisting of 65% White, 30% African American, and 5% Asian American. From the students' self-reports, the racial make-up of the Catholic school sample consisted of Asian American = 5, Hispanic = 2, Native American = 5, Mixed race = 7, African American = 60, White = 101. The Catholic school included in the sample was chosen because it tended to serve White and African-American families who were similar in socioeconomic status and whose status was roughly similar to that of the students in the public school. African-American and White families can afford to send the adolescents to the Catholic school in part because of the relative inexpense of Catholic schools in the city and because of financial assistance provided by the school. The Catholic school students were selected for participation in a manner similar to that used for the public school students. The identifying numbers of those classes designated as a first period study hall were made available to the research staff. Students were then selected for participation by randomly selecting study hall classes. A comparison of the grades of the participating students with the average grades for the entire school revealed no differences. Comparisons were also made to determine whether the academic tracks of students taking a first-period study hall differed in a systematic manner from that of other students. No differences were found. The parents of participants were, on average, high-school educated. The overall school average for parental education based on the entire school was also the completion of high school. Because the total number of individuals in other racial groups was small, our analyses focused on the African-American adolescents in the public school and both the African-American and White students in the Catholic school.[2]

Measures

Perceptions of a discriminatory job ceiling.   Our measure of the respondents' perceptions of discrimination consisted of Mickelson's (1990) Concrete Attitudes Scale. The Concrete Attitudes Scale ($\alpha = .67$) is a 6-item measure that assesses the extent to which the adolescents perceive that their family members have received jobs, wages, and promotions equitable to their level of education. We chose to focus on the adolescents' awareness of the experiences of family members, in particular their parents, because according to Fordham and Ogbu (1986), parents and peers are a primary source from which adolescents learn about the mobility structure operating in the African-American community. Also, given the adolescents' age and status, it was not likely that they would have had extensive experience applying for and

---

[2]There is a discrepancy between the school's reports of their racial composition and the students' self-reports of their ethnicity. In conducting our analyses we relied on the students' reports as a means of separating the students into groups because we believed that the students' self-reports were the better indicator of the students' self-conceptions and affiliations.

not receiving jobs for which they were educationally overqualified (i.e., directly experiencing a job ceiling). A sample item included: "Based on their experiences my parents say people like us are not always paid or promoted according to our education." Participants responded on a scale ranging from *strongly agree* (4) to *strongly disagree* (1). The items on the scale were summed to yield an overall score of the adolescents' perceptions of discriminatory treatment.

Perceptions of the importance of schooling.   The adolescents' perceptions of the importance of schooling were assessed using the measure of Social Bonding to School (Wehlage, Rutter, Smith, Lesko, & Fernandez, 1989). This measure (6 items, α = .76) assesses the value and commitment students have regarding school. A sample item includes "Success in life does not have much to do with the things studied in school." The response format for the scale ranged from *strongly agree* (1) to *strongly disagree* (4). The items of the scale were summed to yield a total score.

Ethnic identity.   The respondents' ethnic identification was assessed using the Multigroup Ethnic Identity Measure (MEIM; Phinney, 1990). The MEIM is a 27-item questionnaire, assessing three aspects of ethnic identity: (a) ethnic group identification, (b) ethnic identity development, and (c) attitudes and orientation toward other groups. In our analyses we used the ethnic identity development subscale (7 items, α = .80), which assessed the degree to which the adolescents have searched, explored, and finally developed a sense of commitment regarding their ethnic identity. An example of an item from the scale included "I have a clear sense of my ethnic background, and what it means for me." The items were scored on a scale ranging from *strongly agree* (6) to *strongly disagree* (1). For each respondent the items of the scale were summed and the average was calculated such that the respondents' scores represented the mean ethnic identity development score.

Self-perceptions of ability.   The measure of the respondents' perceptions of their abilities consisted of their response to the question of "How good are you in the following areas?" This question was asked for three course areas (math, English, social studies) required across all grades and at both schools. The response scale ranged from *very good* (4) to *very bad* (1). The respondents' scores across all course areas were summed to yield a single measure of their perceptions of their abilities.

School performance.   School performance was measured using the respondents' official grades taken from their school records for the three classes (English, math, social studies), which were required of all students across both schools. We also included measures assessing the adolescents' engagement in school (Dornbusch & Steinberg, 1990). These measures examined the degree to which students reported (a) spending time on homework assignments, (b) consistently attending class, (c) concentrating in class, and (d) paying attention to class work. The questions for these measures were asked about the three subject areas assessed in the study. A sample question included: "How often do you cut (an unexcused absence) each of these classes?" The possible responses ranged from *almost every day* (1) to *never cut* (4). A composite measure was created by summing across each question for each course area, and then adding these scores to obtain a single overall measure of engagement. The measure consisted of 12 questions with $\alpha = .86$.

Analysis Plan

The first step in the analyses was the examination of the effects of the demographic characteristics, race, social class, gender, and type of school attended on the independent and dependent variables. The components of the model assessed were then analyzed using a series of path models obtained using simultaneous multiple-regression analyses in which the respondents grades and school engagement were regressed on the components of the theory. This analysis first allows the examination of the effects of perceived discrimination on the variables (perceptions of the importance of school, self-perceptions of ability, ethnic identity) proposed to mediate the relation of discrimination to school performance and engagement. Next, the effects of the mediating variables on school performance and engagement were assessed. The path models were calculated for each subsample separately, and the demographic characteristics of age, socioeconomic status, and sex were entered into each equation to control for their effects.

RESULTS

Descriptive Analyses

Means, standard deviations, ranges of the measures, and correlations among the major variables are shown in Tables 1 and 2. In the first step of the analyses, the effects of race, social class, gender, and type of school attended on the students' scores on the independent and depen-

181

TABLE 1
Means, Standard Deviations, and Ranges for the Major Variables

Variable	M	SD	R
Public school African-American adolescents[a]			
Perceptions of discrimination	12.45	4.51	6–23
Self-concept of ability	12.03	2.17	6–15
Perceptions of importance of school	15.77	2.59	8–20
Ethnic identity development	3.67	1.07	1.50–5.87
Grades	62.41	31.56	47–71.66
School engagement	55.87	13.30	21–60
Catholic school African-American adolescents[b]			
Perceptions of discrimination	12.35	3.92	6–22
Self-concept of ability	12.30	2.00	4–15
Perceptions of importance of school	15.11	2.85	7–20
Ethnic identity development	3.88	.97	1.62–5.87
Grades	66.90	38.35	57.31–76.61
School engagement	58.61	11.21	38–60
Catholic school White adolescents[c]			
Perceptions of discrimination	12.08	3.48	6–20
Self-concept of ability	12.41	1.40	9–15
Perceptions of importance of school	15.01	2.72	7–20
Ethnic identity development	3.41	.84	1.12–5.37
Grades	81.67	29.48	67.38–98.78
School engagement	60.80	7.83	41–60

[a]n = 135. [b]n = 60. [c]n = 100.

dent variables were examined. Separate analyses were conducted comparing public school African-American adolescents to Catholic school African-American adolescents, public school African-American adolescents to Catholic school White adolescents, and Catholic school African-American adolescents to Catholic school White adolescents. This analysis permitted for the African-American students, in particular, the assessment of within-race effects of social class on the students' scores. The assessment of the independent and dependent measures was conducted in a 2 (Social Class) × 2 (Gender) × 2 (School) multivariate analysis of variance (MANOVA). The two social class categories were created by scoring those whose parents had a high-school education or less as 1 and those whose parents had more a high-school education as 2.

Significant multivariate effects were followed by univariate analyses of variance, and mean comparisons were made with Tukey B. The MANOVA comparing public school and Catholic school African-American adolescents revealed a significant overall effect of type of school attended, $F(6, 186) = 51.87$, $p < .0001$. Significant effects of social class, gender, and interaction were not found. Univariate analyses revealed that type of school attended had a significant effect on students' school engagement, $F(2, 191) = 4.08$, $p < .04$, with Catholic school African-American adolescents ($M = 58.61$, $SD = 11.21$) scores higher than those of public school African-American students ($M = 55.87$, $SD = 13.30$). As discussed earlier, significant interaction effects of the variables were not found.

The analysis comparing public school African-American students with Catholic school White students revealed significant effects for social class, $F(6, 256) = 2.12$, $p < .05$, and race/type of school attended, $F(6, 256) = 93.06$, $p < .001$. Gender and interaction effects were not found. Univariate analyses revealed that social class had a significant effect on adolescents' perception of a job ceiling, $F(2, 261) = 4.72$, $p < .03$, with lower social class students ($M = 12.45$, $SD = .35$) more likely to report greater awareness of the existence of a discriminatory job ceiling than higher social class students ($M = 11.82$, $SD = .38$). Also, social class had a significant effect on students' school engagement, $F(2, 261) = 6.00$, $p < .01$, with higher social class students ($M = 15.29$, $SD = .29$) reporting higher engagement in school than lower social class

TABLE 2
Correlations Among Major Variables

Variable	(1)	(2)	(3)	(4)	(5)	(6)
Public school African-American adolescents[a]						
1. Perceptions of discrimination						
2. Self-concept of ability	−.02					
3. Importance of school	−.28*	.12				
4. Ethnic identity development	.002	.21**	.07			
5. Grades	−.009	.31**	.13	.18*		
6. School engagement	−.07	.49***	.23*	.19*	.25**	
Catholic school African-American adolescents[b]						
1. Perceptions of discrimination						
2. Self-concept of ability	−.02					
3. Importance of school	−.34**	−.05				
4. Ethnic identity development	.07	−.07	.02			
5. Grades	.22†	.36**	.02	.11		
6. School engagement	.30*	.08	−.05	−.02	.16	
Catholic school White adolescents[c]						
1. Perceptions of discrimination						
2. Self-concept of ability	−.07					
3. Importance of school	−.06	.04				
4. Ethnic identity development	.04	.28**	.001			
5. Grades	.01	.22*	.30**	−.001		
6. School engagement	−.24**	.24*	.17†	−.18*	.31**	

[a]$n = 135$. [b]$n = 60$. [c]$n = 100$.
*$p < .05$. **$p < .01$. ***$p < .001$. †$p < .10$.

students (M = 14.21, SD = .32). Univariate analyses also revealed that race/type of school attended had a significant effect on school engagement, $F(2, 261)$ = 13.75, p < .04, grades $F(2, 261)$ = 53.95, p < .001, and ethnic identity development $F(2, 261)$ = 4.38, p < .05. The White Catholic school students (M = 60.80, SD = 7.83) had higher school engagement scores than the African-American public school students (M = 55.78, SD = 13.30). The White Catholic school students (M = 81.67, SD = 29.48) also had higher grades than the African-American public school students (M = 62.41, SD = 33.56). Finally, the African-American public school students (M = 3.67, SD = .08) had higher ethnic identity scores than the White Catholic school students (M = 3.41, SD = .08).

The scores of the African-American and White Catholic school students were also compared in a 2 (Race) x 2 (Gender) x 2 (Social Class) MANOVA. An overall effect for race, $F(6, 154)$ = 3.15, p < .05, was found. Univariate analyses revealed that race had a significant effect on the students' ethnic identity, $F(2, 158)$ = 10.35, p < .001, with African-American students' scores (M = 3.88, SD = 12) higher than White students' scores (M = 3.41, SD = .08). Race was also related to students' grades, $F(2, 158)$ = 50.80, p < .001, with African-American students' grades (M = 66.90, SD = 33.35) lower than those of White students (M = 81.67, SD = 29.48). The fact that social class had little effect on the measures was somewhat surprising, though perhaps explainable by the relatively narrow range of social classes represented in the sample. The upper bound of parents' educational level in the study was some college or completion of a 2-year degree. Few of the parents had completed 4 years of college, and fewer still had attended or completed professional or graduate-school programs.

Perceptions of Discrimination
and the Importance of Schooling

The next step in the analyses was to examine the path models examining the hypothesized relations between the independent and dependent variables. The first hypothesis examined was the prediction that the adolescents' perceptions of a job ceiling would negatively affect their views of the importance of school. For African-American adolescents in both school settings, support for this hypothesis was obtained. African-American public school (β = -.15, p < .05) and African-American Catholic school students', (β = -.26, p < .01), perceptions of a discriminatory job ceiling were negatively associated with their perceptions of the importance of school. White Catholic school students' perceptions of a job ceiling and their view of the importance of school were not related. These findings are shown in Figures 2, 3, and 4. The results of the overall regression

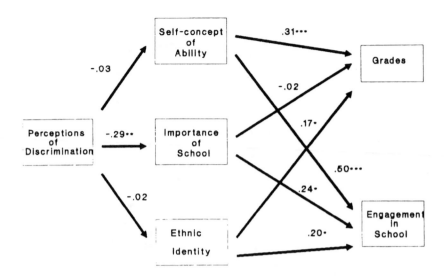

FIGURE 2 Predictors of grades and school engagement for public school African-American adolescents. * $p < .05$. **$p < .01$. ***$p < .001$. †$p< .10$.

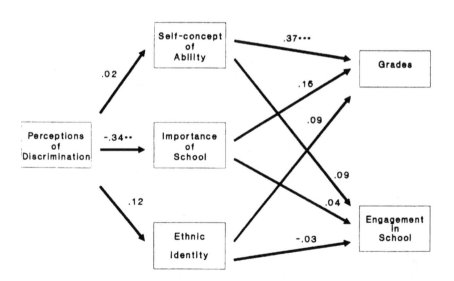

FIGURE 3 Predictors of grades and school engagement for Catholic school African-American adolescents. *$p < .05$. **$p < .01$. ***$p < .001$. †$p < .10$.

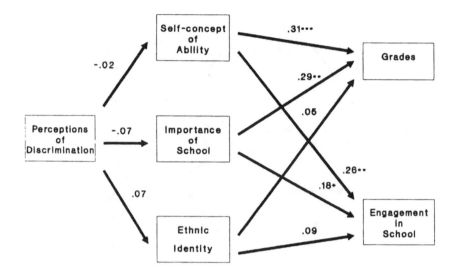

FIGURE 4 Predictors of grades and school engagement for Catholic school White adolescents. $^*p < .05.$ $^{**}p < .01.$ $^{***}p < .001.$ $^{t}p < .10.$

TABLE 3
Regression Model Predicting Students' Grades: Public School African-American
Adolescents

Independent Variable	B	β	T
Perceptions of discrimination	−.009	−.02	−.26
Self-concept of ability	.31	.31	4.12***
Perceptions of importance of school	−.29	−.02	−.28
Ethnic identity development	.39	.17	2.08*
Socioeconomic status	.01	.02	.32
Age	−.005	−.01	.90
Sex	−.16	−.04	−.50
Summary statistics			
Multiple $R = .41$			
$R^2 = .17$			
Standard error = 2.01			
$F(7, 127) = 2.86^{**}$			

$^*p < .05.$ $^{**}p < .01.$ $^{***}p < .001.$

TABLE 4
Regression Model Predicting Students' School Grades: Catholic School African-
American Adolescents

Independent Variable	B	β	T
Perceptions of discrimination	.11	.22	1.88[t]
Self-concept of ability	.37	.37	3.06**
Perceptions of importance of school	1.95	.15	1.11
Ethnic identity development	−.005	−.01	−.07
Socioeconomic status	−.003	−.01	−.05
Age	.01	.20	1.66[t]
Sex	.48	.12	.97
Summary statistics			
Multiple R = .51			
R^2 = .26			
Standard error = 1.84			
$F(7, 52)$ = 2.03*			

*$p < .05$. **$p < .001$. [t]$p < .10$.

TABLE 5
Regression Model Predicting Students' Grades: Catholic School White Adolescents

Independent Variable	B	β	T
Perceptions of discrimination	−.01	−.02	−.18
Self-concept of ability	.21	.31	3.06**
Perceptions of importance of school	.64	.29	2.61*
Ethnic identity development	−.13	−.05	.51
Socioeconomic status	.12	.19	1.87[t]
Age	−.87	−.30	−3.15*
Sex	.008	.18	1.88[t]
Summary statistics			
Multiple R = .47			
R^2 = .22			
Standard error = 1.86			
$F(7, 93)$ = 3.88**			

*$p < .01$. **$p < .001$. [t]$p < .10$.

analyses predicting students' grades are shown in Tables 3, 4, and 5.
The overall regression analyses predicting students' school engagement are shown in Tables 6, 7, and 8.

Perceptions of Discrimination
and Self-Perceptions of Abilities

The second hypothesis examined was the expectation that the perception of a job ceiling would negatively affect African-American students'
perceptions of their academic abilities. Support for this hypothesis was
not revealed in the analyses. There were no significant links between

TABLE 6

Regression Model Predicting Students' School Engagement: Public School African-American Adolescents

Independent Variable	B	β	T
Perceptions of discrimination	.11	.04	.49
Self-concept of ability	3.11	.50	6.41**
Perceptions of importance of school	1.22	.24	2.84*
Ethnic identity development	.39	.20	3.08*
Socioeconomic status	−.17	−.04	−.51
Age	.02	.07	.83
Sex	−1.56	−.06	−.75
Summary statistics			
Multiple R = .52			
R² = .27			
Standard error = 11.43			
F(7, 127) = 6.73**			

*p ≤ .05. **p < .001.

TABLE 7

Regression Model Predicting Students' School Engagement: Catholic School African-American Adolescents

Independent Variable	B	β	T
Perceptions of discrimination	.67	.27	1.92†
Self-concept of ability	.49	.09	.71
Perceptions of importance of school	.02	.04	.96
Ethnic identity development	−.53	−.03	−.07
Socioeconomic status	−.36	−.13	−.95
Age	.03	.11	.80
Sex	.18	.01	.95
Summary statistics			
Multiple R = .33			
R² = .11			
Standard error = 10.00			
F(7, 52) = .96			

†p < .10.

perceptions of a job ceiling and their perceptions of their academic abilities for the African-American public school students (β = -.03), African-American Catholic school students (β = .02), and White Catholic school students (β = -.02).

Perceptions of Discrimination and Ethnic Identity Development

The third hypothesis assessed was the prediction that the African-American adolescents' perceptions of a job ceiling would be positively

TABLE 8
Regression Model Predicting Students' School Engagement Catholic School White Adolescents

Independent Variable	B	β	T
Perceptions of discrimination	−.01	−.02	−.18
Self-concept of ability	1.53	.26	2.58*
Perceptions of importance of school	1.64	.18	1.84†
Ethnic identity development	.70	.09	.51
Socioeconomic status	.48	.18	1.74†
Age	−.008	−.04	−.43
Sex	.76	.06	.62
Summary statistics			
Multiple R = .41			
R² = .17			
Standard error = 7.81			
F(7, 93) = 2.83*			

*p < .01. †p < .10.

associated with the development of their ethnic identity. The data revealed no support for this hypothesis. For the African-American public school students (β = -.02), for the African-American Catholic school students (β = .12), and for the White Catholic school students (β = .07), perceptions of a job ceiling were not related to ethnic identity development.

Importance of Schooling, Self-Perceptions of Abilities, Ethnic Identity Development, and School Achievement and Engagement

The next hypothesis tested concerned the prediction that the variables mediating adolescents' perception of discrimination would be significantly associated with school performance and engagement. Specifically, the links among the adolescents' perceptions of the importance of school, perceptions of academic abilities, ethnic identity, and school achievement and engagement were examined. It should be noted that strong support for the model assessed here required that there be significant associations among the adolescents' perceptions of discrimination, the mediating variables (e.g., perceptions of the importance of school, perceptions of their academic abilities, and their ethnic identity), and the adolescents' school performance and engagement. Such links were evident in one instance. The African-American public school students' perceptions of discrimination and perceptions of the importance of schooling were significantly related, and in turn, their perceptions of the importance of school were significantly associated with their engagement in school (β = .24, p < .05).

Other significant relations among the three variables and the adolescents' grades and engagement revealed, first, that African-American public school students' perceptions of their academic abilities were significantly associated with their grades (β = .31, p < .01) and their school engagement (β = .50, p < .001). Similar findings were obtained for the White Catholic school students, in that their perceptions of their abilities were significantly associated with their grades (β = .31, p < .001) and their school engagement (β = .26, p < .01. A significant association between grades and the adolescents' perception of their abilities was also revealed for the African-American Catholic school students (β = .37, p < .001). Their perceptions of their abilities were not associated with their school engagement scores. The White Catholic school students' perceptions of the importance of school were significantly linked to both their grades (β = .25, p < .01) and their engagement in school (β = .18, p < .05). Finally, the public school African-American students' ethnic identity was significantly associated with both their grades (β = .17, p < .05) and their school engagement (β = .20, p < .05).

DISCUSSION

The main findings of this study concern: (a) the impact of adolescents' perception of discrimination on their perception of the importance of school, and in turn, the impact of their perceptions of the importance of school on their school engagement; (b) the influence of African-American students' ethnic identity on their schooling; and (c) the impact of school setting on adolescents' school performance and engagement. First, the results revealed that for African-American students, the more they perceived that discrimination negatively affects the employment opportunity structure, the less importance they attached to schooling. This finding is apparent for the African-American adolescents in both public and private schools. Lower class adolescents perceived that discrimination had greater effects than higher status adolescents. However, even when the effects of social class were controlled, these findings persisted. For the African-American public school students there was an additional finding, in that their ratings of the importance of school were significantly related to their engagement in school. Thus, the more these adolescents perceived that discrimination diminished employment opportunities, the less importance they attached to schooling, and in turn, the less engaged

190

they were in their school work. For these adolescents, school engagement and grades were positively related, thus indicating that their grades suffer as their school engagement lessens. It would be interesting to know whether there are such areas as adolescents' psychosocial adjustment (e.g., self-reliance, psychological distress, problem behavior) that are also associated with their perceptions of discrimination. It may be, for example, that to the degree that adolescents perceive that discrimination diminishes prospects for social mobility, they may be more likely to engage in delinquency or other problem behaviors that place them at greater risk for problems in school.

A second major finding of this investigation was the positive association of public school African-American adolescents' ethnic identity with their school performance and engagement. Thus, to the extent that the adolescents reported having a clear sense of ethnic identity, they were more likely to report that they engaged in behaviors conducive to school achievement, and they had better grades. This finding complements past results that have shown that parents' encouragement of children's ethnic identity development may also enhance children's school achievement (e.g., Bowman & Howard, 1985). It is curious that a similar finding was not apparent for the African-American Catholic school students. It is possible that, in the integrated, Catholic school setting, the expression of racial or ethnic sentiments were discouraged, either officially or unofficially among the students' peers and by school officials. Adolescent ethnic identity formation may represent an area of psychosocial adjustment for African-American adolescents, that for some students, in some settings, is associated with other areas of their competence, including their schooling.

A third major finding of this study concerned the effects of school setting on adolescents' achievement and engagement in school. In the Catholic school, both African-American and White students reported more engagement in school than the public school African-American students. It is possible, as Coleman and Hoffer (1987) have observed, that the involvement and commitment to schooling of families whose children attend Catholic schools were evident in how engaged the students were in their schooling. The grades of the White Catholic school students were significantly higher than those of the African-American public school students, although the African-American public and Catholic students' grades did not differ. Clearly, grading standards at the two schools may differ so that grades cannot be fairly compared. African-American Catholic school students, were they graded by the same standards as the African-American public schools students, might have had significantly higher grades. It is also possible that for African-American students, the benefits of attending a parochial school are apparent in other areas not assessed in this study—areas like adolescents' aspirations, persistence, or work orientation.

Finally, less focal results revealed that for all adolescents, their perceptions of their academic abilities were positively associated with their grades and (with the exception of the Catholic school African-American adolescents) their school engagement. The Catholic school White adolescents' perceptions of the importance of school were positively associated with their grades and engagement in school. This finding is similar to findings reported by Steinberg et al. (1992).

The results of this investigation offer mixed support for the components of the model examined here. Consistent with the model were the findings that adolescents' perceptions of discrimination, the importance they attached to schooling, and their school engagement were linked. Thus, the more aware adolescents were of discrimination, the less importance they attached to schooling, and in turn, the less engaged they were in school. This finding was apparent for the African-American public school students who were similar to students from Fordham and Ogbus's (1986) ethnographic work. For the African-American Catholic school students, the more aware they were of discrimination, the less importance they attached to school. However, their perceptions of the importance of school were not associated with their school achievement or engagement. This finding could be an anomaly, characteristic of the population of African-American students present in the Catholic school sampled in the study, given that other research has shown a link between African-American adolescents' perceptions of the importance of schooling and their school achievement (e.g., Steinberg et al., 1992).

Further support for the formulation was found in the absence of a link between perceptions of discrimination and the importance attached to school for White Catholic school students. Perhaps, understandably, White adolescents may not believe that they face discrimination in a substantial manner or that it affects their job opportunities. Or, even if they do believe that they face discrimination (e.g., White lower class adolescents), they may not perceive that the positive effects of an education are diminished or unobtainable.

Findings inconsistent with the model were also apparent. The lack of significant relations between the African-American adolescents' awareness of discrimination and either their ethnic identity or their perceptions of their academic abilities are not in line with the predictions from the model. In fact, as discussed earlier, for the African-American public school students, their sense of ethnic identity was positively associated with their school achievement and engagement. Based on these findings, there is some question regarding whether

African-American adolescents with the characteristics of the sample represented in this study develop a stronger sense of racial or ethnic identity as a consequence of their perceptions and awareness of discrimination. African-American adolescents' academic self-confidence also apparently does not suffer as a consequence of their views that there are capricious obstacles to their social mobility in the opportunity structure in American society.

Limitations

Several limitations of our research should be noted. First, the lack of additional findings consistent with the aspects of the model examined may be the result of differences in the methodologies used to conduct the research. Although Ogbu and his associates have employed ethnographic interviews as their principle means of data collection, survey questionnaires were used here. It might be argued that the issues addressed here, for minority youth, are not amenable to examination using questionnaire measures. This explanation is questionable, however, in light of the fact that similar and related issues, like adolescent competence and adjustment and parenting styles, are in fact measurable for African-American adolescents using several methods (e.g., Steinberg, Mounts, Lamborn, & Dornbusch, 1991). Such an explanation also, in fact, argues for research using a variety of methodologies to examine the question of the appropriate measurement approaches in this domain.

A second limitation of the investigation concerns the correlational nature of our study. Thus, it is impossible to know whether perceptions of discrimination lead adolescents to question the benefits of academic accomplishments, or whether adolescents' dim views of the usefulness of academic striving lead them to conclude that they are the victims of discriminatory treatment. Similarly, for the effects of the type of school the adolescents attended, it is possible that practices within Catholic schools contribute to youngsters' greater engagement and, for some, better grades. It is also possible, however, that better, more academically engaged students are more likely to select and remain at Catholic schools. It is also possible that these processes are simultaneously at work. Finally, regarding the direction of causality in the relation between the students' school performance and engagement and ethnicity, it seems clear how adolescents' ethnic identity might enhance their grades and engagement; it is less apparent, however, how these two variables would increase youngsters' ethnicity. Longitudinal data are needed to discover the causal direction of the relations found.

Third, a note of caution needs to be made regarding the nature of our sample and the implications of the results. Our data comes from working-class African-American and White youngsters from two separate school sites. We do not claim that these findings will hold true for middle-class African-American adolescents, middle-class White adolescents, adolescents from other ethnic or racial groups, or younger children of any background. Indeed, these findings may not hold true for working-class African-American adolescents in other school settings, whose characteristics differ from those represented in this study.

In addition, some might argue the adequacy of the measure of discrimination used in our research on the grounds that it does not directly address the issue of strictly racial discrimination. Such a critique appears questionable on the following grounds. First, we employ this measure because Ogbu and associates (Fordham & Ogbu, 1986) argue that adolescents acquire their knowledge of a job ceiling and discrimination from their parents and peers. The measure allows the adolescents to report both on their own knowledge and knowledge and perceptions acquired from their parents. Second, in data analyses currently being conducted in research assessing the psychosocial correlates of adolescents' perceptions of discrimination, we have found a correlation of .74 between the Concrete Attitudes Scale and a measure developed to assess adolescents' general understanding and knowledge of racial discrimination across racial groups (Taylor, 1992). The size of this correlation indicates that these measures overlap to a significant extent and argues for the adequacy of the Concrete Attitudes Scale as a measure of adolescents' perceptions of discrimination.

Implications and Directions for Future Research

In future research it is important to assess the broader effects of adolescents' perceptions of being a target of discrimination. It would be interesting to know, for example, whether the adolescents' perceptions of discrimination affect factors like their psychosocial adjustment. Specifically, adolescents who are more aware of discrimination may be more prone to experience psychological distress (depression and anxiety) and may be more inclined to engage in problematic forms of behavior. Adolescents' awareness of discrimination may also have a negative impact on their sense of self-reliance and autonomy. Indeed, it is possible that if adolescents are less self-reliant and autonomous, the more they perceive or experience the effects of discrimination, they may be more vulnerable to factors among their peers or in their neighborhoods that undermine their school achievement. These processes are similar to, but not identical to, those that Ogbu and associates stress as important. Also, the finding that public school African-American adolescents' ethnic identity development is positively associated with their schooling is an interesting initial finding. It is important now to understand the mechanisms through which ethnic identity development may operate to influence school performance and engagement. Further research on these and relevant issues is clearly needed.

The results also suggest that adolescents' understanding of discrimination and the opportunity structure may be important areas on which to focus intervention efforts for at-risk students. African-American adolescents rightly believe that there are obstacles to their social mobility. It is important, however, that they also understand that in terms of their long-term well-being, and in spite of the obstacles, the benefits of educational accomplishments still outweigh the costs of the lack of an adequate education. This is especially true in light of the changing nature of the economy in the United States. It is just as important to recognize that changes in the opportunity structure aimed at greater inconclusiveness of participation are also necessary. It is neither sufficient, nor perhaps moral, to change adolescents' attitudes when their attitudes may accurately reflect the reality of their lives.

ACKNOWLEDGMENTS

This research was conducted while Ronald D. Taylor was supported by a Post-Doctoral Fellowship from the Social Science Research Council.

We are indebted to Thu Tran and Chanta Chum for their assistance in coding the questionnaires, and Paula Boffa-Taylor for helpful comments on this article.

REFERENCES

Bowman, P., & Howard, C. (1985). Race-related socialization, motivation, and academic achievement: A study of Black youth in three-generation families. *Journal of the American Academy of Child Psychiatry, 24,* 134–141.

Coleman, J. S., & Hoffer, T. (1987). *Public and private high schools: The impact of communities.* New York: Basic Books.

Dornbusch, S. M., & Steinberg, L. (1990). *Ethnic differences in beliefs about the value of school success: An empirical assessment of Ogbu's hypothesis.* Unpublished manuscript.

Fordham, S. (1988). Racelessness as a factor in Black students' school success: Pragmatic strategy or pyrrhic victory? *Harvard Educational Review, 58,* 54–84.

Fordham, S., & Ogbu, J. (1986). Black students' school success: Coping with the burden of "acting White." *Urban Review, 18,* 176–206.

Humphreys, L. G. (1988). Trends in levels of academic achievement of Blacks and other minorities. *Intelligence, 12,* 231–260.

Norman, C. (1988). Math education: A mixed picture. *Science, 241,* 408–409.

Mickelson, R. A. (1990). The attitude–achievement paradox among Black adolescents. *Sociology of Education, 63,* 44–61.

Ogbu, J. (1986). The consequences of the American caste system. In U. Neisser (Ed.), *The school achievement of minority children: New perspectives* (pp. 19–56). Hillsdale, NJ: Lawrence Erlbaum Associates, Inc.

Ogbu, U. L. (1987). Variability in minority school performance: A problem in search of an explanation. *Anthropology and Education Quarterly, 18,* 312–334.

Phinney, J. S. (1990). *The multigroup ethnic identity measure: A new scale for use with adolescents and young adults from diverse groups.* Unpublished questionnaire.

Spencer, M. B. (1987). Black children's ethnic identity formation: Risk and resilience of castelike minorities. In J. S. Phinney & M. J. Rotheram (Eds.), *Children's ethnic socialization: Pluralism and development* (pp. 103–116). Newbury Park, CA: Sage.

Steinberg, L., Dornbusch, S. M., & Brown, B. B. (1992). Ethnic differences in adolescent achievement. *American Psychologist, 47,* 723–729.

Steinberg, L., Mounts, N. S., Lamborn, S. D., & Dornbusch, S. M. (1991). Authoritative parenting and adolescent adjustment across varied ecological niches. *Journal of Research on Adolescence, 1,* 19–36.

Taylor, R. D. (1992). [Adolescents' perceptions of discrimination: A comparison of measures]. Unpublished raw data.

Wehlage, G. G., Rutter, R. A., Smith, G. A., Lesko, N., & Fernandez, R. R. (1989). *Reducing the risk: Schools as communities of support.* New York: The Falmer Press.

Wetzel, J. (1987). *American youth: A statistical snapshot.* New York: William T. Grant Foundation Commission on Work, Family, and Citizenship.

Received January 6, 1992
Revision received October 30, 1992
Accepted May 24, 1993

JOURNAL OF RESEARCH ON ADOLESCENCE, 1(2), 135–154
Copyright © 1991, Lawrence Erlbaum Associates, Inc.

The Influence of Perceived Family and Personal Factors on Self-Reported School Performance of Chinese and Western High School Students

Doreen A. Rosenthal
The University of Melbourne

S. Shirley Feldman
Stanford University

This study investigated factors contributing to the school performance of first- and second-generation Chinese immigrant students and their Western peers in Australia and the United States. Chinese high schoolers of both generations reported that they put more effort into school than did the Euro-Americans and the Anglo-Australians and reported higher grades than did their American but not their Australian peers. Patterns of relationships between self-reports of educational outcomes and reported family and personal factors were similar across cultures and across generations of Chinese students. Moreover, these patterns were replicated in our Australian and American samples. The family factor most associated with both high achievement and greater effort was a demanding but nonconflictual family environment whereas a negative reaction by parents to school grades was associated with poor performance. The personal qualities of restraint and industry were both associated with positive educational outcomes. It was concluded that explanations of differences in the school performance of Chinese and Western students need to take other aspects of cultural difference into account.

The academic success of Chinese students and those from other Asian minority groups in the U.S. has been a consistent theme in the popular

Requests for reprints should be sent to Doreen A. Rosenthal, Department of Psychology, The University of Melbourne, Parkville 3052, Australia.

press (e.g., Brand, 1987; "Why Asians," 1986), and the superior performance of these students has been demonstrated in a number of studies (Dornbusch, Ritter, Leiderman, Roberts, & Fraleigh, 1987; Hirschman & Wong, 1986; Stevenson, Lee, & Stigler, 1986; Sue & Zane, 1985; Vernon, 1982). Although there has been little focus on the achievements of students of Asian descent in other Western countries, the few studies conducted in Australia confirm the academic success of Chinese students (Anderson & Vervoorn, 1983; Chan, 1987; Chiu & Tan, 1986; McAdam, 1972). Coupled with the greater academic achievement of Asian students in the U.S. has been research indicating that these children, as well as Asian students in their own countries, put more effort into school and academic activities than do their American counterparts (Chen & Stevenson, 1989; Dornbusch, Prescott, & Ritter, 1987; Stevenson & Lee, 1990; Stevenson et al., 1986). Linking these two sets of findings, it has been suggested, but not well documented, that in the U.S., the academic superiority of immigrant Asian students may decline over generations when assimilation into the mainstream culture results in less academic effort (Dornbusch, Prescott, & Ritter, 1987; Sue & Zane, 1985).

This research sought to confirm the differences between Chinese immigrant and Western youth on self-report measures of school performance and to investigate the factors associated with school success in these youth. Our central aim was to examine whether the patterns of relationships between school performance (achievement and effort) and perceived family environments and personal qualities are similar across cultures and whether length of residence in a Western culture has an impact on these relationships.

Most explanations of the success of Asian-American students have looked to cultural interpretations invoking characteristics of the traditional culture as the primary cause (Hirschman & Wong, 1986). For example, the Chinese culture has been typically described as embedded in the Confucian ethic in which education is valued as a means for developing fully as an individual (Bond & Hwang, 1986; Harrison, Serafica, & McAdoo, 1984), as collectivist rather than individualistic (Bond & Hwang, 1986; Hofstede, 1980), and as emphasizing conformity to adult demands (Ho, 1986; Vernon, 1982). Thus, Chinese students are assumed to bring with them values and behaviors from their culture of origin, some of which may be at variance with those of the host culture, but which converge to make educational objectives salient.

There are at least two shortcomings in evoking general cultural explanations for the better performance of Chinese immigrants in Western schools. First, we need to determine empirically that immigrants bring with them a culture that actually differs from the host culture in ways significantly related to educational outcomes. Although the Chinese culture and patterns of family functioning differ in significant respects from those of Western countries (Lin & Fu, 1990; Rosenthal & Feldman, 1990; Triandis et al., 1986), we do not know if or in what way these differences bear on the educational achievement of immigrant youth.

Second, we need to understand the processes or mechanisms which underlie cultural variation rather than merely documenting intergroup differences (Poortinga & Van de Vijver, 1987). Are the same processes associated with school-related objectives in Chinese and Western students, or are the processes different in the diverse cultural groups? We might speculate that some variables (e.g., valuing of education) would be associated with positive educational outcomes in both cultures. Other variables may be related to positive educational outcomes in one cultural context, and either unrelated or related to negative outcomes in another. For example, authoritarian parenting has been shown to undermine educational objectives in the U.S. (Dornbusch, Ritter, Leiderman, Roberts, & Fraleigh, 1987) whereas in the Chinese culture, where parents have a more authoritarian style of relating to children (Ho, 1986), negative effects may not be apparent (Harrison et al., 1984).

In this study we investigated two classes of variables, family environment and personal qualities, both of which are linked to cultural values. A considerable amount of research has identified family environment as a potent influence on school performance of both Western and Chinese students (see e.g., Emery, Weintraub, & Neale, 1982; Marjoribanks, 1987; Slaughter-Defoe, Nakagawa, Takanishi, & Johnson, 1990; Stevenson & Lee, 1990; Wood, Chapin, & Hannah, 1988).

There is evidence, too, that Chinese and Western families differ on beliefs specific to school outcomes. These include, in Chinese families, greater importance given to effort and diligence as a route to academic success (Chang, 1985; Chen & Stevenson, 1989; Dornbusch, Prescott, & Ritter, 1987; Hess, Chih-Mei, & McDevitt, 1987; Stevenson & Lee, 1990); higher levels of achievement motivation, aspirations, and expectations (Chan, 1987; Lin & Fu, 1990; Mak, Schludermann, & Schludermann, 1988); and more acceptance of responsibility for assisting children in their efforts to master school work (Chen & Stevenson, 1989; Stevenson & Lee, 1990). We might expect, as a result, that Chinese students would put more effort into school than their Western peers while Chinese parents would be more supportive than Western parents of their children's educational needs.

Although family beliefs and values may have a direct impact on educational outcomes, they may also be mediated through their effects, via child-rearing and socialization goals, on the personal development and adjustment of students. Personality studies of Chinese (Vernon, 1982) suggest that Chinese show relatively high levels of anxiety, deference, conformity, and order, and low levels of aggression and autonomy. This suggests that Chinese students would be more likely than their Western peers to show qualities of perseverance and concentration, and less likely to be aggressive and disruptive in school. Given the stress on conformity in the Chinese culture, we might also expect that these students would show less initiative than the Western students whose cultural milieu stresses autonomy and independence. Although we cannot predict the precise ways in which these personal qualities may relate to school outcomes in each culture, there is evidence from Western students that high levels of restraint (and low levels of aggression) are related to better school outcomes (Parker & Asher, 1987; Wentzel, Weinberger, Ford, & Feldman, in press). In addition, Kohn and Roseman (1974) found that two dimensions of social–emotional functioning that could be broadly defined as initiative and industry predicted school achievement in elementary school children.

In this study, then, we examined school performance and its correlates in Chinese and Western youth. Most cross-cultural studies of Chinese immigrant youth have involved comparisons only with U.S. youth and have investigated only one generation of immigrant youth (see, e.g., a review by Slaughter-Defoe et al., 1990). We extended this by including two generations of Chinese students so that the effect of length of residence in a Western culture could be explored. We also replicated our study in Australia, providing an opportunity to test the generalizability of Chinese–U.S. comparisons.

First we examined differences between Chinese immigrant youth of two generations and Western youth in self-reported school performance, family environment, and personal qualities. Second, we addressed the central issue of the research (i.e., whether the factors contributing to good school outcomes are the same or different across cultures and generations).

METHOD

Methodological Issues

In any cross-cultural study, it is important but difficult to achieve comparability of samples. In this study we aimed at comparability with respect to school systems within our two Western countries, age of students, gender composition, urban setting, and country of origin of our Chinese respondents.

A second important issue is the need to use measures which are cross-culturally valid. In this research we used measures designed originally for Western respondents, most of which had been used in earlier cross-cultural research (e.g., Dornbusch, Elworth, & Ritter, 1988; Dornbusch, Ritter, Leiderman, & Fraleigh, 1987) or had been normed on samples which included ethnic minorities (Moos & Moos, 1974).[1] We had two experienced Western-trained Chinese psychologists residing in Hong Kong check that our constructs had similar meanings in the Chinese and Western cultures (conceptual/functional equivalence, Hui & Triandis, 1985) and that the criterion of item equivalence (Hui & Triandis, 1985) was reasonably met.

The use of self-reports warrants some comment. Although respondents' honesty and objectivity in providing such information may be open to question, especially in reporting school performance, self-reports have been found to be reliable indices of psychosocial measures derived from the ratings of others (Lenerz, Kucher, East, J. V. Lerner, & R. M. Lerner, 1987). In particular, several studies have demonstrated the validity of self-reports of academic competence (Dornbusch et al., 1987; Lenerz et al., 1987; Stevenson & Lee, 1990; Talwar, Schwab, & R. M. Lerner, 1989). Nevertheless, especially in interpreting the contribution of home environment to school outcomes, we need to bear in mind that our data reflect respondents' perceptions of their environment rather than those of their parents or an external observer.

Subjects

Respondents, drawn from Melbourne, Australia and San Francisco, U.S., were participating in a larger study of the acculturation of Chinese immigrant families.

The Australian sample consisted of 16 year olds in Grades 10 and 11 of high school. There were 96 Anglo Australians (Australian-born adolescents of Anglo-Celtic descent), 62 first-generation Chinese Australians (adolescents born in Hong Kong or Canton of Chinese descent), and 34 second-generation Chinese Australians (Australian-born adolescents of Chinese descent whose parents were born in Hong Kong or Canton). All first-generation Chinese-Australian adolescents had been living in Australia with their families for at least 3 years and all Chinese respondents were fluent in English. Students were drawn from private and public high schools. In each school, all the Chinese-Australian students who were eligible participated, together with randomly se-

---

[1]For a more detailed discussion of family environment see Rosenthal and Feldman (1990).

lected Anglo-Australian classmates. Demographic characteristics of the groups are shown in Table 1.

The groups did not differ in grade level, family type, ratio of males to females, or father's level of education. Although there were differences on the remaining demographic characteristics, these were not expected to influence results given that the majority of respondents in each group were clustered within the same categories.

The U.S. sample consisted of 16 year olds of whom 149 were Euro Americans (White adolescents), 77 first-generation, and 64 second-generation Chinese Americans, all in Grades 10 or 11 of high school. All Chinese Americans were fluent in English. Most Euro-American students were drawn from a large, ethnically diverse suburban public high school. Chinese students were drawn primarily from three city public high schools, all of which had substantial Asian enrollment (i.e., approximately 40%). Demographic characteristics of the groups are shown in Table 1.

The American groups did not differ in age, ratio of males to females, or in father's work commitment. Differences in the remaining demographic characteristics were not expected to influence results once again, given the narrow range of categories into which most respondents were classified.

TABLE 1

Demographic Characteristics of the Respondents in the Australian and U.S. Studies as a Function of Group (in Percentage)

	Australian Study			U.S. Study		
	AA	CA2	CA1	EUS	CUS2	CUS1
Females	59	50	64	56	65	52
Intact families	83	94	91	58	89	84
First-born or						
second-born	76	78	78	78	70	61
Father full-time work	94	88	81	95	90	86
Mother full-time or						
part-time work	76	75	51	76	80	77
Father's education						
Primary (grade) school	1	3	8	0	5	14
High school	35	31	26	24	22	39
College/university	63	65	64	75	72	46
Mother's education						
Primary (grade) school	0	7	10	1	5	29
High school	51	50	44	26	34	38
College/university	48	43	45	72	60	32

Note. AA = Anglo Australian; CA1/CUS1 = First-generation Chinese Australian/American; CA2/CUS2 = Second-generation Chinese Australian/American; EUS = Euro American.

Measures

Students completed a battery of questionnaires in their classrooms during two sessions spaced 1-week apart.

Education measures. There were two measures relating to educational outcomes, achievement, and effort or engagement. School achievement was measured by asking respondents to describe the grades they had received so far in high school. Possible responses ranged from *mostly below D* (1), *mostly Ds* (2), *half Ds and half Cs* (3), to *mostly As* (8).

The effort students put into their schoolwork was measured by four questions: how hard they tried in class, *not at all* (1) to *extremely hard* (5); how much time they spent on homework each day, *none* (1) to *4 or more hours* (6); how often they cut classes, *almost every day* (1) to *never* (5); and the extent to which they paid attention in class, *never* (1) to *always* (5), with a low score indicating low effort. Each question was asked of four subject areas (mathematics, science, English, social studies) and responses to each question were averaged over the four areas. A composite score based on the total of responses to the four questions was computed and the resultant scale had satisfactory internal reliability (Cronbach's α = .62 and .68 for the Australian and U.S. samples, respectively).

Family measures. Two measures directly related to parental support for education: Mother's and father's involvement was assessed separately by a seven-item scale containing questions such as "How often does your mother (father) help with homework when you ask?" and "How often does your mother (father) go to school programs for parents?" Responses ranged from *never* (0) to *usually* (2) with the scales exhibiting satisfactory internal consistency (Mother involvement: α = .69 and .74; Father involvement: α = .68 and .74, for the Australian and U.S. samples, respectively). Because correlations between mother's and father's involvement were extremely high for both samples (r = .99), these measures were combined to form an index of parent involvement.

Following Dornbusch et al. (1988), students were given a list of possible parental reactions to good and poor grades, and asked whether parents responded in that way. Possible responses were *never* (1), *sometimes* (2), to *usually* (3). A principal component analysis yielded three parental reactions, consistent with those of Dornbusch et al.: (a) uninvolved (four items, e.g., parents do not know about grades); (b) punitive, negative response (three items, e.g., parents punish me); and (c) supportive, positive response (three items, e.g., parents encourage me). Scores for the three types of reactions to grades were calculated by giving items defining the factors unit weighting and summing respondents' scores for each factor.

In addition, students completed a battery of 18 questionnaires relating to home environment. The scales were derived from two sources: the 10 subscales of the Family Environment Scale (FES; Moos & Moos, 1974) and eight measures of parenting used by Dornbusch, Ritter, Leiderman, Roberts, and Fraleigh (1987). The FES measures included the following nine-item scales: Cohesion, Expressiveness, Conflict, Independence, Achievement Orientation, Intellectual–Cultural Orientation, Active–Recreational Orientation, Moral–Religious Emphasis, Organization, and Control. The Dornbusch measures included Monitoring of the Adolescent, Mother and Father Authoritativeness, Mother and Father Authoritarianism, Parental Involvement in Adolescent Decision Making, Acceptance of Diversity, and Emphasis on Conformity. These measures are reported in more detail elsewhere in a study of change in Chinese immigrant families' practices and functioning (Rosenthal & Feldman, 1990).

In order to reduce the complexity of the family measures, the multivariate analysis of variance (MANOVA) procedure was used to obtain an error-free correlation matrix for the scales (i.e., a matrix of correlations adjusted for group differences). A principal component analysis was performed on this matrix for the total sample. Following varimax rotation, only scales with loadings of .40 or greater and that loaded substantially on only one factor were selected. The result was that 16 of the 18 scales loaded on the factors. Raw scores on each scale were then standardized separately for each sample. We then gave unit weighting to the scales that were identified through the principal component analysis as belonging together and averaged these to form a composite.

The three composites were named and constituted as follows: (a) The Accepting–Engaged family factor consisted of Acceptance of Diversity (loading .70), Intellectual–Cultural Orientation (.70), Cohesion (.65), Active–Recreational Orientation (.62), Authoritative Mother (.50), Authoritative Father (.49), Independence (.49), and Expressive (.49). Alpha coefficients ranged from .73 to .80; (b) the Demanding family factor was comprised of Control (.75), Parental Involvement in Decision Making (.67), Conformity (.52), Organization (.45), and Achievement Orientation (.45). Alpha coefficients for the five-item composite ranged from .55 to .65; and (c) the Autocratic family factor, a three item composite, was comprised of Conflict (.71), Authoritarian Mother (.64), and Authoritarian Father (.57) with alpha coefficients ranging from .56 to .66.

Intercorrelations between the three composite measures were low to moderate: $r_{a,b} = -.08$; $r_{a,c} = -.27$, $r_{b,c} = .35$.

Personal development and adjustment measures. Three measures of personal qualities were also included as predictors of educational outcomes. The first of these was restraint (i.e., the extent to which respondents exhibit self-control and socially acceptable behavior, Weinberger, 1990). Respondents were asked to rate whether a statement corresponded to what they were usually like (e.g., "I have done some things that weren't right and felt sorry about it later"), ranging from *false* (1) to *true* (5), or how often they acted or thought in a particular way (e.g., "I lose my temper and 'let people have it' when I'm angry"), ranging from *almost never* (1) to *almost always* (5). Weinberger (1990) reported an alpha coefficient of .85 for his normative sample of adolescents.

The extent to which individuals demonstrate qualities of industry and initiative was assessed using two scales from the Erikson Psychosocial Stage Inventory (EPSI; Rosenthal, Gurney, & Moore, 1981). Initiative and industry are two of Erikson's psychosocial stages whose resolution is assumed to be achieved by adolescence. Each scale contains six items, for example, "I'm a hard worker" (Industry) and "I am able to be first with new ideas" (Initiative), which respondents rate from *hardly ever true* (1) to *almost always true* (5). Rosenthal et al. (1981) reported alpha coefficients of .79 and .81 for Industry and Initiative respectively for their sample of adolescents.

RESULTS

Results are presented in two sections. First, analyses of variance (ANOVAs) were conducted to address the question of cultural differences in educational outcomes. Sex was entered as a factor in order to check whether any Group × Sex interactions occurred. Similar analyses were conducted for the measures of parental support for education, family environment, and personal qualities. Second, the MANCOVA test of the parallelism of regression planes was used to address the central question of whether school outcomes showed similar patterns of relationships to family measures and personal qualities in two generations of Chinese immigrant youth and their Western peers.

The Australian and U.S. data are presented separately because the measure of achievement, school grades, is not comparable across the two samples (i.e., the scales used for the allocation of grades are different in Australia and the U.S.). Given these differences, there would be serious problems in interpreting main effects and interactions if location (Australia and U.S.) was entered as a third factor in the ANOVAs.

The Australian Study

Mean differences between groups. Differences between the three groups on educational outcomes, parental support for education, family environment, and personal qualities were assessed by two-factor, 3 (Group) × 2 (Sex), ANOVA. Mean scores, values of F, and results of post-hoc comparisons conducted on all pairs of groups are shown in Table 2.

The groups did not differ on achievement level but there were significant differences on effort. Post-hoc comparisons indicated that the first-generation Chinese Australians put more effort into schoolwork than did the Anglo Australians. Involvement in schooling was greater for Anglo-Australian parents than for the Chinese Australians, whereas mothers of second-generation Chinese Australians were more involved

TABLE 2
Mean Scores, Values of F, and Post-Hoc Comparisons for Education, Family, and Personal Measures by Group: The Australian Study

Measure	AA	CA2	CA1	F
Educational outcomes				
Achievement	6.67	6.65	7.07	2.38
Effort	16.41[a]	17.25[a,b]	17.56[b]	4.05*
Parental support for education				
Parent involvement	7.63[a]	6.30[b]	5.74[c]	10.73***
Parent reaction to grades				
Uninvolved	5.75	6.04	5.96	.69
Negative, hostile	4.28[a]	5.44[b]	5.02[b]	10.40***
Positive, supportive	7.69[a]	6.71[b]	6.63[b]	13.43***
Family environment				
Accepting–Engaged	55.0[a]	52.3[b]	52.1[b]	6.52**
Demanding	48.0[a]	54.1[b]	52.9[b]	17.38***
Autocratic	48.9	51.3	49.4	1.21
Personal qualities				
Restraint	3.60	3.54	3.61	.50
Initiative	3.74	3.60	3.53	2.34
Industry	3.60	3.67	3.51	.47

Note. AA = Anglo Australian; CA2 = second-generation Chinese Australian; CA1 = First-generation Chinese Australian. Entries that share a superscript do not differ significantly from each other on post-hoc comparisons ($p < .05$).
$*p < .05. **p < .01. ***p < .001.$

than were mothers of the first-generation group. Anglo-Australian parents were less likely to react negatively to their adolescent's school grades and were more supportive than were the Chinese-Australian parents. There were no significant Group × Sex interactions on any educational measures. Anglo-Australian adolescents perceived their family environment as significantly more accepting–engaged and less demanding than did their Chinese peers.[2] There were no significant differences between the groups on autocratic family environment or on the personal qualities of restraint, initiative, and industry.

In summary, there were no differences between the first- and second-generation Chinese Australians on any measure and on most measures the Anglo Australians differed from one or both Chinese groups.

Group differences in patterning of relationships. The central focus of this study was whether educational outcomes showed similar nomological networks (i.e., patterns of relationships with family and personal measures) among Chinese immigrant and Western youth. We examined this issue first by conducting multiple regressions for each of the school outcome measures to determine the extent to which family and personal variables accounted for the variance in school outcomes. Analyses were conducted separately for each group, and, given the relatively small sample sizes, we also conducted separate analyses for family and for personal variables. Following these analyses, we compared the slopes of the regression planes generated for each of the three groups using an analysis of covariance (ANCOVA) procedure. This test indicated that the assumption of parallel or homogeneous slopes was supported (i.e., the patterning of predictors, both family and personal, was similar across groups). Consequently we pooled the data for the three groups and carried out two further multiple regressions for each of the two educational outcomes. In the first, family variables were entered as predictors whereas in the second, the predictors were personal variables. Standardized regression weights (betas) for the predictors together with R^2 are summarized in Table 3.

Family variables accounted for relatively high levels of the variance in achievement, whereas personal variables accounted for less variance in both educational outcomes. Of the family measures, achievement was best predicted by the absence of a negative, punitive reaction to grades. Other predictors of high achievement were a demanding family environment, high levels of parental involvement, and, somewhat curiously, an unresponsiveness or uninvolved reaction to grades, that is not

---

[2]The original normative sample (Moos & Moos, 1974) included Blacks and Hispanics but not Asian-Americans.

TABLE 3
Beta Weights for Predictors of Achievement and Effort in the Australian
and U.S. Samples

Measures	Australia		U.S.	
	Achievement	Effort	Achievement	Effort
Family measures				
Accepting–Engaged	.04	−.10	.24****	.23****
Demanding	.23***	.33****	.19***	.24****
Autocratic	−.05	−.06	.00	−.02
Unresponsive to grades	.22***	.01	.16***	.03
Negative reaction to grades	−.40****	−.19**	−.23****	−.20***
Positive reaction to grades	−.12	−.06	−.01	−.08
Parent involvement	.23***	.11	.01	.02
R^2	.21	.11	.12	.11
Personal measures				
Restraint	.14**	.18***	.11*	.24****
Initiative	.06	−.15***	−.08	−.10*
Industry	.24***	.32****	.36****	.39****
R^2	.11	.14	.15	.24

$*p < .10. **p < .05. ***p < .01. ****p < .001.$

acknowledging performance as good or bad. Industry and, to a lesser extent, restraint were the personal qualities which significantly predicted achievement. A demanding family environment was significantly predictive of effort whereas a negative reaction to grades predicted lower levels of effort. Restraint and industry positively predicted effort whereas lack of initiative was, unexpectedly, associated with higher levels of effort.

The parallelism of regression planes suggested that group membership had little differential impact on the patterning of predictors of achievement and effort. The relationship of school outcomes to family and personal measures did not differ with cultural background or length of residence in Australia.

The U.S. Study

Mean differences between groups.   The major findings of the Australian study were replicated in the U.S. sample (see Table 4) except that, in addition, there was a significant difference between the U.S. groups on achievement. Euro Americans reported lower levels of achievement and less effort than did either of the Chinese-American groups. The first- and second-generation Chinese Americans did not differ on either of these measures.

There were significant differences between each of the groups on all

TABLE 4

Mean Scores, Values of F, and Post-Hoc Comparisons for Education, Family, and Personal Measures by Group: The U.S. Study

Measure	EUS	CUS2	CUS1	F
Educational outcomes				
Achievement	5.77[a]	6.70[b]	6.61[b]	16.05***
Effort	15.71[a]	16.74[b]	16.48[b]	4.06*
Parental support for education				
Parent involvement	7.49[a]	5.67[b]	4.13[c]	41.53***
Parent reaction to grades				
Uninvolved	5.46[a]	5.89[b]	6.86[c]	20.09***
Negative, hostile	7.71[a]	7.16[b]	6.18[c]	27.67***
Positive, supportive	5.66	5.59	5.93	0.58
Family environment				
Accepting–Engaged	53.8[a]	51.3[b]	49.5[b]	14.99***
Demanding	49.9[a]	52.5[a,b]	53.1[b]	8.96***
Autocratic	48.9[b]	50.5[b]	51.0[b]	3.70*
Personal qualities				
Restraint	3.61	3.48	3.72	2.45
Initiative	3.71[a]	3.23[c]	3.46[b]	17.49***
Industry	3.57	3.43	3.50	1.13

Note. EUS = Euro American; CUS2 = Second-generation Chinese American; CUS1 = First-generation Chinese American. Entries which share identical superscripts do not differ significantly from each other on post-hoc comparisons ($p < .05$).
*$p < .05$. **$p < .01$. ***$p < .001$.

parental measures except supportive reaction to grades. Euro-American parents were most involved, were least likely not to react to grades, and were most likely to react in a hostile fashion. Conversely, the parents of first-generation Chinese Americans were least involved, were most likely to be unresponsive to grades, and were least likely to be hostile. There were no significant Sex × Group interactions.

The Euro Americans perceived their families as significantly more accepting–engaged and less demanding and autocratic than did their Chinese peers. In addition, Chinese students had significantly lower scores on initiative than did the Euro Americans. As in the Australian study, the White students differed from one or both Chinese groups on most measures.

Group differences in patterning of relationships. A test of the parallelism of regression planes which indicated that there were no significant differences between the three groups in the patterning of predictors of either achievement or effort. Multiple regressions on the pooled data for the three groups are reported in Table 3 where it can be seen that there are close parallels with the Australian results, although family measures accounted for relatively less variance in achievement, and personal qualities accounted for relatively more variance in effort for the U.S. than the Australian sample. The major differences, however, were that an accepting–engaged family environment was highly predictive of both achievement and effort for these American students whereas parent involvement in education no longer predicted achievement significantly. As a final step, we tested whether the patterns of predictors of achievement and effort were similar across the two samples. In all four cases reported in Table 3, the assumption of parallel slopes was met. Thus, for both achievement and effort, the relationships with family and personal measures were the same for our Australian and U.S. samples.

DISCUSSION

Our results confirmed that differences exist between these Chinese immigrant and Western youth on self-report measures of school effort, and, to a lesser extent, grades and on factors which were assumed to support or undermine educational outcomes. Moreover, those factors which were associated with good outcomes in two Western cultures were similar to those in two generations of Chinese immigrants. Bearing in mind the methodological considerations raised earlier, we can draw some interesting conclusions from this research.

As predicted, Chinese students report putting more effort into academic activities than their Western peers in both samples, but only in the U.S. did they report higher levels of academic achievement. This latter finding may be due to the particular Australian school population sampled. Most Australian respondents were enrolled at private schools or special high schools drawing on populations where expectations of academic achievement are high for all students, including non-Chinese. This was not the case for the U.S. sample which was drawn primarily from schools in the public school system. Given the importance of academic achievement and greater expectations of such achievement among Chinese parents relative to their American peers (Stevenson & Lee, 1990), Chinese students in these American schools may have an advantage over their Western peers.

Speculation about less positive educational outcomes in longer term immigrants was, in general, not confirmed. Although Dornbusch, Prescott, and Ritter (1987) reported a decrease in effort across three generations for their sample of Chinese students and a nonsignificant trend for this to occur with achievement, examination of their findings reveals no differences between first- and second-generation students. In their sample, change occurs in the third generation. Clearly the question of erosion of academic achievement and effort in third- and subsequent generations warrants further investigation. We speculate, however, that the view held of the Chinese as a model minority would lead to continuing expectations of high achievement, expectations that would persist for this visible minority irrespective of length of residence in a Western culture.

We found group differences in perceived parental support for education with evidence for differences between generations in the American sample only. Contrary to our predictions and some (Stevenson & Lee, 1990) but not other research (Yao, 1985), the perception of parents' involvement in education was higher among Western than Chinese students, with greater support for the second-generation Chinese students (although not significantly so for the Australian sample). There are a number of possible reasons for these findings. First, Chinese parents may have less facility with English and thus difficulty in providing assistance to their student children. Chinese parents may be less likely to interact with school personnel because of language difficulties or cultural barriers. Second, although Chinese parents may be more helpful to young children than Western parents (Stevenson & Lee, 1990), they expect adolescents to be mature and thus more independent. Third, our measure of help and involvement may indeed have a Western bias. Rather than helping with homework or attending school meetings, Chinese parents may support their childrens' academic activities by, for example, providing books or a room for study or by relieving them of household or other chores.

Perceptions of parents' reactions to school grades took different forms in the two cultures. Anglo-Australian parents were perceived as offering more positive support while Chinese parents reacted negatively, either by punishing students for poor grades or exhorting them to do better if they achieved good grades. In the U.S., however, it was the Euro-American parents more than the Chinese who were perceived to adopt this negative response while Chinese parents were more likely than their Western peers to be unresponsive and uninvolved. It is unclear why these differences across samples occurred. Negative responses to grades may derive from Chinese parents' greater expectations for academic achievement and their belief in the importance of hard work as a basis for this achievement (Stevenson & Lee, 1990). On the other hand, unresponsive attitude to grades may be due to a cultural belief in emotional restraint and modesty.

Turning to the central issue of the research, in exploring the factors which support or undermine educational outcomes, we questioned whether there would be different patterns of relationships with educational outcomes for our Western and Chinese students. We found that

the factors which influenced these outcomes were remarkably consistent, not only across our Western and Chinese groups but also in our
Australian and American samples. This similarity in nomological networks (i.e., in patterns of associations) is in fact good evidence according to Hui and Triandis (1985) for the cross-cultural equivalence of
the constructs measured.

Of the family measures, not unexpectedly, a family environment,
which was perceived to be organized and focused on achievement in the
context of control without conflict, a demanding environment, was
strongly associated with positive achievement and greater effort. Conversely, parents who were perceived to react negatively to school grades
had lower achieving and less effortful students. Thus, our results are
consistent with those reported by Dornbusch et al. (1988). Coupled with
the relatively poor predictive power both of the measures of parents'
involvement in school and of parents' positive reaction to grades, this
suggests that supportive parental behavior targeted specifically at the
educational context has less impact than does negative, punitive behavior.

It is not possible, of course, to determine unequivocally whether
negative parental responses to grades contribute to or are a consequence
of poor student performance. However, the former interpretation may
be more accurate because parents were perceived to respond in this way
to good as well as to poor grades. Furthermore, Dornbusch et al. (1988)
found that a negative reaction to poor grades by parents was associated
with subsequent poorer student performance.

The relationship between educational outcomes and restraint and
industry is consistent with earlier research with Western students (Kohn
& Roseman, 1974; Parker & Asher, 1987; Wentzel et al., in press), but
the linking of initiative with less effort is surprising. Inspection of items
on the initiative scale suggests that low scores reflect a conformity which
may, in fact, fit well with school demands (e.g., paying attention in class
or doing one's homework).

One clear finding is that our results are not consistent with an
individual-level approach to cultural differences (Leung, 1989), where
the aim is to identify a common set of factors or antecedents that
accounts for both individual differences within a culture as well as
intergroup differences in outcomes. In this study, knowledge of the
factors that differentiated cultural groups in many cases did not account
for individual differences within a culture. Conversely, factors contributing to individual differences in school performance were not always
those which yielded cultural differences between groups. For example,
although Chinese students did report a more demanding family environment than their Western peers, an environment conducive to en-

hanced educational outcomes, negative reactions by parents to school grades (a strategy associated with poorer academic performance), was more common among Chinese Australians than their Anglo-American peers. On the other hand, neither restraint nor industry differentiated between groups, however in both samples these were significant predictors of effort and achievement. Importantly, in other cross-cultural studies there have been similar failures of this individual-level approach to cultural differences, in school outcomes (Dornbusch, Ritter, Leiderman, Roberts, & Fraleigh, 1987) as well as adolescent expectations for autonomy and levels of misconduct (Feldman & Rosenthal, in press; Feldman, Rosenthal, Mont-Reynaud, Leung, & Lau, 1991).

The finding of similar and robust patterns of relationships between school performance and our predictors for Chinese and Western students, replicated in two Western countries, suggests that cultural explanations based on family processes and personal characteristics, at least as measured in this research, do not explain Chinese students' superior school performance. However, further research, using more fine-grained measures, is needed if we are to tease apart the contributions of home and culture to students' academic performance. Moreover, we should not overlook other cultural characteristics such as the value accorded to education and cultural variations in parents' beliefs about children's competence (Hess et al., 1987; Rosenthal & Gold, 1989). We may need as well to look more closely at structural factors that differentiate Chinese immigrants from their Western peers. Possible candidates, we suggest, include family structure and the place of the Chinese community in the broader societal context.

ACKNOWLEDGMENTS

This research was supported by a grant to Doreen A. Rosenthal from the Spencer Foundation, and to S. Shirley Feldman from the Stanford Center for the Study of Families, Children, and Youth.

We are indebted to Dr. Kwok Leung and Dr. Sing Lau for their diverse contributions to this study and to anonymous reviewers for their constructive comments on an earlier draft of this article.

REFERENCES

Anderson, D. S., & Vervoorn, A. E. (1983). *Access to privilege: Patterns of participation in Australian post-secondary education.* Canberra: Australian National University Press.

Bond, M. H., & Hwang, K. (1986). The social psychology of the Chinese people. In M. H. Bond (Ed.), *The psychology of the Chinese people* (pp. 213–264). Hong Kong: Oxford University Press.

Brand, D. (1987, August). The new whiz kids: Why Asian-Americans are doing so well and what it costs them. *Time Magazine*, 42–51.

Chan, H. K-Y. (1987). *The adaptation, life satisfaction and academic achievement of Chinese senior school students in Melbourne.* Unpublished doctoral dissertation, Monash University, Melbourne.

Chang, C. (1985). Family influences on school achievement in China. *U.S.–China Friendship, 9*(4), 20.

Chen, C., & Stevenson, H. W. (1989). Homework: A cross-cultural examination. *Child Development, 60*, 551–561.

Chiu, E., & Tan, E. S. (1986, May). *Socialization of Australian-born Chinese.* Paper presented at the Ethnicity and Multiculturalism National Research Conference, Melbourne.

Dornbusch, S. M., Elworth, J. T., & Ritter, P. L. (1988). *Parental reaction to grades: A field test of the over-justification approach.* Unpublished manuscript.

Dornbusch, S. M., Prescott, B. L., & Ritter, P. L. (1987, April). *The relation of high school academic performance and student effort to language use and recency of migration among Asian- and Pacific-Americans.* Paper presented at the Annual Meeting of the American Educational Research Association, Washington, DC.

Dornbusch, S. M., Ritter, P. L., Leiderman, P. H., Roberts, D. F., & Fraleigh, M. J. (1987). The relation of parenting style to adolescent school performance. *Child Development, 58*, 1244–1257.

Emery, R., Weintraub, S., & Neale, J. M. (1982). Effects of marital discord on the school behavior of schizophrenic, affectively disordered and normal parents. *Journal of Abnormal Child Psychology, 10*, 215–228.

Feldman, S. S., & Rosenthal, D. A. (in press). The influence of family variables and adolescents' values on age expectations of behavioral autonomy: A cross-cultural study of Hong Kong, Australian, and American youth. *International Journal of Psychology.*

Feldman, S. S., Rosenthal, D. A., Mont-Reynaud, R., Leung, K., & Lau, S. (1991). Ain't misbehavin': Adolescent values and family environments as correlates of misconduct in Australia, Hong Kong, and the United States [this issue]. *Journal of Research on Adolescence, 1*, 109–134.

Harrison, A., Serafica, F., & McAdoo, H. (1984). Ethnic families of color. In R. D. Parke (Ed.), *Review of child development research 7: The family* (pp. 329–371). Chicago: University of Chicago Press.

Hess, R. D., Chih-Mei, C., & McDevitt, T. M. (1987). Cultural variations in family beliefs about children's performance in mathematics: Comparisons among People's Republic of China, Chinese-American, and Caucasian-American families. *Journal of Educational Psychology, 79*, 179–188.

Hirschman, C., & Wong, M. G. (1986). The extraordinary attainments of Asian-Americans: A search for historical evidence and explanations. *Social Forces, 65*, 1–27.

Ho, D. Y. F. (1986). Chinese patterns of socialization: A critical review. In M. H. Bond (Ed.), *The psychology of Chinese people* (pp. 1–37). Hong Kong: Oxford University Press.

Hofstede, G. (1980). *Culture's consequences.* Beverly Hills: Sage.

Hui, C. H., & Triandis, H. C. (1985). Measurement in cross-cultural psychology: A review and comparison of strategies. *Journal of Cross-Cultural Psychology, 16*, 131–152.

Kohn, M., & Roseman, B. L. (1974). Social-emotional, cognitive, and demographic determinants of poor school achievement: Implications for a strategy of intervention. *Journal of Educational Psychology, 66*, 277–284.

Lenerz, K., Kucher, J. S., East, P. L., Lerner, J. V., & Lerner, R. M. (1987). Early adolescents' physical organismic characteristics and psychosocial functioning: Findings from the Pennsylvania early adolescent transitions study (PEATS). In R. M. Lerner & T. T. Foch (Eds.), *Biological-psychosocial interactions in early adolescence* (pp. 225–248).

Hillsdale, NJ: Lawrence Erlbaum Associates, Inc.

Leung, K. (1989). Cross-cultural differences: Individual-level vs. culture-level analysis. *International Journal of Psychology, 24*, 703–719.

Lin, C-Y. C., & Fu, V. R. (1990). A comparison of child-rearing practices among Chinese, immigrant Chinese, and Caucasian-American parents. *Child Development, 61*, 429–433.

Mak, M., Schludermann, S., & Schludermann, E. (1988, March). *A cross-cultural study on achievement behavior, causal attribution, and parent–child interactions among Hong Kong Chinese, Euro-Canadian, and Chinese-Canadian adolescents.* Paper presented at the Society for Research on Adolescence Conference, Alexandria, VA.

Marjoribanks, K. (1987). Ability and attitude correlates of academic achievement: Family–group differences. *Journal of Educational Psychology, 79*, 171–178.

McAdam, K. (1972). The study methods and academic results of overseas students. In S. Bochner & P. Wicks (Eds.), *Overseas students in Australia* (pp. 97–104). Sydney: University of New South Wales Press.

Moos, R., & Moos, B. S. (1974). *Family environment scale.* Palo Alto, CA: Consulting Psychologist Press.

Parker, J. G., & Asher, S. R. (1987). Peer relations and later personal adjustment: Are low-accepted children at risk? *Psychological Bulletin, 102*, 357–389.

Poortinga, Y. H., & Van de Vijver, F. J. R. (1987). Explaining cross-cultural differences: Bias analysis and beyond. *Journal of Cross-Cultural Psychology, 18*, 259–282.

Rosenthal, D. A., & Feldman, S. S. (1990). The acculturation of Chinese immigrants: Perceived effects on family functioning of length of residence in two cultural contexts. *Journal of Genetic Psychology, 151*, 493–514.

Rosenthal, D. A., & Gold, R. (1989). A comparison of Vietnamese-Australian and Anglo-Australian mothers' beliefs about intellectual development. *International Journal of Psychology, 24*, 179–193.

Rosenthal, D. A., Gurney, R. M., & Moore, S. M. (1981). From trust to intimacy: A new inventory for examining Erikson's stages of psychosocial development. *Journal of Youth and Adolescence, 10*, 525–537.

Slaughter-Defoe, D. T., Nakagawa, K., Takanishi, R., & Johnson, D. J. (1990). Toward cultural/ecological perspectives on schooling and achievement in African- and Asian-American children. *Child Development, 61*, 363–383.

Stevenson, H. W., & Lee, S. Y. (1990). Contexts of achievement. *Monographs of the Society for Research in Child Development, 55*(1–2, Serial No. 221).

Stevenson, H. W., Lee, S. Y., & Stigler, J. (1986). Mathematics achievement of Chinese, Japanese and American children. *Science, 231*, 693–699.

Sue, S., & Zane, N. S. W. (1985). Academic achievement and socioemotional adjustment among Chinese university students. *Journal of Counseling Psychology, 32*, 570–579.

Talwar, R., Schwab, J., & Lerner, R. M. (1989). Early adolescent temperament and academic competence: Tests of "direct effects" and developmental contextual models. *Journal of Early Adolescence, 9*, 291–309.

Triandis, H. C., Bontempo, R., Betancourt, H., Bond, M., Leung, K., Brenes, A., Georgas, J., Hui, C. H., Marin, G., Setiadi, B., Sinha, J. B. P., Verma, J., Spangenberg, J., Touzard, H., & de Montmollin, G. (1986). The measurement of the etic aspects of individualism and collectivism across cultures. *Australian Journal of Psychology, 38*, 257–268.

Vernon, P. E. (1982). *The abilities and achievements of Orientals in North America.* New York: Academic.

Weinberger, D. A. (1990). *Socio-emotional adjustment in older children and adults: I. Psychometric properties of the Weinberger Adjustment Inventory.* Manuscript submitted for publication.

Wentzel, K., Weinberger, D., Ford, M., & Feldman, S. (in press). Academic achievement in pre-adolescence: The role of motivational, affective, and self-regulatory processes. *Journal of Applied Developmental Psychology.*

Why Asians are going to the head of the class. (1986, August 3). *New York Times,* pp. 18–23.

Wood, J., Chapin, K., & Hannah, M. E. (1988). Family environment and its relationship to underachievement. *Adolescence, 23,* 283–290.

Yao, E. L. (1985). A comparison of family characteristics of Asian-American and Anglo-American high achievers. *International Journal of Comparative Sociology, 26,* 198–208.

Received March 8, 1990
Revision received October 29, 1990
Accepted October 31, 1990

Stability of Intelligence from Preschool to Adolescence: The Influence of Social and Family Risk Factors

Arnold J. Sameroff
University of Michigan

Ronald Seifer
E. P. Bradley Hospital and Brown University Program in Medicine

Alfred Baldwin and Clara Baldwin
University of Rochester

SAMEROFF, ARNOLD J.; SEIFER, RONALD; BALDWIN, ALFRED; and BALDWIN, CLARA. *Stability of Intelligence from Preschool to Adolescence: The Influence of Social and Family Risk Factors.* CHILD DEVELOPMENT, 1993, 64, 80–97. Intelligence scores of children in a longitudinal study were assessed at 4 and 13 years and related to social and family risk factors. A multiple environmental risk score was calculated for each child by counting the number of high-risk conditions from 10 risk factors: mother's behavior, mother's developmental beliefs, mother's anxiety, mother's mental health, mother's educational attainment, family social support, family size, major stressful life events, occupation of head of household, and disadvantaged minority status. Multiple risk scores explained one-third to one-half of IQ variance at 4 and 13 years. The stability between 4- and 13-year environmental risk scores (r = .77) was not less than the stability between 4- and 13-year IQ scores (r = .72). Effects remained after SES and race, or maternal IQ, were partialled; multiple risk was important in longitudinal prediction, even after prior measurement of child IQ was accounted for; the pattern of risk was less important than the total amount of risk present in the child's context.

Understanding the development of child behavior increasingly has required attention to aspects of the environment as moderators of performance. Although the perception of the child as constitutionally separate from the environment frequently leads to the belief that the child's behavior is also separate from the environment, organismic and contextualist worldviews have emphasized the importance of experience in understanding individual developmental outcomes (Baltes, Reese, & Lipsitt, 1980; Lerner, Skinner, & Sorell, 1980; Sameroff, 1983; Wachs & Gruen, 1982).

Broman, Nichols, and Kennedy (1975) compared the effects of 169 individual biomedical and behavioral variables during infancy on 4-year intellectual performance in a sample of 26,760 children from the National Institute of Neurological and Communicative Disorders and Stroke Collaborative

Perinatal Project. Although only 11 (7%) of these variables could be said to constitute social or family behavioral factors, two of these, SES and mother's education, were the most predictive of all the variables. This study demonstrated the importance of early environmental factors but did not reveal the aspects of the environment that were the most salient predictors.

Despite the nominal interest of developmentalists in the effects of context, the analysis and assessment of environments has fallen more in the domain of sociology than of developmental psychology (Clausen, 1968; Elder, 1984; Kohn & Schooler, 1983; Mayer & Jencks, 1989). The magnitude of a social ecological analysis involving multiple settings and multiple systems (Bronfenbrenner, 1979) has daunted researchers primarily trained to focus on individual behavioral processes. A further daunting factor

This research was supported by grants from the National Institute of Mental Health and the W. T. Grant Foundation. Requests for reprints should be sent to Arnold J. Sameroff, Center for Human Growth and Development, University of Michigan, 300 N. Ingalls, Ann Arbor, MI 48109-0406.

has been the increasing necessity to use multicausal models to explain developmental phenomena (Sameroff, 1983).

Although SES is a powerful distal predictor of developmental outcomes, it is ultimately unsatisfying to behaviorists because it does not reveal the proximal differences in family experience in different SES groups that produce differences in child developmental outcome. In the current study we have tried to examine the longitudinal effects of a number of social and family risks that have been found to play a major role in influencing child development. Each of these factors is found more frequently in poverty samples than in affluent samples, but each can be found at any SES level.

We attempted to answer four questions in this study: (1) whether intelligence was related to environmental risk factors and, if so, whether this relation was partially independent of social status and minority racial status, (2) whether the contextual risks were partially independent of maternal intelligence, (3) whether the longitudinal predictive power of these risk factors was partially independent of previous assessments of child intelligence, and (4) whether there were patterns of risk factors that were more predictive of outcome than other patterns (i.e., whether the quality or quantity of risk factors was the more important predictive aspect).

Preliminary Findings on Risk and Development
This report is based on data from the Rochester Longitudinal Study (RLS), an investigation of the development of a group of children from the prenatal period through adolescence living in a socially heterogeneous set of family circumstances. Approximately half of the families originally were selected because of maternal emotional problems. The other half were selected so that ill and non-ill groups were roughly equivalent on a number of demographic variables including SES, race, age of mother, education of mother, and family size. A full report of the selection and recruitment of families and the development of the children through 2½ years of age can be found in Sameroff, Seifer, and Zax (1982).

When the children were 4 years old we calculated a multiple environmental risk score from 10 factors and compared the intelligence scores of children with differing numbers of risks (Sameroff, Seifer, Barocas, Zax, & Greenspan, 1987). We found a linear

relation; the average IQ of the children with no risk factors was 118, whereas the average IQ of the children with the most risk factors (seven or eight) was 85, a range of over 2 SD. We examined by cluster analysis if there was any consistency in the distribution of risk factors that affected the IQ scores. We found that it was the number of risk factors and not the kind of risk factor that was the determining influence. Several clusters were identified with the same number, but different kinds, of risks—groups of children with different clusters of risks had similar IQ scores. These results fit a multicausal model of development in which outcome is multiply determined and cannot be attributed to any single factor. That is, different patterns of risk can produce similar outcomes.

Since the initial report of the effect of multiple risk factors on 4-year IQ scores we have completed an assessment of the RLS sample when the children were 13 years old. This report is a comparison of the relation of children's intelligence to environmental risk at each age. We also report on the relation between these measures across the 9-year interval between assessments.

Single- versus Multiple-Risk Models
Although statistically significant differences in outcome are frequently associated with single risk factors, these differences rarely explain large proportions of outcome variance. Parmelee (Parmelee & Haber, 1973) was a pioneer in attempts to use cumulative risk factors for predicting early intelligence, but most of his variables were dimensions of child health and physical status. Cumulative indices of environmental risk were more often used in the study of mental health outcomes. In a much-cited study, Rutter (1979) argued that it was not any particular risk factor but the number of risk factors in a child's background that led to psychiatric disorder. Psychiatric risk for a sample of 10-year-olds rose from 2% in families with zero or one risk factors to 20% in families with four or more. The six risk factors studied included severe marital distress, low SES, large family size or overcrowding, paternal criminality, maternal psychiatric disorder, and admission to care of the local authority. Williams, Anderson, McGee, and Silva (1990) related behavioral disorders in 11-year-olds to a cumulative disadvantage score based on number of residence and school changes, single parenthood, low SES, marital separation, young motherhood, low maternal cognitive ability, poor family rela-

tions, seeking marriage guidance, and maternal mental health symptoms. The sample was divided into five groups, and a strong relation was found between disadvantage and child behavior score. For the children with fewer than two disadvantages only 7% had behavior problems, whereas for the children with eight or more disadvantages the rate was 40%. In the RLS 4-year data, we found a comparable relation between our multiple environmental risk score and the child's social emotional competence (Sameroff, Seifer, Zax, & Barocas, 1987). The number of children rated as clinically disturbed rose from 3% in the zero-risk group to 30% in the highest risk group (seven or eight risk factors).

Summary of Research Plan

A longitudinal sample of 152 families was examined at 4 and 13 years of age in terms of 10 risk factors and their relation to cognitive outcomes (IQ). The 10 risk factors were aggregated into a composite environmental multiple risk index. Questions addressed were (1) the magnitude of the relation between risk and IQ, (2) the influence of maternal IQ, (3) relative predictive power from prior assessments of risk and IQ, and (4) whether specific patterns of risk were important to consider.

Method

Sample

Families in this report were participants in the Rochester Longitudinal Study (Sameroff et al., 1982). The 152 families who completed the 13-year assessment have been studied since the mothers were pregnant with the study children. The original purpose of the study was to examine the transmission of serious mental disorder across generations. About half of the mothers were identified through a county-wide psychiatric registry as having mental illness that was documented by two psychiatric interviews conducted by project staff (Current and Past Psychopathology Scales [CAPPS] done prenatally and when the child was 2½ years old). Socioeconomic status was broadly represented. Mean four-factor Hollingshead (1975) scores were 3.18 (SD = 1.34) at 4 years of age and 2.84 (SD = 1.36) at 13 years (all five SES categories were represented at each age, with group sizes ranging from 17 to 39). The families also varied on race: 99 were white, 52 were black, and 1 was Puerto Rican. Most of the nonwhite families were in lower SES groups—at 4 years 41 of the 53 were in SES 4 or 5, and at 13 years 34 of the

53 were in the lowest two SES groups. In contrast, 21 (at 4 years) and 19 (at 13 years) of the 99 white families were in SES 4 or 5. At the time their children were born, mothers' average age was 24.5 (SD = 4.8). All mothers were recruited from obstetric services where they received prenatal care for the index child.

Note that these procedures for selecting families resulted in a broad range of pathology, with some oversampling of ill families. About one-fourth of the mothers originally recruited to be no-illness cases turned out to have diagnosable mental disorders when interviewed prenatally. The illnesses were typically mild to moderate in severity. As a result, a broad range of pathology was represented in the final study sample, and the extreme groups feature of the original sampling scheme was reduced.

History of RLS sample.—The RLS sample included 270 families assessed during the first year of life. About 20% of these families were lost to the study between 1 and 4 years of age—leaving a group of 214 families at the 4-year assessment whom we attempted to contact 9 years later. We succeeded in locating 185 families (86%). Of these, 12 (6%) had moved out of the area, 6 (3%) had a change of primary caregiver, and 15 (8%) refused to participate. This left a sample of 152 families with complete data at both ages. We compared the families in the study (n = 152) with those who dropped out between 4 and 13 years (n = 62) and those who dropped out between 1 and 4 years (n = 56); there were no significant differences on socioeconomic status, proportion of minority families, father absence, family size, or severity of maternal illness. Thus, although many of these high-risk families were lost to follow-up over a 13-year period, the families who dropped out were not a select group of the highest-risk families.

Procedures

When the children in the RLS were 4 years old, and again when they were 13 years old, they came to the research laboratory with their mothers for a 2-hour session. The child and mother were separated, and each completed a battery of assessments.

Assessment of Child IQ

At 4 years Wechsler Preschool and Primary Scale of Intelligence (WPPSI) subscales of Similarities, Comprehension, Information, and Vocabulary were used; at 13 years the Revised Wechsler Intelligence Scales for Children (WISC-R) Information, Similarities, Picture Arrangement, and Block Design subscales were used. The subscales chosen at each age are highly correlated with the Wechsler Full Scale IQ scores (Wechsler, 1967, 1974) and served as a reliable index of child test performance. Because of the length of the battery we were not able to use all of the Wechsler subscales. Eight of the children did not complete the IQ test at 4 years of age.

The use of short forms on IQ tests results in good estimates of full-scale IQ (Kaufman, 1979). Four-scale short forms typically have correlations with full-scale IQ of about .90, depending on the specific scales used and age of children examined (e.g., Kaufman, 1972).

Assessment of Maternal IQ

Two short IQ tests were given to the mothers at the 13-year assessment, and the scores were averaged: the Shipley (1967) Institute of Living Scale and the Quick Test (Ammons & Ammons, 1962). Four of the mothers did not complete the IQ tests.

Assessment of Contextual Risk

At both 4 and 13 years of age an environmental multiple-risk index was developed for each family. At both ages each family was assigned a score for presence or absence of 10 risk factors. These 0–1 scores were then summed to obtain the multiple-risk index. The 10 risk factors were the same at both ages, although there were differences in the specific measures used in some cases. The measure of each domain is provided below for the 4- and 13-year assessments and is summarized in Table 1. In the case of continuous variables where an objective categorical definition of risk was not available, families in the top quartile were placed in the hazardous category.

4-Year Risk Assessment

Minority group status.—Black and Puerto Rican families were included in the risk group (35%).

Occupation of head of household.—The head of household occupation was classified on the Hollingshead (1975) nine-point scale. Those scoring 1 or 2 (i.e., unemployed, laborers, or semiskilled) were assigned to the risk category (27%).

Maternal education.—Mothers who did not complete high school were in the risk category (33%).

Family size.—Families with four or more children living at home were placed in the risk group (16%).

Father absence.—Families where a father or stepfather was not present in the household were assigned to the risk category (24%).

Stressful life events.—During the first 4 years of the RLS mothers were questioned about events that affected the child and the family at 4-, 12-, 30-, and 48-month assessments. A measure of stressful negative life events was developed (Rosenzweig, Seifer, & Sameroff, 1982) patterned after the inventories of Holmes and Rahe (1967) that included events such as loss of job, deaths in the family, or physical illness. The risk group had 20 or more stressful events during the first 4 years of study on this measure (23%).

Parental perspectives.—For this dimension we combined the standardized scores of two measures that reflected rigidity versus flexibility in the attitudes, beliefs, and values that parents had in regard to their child's development. The Concepts of Development Questionnaire (CODQ; Sameroff & Feil, 1985) evaluates parents' understanding of development on a dimension ranging from categorical to perspectivistic. At the *categorical* end, child development is seen as a determined expression of single causes like constitution or environment. At the *perspectivistic* end, child behavior is seen as the outcome of complex, transactional processes. The Kohn (1977) parental values scale measures the behaviors that parents desire for their children. The primary dimension derived from this scale ranges from conformity to self-direction. An orientation toward child *conformity* emphasizes values of obedience, neatness, good manners, and appropriate sex role behavior. An orientation toward child *self-direction* emphasizes values of responsibility, consideration of others, and curiosity. The two scores were standardized and summed to yield a summary score. Those scoring .60 or above were assigned to the risk category (21%).

Maternal anxiety.—Anxiety was used to assess variation in the subclinical range of emotional functioning. Those with scores of 6 or higher on the Rutter Malaise Scale (Rutter, 1976) were assigned to the risk category (23%).

Maternal mental health.—The mental health status of the mother was determined from structured psychiatric interviews (Endicott & Spitzer, 1972) conducted when the mother was pregnant with the study child and when the study child was 30 months of age. Psychopathology present on either interview resulted in assignment to the risk category (46%).

Interaction.—The mother and child were videotaped in an interaction task to assess maternal teaching style (Barocas et al., 1991). Four five-point scales rating the affect of the mother in this situation were scored: Positive, Negative, Flattened, and Involved. These four scales were summed (with Negative and Flattened reversed) to yield a single summary score. Those scoring 12 or less on this scale (21%) were assigned to the risk group.

13-Year Risk Assessment

Minority group status.—Black and Puerto Rican families were included in the risk group (35%).

Occupation of head of household.—The head of household occupation was classified on the Hollingshead (1975) nine-point scale. Those scoring 1 or 2 (i.e., unemployed, laborers, or semiskilled) were assigned to the risk category (21%).

Maternal education.—Mothers with less than a high school education were in the risk category (22%).

Family size.—Families with four or more children living at home were placed in the risk group (11%).

Father absence.—Families where a father or stepfather was not present in the household were assigned to the risk category (41%).

Stressful life events.—The Life Events Questionnaire was used (Garmezy & Tellegen, 1984), a modified version of the Coddington (1972a, 1972b) scale. The risk group had 24 or more stressful events during the previous decade (i.e., the period between the 4- and 13-year assessments) on this measure (27%).

Parental perspectives.—The scales and scoring procedures from the 4-year assessment were used again here. Those scoring .60 or above were assigned to the risk category (28%).

Maternal anxiety.—As at 4 years, those with scores of 6 or higher on the Rutter Malaise scale were assigned to the risk category (27%).

Maternal mental health.—A diagnostic interview for psychiatric conditions was not conducted at the 13-year assessment. Instead, the interviewers who conducted the

2-hour parent interview assessment systematically rated the mother on the Psychological Impairment Rating Scale (World Health Organization, 1973). This scale has items for outgoing/withdrawn, open/defensive, uncooperative, likability, coherence of thought, judgment and reasoning, intelligence, appearance, and coping skills. A summary score, the mean of the nine five-point ratings, was made. Those scoring above 1.9 were assigned to the risk category (50%).

Interaction.—At 13 years there were no direct observations of interaction tasks with the child. Instead the mother completed the Camberwell Family Interview (Brown & Rutter, 1966), which assesses the parent's affective relationship to the child by examining measures of expressed emotion when discussing the child. A composite measure of expressed emotion was created by summing standardized scores for the Dissatisfaction, Criticism, Hostility, Positive, Enthusiasm, Enjoyment, Understanding, and Warmth scales (note that the Positive through Warmth scales were reversed so that all indexed negative expressed emotion). Families scoring greater than .28 on this variable were assigned to the risk category (25%).

Results

Two basic approaches to data analysis are included in the presentation of results below, each with its own advantages and disadvantages. The first approach involved the creation of a single multiple risk index, based on the 10 dichotomous risk ratings. The advantages of this approach include the use of a single composite predictor in the analyses and the ability to translate the results into meaningful graphic representations; disadvantages include the loss of predictive power due to the partly arbitrary reduction of 10 measures into a single composite. The second approach was to use each of the 10 risk measures in multiple regression analyses. The advantages of this approach include retention of full predictive power of the original variable set; disadvantages include the loss of statistical power to detect significant relations, particularly in subsample analyses (where subject to predictor ratios were about 4:1). To differentiate these two strategies, the first will be referred to using the term *composite*, while the second will be indicated by *multiple predictor.*

Where relevant, effect sizes will be presented in terms of Cohen's (1988, 1990) stan-

TABLE 1

Risk Factor Definitions at 4 and 13 Years and Percent of Families
That Did or Did Not Change Status (n = 152)

Risk Factor	4-Year Definition	13-Year Definition	Same	Worse	Better	Kappa
Minority status	Nonwhite (35%)	Nonwhite (35%)	100	0	0	1.00
Occupation	Hollingshead 1–2 (27%)	Hollingshead 1–2 (21%)	80	7	13	.44
Mother education	HS not complete (33%)	HS not complete (22%)	86	1	13	.66
Family size	≥ 4 children (16%)	≥ 4 children (11%)	85	5	10	.35
Family support	Father absent (24%)	Father absent (41%)	61	28	11	.13
Life events	20 or more (23%)	24 or more (27%)	70	17	13	.20
Parenting perspectives	Composite ≥ .60 (20%)	Composite ≥ .60 (27%)	82	12	6	.50
Anxiety	Malaise ≥ 6 (23%)	Malaise ≥ 6 (27%)	82	11	7	.51
Mental health	Severity > 1 (47%)	PIRS > 1.90 (50%)	59	22	19	.19
Interaction	Composite ≤ 12 (19%)	Composite > .28 (25%)	68	19	13	.06

Note.—Table entries are percentage of cases in each category.

dards for small, medium, and large effects. Medium effects (e.g., Pearson correlations of .30, or t test differences of one-half standard deviation) are those typical of the behavioral sciences (Cohen, 1990; Sedlmeier & Gigerenzer, 1989).

Multiple Risk at 4 and 13 Years of Age
The individual risk factors are listed in Table 1. In general, about 25% of the sample was classified in the risk category for any one item, although there was a range from 11% to 50%. The highest percentage was for mental health, which was expected since this study oversampled for mothers with mental health problems.

The average number of risk factors was 2.63 (SD = 2.35) with a range from 0 to 9 at 4 years, and 2.85 (SD = 2.22) with a range from 0 to 8 at 13 years. Because of low frequencies, families scoring higher than 7 were combined with the group of families having seven risk factors; the result was that the smallest group at each age had eight families. The correlation of these composite risk scores across the 9-year span was .77.

Stability in Individual Risk Factors
The stability of the 10 risk factors examined at 4 and 13 years of age is described in Table 1. Across these 10 factors, the range of

percent agreement was from a low of 59% for mental health to a high of 100% for minority status, with a median of 81%. Kappa statistics, indexing chance-corrected rates of agreement, indicate that, for half of the risk factors, there was moderate to high agreement at the two ages. There was no particular trend toward an increase or decrease in total risk between the two assessment ages. The factor where risk most clearly increased was father absence, which rose from 24% to 41%. The most notable decrease in risk was in mother education, where the percent of mothers who had not completed high school fell from 33% to 22%.[1] Thus, with moderate or lower stability for most of the individual risk factors, the composite multiple risk score still had impressive cross-time stability over the 9-year period (see above).

Relation of Individual Risk Factors to IQ Outcomes
At 4 years of age, all 10 risk items were significantly related to lower child IQ scores (see Table 2). Not surprisingly, the strongest differences were in the race and social status domains: minority status, head of household occupation, and mother education. However, there were other variables that had differences of equivalent magnitude: parent-child interaction and parenting perspectives.

[1] Our data in Table 1 indicate that one mother classified as having completed high school at 4 years was in the not-completed group at 13 years. As in any data set, we assume some degree of measurement error (probably in excess of one misclassification on one variable) either in respondents' reports or transcription error. Without any means to verify such data, we have left the values in their seemingly contradictory form.

TABLE 2

CHILDREN'S IQ SCORES AND INDIVIDUAL RISK FACTORS AT 4 AND 13 YEARS

RISK FACTOR	4-YEAR IQ SCORES			13-YEAR IQ SCORES		
	Low Risk	High Risk	F Value	Low Risk	High Risk	F Value
Minority status	110.2 (17.0)	90.5 (13.3)	50.89**	110.3 (15.7)	86.4 (13.2)	89.94**
Occupation	108.2 (17.5)	90.0 (13.3)	34.45**	106.0 (17.4)	87.0 (15.9)	30.93**
Mother education	108.9 (18.0)	91.5 (12.6)	35.14**	105.6 (18.2)	89.0 (14.5)	23.35**
Family size	104.8 (18.7)	94.3 (13.7)	6.35*	103.7 (18.3)	88.1 (16.5)	11.29**
Family support	105.7 (18.2)	94.8 (16.4)	9.53**	105.6 (18.1)	96.7 (18.5)	8.66**
Life events	105.2 (18.4)	97.4 (17.4)	4.68*	101.8 (18.8)	102.5 (18.7)	.04
Parenting perspectives	107.3 (17.0)	91.7 (15.9)	19.69**	107.8 (16.7)	87.4 (14.7)	47.82**
Anxiety	105.4 (18.5)	97.4 (15.5)	4.98*	103.7 (18.6)	97.3 (18.5)	3.50
Mental health	106.6 (19.2)	99.3 (16.6)	5.86*	110.5 (15.5)	93.7 (18.2)	36.72**
Interaction	107.2 (17.9)	87.8 (11.4)	31.67**	104.2 (17.8)	98.6 (19.9)	2.62

NOTE.—Table entries are means with standard deviations in parentheses.
* $p < .05$.
** $p < .01$.

Seven of the 10 risk factors were still significantly related to child IQ at 13 years of age. Again, the social status variables were robust predictors, joined by parenting perspectives and maternal mental health. Life events, maternal anxiety, and family interaction failed to significantly predict 13-year child IQ. The correlations among the risk factors and child IQ at age 4 are presented in Table 3 and at age 13 in Table 4.

Relation of Multiple Risk Score to Child IQ

The first major question addressed in the analysis was whether the multiple environmental risk score was strongly related to 4- and 13-year child IQ. The simple correlation of the composite multiple risk score with child IQ was $-.58$ at 4 years and $-.61$ at 13 years of age. In the corresponding multiple predictor analyses, total R^2 was .50 at 4 years and .51 at 13 years (both $p < .01$). As can be seen in Figures 1 and 2, the difference between the highest and lowest risk groups was about 30 points (for linear trend, $F = 52.46$, $p < .01$ at 4 years; $F = 83.59$, $p < .01$ at 13 years; deviation from linear effects did not approach significance).

A corollary question was whether the multiple risk index significantly improved prediction of child IQ at 4 and 13 years of age beyond that of social status indicators. The significant relations of the composite multiple risk score and child IQ remained after SES and minority status were partialled (see the dashed lines on Figs. 1 and 2). For the linear component in the analysis of covariance, $F = 6.63$, $p < .05$ at 4 years; $F = 5.80$, $p < .05$ at 13 years; the deviation from linear components did not approach significance. Even with the strongest individual predictors of child IQ partialled, the multiple risk index still differentiated the highest and lowest groups by about 15 points. The corresponding effect sizes (Cohen, 1988) for these analyses of covariance were $f = .35$ at 4 years and $f = .22$ at 13 years. Both effects sizes are near the medium range (i.e., $f = .25$) as defined by Cohen.

When using the multiple predictor strategy, the 4-year results were similar—R^2 change after entering the covariates on the prior step was .133 ($p < .01$). However, for the 13-year data, the R^2 change was .04 after partialling SES and minority status, which was not significant. Since more than half of the total variance was explained by the covariates and predictors, the effect size at 4 years was $f^2 = .36$, and at 13 years $f^2 = .09$. These compare with Cohen's effect sizes,

where $f^2 = .02$ is a small effect, $f^2 = .15$ is a medium effect, and a large effect is $f^2 = .35$.

Multiple Risk within Minority Status Groups

There is strong evidence from the covariance analysis that statistically controlling minority status did not eliminate the effect of multiple risk on child IQ. The ANCOVA analysis, however, did not address the question of whether the multiple risk effect was present within the black and white groups when they were analyzed separately. The data within black and white groups are presented in Figures 3 and 4 (the one Puerto Rican family in this sample was not included in these analyses).

At 4 years of age, the effect of composite multiple risk was present only among the white families (linear trend $F = 12.99$, $p < .01$; deviation from linear not significant). The IQs of the children in the black families were uniformly low (linear trend $F = .19$, $p = .66$). However, by 13 years of age, there was an effect of multiple risk within both the white (linear trend $F = 17.80$, $p < .01$; deviation from linear not significant) and the black families (linear trend $F = 9.56$, $p < .05$; deviation from linear not significant).

When examined from the multiple predictor strategy, a strong effect was found within the white families, $R^2 = .44$ at 4 years ($p < .01$) and $R^2 = .23$ at 13 years ($p < .01$). At both ages, there was substantial variance explained by the multiple predictors in the black subsamples ($R^2 = .19$ at 4 years; $R^2 = .23$ at 13 years), but neither regression was significant in this smaller group.

Influence of Maternal IQ

A second important question was whether environmental risk effects would be substantial after the effects of maternal IQ were accounted for. At both ages, the linear trend for composite multiple risk was significant in analysis of covariance with maternal IQ partialled ($F = 16.20$, $p < .01$ at 4 years; $F = 19.92$, $p < .01$ at 13 years; deviation from linear components did not approach significance). The group means and means adjusted for the covariation of maternal IQ are presented in Figures 5 and 6. Effect sizes for these analyses of covariance were $f = .34$ at 4 years and $f = .35$ at 13 years. These fall between standards for medium ($f = .25$) and large ($f = .40$) effects as defined by Cohen.

Conclusions were the same using the multiple predictor strategy (R^2 change $= .19$

TABLE 3

Correlations among Child IQ and Risk Variables at 4 Years

Variable	1	2	3	4	5	6	7	8	9	10	11
1. Minority status	···										
2. Occupation	-.53	···									
3. Mother education	.55	-.71	···								
4. Family size	.25	-.25	.37	···							
5. Family support	.25	-.33	.33	.14	···						
6. Life events	.11	-.21	.32	.25	.05	···					
7. Parenting perspectives	.51	-.38	.44	.17	.17	.25	···				
8. Anxiety	.16	-.33	.41	.15	.30	.23	.16	···			
9. Mental health	-.09	-.23	.34	.20	.28	.20	.02	.45	···		
10. Interaction	-.55	.47	-.48	-.20	-.07	-.14	-.48	-.29	-.05	···	
11. Child IQ	-.51	.55	-.57	.37	-.25	.28	-.44	-.19	-.09	.54	···

NOTE.—Table entries are Pearson correlations. With n = 144, correlations above .17 are significant, p < .05, and above .22 are significant, p < .01.

TABLE 4

Correlatons among Child IQ and Risk Variables at 13 Years

Variable	1	2	3	4	5	6	7	8	9	10	11
1. Minority status	···										
2. Occupation	-.53	···									
3. Mother education	-.48	.63	···								
4. Family size	.29	-.26	-.15	···							
5. Family support	-.21	.46	.24	.11	···						
6. Life events	-.09	-.06	-.08	.05	-.16	···					
7. Parenting perspectives	.56	-.60	-.57	.11	-.23	-.03	···				
8. Anxiety	.06	-.29	-.30	-.05	-.20	.35	.15	···			
9. Mental health	.34	-.51	-.47	.16	-.14	-.06	.50	.25	···		
10. Interaction	.17	-.34	-.20	.14	-.07	.01	.21	.21	.49	···	
11. Child IQ	-.61	.55	.48	-.27	.23	.03	-.55	-.18	.34	-.17	···

NOTE.—Table entries are Pearson correlations. With n = 152, correlations above .16 are significant, p < .05, and above .21 are significant, p < .01.

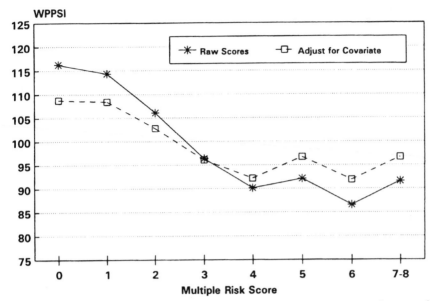

Fig. 1.—Mean 4-year IQ scores, and means adjusted for covariation of SES and race, within multiple risk groups.

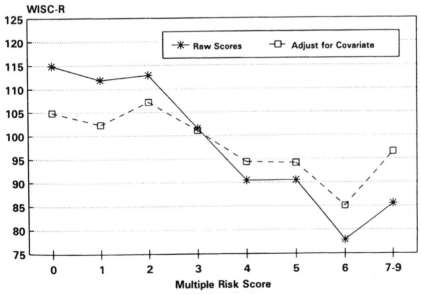

Fig. 2.—Mean 13-year IQ scores, and means adjusted for covariation of SES and race, within multiple risk groups.

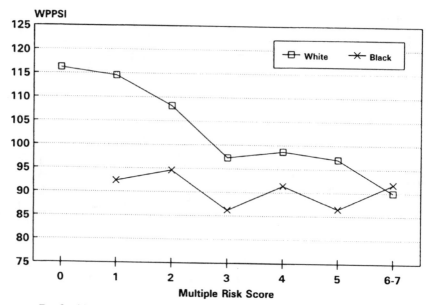

FIG. 3.—Mean 4-year IQ scores of whites and blacks within multiple risk groups

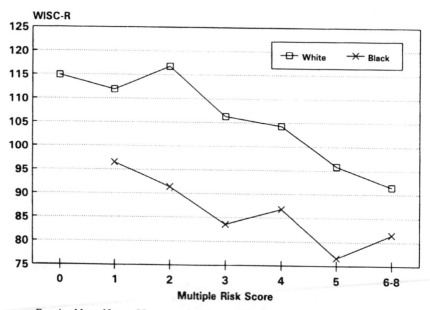

FIG. 4.—Mean 13-year IQ scores of whites and blacks within multiple risk groups

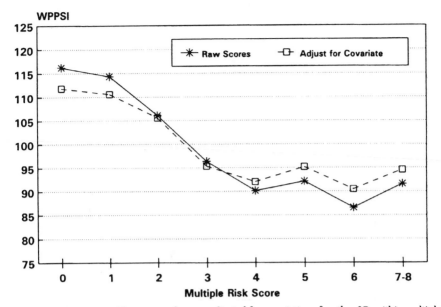

FIG. 5.—Mean 4-year IQ scores, and means adjusted for covariation of mother IQ, within multiple risk groups.

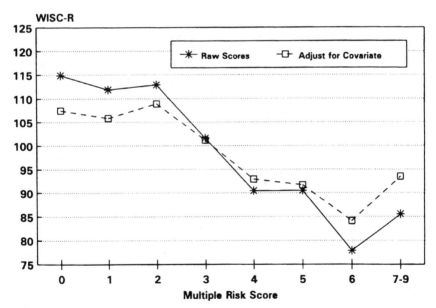

FIG. 6.—Mean 13-year IQ scores, and means adjusted for covariation of mother IQ, within multiple risk groups.

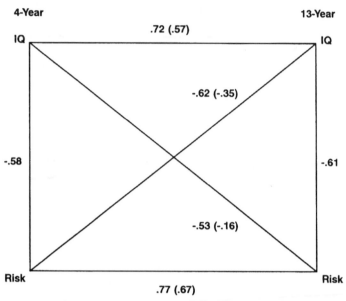

4-Year   13-Year

.72 (.57)

IQ   IQ

-.62 (-.35)

-.58   -.61

-.53 (-.16)

Risk   Risk

.77 (.67)

Fig. 7.—Summary of correlations among composite multiple risk scores and child IQ scores at 4 and 13 years. (Partial correlations are in parentheses.)

at 4 years; R^2 change = .12 at 13 years; $p <$ .01). The effect sizes for these two analyses were f^2 = .38 and f^2 = .24 at 4 and 13 years, respectively. These are in the medium (f^2 = .15) to large (f^2 = .40) range.

Longitudinal Prediction of Child IQ

The third major question was the degree to which individual, contextual, and parental variables predicted 13-year child IQ. The highest single correlate of child IQ at 13 years of age was child IQ at 4 years of age (r = .72). Mother IQ (r = .62) and 4-year composite multiple risk (r = −.62) were comparable in their ability to predict 13-year child IQ. However, the 4-year child IQ did not comprise all of the significant explanation of 13-year IQ. The partial correlation of 4-year composite risk with 13-year child IQ (partialling 4-year child IQ) was −.35 (t = 4.49; $p <$ .01). It is interesting to note in this context that the magnitude of stability in multiple risk (r = .77) was about the same as that for child IQ. Child IQ at age 4 was also a good predictor of composite risk at age 13 (r = −.53); however, when 4-year composite risk was covaried, the partial correlation dropped to −.16. To provide a full appreciation of the longitudinal relations among risk and IQ variables, these data are presented in the format of a cross-panel analysis (see Fig. 7). Note that, in line with cri-

tiques of cross panel analysis (Rogosa, 1980), we do not interpret these data from a causal perspective. They are included for descriptive purposes only.

Specificity of Individual Risk Influences

The final major question was whether any specific patterns of risk were better predictors of child outcomes. Ideally, such an analysis would examine outcomes in families who have different patterns of risk, but the same number of risk factors. We examined this question only with families who had enough risk factors so that questions about patterns of risk would be meaningful. Those families with more than two risk factors were included in the analysis. Because of the wide range of number of risk factors in the final clusters used, number of risks was used as a covariate when examining group differences on IQ scores.

To discern patterns among the families, cluster analysis was performed at each age on the 10 risk factors using the complete linkage method. At each age four clusters were retained, which resulted in adequate group sizes for subsequent analyses. The characteristics of these groups of families are described in Table 5.

At 4 years of age two of the clusters had maternal mental health and education as

TABLE 5

SUMMARY OF CLUSTER ANALYSES

	Number of Risk Factors	Child IQ	Adjusted Child IQ
4-year cluster risk factors:			
Mental health, education, anxiety (n = 20)	4.7 (1.7)[a]	95.4 (13.0)	95.1 (12.8)
Mental health, education, perspectives, occupation, minority status (n = 12)	6.1 (1.4)	91.7 (12.8)	93.7 (12.5)
Education, occupation, minority status, interaction (n = 29)	4.7 (1.2)	89.7 (11.6)	89.5 (11.3)
Perspectives, minority status (n = 10)	3.8 (.8)	90.0 (19.1)	88.5 (19.3)
13-year cluster risk factors:			
Mental health, life events, father absent, occupation, anxiety (n = 18)	5.3 (1.6)[b]	94.2 (17.9)	97.3 (16.5)
Mental health, father absent, minority (n = 23)	3.7 (.9)	92.4 (16.3)	88.7 (14.9)
Mental health, interaction (n = 15)	4.0 (.8)	98.2 (19.5)	95.7 (18.5)
Mental health, education, perspectives, father absent, minority (n = 24)	5.3 (1.7)	85.3 (13.0)	88.4 (12.5)

NOTE.—Table entries are means (standard deviations in parentheses). IQ means were adjusted for covariate of number of risk factors. Risk factors listed for each cluster are those where more than 50% of the members had that factor.

[a] Number of risk factors significantly different, $F = 5.43$, $p < .01$.

[b] Number of risk factors significantly different, $F = 7.92$, $p < .01$.

231

risks; these clusters were differentiated in that one had anxiety and the other had parenting perspectives, family occupation, and minority status. A third cluster had maternal education, family occupation, minority status, and interaction as risk factors. The final cluster had parenting perspectives and minority status as risks. The mean number of risk factors in the four groups ranged from 3.8 to 6.1, which was significant (see Table 5). When number of risk factors was partialled from the analysis, adjusted means of child IQ scores ranged from 88.5 to 95.1, which was not a significant difference ($F = 0.92$, $p = .44$).

At 13 years, all of the clusters had maternal mental health as a risk. They were differentiated as follows. The first cluster had life events, father absence, family occupation, and anxiety as risks; the second had father absence and minority status as risks; the third cluster had interaction as a risk; the final cluster had maternal education, parenting perspectives, father absence, and minority status as risks. As at 4 years, the mean number of risk factors was significantly different (see Table 5), ranging from 3.7 to 5.3, but the child IQ scores were not different among the four groups ($F = 1.74$, $p = .17$) when number of risk factors was partialled. The adjusted means ranged from 88.7 to 97.3.

Discussion

The current study was a further attempt to examine the effects of environment on the intellectual development of children at 4 and 13 years of age. Analysis involved 10 risk factors that are predominantly found in lower SES groups but affect the development of children at all SES levels. Because of the potent effects of our multiple risk index found at 4 years (Sameroff, Seifer, Barocas, Zax, & Greenspan, 1987), we calculated a new multiple environmental risk score for each family based on their situation 9 years later.

Environmental Risk and Intellectual Development

The single composite multiple risk score at 4 years explained 34% of the variance in the child's IQ. At 13 years the composite risk score explained 37% of the variance in the child's IQ. Corresponding proportion of variance estimates using the 10-variable multiple-regression approach were 50% at both ages.

It should be remembered that there was no direct measure of child behavior in the risk index. The child was involved in these measurements only in a minor way—as the interactive partner in one of the 10 risk assessments at 4 years of age, and in that case, only scores of mothers' behavior during that interaction were used. Thus, without specifically looking at the child we were able to predict one-third to one-half of the variance (depending on the analysis method used) in his or her intelligence from preschool through adolescence.

The results are clear in demonstrating: (1) multiple risk was related to child IQ at 4 and 13 years with effects remaining after SES and race were controlled (particularly when the composite multiple risk strategy was used); (2) maternal IQ did not account for all of these effects; (3) multiple risk was important in longitudinal prediction, even after prior measurement of child IQ was accounted for—stability in contextual risk was of the same magnitude as stability of child IQ; and (4) for families with multiple risks (i.e., with three or more risks), the pattern of risk was less important than the total amount of risk present in the child's context. These findings represent a replication at 13 years of age of findings previously reported for this sample for multiple risks assessed during the first 4 years of life (Sameroff, Seifer, Barocas, Zax, & Greenspan, 1987).

Although we found that the more risk factors, the worse the developmental outcome, an argument could be made that the multiple risk score was merely a surrogate for social status. In order to demonstrate that the multiple risk score was a correlate of IQ independent of social status, we covaried SES and race and still found a major effect of multiple risk score. The corresponding biological argument is that the environmental multiple risk score is a surrogate for genetic influences. Mothers with poor IQ genes provide poor environments for their children with poor IQ genes. To examine this hypothesis we covaried mother's IQ and still found a major effect of multiple risk score.

When interpreting these results, the unique nature of the subjects should be considered. First, risk factors in this study are overrepresented compared with the general population, which may serve to accentuate the relative predictive power of risk on IQ. This may also serve to enhance the nonspecific nature of the risk effects, since many of these families suffered from simultaneous risk conditions. Second, the absolute size of the relations found between risk and outcome may be sample specific; factors such as the amount and type of risk may be unique to this study. Third, as discussed below, the high incidence of mental illness in this sample may also mask specificity of risk, especially at 13 years where it was difficult to find clusters of risk patterns that did not include maternal mental illness.

Stability of Environmental Risk

Within the RLS our attention has been devoted to the source of stability and instability in child performance. The typical statistic reported in longitudinal research is the correlation between early and later performance of the children. We too found such correlations. Intelligence at 4 years correlated .72 with intelligence at 13 years. The usual interpretation of such a number is that there is a continuity of competence or incompetence in the child. Such a conclusion cannot be challenged if the only assessments in the study are of the children. In the RLS we examined environmental as well as child factors. We were able to correlate environmental characteristics across time as well as child ones. We found that the correlation between composite multiple risk scores at the two ages was .76, as great as or greater than any stability within the child. Those children had poor family and social environments when they were born (Sameroff, Seifer, Barocas, Zax, & Greenspan, 1987), still had them when they were 13, and probably would continue to have them for the foreseeable future.

When children's 4-year IQ scores were partialled from the 13-year IQ score, there was still a highly reliable proportion of variance associated with environmental risk. Whatever the child's ability for achieving high levels of competence, it was severely undermined by the continuing paucity of environmental support. Whatever the capabilities provided to the child by individual factors, the environment nevertheless placed additional constraints on the opportunities for further development.

A methodological point regarding data analysis strategy is also important to consider. Studies such as the one reported here, involving the longitudinal assessment of families that are difficult to identify and difficult to maintain in longitudinal samples, are expensive and not often replicated. A sample size of 152 is relatively large for such studies. Yet, the use of statistical techniques

that would yield the highest degree of prediction (i.e., the multiple regression approach) were limited by issues of statistical power. When partial regressions were examined, the use of 10 predictors precluded finding statistical significance in the multiple regression strategy even though meaningful proportions of variance were explained. In contrast, the single composite risk score strategy resulted in findings that were more often statistically significant, were amenable to graphical presentation, and were less affected by issues of statistical power.

Quantity versus Quality of Risk

The final issue was related to the quality of the risk factors. In this study we tested whether it was the number or kind of risk factors that most strongly affected child behavior. At both 4 and 13 years we found that the number of risk factors was the more important consideration. When we cluster analyzed the risk factors, we found generally that, independent of the number of risk factors, different patterns of risk were not related to child IQ.

Some limitations of the cluster analysis of patterns of risk should be noted. First, this analysis was exploratory; we did not recruit families into this study based on the presence of different patterns of risk. Second, at 13 years of age all clusters had more than half of the families with maternal mental illness as a risk factor. Thus, this analysis did not differentiate groups with respect to this individual risk factor. Third, because families that had low numbers of risks (i.e., did not have meaningful patterns) were eliminated from the analysis, there were fewer cases with which to examine group differences. Thus, generalizability is appropriate only to families with several risk factors, and the power of these tests to detect group differences is not as high as one would like.

Risk and Protective Factors

In this study we identified risk factors for low intelligence in children. From these data we concluded that there are many sources of risk that affect child outcome ranging from distal factors like the economic status of the family to proximal factors like the parent's interaction with the child. From a psychological perspective distal experiential factors must affect the child through the operation of proximal factors. Where distal variables continue to have an impact, it is an indication that the relevant proximal variables have not been identified or assessed.

The finding that parent interaction is a risk variable at 4 years but not at 13 years is a case in point. For the adolescent, peer and school influences may be much more salient for development than parent influences, yet these peer variables were not assessed in this study. An alternative explanation is that the assessment strategy, the Camberwell Family Interview, was ill suited for measuring interaction in this context.

The analysis of risk factors addresses only one of the multiple influences that regulate developmental outcomes. Others, from the more optimistic perspective, have directed their attention to identifying resilient children and protective factors (Luthar & Zigler, 1991; Masten & Garmezy, 1985; Seifer, Sameroff, Baldwin, & Baldwin, in press). Whether reducing risk or increasing protection is the more useful strategy for future interventions will be determined by scientific and social experiments beyond the scope of this report. The variables that we did assess point to the multiple levels of social influence and the complexity of the dynamic interactions and transactions that will have to be analyzed before a comprehensive view of the developmental process will be revealed.

References

Ammons, R. B., & Ammons, C. H. (1962). *The Quick Test (QT): Provisional manual*. Missoula, MT: Psychological Test Specialists.

Baltes, P. B., Reese, H. W., & Lipsitt, L. P. (1980). Life span developmental psychology. *Annual Review of Psychology, 31*, 65–110.

Barocas, R., Seifer, R., Sameroff, A. J., Andrews, T. A., Croft, R. T., & Ostrow, E. (1991). Social and interpersonal determinants of developmental risk. *Developmental Psychology, 27*, 479–488.

Broman, S. H., Nichols, P. L., & Kennedy, W. A. (1975). *Preschool IQ: Prenatal and early developmental correlates*. Hillsdale, NJ: Erlbaum.

Bronfenbrenner, U. (1979). *The ecology of human development*. Cambridge, MA: Harvard University Press.

Brown, G. N., & Rutter, M. (1966). The measurement of family activities and relationships: A methodological study. *Human Relations, 19*, 214–263.

Clausen, J. A. (1968). *Socialization and society*. Boston: Little, Brown.

Coddington, R. D. (1972a). The significance of life events as etiologic factors in the diseases of children: I. A survey of professional workers. *Journal of Psychometric Research, 16*, 7–18.

Coddington, R. D. (1972b). The significance of life events as etiologic factors in the diseases of children: II. A study of normal population. *Journal of Psychometric Research, 16*, 205–213.

Cohen, J. (1988). *Statistical power analysis for the social sciences* (2d ed.). Hillsdale, NJ: Erlbaum.

Cohen, J. (1990). Some things I have learned (so far). *American Psychologist, 45*, 1304–1312.

Elder, G. H., Jr. (1984). Families, kin, and the life course: A sociological perspective. In R. D. Parke (Ed.), *Review of child development research: The family* (Vol. 7). Chicago: University of Chicago Press.

Endicott, J., & Spitzer, R. L. (1972). Current and past psychopathology scales (CAPPS). *Archives of General Psychiatry, 27*, 678–687.

Garmezy, N., & Tellegen, A. (1984). Studies of stress-resistant children: Methods, variables, and preliminary findings. In F. Morrison, C. Lord, & D. Keating (Eds.), *Advances in applied developmental psychology* (Vol. 1, pp. 231–287). New York: Academic Press.

Hollingshead, A. B. (1975). *Four-Factor Index of Social Status*. Unpublished manuscript, Yale University.

Holmes, T. H., & Rahe, R. H. (1967). The social readjustment rating scale. *Journal of Psychosomatic Research, 11*, 213–218.

Kaufman, A. S. (1972). A short form of the Wechsler Preschool and Primary Scale of Intelligence. *Journal of Consulting and Clinical Psychology, 39*, 361–379.

Kaufman, A. S. (1979). *Intelligent testing with the WISC-R*. New York: Wiley.

Kohn, M. L. (1977). *Class and conformity: A study in values* (2d ed.). Chicago: University of Chicago Press.

Kohn, M., & Schooler, C. (1983). *Work and personality: An inquiry into the impact of social stratification*. Norwood, NJ: Ablex.

Lerner, R. M., Skinner, E. A., & Sorell, G. T. (1980). Methodological implications of contextual/dialectic theories of development. *Human Development, 23*, 225–235.

Luthar, S. S., & Zigler, E. (1991). Vulnerability and competence: A review of research on resilience in childhood. *American Journal of Orthopsychiatry, 61*, 6–22.

Masten, A. M., & Garmezy, N. (1985). Risk, vulnerability, and protective factors in developmental psychopathology. In B. B. Lahey & A. E. Kazdin (Eds.), *Advances in clinical child psychology* (Vol. 8, pp. 1–52). New York: Plenum.

Mayer, S. E., & Jencks, C. (1989). Growing up in poor neighborhoods: How much does it matter? *Science, 243*, 1441–1445.

Parmelee, A. H., & Haber, A. (1973). Who is the

at risk infant? *Clinical Obstetrics and Gynecology, 16,* 376–387.

Rogosa, D. (1980). A critique of cross-lagged correlation. *Psychological Bulletin, 88,* 245–258.

Rosenzweig, L., Seifer, R., & Sameroff, A. J. (1982). *The impact of stressful life events on high-risk infants.* Unpublished manuscript.

Rutter, M. (1976). Research report: Isle of Wight studies, 1964–1974. *Psychological Medicine, 6,* 313–332.

Rutter, M. (1979). Protective factors in children's responses to stress and disadvantage. In M. W. Kent & J. E. Rolf (Eds.), *Primary prevention of psychopathology: Vol. 3. Social competence in children* (pp. 49–74). Hanover, NH: University Press of New England.

Sameroff, A. J. (1983). Developmental systems: Contexts and evolution. In W. Kessen (Ed.), P. H. Mussen (Series Ed.), *Handbook of child psychology: Vol. 1. History, theory, and methods* (pp. 237–294). New York: Wiley.

Sameroff, A. J., & Feil, L. (1985). Parental concepts of development. In I. E. Sigel (Ed.), *Parental belief systems: The psychological consequences for children* (pp. 84–104). Hillsdale, NJ: Erlbaum.

Sameroff, A. J., Seifer, R., Barocas, R., Zax, M., & Greenspan, S. (1987). Intelligence quotient scores of 4-year-old children: Social environmental risk factors. *Pediatrics, 79,* 343–350.

Sameroff, A. J., Seifer, R., & Zax, M. (1982). Early development of children at risk for emotional disorder. *Monographs of the Society for Research in Child Development, 47*(7, Serial No. 199).

Sameroff, A. J., Seifer, R., Zax, M., & Barocas, R. (1987). Early indicators of developmental risk: The Rochester Longitudinal Study. *Schizophrenia Bulletin, 13,* 383–394.

Sedlmeier, P., & Gigerenzer, G. (1989). Do studies of statistical power have an effect on the power of studies? *Psychological Bulletin, 105,* 309–316.

Seifer, R., Sameroff, A. J., Baldwin, C. P., & Baldwin, A. (in press). Child and family factors that ameliorate risk between 4 and 13 years of age. *Journal of the American Academy of Child and Adolescent Psychiatry.*

Shipley, W. C. (1967). *Shipley Institute of Living Scale: Manual of directions and scoring key.* Hartford, CT: Institute of Living.

Wachs, T. D., & Gruen, G. (1982). *Early experience and human development.* New York: Plenum.

Wechsler, D. (1967). *The Wechsler Preschool and Primary Scale of Intelligence.* New York: Psychological Corp.

Wechsler, D. (1974). *Wechsler Intelligence Scale for Children—Revised.* New York: Psychological Corp.

Williams, S., Anderson, J., McGee, R., & Silva, P. A. (1990). Risk factors for behavioral and emotional disorder in preadolescent children. *Journal of the American Academy of Child and Adolescent Psychiatry, 29,* 413–419.

World Health Organization (1973). *The international pilot study of schizophrenia* (Vol. 1). Geneva: World Health Organization.

JOURNAL OF RESEARCH ON ADOLESCENCE, 6(4), 629–648
Copyright © 1996, Lawrence Erlbaum Associates, Inc.

School Outcomes for Minority-Group Adolescent Mothers at 28 to 36 Months Postpartum: A Longitudinal Follow-Up

Bonnie J. Leadbeater

Department of Psychology
Yale University

Following up on a 12-month prospective study (Linares, Leadbeater, Kato, & Jaffe, 1991), stability and predictors of delayed grade-placement for 84 inner-city, African American and Puerto Rican adolescent mothers were investigated. Based on school attendance before pregnancy and up to 28 to 36 months postpartum, mothers were classified as continuous attenders, returners, before-pregnancy dropouts, and after-pregnancy dropouts. A majority (78.5%) of the mothers were in the same school-outcome groups at both assessment points. Predelivery school performance was the strongest predictor of delayed grade-placement. Compared to the dropout groups, mothers who were in school or graduated reported fewer repeat pregnancies, and more of them sought postsecondary education. Mothers who returned to school reported fewer stressful life events, more family support, fewer depressive symptoms, and stronger career commitments than did mothers in the dropout groups. The implications of early school failure and inadequate emphasis on girls' career development for adolescent mothers' school outcomes are discussed.

Although school-age parenting is typically believed to disrupt optimal school achievement, past research demonstrated that there is considerable diversity in educational outcomes for adolescent mothers (Furstenburg, Brooks-Gunn, & Morgan, 1987; Haggstrom, Kanouse, & Morrison, 1986; Henshaw, Kenney,

---

Requests for reprints should be sent to Bonnie Leadbeater, Department of Psychology, Yale University, P.O. Box 208205, New Haven, CT, 06520–8205.

Somberg, & Van Vort, 1989; Linares, Leadbeater, Kato, & Jaffe, 1991; Moore et al., 1993; Mott & Marsiglio, 1985; Scott-Jones, 1991; Scott-Jones & Turner; 1990; Upchurch, 1993). National statistics indicated that a majority of adolescent mothers (71%) eventually do complete high school; however, few (20%) pursue college education (Alan Guttmacher Institute, 1994). Those who graduate from high school face staggering competition in a job market that demands increasing levels of education (Strawn, 1992).

Multivariate, longitudinal analyses of large-scale surveys of adolescent mothers illuminated important predictors of high school graduation or obtaining a General Equivalency Diploma (GED). These include antecedent factors (i.e., poverty; race/ethnicity; and parents' educational, employment, and marital status) and events that occur subsequent to the first birth (i.e., stressful life events and repeat pregnancies). Adolescents from disadvantaged family backgrounds who become mothers before the age of 18 appear to be at particular risk for negative outcomes (see reviews in Alan Guttmacher Institute, 1994; Linares et al., 1991; Scott-Jones & Turner, 1990; Upchurch, 1993; Upchurch & McCarthy, 1990, 1991).

Despite the availability of these large-scale datasets, the *relative* importance of family background characteristics, school-age childbearing, and subsequent events for the educational and economic outcomes of adolescent mothers is the subject of ongoing debate (Geronimus & Korenman, in press; Hoffman, Foster, & Furstenberg, 1992). These large-scale studies generally did not account for the prepregnancy school achievement of adolescent mothers in assessing the effects of childbearing on subsequent educational success. Moreover, little prospective research went beyond demographic factors to investigate what differentiates those adolescent mothers who persist in high school, despite high-risk circumstances, from those who drop out.

Upchurch (1992) prospectively assessed relations between early schooling and childbearing experiences in a sample of women who were 14 to 18 years old in initial interviews. Using data from the National Longitudinal Survey of Youth (NLSY) collected annually from 1979 to 1986, she reported that 53.1% of White, 59.5% of Black, and 36.7% of Hispanic women who became mothers before the age of 18 graduated from high school or got a GED. Those who dropped out of school *before* they became pregnant came from the least educated family backgrounds and were more likely to be White or Hispanic than to be Black. Blacks were more likely to drop out of school *after* becoming pregnant than were Whites or Hispanics.

Differences among these subgroups were also suggested in a study of 120 inner-city, poor, African American and Puerto Rican adolescents who became mothers when they were 14 to 18 years old (Linares et al. 1991). By 12-months postpartum, 40.7% of the mothers were in school or had graduated, a further 21.2% had returned, 12.4% had dropped out prior to the pregnancy, and 25.7% dropped out after the pregnancy. School performance before the delivery was the strongest predictor of their delayed grade-placement (ideal age for grade minus last grade completed). Group differences were also found: Fewer mothers (18%) who attended continuously in this 1st year postpartum had repeat pregnancies compared to those (69%) who had dropped out before the pregnancy. Before-pregnancy dropouts also reported more depressive symptoms at delivery than did any of the other mothers. Returners (32%) and after-pregnancy dropouts (63%) also had more repeat pregnancies than did continuous attenders. These subgroups did not differ on measures of occupational aspirations, stressful life events, or quality of support from their families or their children's biological fathers. However, measures of occupational aspirations failed to distinguish ideal from realistic career goals, and assessments of support from the children's fathers were limited to instrumental support to the children rather than emotional support to the adolescent mothers.

This study presents results from analyses of longitudinal data collected from a sample of adolescent mothers at 28 to 36 months postpartum. The goals in conducting this follow-up were to (a) assess the stability of the school-outcome groups, (b) compare the relative importance of predelivery educational achievements and postdelivery risk and protective factors for school outcomes at 28 to 36 months postpartum, and (c) identify factors that distinguish between mothers who drop out from those who remain in school, graduate, or return to school after a period of absence. This intensive follow-up of a sample of disadvantaged, inner-city, minority-group adolescent mothers offers to illuminate the forces that predict negative outcomes while providing a window into the lives of those who succeed despite high-risk circumstances. Prospective predictors included variables that preceded the delivery (ethnicity and predelivery school achievement), variables that tapped postdelivery risk factors (maternal depressive symptoms, stressful life events, and repeat pregnancies), and protective factors (living with the adolescent's mother [called the grandmother in this report]; child care help; and emotional support from family, peers, and boyfriends).

Given the extensive literature suggesting causal links between early childbearing and negative school outcomes, it was expected that risk and protective factors occurring subsequent to the delivery would better predict school outcomes at almost 3 years postpartum than would prepregnancy school achievement. Dropouts were expected to be experiencing higher levels of the postpartum risk factors and fewer protective factors than were consistent attenders and graduates. Support from the children's fathers was not expected to relate to the mothers' educational outcomes because of the instability of these relationships (Chase-Lansdale & Vinovskis, 1987).

239

METHOD

Participants

One hundred and twenty adolescent mothers and their children were participants in the original sample. They were recruited consecutively in 1987 and 1988 from adolescent mothers who at 3 to 4 weeks postpartum brought their infants for well baby care to an urban adolescent health center. They represented approximately 89% of the adolescent mothers who were enrolled at the clinic during that time. Details of the sample, procedures, and measures were elaborated in Leadbeater and Linares (1992).

Mothers were 14 to 19 years old at delivery ($M = 17.1$, $SD = 1.2$) and were primarily African American (53.1%) or Puerto Rican (42.5%). All but 2 were primiparous, and most lived with their own mothers (71.7%) and came from families on welfare (64.6%). On average, they had completed 9.5 ($SD = 1.3$) years of school, and half remained in school or had graduated at delivery (Linares et al., 1991). The majority of the children were from full-term deliveries and were of normal birth weight. At 28 to 36 months postpartum, the mothers' average age was 19.7 years ($SD = 1.2$). The majority lived with their mothers (52.4%) and were supported on their own (17.9%) or their mothers' public assistance (52.4%). Only 6 of the mothers (7.9%) were married.

Procedure

Mothers were seen in individual interviews five times. All data were collected by research assistants with at least a master's degree in social work, counseling, or developmental psychology. At 3 to 4 weeks postpartum (Time 1), initial questionnaire data were collected. Similar questionnaire data were collected again at 6 months (Time 2), 12 months (Time 3), and 28 to 36 months (Time 5) postpartum. The wider gap at Time 5 ($M = 32$ months postpartum, $SD = 4$ months) reflected increased difficulties finding the mothers. Timing of the Time 5 interview was not related to school-outcome group, $F(3, 80) = .15$, $p < .92$, or to delayed educational achievement, $r = -.01$, and was not expected to influence the findings reported here. Data collected at 20 to 24 months (Time 4) consisted of child language assessments and videotapes of mother–child interactions, which were not used in these analyses.

Numbers used in the analyses vary somewhat at each time point due to difficulties in locating the mothers or in scheduling the interviews in the short time frames between assessments. Questionnaire data were complete for 113 (94%) mothers from Time 1 to Time 3 and 84 (71%) mothers at Time

5. Mothers not in the sample at 28 to 36 months did not differ significantly from the remaining participants on any of the initial demographic or predictor variables except for levels of depressive symptoms, $t(116) = 2.13$, $p < .04$. At delivery, mothers remaining in the study reported significantly more depressive symptoms ($M = 13.9$, $SD = 7.8$) than did those not interviewed ($M = 10.7$, $SD = 7.2$). This difference of 3.0 points is unlikely to be of practical or clinical significance.

At the 28 to 36-month assessment, ethnographic data were also collected in an audiotaped, semistructured interview that was designed to elicit the mothers' descriptions of their daily lives since their children were born, their aspirations for themselves and their children, their plans to accomplish these goals, their views of themselves as women and as mothers, and the stability and quality of their social support networks. Interviews were transcribed and subjected to content coding as described later. These data were available for 79 of the 84 mothers who completed questionnaires at Time 5 (2 mothers left before completing the interview, and 3 audiotapes were inaudible).

Measures

Questionnaire Data

As in Linares et al. (1991), the school-outcome groups were determined from the adolescent mothers' responses to questions about type of school enrolled in, when last attended, last grade completed, and current grade level at Times 1, 2, 3, and 5. The criterion for in-school status was defined as current school attendance (not merely school enrollment) or, if interviewed during the summer months, attendance in the last marking period. The sample was divided into four groups: *Continuous attenders/graduates* were 28 (33%) mothers who attended school through the pregnancy and at Times 1, 2, 3, and 5, or had graduated from high school or a GED program (68% of attenders). *School returners* were 16 (19%) mothers who were not in school during the pregnancy or at Times 1, 2 or 3 but reported returning or graduating by Time 5. *Before-pregnancy dropouts* were 10 (12%) mothers who had dropped out before the pregnancy and were not attending school at Times 1, 2, 3, or 5. *After-pregnancy dropouts* were 30 (36%) mothers who had dropped out of school during the pregnancy or by Times 1, 2, or 3 and had not returned by Time 5.

Delayed grade-placement.   Being "overage" for grade level, a correlate of eventual school dropout (Hahn, Danzberger, & Lefkowitz, 1987), was calculated as the discrepancy score between the mother's last grade completed and her "ideal" grade-placement if she had entered Grade 1 by age 6 and had not been retained subsequently (Foltz, Klerman, & Jekel, 1972). High school graduation or attainment of a GED was set as the highest ideal level of achievement because only 5 of the mothers had any postsecondary education by Time 5.

Depressive symptoms.   The Beck Depression Inventory (Beck, 1967) is a widely used, 21-item questionnaire that assesses cognitive, behavioral, affective, and somatic symptoms of depression. Weighted response categories are scored 0 to 3 for each of the 21 items and are summed to yield a single score.

Perceived social support.   The Perceived Social Support From Family and Perceived Social Support From Friends (Procidano & Heller, 1983) scales were used as measures of the perceived emotional support received. Although many social support measures were available, these had the advantage of focusing specifically on the quality of emotional relationships with family and friends (Tardy, 1985).

As an assessment of concrete support provided by the maternal or paternal grandmothers, *day care help* was coded from a time line chart as 0 *(No, grandmother does not help or helps very rarely)* or 1 *(Yes, grandmother shares in the child's care).* Residence with the grandmother at Time 5 was also coded as *yes* or *no.*

Life stress.   The Life Events Scale (Egeland, Breitenbucher, & Rosenberg, 1980) is a structured interview that investigates the occurrence of, and the circumstances surrounding, 44 events common to low-income, primiparous women. For example, frequently reported events included unemployment for themselves or someone they were dependent on, school problems, moves, inadequate housing, chronic illnesses in immediate family, deaths of family members or close friends, involvement in physical fights, changes in social life, problems with relatives, and unstable relationships with boyfriends. Higher scores (on a scale of 0 to 3) reflect disruption due to the greater frequency or longer duration of the event, or the closeness of the relationships involved.

Repeat pregnancies and their outcomes were based on self-reports at Times 3 and 5. At Time 3, these reports were also verified through a search of medical records available for 61% of the participants. Agreement between the medical records and self-reports was high 95% ($\kappa = .91$) at that time.

Ethnographic Data

Content coding of the interview data involved an iterative process by which response themes were identified in about one third of the transcripts. These were refined and applied to the remaining interview. Codes were then taught to new raters for reliability assessments.

Occupational commitment was coded from mothers' responses to open-ended questions that explored current work aspirations: "Would you like to be working?" "At what?" "What would your ideal job be say in 5 years?" "How do you plan to achieve your goals?" "Have you begun to work toward these goals?" These were coded for work aspirations: 0 *(no choice elicited)*, 1 *(gives a vague choice or several possible choices)*, 2 *(gives a clear statement of work aspirations)*; has plans for achieving goals: 1 *(yes)*, 0 *(no)*; and is currently pursuing goals: 1 *(yes)*, 0 *(no)*. Scores were summed to give a score for overall occupational commitment, with high scores reflecting a clear choice with plans for achieving that goal as well as active pursuit of it. Agreement on codes for two coders for a third of the interviews was 79% for choice, 85% for having plans, and 89% for active pursuit.

Plans to seek postsecondary education was coded as *yes* or *no* from mothers' responses to questions about their plans for achieving their career goals. Agreement for two coders for a third of the interviews was 89%.

Father's support of the child was coded from the mother's descriptions of the child's relationship with the father from the interview data as 1 *(little or no contact)*, 2 *(sees child but does not have a good relationship)*, or 3 *(sees child frequently and has a close relationship)*. Descriptions of his *relationship to the mother* were coded as 1 *(little or no contact)*, 2 *(neutral relationship)*, or 3 *(sees frequently in a warm, emotionally supportive relationship)*. Agreements for two coders for a third of the interviews were 95% for relationship with the child and 89% for relationship with the mother.

Reasons for noninvolvement with the child's father were coded as 0 *(no problems mentioned)*, 1 *(immature, irresponsible, seeing other women)*, 2 *(excessively macho, restrictive, or physically abusive)*, 3 *(involved in selling or using drugs)*, 4 *(in prison)*, or 5 *(dead)*. All categories mentioned were noted; however, scores analyzed reflected the highest category given, reasoning that the problems overlapped (i.e., prison terms and violent deaths were often for drug-related reasons), and those at higher levels reflected greater likelihood that fathers were unavailable. Agreement between two coders was 84%.

Romantic partners' support. The mothers' descriptions of relationships with men other than their children's fathers were coded as 1 *(no
relationship)*, 2 *(seeing someone in a conflicted or neutral relationship)*, or 3 *(sees
frequently in a warm, emotionally supportive relationship)*. Agreement between
two coders for a third of the interviews was 95%.

RESULTS

Delayed Grade-Placement at 28 to 36 Months Postpartum

Correlations and hierarchical regression analyses were used to assess the
associations of the demographic, individual, support, and stress variables
with Time 5 delayed grade-placement. Intercorrelations among the variables are presented in Table 1. Greater risk of Time 5 delayed grade-placement was associated significantly with being more delayed in grade-placement for age at delivery and reporting more stressful life events 1 year after
delivery. Mothers who were more delayed also reported higher levels of
concurrent depressive symptoms, more repeat pregnancies, and lower
occupational commitments by Time 5.

Intercorrelations among the items also suggest associations among variables that may indirectly affect school outcomes: Being African American
tends to be related to less initial and Time 5 delayed grade-placement ($p <$
.10) and is significantly associated with higher work commitment scores.

Mothers on public assistance at Time 3 were more delayed in their
grade-placement at delivery than were those mothers not receiving public
assistance.

Receiving day care help from the grandmothers during the first 28 to 36
months postpartum was related to more perceived family support and to
fewer repeat pregnancies up to that time. Fewer repeat pregnancies in this
period were also associated with higher work commitment scores.

As reported in Leadbeater and Linares (1992), depressive symptoms,
stressful life events, and social supports from family and friends were
slightly to moderately intercorrelated.

A hierarchical regression equation was computed to examine the relative
contributions of the prospective predictor variables that were significantly
correlated with delayed grade-placement at Time 5. Delayed grade-placement at Time 1 was entered before Time 3 risk and protective factors and
repeat pregnancies by Time 5 to assess their effects after controlling for
prepregnancy school performance. Race/ethnicity was entered into the
equation last to see if it added to the explained variance once other differ-

TABLE 1
Intercorrelations Among Predictors of Time 5 Delayed Grade-Placement

	1	2	3	4	5	6	7	8	9	10	11	12	13
1. T5 delayed grades													
Antecedent factors													
2. T1 delayed grades	56***												
3. Ethnicity/race[a]	-21*	-25**											
Risks assessed at 12 months postpartum (Time 3)													
4. Depressive symptoms	06	04	00										
5. Stressful life events	21**	04	00	66***									
Protectors assessed at 12 months postpartum (Time 3)													
6. Support from family	00	02	-06	-41***	-40***								
7. Support from friends	-16	-08	00	-43***	-36***	23**							
8. On public assistance	16	33**	-13	05	09	-04	12						
Risks assessed at 28 to 36 months postpartum (Time 5)													
9. Depressive symptoms	23**	17*	08	51***	29**	-17*	-23**	-23**					
10. Repeat pregnancies	29***	28***	-03	09	20*	02	00	00	15				
Protectors at 28 to 36 months postpartum (Time 5)													
11. Child care help	-08	-29***	-17*	-21*	43***	09	13	-09	-26**	07			
12. Child's fathers' support	04	17*	02	-21*	-11	15	07	06	08	03	-15		
13. New partners' support	-17*	-16	00	09	04	08	13	-03	-18*	03	05	-49***	
14. Occupational commitment	22**	-10	33***	-03	05	04	03	11	-15	-31***	18*	-15	09

Note. Decimals are omitted from all correlations. Numbers range from 79 to 84 due to missing data points.
[a] African American = 1, Hispanic = 0.
*p < .10. **p < .05. ***p < .01.

ences were accounted for. Mean substitutions were made for occasional missing predictors for all African American and Hispanic mothers who had Time 5 delayed grade-placement scores ($n = 79$). As shown in Table 2, this equation explained a total of 33% of the variance in Time 5 delayed grade-placement, $F(5, 73) = 7.29$, $p < .001$). Only prepregnancy delayed grade-placement at Time 1 added independently to the explained variance.

For comparison with findings from other studies, this regression equation was computed a second time without controlling for predelivery delayed grade-placement. As seen in Table 2, a total of 13% of the variance in delayed grade-placement at Time 5 was explained by this equation, $F(4, 74) = 2.89$, $p < 02$. Occurrence of a repeat pregnancy and race/ethnicity each added independently ($p < .05$) to the explained variance in predicting more negative outcomes.

Characteristics of Time 5 School-Outcome Groups

Although multivariate regression analyses reveal information about the relative importance of predictors, they may obscure within group differences. Chi-square tests of independence and multivariate analyses of variance (MANOVAs) with follow-up univariate analyses and Newman–Keuls Multiple Range tests were used to test for group differences. Distributions and stability of Time 5 school-outcome groups with the Time 3 groups that were previously reported in Linares et al. (1991) were also assessed.

TABLE 2
Summary of Hierarchical Multiple Regression Analysis for Prospective Predictors of Delayed Grade-Placement at Time 5

Variables	Multiple R	R-Square	R-Square Change	F-Change	β	T
Time 1 delayed placement	.53	.28	.28	30.62***	.49	4.66***
Time 3 on public assistance	.53	.28	.00	ns	−.03	ns
Time 3 stressful events	.55	.30	.01	ns	.12	ns
Repeat pregnancies	.56	.31	.01	ns	.13	ns
Ethnicity/race	.58	.33	.01	ns	−.14	ns
Time 3 on public assistance	.20	.03	.02	3.15*	−.14	ns
Time 3 stressful events	.22	.04	.01	ns	.07	ns
Repeat pregnancies	.30	.08	.04	3.42*	.23	2.03**
Ethnicity/race	.37	.13	.04	3.87**	−.21	−1.97**

*$p < .10$. **$p < .05$. ***$p < .01$.

Distribution and Stability of Times 3 and 5
School-Outcome Groups

Delayed grade-placements at Times 3 and 5 were correlated .73. As seen in Table 3, a majority (78.5%) of the mothers remained in the same school-outcome group at both assessments. Almost half of those who had dropped out and returned by Time 3 dropped out again by Time 5 without graduating. None of those who dropped out before their first pregnancy returned. One third ($n = 5$) of the Time 3 after-pregnancy dropouts returned to school by Time 5.

Psychosocial variables. A MANOVA used to assess group differences in the risk and protective factors assessed as continuous variables at Times 3 and 5 (including depressive symptoms, supports from family and friends, and stressful life events) was significant, $F(18, 209) = 2.91, p < .001$. As seen in Table 4, by Time 3 returners had reported significantly fewer stressful life events compared to the dropout groups, and they tended (p .08) to have seen their families as more supportive. Group differences in support from friends were not significant. By Time 5, returners concurrently reported fewer depressive symptoms, and they had higher occupational commitments than did the dropout groups. Findings were nearly identical when race/ethnicity was entered as a covariate.

Demographics. Race/ethnicity differences for the African American ($n = 47$) and Puerto Rican mothers ($n = 32$) and the school-outcome groups were not statistically significant. However, as expected from previous research, consistent attenders and returners were more likely to be African American than Puerto Rican (72% and 60%, respectively). A small majority

TABLE 3
Cross-Tabulations of School-Outcome Groups at Times 3 and 5

| | Time 3 | | | | |
	Attenders	Returners	Dropped Out Before	Dropped Out After	Totals
Time 5					
Attenders	28	—	—	—	28
Returners	—	11	—	5	16
Dropped out before	—	—	10	—	10
Dropped out after	5	8	—	17	30
Totals	33	19	10	22	84

247

TABLE 4
Means, Standard Deviations, and Univariate F Tests for Continuous Predictors of School-Outcome Groups

	Attenders $(n = 27)$	Returners $(n = 15)$	Dropped Out		Univariate $F(3, 76)$
			Before $(n = 10)$	After $(n = 28)$	
Time 3 (depressive symptoms)					
M	11.3	7.4	13.5	10.9	ns
SD	7.4	6.4	12.7	8.3	
Time 3 (family support)					
M	12.0	14.8	8.7	10.8	2.31*
SD	6.3	5.3	6.1	6.1	
Time 3 (friends support)					
M	12.0	14.8	8.6	10.8	ns
SD	6.2	5.2	6.1	6.5	
Time 3 (stressful events)					
M	7.7_a	7.2_a	11.9_b	11.6_b	2.79**
SD	6.1	5.9	7.6	6.7	
Time 5 (depressive symptoms)					
M	9.4_{ab}	4.1_a	13.2_b	11.6_b	3.58*
SD	6.1	5.6	9.3	9.9	
Time 5 (occupational commitment)					
M	2.8_a	3.0_a	2.0_{ab}	1.5_b	6.42***
SD	1.4	1.3	1.1	1.4	

Note. Subscripts denote pairs of groups that differ significantly at $p < .05$ on Student–Newman–Keuls Multiple Range Tests.
*$p = .07$. **$p < .01$. ***$p < .001$.

of the after-pregnancy dropouts were African American (55%), whereas more before-pregnancy dropouts were Puerto Rican (60%).

Cross-tabulations and the results of chi-square tests of independence for categorical predictors of the Time 5 school-outcome groups are shown in Table 5. The percentages of mothers on public assistance in each of the school-outcome groups did not differ significantly.

Postsecondary school aspirations.   Attenders and returners were significantly more likely to say they planned to seek postsecondary education (70% of attenders and 60% of returners) compared to the before-pregnancy dropouts (40%) or after-pregnancy dropouts (29%).

Support from grandmothers.   Approximately half of each school-outcome group lived with their mothers. Group differences in the provision of child care support by the maternal (or occasionally paternal) grandmother

TABLE 5
Cross-Tabulations for Categorical Predictors (Assessed at Time 5)
of School-Outcome Groups

			Dropped Out		
	Attenders (n = 28)	Returners (n = 16)	Before (n = 10)	After (n = 30)	Chi-square Tests (df = 3)
On public assistance	68	56	70.0	80.0	ns
Plans to attend college	70	60	40	29	10.62**
Lives with grandmother	54	50	36	50	ns
Had help with child care	61	62	30	33	7.04*
Has close relationship					
With child's father	23	20	29	40	ns
With new partner	42	53	40	32	ns
Not married or planning	59	73	80	68	ns
Had repeat pregnancy	39	68	70	93	19.43***

$*p < .10.$ $**p < .05.$ $***p < .01.$

tended toward significance ($p = .07$). Only 30% of before-pregnancy drop-outs and 33% of after-pregnancy dropouts reported that their mothers helped with child care, compared to 62.5% of the returners and 60.7% of the consistent attenders/graduates. Collapsing cells to compare both dropout groups with attenders, graduates, and returners yielded a significant chi-square, $\chi^2(1, n = 84) = 5.5, p < .02$.

Support from baby's father or new romantic partner.   Overall, 41% of the mothers said they were involved in a close relationship with a new romantic partner, and 25.7% said they were involved in a close relationship with the baby's father. The school-outcome group differences were not significant. Being married or planning to be married was also not signifi-cantly related to school outcomes. The majority of the mothers in all groups were not married and did not plan to be.

The mothers' descriptions of problems encountered in relationships with their children's fathers suggest that serious problems limited their involve-ment overall (Leadbeater, Way, & Raden, 1996). Only 19.5% of the adoles-cent mothers reported no problems. The others said their children's fathers were immature, irresponsible, or seeing other women (32.1%); excessively macho, restrictive, or physically abusive (11.5%); selling or using drugs (14.1%); in jail (19.2%); or dead (3.8%).

Repeat pregnancies.   As expected, the school-outcome groups differed significantly in the percentages having a repeat pregnancy by Time 5. Only

39% of the consistent attenders had had one or more pregnancies sinc
1, compared to 68% of the returners, 93% of the after-pregnancy dropouts,
and 70% of the before-pregnancy dropouts. In addition, only 2 (7%) attenders had a full-term delivery, compared with 3 (19%) returners, 14 (47%)
after-pregnancy dropouts, and 3 (30%) before-pregnancy dropouts.

DISCUSSION

The trend toward increasing dropout rates in this sample is clear. At 12
months postpartum, 62% of the adolescent mothers were in school or
graduated. By 28 to 36 months postpartum, only 52% (41% of Puerto Ricans
and 57% of African Americans) were in school or graduated. Only 5 mothers
were pursuing postsecondary education. Few (6%) who had dropped out
by 12 months postpartum returned, and more (15%) had dropped out by
28 to 36 months postpartum. Overall rates of graduation (71%) for adolescent mothers in the 1987 National Survey of Families and Households were
somewhat higher (Alan Guttmacher Institute, 1994). However, rates for
Blacks and Hispanics from the 1986 NLSY (Upchurch, 1992) were similar.
The latter showed that only 59% of blacks and 37% of Hispanics who
became mothers at less than 18 years of age graduated from high school.
These similarities held despite the concentration of inner-city, disadvantaged mothers in our sample (which might result in lower graduation rates)
and the older cohort represented in the NLSY data (who would have had
more years to complete high school).

In our data, school performance *prior* to the delivery was the strongest
predictor of delayed grade-placement at almost 3 years postdelivery. Although there is evidence that early intervention programs can impact
school outcomes for some adolescent mothers (Klerman & Horwitz, 1992;
Seitz, Apfel, & Rosenbaum, 1991), the educational success of minority-
group adolescent mothers clearly depends on the attention given to reducing school failure in adolescent girls *before* they become parents. It is possible
that some of the mothers in our sample will return to school or job training
programs as their children enter school. However, Scott-Jones and Turner
(1990) found no cohort differences in educational outcomes for nationally
representative samples of Blacks (ages 20 to 24, 25 to 34, or 35 to 44) who
had all become mothers as adolescents. This suggests that further changes
in school outcomes with age are unlikely.

Educational attainment is higher in African American than in Puerto
Rican teenagers in the communities represented by this sample ("New
York's Dropouts-to be," 1989), thus it is not surprising that the adolescent
mothers in our sample reflect the same pattern. The African American

adolescent mothers also had somewhat higher work commitment scores than did the Puerto Ricans. Women's positive identities as mothers are strong in traditional Hispanic cultures (De Leon, 1996; Garcia-Coll, Escobar, Cebollero, & Valcarcel, 1989). This positive valuing of motherhood may reduce social pressures to pursue work and child care goals simultaneously. The mothers of the African American adolescents were more educated compared to those of Puerto Rican descent, and the former may have provided more support for their daughters' education. However, the ethnographic data also suggest that occupational goals and plans for achieving them were vague for many of the mothers. Many aspired to generally low-paying jobs including licensed practical nurse, receptionist, toll both operator, and so forth. Many also did not know what annual, or even weekly, income would allow them to meet their basic needs. Similarly, they did not anticipate problems meeting their basic needs with a single income from a low-paying job. Many also aspired to occupations for which they did not know the educational requirements, duties, or average income. The literature on career development for adolescent girls is almost nonexistent (De Leon, 1996). Given the current need for many single mothers to support themselves and their children on a single income, school-based vocational counseling directed at career development for middle school girls is badly needed.

Despite small cell numbers in this study, findings of within-group differences in school outcomes among these young mothers importantly begin to demonstrate the very different pathways that they take into young adulthood. Compared to both dropout groups, returners reported fewer stressful life events, perceived their families as more supportive, and were less likely to report concurrent levels of depressive symptoms. As one returner who was attending a Job Core Program in northern New York state said in the Time 3 ethnographic interview, "I feel good about going away to school for my mother and my kids. I want to make everyone proud of me and succeed in my life" (Participant #003, p. 1). We need to know more about the social contexts that help some young mothers to maintain positive aspirations despite a period of absence from school or the occurrence of traumatic or stressful life events that have the potential to derail their educational achievement (see Way & Leadbeater, 1995).

On the other hand, for mothers who drop out, subsequent school achievement and occupational commitments may be further limited by repeat pregnancies, less day care assistance from grandmothers, and more stressful life events. In the words of one mother who was pregnant with her third child, "If I didn't have the kids, I guess I'd be working right now. I'd be a computer operator or working somewhere with computers because it has always fascinated me. But now that I have a family to deal with, you

251

know, I don't think I have all that mind and attention to put in all my work. Some of it would have to go into the family too. I don't think I'd be able to do that. (Participant #055, p. 5). The desirability of having more children is increased because, as some mothers said, "I am at home anyway." In a situation in which the grandmothers are less involved with child care, responsibility falls to the adolescent mother herself (possibly also recipro- cally reflecting the greater likelihood that an adolescent mother who drops out of school will be caring for her own children). Lack of day care support may finalize their entrenchment into a trajectory that deters returning to school.

Our findings also suggest that different sources and types of social supports differentially affect educational outcomes for these mothers. How variations in timing, as well as types and amounts of support are implicated in positive and negative outcomes for adolescent mothers at 6 years post- partum are being explored in research with this sample (Way & Leadbeater, 1995). In this study, however, the effects of emotional support from families on delayed grade-placement at about 3 years postpartum did not appear to be direct. The quality of these relationships may serve to ameliorate depressive symptoms and the occurrence of stressful life events and im- prove child care for some adolescent mothers (Apfel & Seitz, 1991; Chase- Lansdale, Brooks-Gunn, & Zamsky, 1994; Leadbeater & Bishop, 1994; Lead- beater & Linares, 1992). On the other hand, long-term dependence on families for emotional, residential, and child care support may be associated with difficulties in gaining financial and residential self-sufficiency.

The absence of support from male partners is consistent with our find- ings for the children's fathers at 12 months postpartum (Linares et al., 1991). Only one fourth of the adolescent mothers were involved in an emotionally supportive relationship with the children's fathers. Although it might be hypothesized that adolescent mothers, following their own mothers, see single parenthood as a viable and acceptable alternative to marriage (Caldas, 1993), our data suggest an alternative interpretation. Social factors including norms undermining commitments to one relationship and con- doning excessively macho behavior, as well as involvement in drug-related or violence-related crimes (on the part of 37% of the children's fathers), severely limit the likelihood that these young men could become long-term partners. The "ideal man" is described by several of the adolescent mothers as a "provider" and "someone who accepts me and is there for me and my child." The problems the mothers describe, together with high levels of unemployment in minority youths, mean this individual is not prevalent in their social networks. Marriage is too often not a viable alternative (Leadbeater et al., 1996). Many mothers also expressed their reluctance to become involved in new relationships, given, as one mother said, "I came out of one relationship that ended bad, so I can't see myself in another one" (Participant #064, p. 13). The long-term effects of involvement in new relationships are uncertain. Will these relationships also break up in the face of similar problems?

Mothers who were receiving public assistance 1 year postpartum were more likely to have already been delayed in their educational achievement at delivery. Future research needs to address how public assistance affects stressors that impede educational progress subsequent to delivery (e.g., illness, residential instability, repeat pregnancies) only after taking account of the pregnancy risk factors.

Mothers with greater delayed grade-placement reported more depressive symptoms at 28 to 36 months postpartum than those who were less delayed, perhaps reflecting their discouragement with the future. Demands of dealing with current stresses and responsibilities may preclude their engagement in activities that could improve their long-term outcomes (see Leadbeater & Linares, 1992).

In summary, only slightly more than half the adolescent mothers in this study are likely to finish high school and go on to pursue their occupational goals. Risk and protective factors occurring subsequent to their first delivery had little effect on the mothers' educational outcomes once previous school performance was controlled. This gives little support to the belief that even adolescent mothers who have supportive families and who are not psychologically distressed will be able to alter their prepregnancy educational trajectories. As Klerman and Horwitz (1992) wrote in reviewing the role of service programs in reducing the negative consequences for adolescent mothers: "Even though programs are expanding in number, scope, and sophistication, the problems faced by the adolescents involved appear to be outstripping them" (p. 312).

The social policy implications of this research are clear: Poor educational and economic outcomes for adolescent mothers are largely determined by their educational success before the pregnancy. Programs for the prevention and early remediation of learning problems among girls living in poverty are needed. Moreover, the development of middle school curricula focusing on career development and costs of daily life (rent, utilities, phone, etc.) would stimulate girls to think about realistic economic and occupational goals. Career development programs must also seek to increase middle school girls' exposure to work opportunities beyond low-paying jobs. Living in communities with high concentrations of joblessness and poverty, girls may have difficulty in gaining information about and motivation for career opportunities beyond low-wage jobs (Wilson, in press).

Ambivalence over providing school-based and community-based, high-quality, day care centers for the children of adolescent mothers for fear of increasing the likelihood of adolescent childbearing (Nathanson, 1991) needs to be weighed against the likelihood of long-term negative outcomes for them. Incentives are also needed for relatives of adolescent mothers to provide day care for preverbal infants because this is seen as the safest mode of infant day care. Effective, long-term birth control methods now exist and must be made more available to adolescent mothers, given their high risk for unintended repeat pregnancies.

The effects of concentrations of poverty, joblessness, and the drug culture on the maintenance of poverty among inner-city, single mothers need to be addressed. Many disadvantages for young mothers and their children stem directly from these problems. Potential support from the children's fathers is reduced or eliminated by their premature deaths, imprisonment for drug-related crimes, drug use, or missed education. The probability of increasing financial security through marriage is sharply curtailed. Recent increases in poverty to both children under 6 and adolescents under 18 (Strawn, 1992), as well as simultaneous increases in births to adolescents, demand renewed attention to the context of adolescent parenting. As a society, we can no longer afford to neglect the social disadvantages that create and maintain negative outcomes for adolescent mothers and their children.

ACKNOWLEDGMENTS

Preliminary results of this study were presented in a poster at the Society for Research on Adolescence, Washington, D.C., March 1991. This research was supported in part by grants from the Smith-Richardson and Spencer foundations and a William T. Grant, Faculty Scholars Award. I appreciate the assistance of L. Oriana Linares and Pam M. Kato, in data collection, and of Sandra Bishop, in data analyses. Continuing thanks to all mothers who participated in the study.

REFERENCES

Alan Guttmacher Institute. (1994). *Sex and America's teenagers*. New York: Author.

Apfel, N., & Seitz, V. (1991). Four models of adolescent-mother grandmother relationships in black, inner-city families. *Family Relations, 40*, 421–429.

Beck, A. (1967). *Depression: Causes and treatment*. Philadelphia: University of Pennsylvania Press.

Caldas, S. J. (1993). Current theoretical perspectives on adolescent pregnancy and childbearing in the United States. *Journal of Adolescent Research, 8*, 4–20.

Chase-Lansdale, P. L., Brooks-Gunn, J., & Zamsky, E. (1994). Young African-American multigenerational families in poverty: Quality of mothering and grandmothering. *Child Development, 65*, 638–648.

Chase-Lansdale, P. L., & Vinovskis, M. A. (1987). Should we discourage teenage marriage? *The Public Interest, 87*, 23–27.

De Leon, B. (1996). Career development of Hispanic adolescent girls. In B. Leadbeater & N. Way (Eds.) *Urban adolescent girls: Resisting stereotypes* (pp. 380–398). New York: New York University Press.

Egeland, B., Breitenbucher, M., & Rosenberg, D. (1980). Prospective study of the significance of life stress in the etiology of child abuse. *Journal of Consulting and Child Psychology, 48,* 195–205.

Foltz, A. M., Klerman, L., & Jekel, J. F. (1972). Pregnancy and special education: Who stays in school? *American Journal of Public Health, 62,* 1612–1619.

Furstenberg, F. F., Brooks-Gunn, J., & Morgan, S. P. (1987). *Adolescent mothers in later life.* New York: Cambridge University Press.

Garcia-Coll, C. T., Escobar, M., Cebollero, P, & Valcarcel, M. (1989). Adolescent pregnancy and childbearing: Psychosocial consequences during the postpartum period. In C. T. Garcia-Coll & M. de Mattei (Eds.), *The psychosocial development of Puerto Rican women* (pp. 84–114). New York: Praeger.

Geronimus, A. T, & Korenman, S. (1992). The socioeconomic consequences of teen childbearing reconsidered. *Quarterly of Economics, 107,* 1187–1214.

Haggstrom, G., Kanouse, D., & Morrison, P. (1986). Accounting for the educational shortfalls of mothers. *Journal of Marriage and the Family, 48,* 175–186.

Hahn, A., Danzberger, J., & Lefkowitz, B. (1987). *Dropouts in America: Enough is known for action.* Washington, DC: Institute for Educational Leadership.

Henshaw, S., Kenney, A. M., Somberg, D., & Van Vort, J. (1989). *Teenage pregnancy in the United States: The scope of the problem and state responses.* New York: Alan Guttmacher Institute.

Hoffman, S. D., Foster, E. M., & Furstenberg, F. F. (1992, May). *Re-evaluating the costs of teenage childbearing.* Paper presented at the National Institute of Child Health and Human Development (NICHD) conference, Bethesda, MD.

Klerman, L. V., & Horwitz, S. M. (1992). Reducing the adverse consequences of adolescent pregnancy and parenting: The role of service programs. *Adolescent Medicine: State of the Art Reviews, 3,* 299–316.

Leadbeater, B. J., & Bishop, S. (1994). Predictors of behavior problems in preschool children of inner-city, Afro-American and Puerto Rican adolescent mothers. *Child Development, 65,* 638–648.

Leadbeater, B. J., & Linares, O. (1992). Depressive symptoms in black and Puerto Rican adolescent mothers in the first year postpartum. *Development and Psychopathology, 4,* 451–468.

Leadbeater, B. J., Way, N., & Raden, T. (1996). Effects of involvement of the biological fathers for toddlers of African American and Puerto Rican adolescent mothers. In B. Leadbeater & N. Way (Eds.) *Urban adolescent girls: Resisting the stereotypes* (pp. 193–212). New York: New York University Press.

Linares, L. O., Leadbeater, B. J., Kato, P. M., & Jaffe, L. (1991). Predicting school outcomes for minority group adolescent mothers: Can subgroups be identified? *Journal of Research on Adolescence, 1,* 379–400.

Moore, K. A., Myers, D., Morrison, D. R., Nord, C. W., Brown, B., & Edmonston, B. (1993). Age at first childbirth and later poverty. *Journal of Research on Adolescence, 3,* 393–422.

Mott, F., & Marsiglio, W. (1985). Early childbearing and completion of high school. *Family Planning Perspectives, 17,* 234–237.

Nathanson, C. A. (1991). *Dangerous passage: The social control of sexuality in women's adolescence.* Philadelphia: Temple University Press.

New York's Dropouts-to-be: A grim class portrait. (1989, April). *The New York Times,* p. B1.

Procidano, M., & Heller, K. (1983). Measure of perceived social support from friends and family. *American Journal of Psychology, 11,* 1–24.

Scott-Jones, D. (1991). Adolescent childbearing, risks and resilience. *Education and Urban Society, 24,* 53–64.

Scott-Jones, D., & Turner, S. L. (1990). The impact of adolescent childbearing on educational attainment and income of black females. *Youth and Society, 22,* 35–53.

Seitz, V., Apfel, N. H., & Rosenbaum, L. K. (1991). Effects of an intervention program for pregnant adolescents: Educational outcomes at 2 years postpartum. *American Journal of Community Psychology, 19,* 911–930.

Strawn, J. (1992). The states and the poor: Child poverty rises as the safety net shrinks. *Social Policy Report, 6,* 1–19.

Tardy, C. H. (1985). Social support measures. *American Journal of Community Psychology, 13,* 187–202.

Upchurch, D. M. (1992, May). *Early schooling and childbearing experiences: Implications for post-secondary school attendance.* Paper presented at the National Institute of Child Health and Human Development (NICHD) conference, Bethesda, MD.

Upchurch, D. M. (1993). Early schooling and childbearing experiences: Implication for post-secondary school attendance. *Journal of Research on Adolescence, 3,* 423–443.

Upchurch, D. M., & McCarthy, J. (1990). The timing of a first birth and high school completion. *American Sociological Review, 55,* 224–243.

Upchurch, D. M., & McCarthy, J., (1991). Adolescent childbearing and high school completion in the 1980: Have things changed? *Family Planning Perspectives, 21,* 199–202.

Way, N., & Leadbeater, B. J. (1995). *Pathways towards the educational success of adolescent mothers: Reconsidering the role of grandmothers.* Manuscript submitted for publication.

Wilson, W. J. (in press). *Jobless ghettos: The disappearance of work and its effect on urban life.* New York: Knopf.

Received February 8, 1993
Revision received August 25, 1994
Accepted September 29, 1995

Parental Child Rearing and
Academic Achievement in Boys:
The Mediational Role of Social-Emotional Adjustment

Kathryn R. Wentzel
University of Maryland
S. Shirley Feldman
Stanford University
Daniel A. Weinberger
Case Western Reserve University

This study investigated two nonintellectual factors that may partly explain the relation between parenting and academic achievement—sons' self-restraint and emotional adjustment—in a sample of 85 sixth-grade boys. Results of multiple regression techniques indicated that sons' reports of mothers' harsh and inconsistent discipline were related both directly and negatively to sons' classroom grades and indirectly via sons' global distress and low cognitive self-worth. Fathers' harsh and inconsistent discipline was related only indirectly to sons' grades by way of its independent association with sons' distress and low self-restraint. In general, these results were replicated when standardized test scores were substituted into the model. These findings underscore the critical contribution of social and emotional development to academic and intellectual achievements, and the key role of parent-child relationships in influencing such development.

A growing body of research on the development of children's cognitive competence indicates substantial links between the quality of parent-child relationships and children's performance on academic tasks. In general, nurturant, consistent, and authoritative parenting styles are positively related to a child's cognitive competence, whereas critical, inconsistent, and authoritarian styles are related to less advanced cognitive development (Baumrind, 1973; Bing, 1963; Dornbusch, Ritter, Leiderman, Roberts, & Fraleigh, 1987;

This research was supported by grants from the Center for the Study of Families, Children, and Youth at Stanford University and the Spencer Foundation.

Journal of Early Adolescence, Vol. 11 No. 3, August 1991 321-339
© 1991 Sage Publications, Inc.

257

Hess, Holloway, Dickson, & Price, 1984; Hess & McDevitt, 1984; Radin, 1972, 1973). For the most part, researchers have suggested that parenting practices directly facilitate or constrain the development of cognitive skills. However, the types of parenting that predict academic achievement also predict general social and emotional adjustment. Given that nonintellectual factors are often powerful predictors of a child's performance at school, parenting practices also may be related indirectly to school achievement by contributing to the development of these noncognitive skills.

The focus of the present study was on two nonintellectual factors that may partly explain the relation between parenting and academic achievement — children's self-restraint and emotional adjustment. Self-restraint refers to self-regulation in the interest of achieving long-term goals or a balance between personal needs and those of others. Tendencies to control impulses, to suppress aggressive behavior, to be considerate of others, and to be responsible characterize restraint-related behavior (Weinberger, 1989; Weinberger & Schwartz, 1990). Emotional adjustment was defined in terms of feelings of cognitive self-worth and global distress as reflected in general states of anxiety, depression, low self-esteem, and low emotional well-being. The present research investigated the link between parenting and achievement in early adolescence; studies in this area have focused primarily on young children (see Dornbusch et al., 1987; and Steinberg, Elman, & Mounts, 1989 for exceptions).

Children's self-restraint is an especially important characteristic in that it is strongly related to both the quality of family functioning as well as children's competence in nonfamilial settings. In particular, parent-child interactions characterized by hostility and inappropriate forms of parental control are associated with displays of low restraint in the classroom (Feldman & Wentzel, 1990). In turn, such behavior can have negative consequences for achievement. Students who exhibit low impulse control and express their needs in aggressive ways, who are inconsiderate of others, and are socially irresponsible tend to have lower grades than students who display these skills (Wentzel, Weinberger, Ford, & Feldman, 1990). This relationship may be explained in part, by findings that students who misbehave and are irresponsible tend to have low school motivation, are treated negatively by teachers, and are likely to receive less one-on-one instruction than other children (Brophy & Good, 1974; Wentzel et al., 1990).

To date, research identifying sons' self-restraint as a mediator between parenting and academic achievement has focused on the quality of observed parent-child interactions in the home (Feldman & Wentzel, 1990). Presumably, these interactions teach children restraint-related skills that are used in other social settings such as the classroom. In early adolescence, however, children's increased social-cognitive skills as well as their greater experience as family members allow them to assess and interpret the nature of their relationships with their parents subjectively (Smetana, 1988). As such, the meaning that children attach to their parents' behavior may be related to self-restraint in ways that are different from parenting as assessed by observers. Thus, in the present study, sons' reports of parental child-rearing practices were used to assess the quality of parenting techniques.

Several types of evidence suggest that aspects of children's emotional adjustment may also partly mediate the link between parenting and academic achievement. First, a child's affective functioning tends to generate motivational orientations that can interfere with academic performance (Harter, 1983, in press). At a general level, emotional distress has been consistently linked to disengagement from goal pursuit (Klinger, 1975), perceived helplessness, and withdrawal from situational and task demands (Dweck & Leggett, 1988; Pyszczynski & Greenberg, 1986; Seligman & Garber, 1980). Perceptions of low cognitive self-worth have been negatively associated with specific indices of achievement such as grades and standardized test scores (e.g., Meece, Blumenfeld, & Hoyle, 1988; Harter & Connell, 1984).

Children's emotional adjustment in the form of low self-esteem, depression, and low emotional well-being is also related to parents' use of harsh and inconsistent discipline (Armentrout, 1971; Cole & Rehm, 1986; Walker & Greene, 1986; Litovsky & Dusek, 1985; Yee & Flanagan, 1985). Thus negative forms of parenting may affect school performance by generating high levels of emotional distress as well as low levels of self-restraint. Moreover, emotionally distressed children, especially boys, are likely to display conduct disorders and other behavior characterized by a lack of self-restraint (Achenbach & Edelbrock, 1978; Leung & Drasgow, 1986; Ney, Colbert, Newman, & Young, 1986). As such, a link between emotional adjustment and classroom self-restraint may provide yet another path by which family functioning is related to both maladaptive classroom behavior and academic problems of early adolescent boys.

To summarize, relations between parents' harsh and inconsistent discipline, sons' self-restraint, emotional adjustment, and achievement were investigated. The specific set of relations that were of interest are shown in Figure 1. Because there is evidence to suggest that mother-son and father-son interactions are differentially related to sons' social, emotional, and academic competence (Feldman & Wentzel, 1990; Radin, 1972, 1973), both mothers' and fathers' parenting were assessed separately. Specifically, sons' reports of their parents' harsh and inconsistent discipline were used to assess parenting.

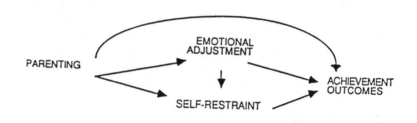

Figure 1:   Hypothesized Relations Among Parents' Child Rearing, Sons' Emotional Adjustment, Self-Restraint, and Achievement Outcomes.

Emotional adjustment was assessed at two levels potentially relevant to classroom functioning: global distress and cognitive self-worth. Although often significantly correlated, classroom-specific indices of self-worth are generally more predictive of academic performance than more global measures of emotional distress (Byrne, 1984; Byrne & Shavelson, 1986). In contrast, it is likely that global distress is more strongly related to general parenting than classroom-specific indices of self-worth.

Academic achievement was assessed using both classroom grades and standardized test scores. Most research relating family functioning to children's cognitive competence has used these outcomes interchangeably (Hess & Holloway, 1984). However, standardized tests are designed to measure basic or specialized academic abilities, whereas evaluations of classroom performance often reflect a variety of noncognitive as well as cognitive skills (see Wentzel, 1991, for a review of this literature). If social and emotional adjustment skills contribute directly to intellectual development, they should predict both types of achievement.

Finally, only boys were studied in this research. Several factors prompted this decision. First, by sixth grade, in contrast to girls, very few boys have entered puberty (Petersen & Taylor, 1980; Tanner, 1962) and pubertal status is known to influence both parent-child relationships (Papini & Sebby, 1987; Steinberg, 1987) and social-emotional adjustment (Paikoff & Brooks-Gunn, in press). Thus, to limit as much as possible the confounding influence of pubertal status, this investigation focused on only one sex. Second, boys were of special interest because they are more prone to almost every major adjustment problem of childhood (e.g., Clarizio & McCoy, 1983) and appear to be especially at risk for academic problems resulting from family functioning (Emery, 1982; Emery & O'Leary, 1982).

METHOD

Sample

The subjects participating in this research were 85 sixth-grade boys (ages ranged from 11 years to 12.6 years) drawn from a larger nonclinical sample of sixth-grade boys and their families recruited from two school districts in the San Francisco Bay Area. This larger study was a collaborative investigation of early adolescent boys' social, emotional, and academic functioning requiring a significant amount of time and commitment by participating families. Sixty-eight percent of the families invited to take part in the research agreed to do so (see Weinberger, Tublin, Ford, & Feldman, 1990, for a more detailed description of this sample).

For the present study, boys were selected if complete data were available from them. Of these students, 65% were Caucasian, 9% were Hispanic-American, 13% were Asian-American, and the remaining 13% represented other ethnic groups. Primarily middle class, 68% ($n = 58$) of the boys came from intact families and 32% ($n = 27$) from either single-parent or blended families.

Measures

Both self-report questionnaires and teacher and peer ratings were used in this research. Measures of global distress, cognitive self-worth, and teacher and peer rating forms were administered 9 weeks after the beginning of the school year. Students were seen during class periods and teachers outside of class. Teachers received $15 for completing ratings of each member of the class. Students had one teacher for all subjects. Questionnaires assessing parenting practices were mailed to students at home and collected approximately 1 week later. Follow-ups were conducted after the questionnaires were mailed to answer questions and to assure the boys that their responses would remain strictly confidential.

Harsh and inconsistent discipline was assessed using a subscale of the Weinberger Parenting Inventory (WPI; Weinberger, Feldman, & Ford, 1989). The 24-item scale measures the tendency for parents to be inconsistent, and harsh in terms of being both authoritarian and prone to using severe punishment. It has an internal consistency of .91 (Cronbach's alpha) and 2-week test-retest of .86. Sample items include "she wants me to obey her without asking any questions," "she makes sure my punishments are severe enough that I will remember them for a long time," and "whether she punishes me often depends on what mood she's in." Boys completed the scale twice, once for mothers and once for fathers ($\bar{X}$s and SDs = 19.47/5.65 and 20.12/5.81, respectively). The sons from single parent and blended families filled out scales for either their natural fathers or stepfathers. Sons filled out scales about their fathers if they maintained ongoing relationships with them and perceived them as playing a significant role in their lives. All of the items were rated on 5-point Likert-type scales.

The Harsh and Inconsistent Discipline Scale was validated in a separate sample of early adolescents in relation to the Schludermann and Schludermann (1970) revision of the Child Report of Parent Behavior Inventory (CRPBI; Schaefer, 1965). Correlations with conceptually related scales were highly significant ($p < .001$) (see Feldman, Wentzel, Weinberger, & Munson, 1990).

Emotional adjustment. Sons' emotional adjustment was assessed at a global level as well as within the classroom. Global distress was measured using the Weinberger Adjustment Inventory (WAI; Weinberger, 1989). The distress score is derived from 29 items (alpha = .91) tapping four affective dimensions: anxiety (e.g., "I worry too much about things that aren't important"), depression (e.g., "I often feel sad or unhappy"), affect associated with low self-esteem (e.g., "I'm not very sure of myself"), and low emotional well-being (e.g., "I'm the kind of person who has a lot of fun" [reverse scored]).

The WAI distress score has been validated in a larger early adolescent sample. With respect to concurrent validity, distress correlated .71 with Spielberger STAI-C Anxiety (Spielberger, 1973), .64 with the Child Depression Inventory (Kovacs, 1980), and –.60 with the global self-worth subscale on the Perceived Competence Scale for Children (Harter, 1982). Test-retest stability was over .70 across a 7-month period.

Cognitive self-worth was assessed using the cognitive subscale of the Harter (1982) Perceived Competence Scale for Children. The 7-item scale measures children's perceptions of their cognitive ability at school. The scale has internal consistency of .76 (Cronbach's alpha) and test-retest reliability of .78 over a 3-month period. In the present sample, the mean score was 18.34 ($SD = 4.06$).

Sons' restraint. Sons' restraint scores represent composites of teacher ratings and peer nominations. Using 5-point scales (1 = *almost never, 5 = almost always*), teachers rated each student in the class on four items (alpha = .87): considerate of others; impulsive, acts without thinking (reverse coded); follows rules, responsible; fights with others, loses temper (reverse coded).

Scores were subsequently standardized within classrooms to enable across-classroom comparisons.

Peer nominations of restraint were also collected. Classmates nominated two male peers on four restraint items (alpha = .85) corresponding to those rated by teachers. The number of nominations received by each boy was converted into a within-classroom z score to control for class size. The teacher ratings and peer nominations were correlated significantly with each other (r = .82, $p < .001$). Consequently, the scores were averaged to form a composite restraint score.

Sons' academic performance. Student grades were obtained from student files at the end of the year. Reading, mathematics, English, spelling, social studies, and science grades were averaged to form an overall grade-point average (GPA; $\overline{X}$ = 2.80, SD = .73). Sixth-grade reading, spelling, language, and mathematics scores from the *Comprehensive Test of Basic Skills* (CTB/ McGraw-Hill, 1983) were averaged to form a composite standardized test score.

RESULTS

Two sets of findings are reported. First, zero-order correlations between achievement outcomes, sons' distress, cognitive self-worth, and perceived parenting were examined. Next, using multiple-regression techniques, relations between perceived parenting, sons' social and emotional functioning, and achievement were investigated.

Intercorrelations among perceived parenting, sons' distress, cognitive self-worth, self-restraint, and achievement outcomes are shown in Table 1. GPA was significantly and negatively related to mothers' and fathers' harsh and inconsistent discipline as well as to sons' global distress, and positively related to sons' cognitive self-worth and self-restraint. Standardized test scores were significantly related to these same variables with the exception of global distress. Self-restraint, distress, and cognitive self-worth were related to perceived parenting as well as with each other. Mothers' and fathers' harsh and inconsistent disciplinary styles were related significantly and positively. Preliminary analyses indicated that family structure (single vs. intact) was not significantly correlated with any of the variables under study. Consequently, final analyses did not include this variable.

Multiple regression analyses were used to assess the various paths by which perceived parenting and sons' social and emotional functioning were related to achievement. First, simultaneous regressions including all of the

TABLE 1:   Intercorrelations of Perceived Parenting, Sons' Social-Emotional
Adjustment, and Achievement Outcomes

	GPA	Test Scores	Discipline		Global Distress	Self-Worth
			Mother	Father		
Standardized test scores	.68***	—				
Harsh and inconsistent discipline: MO	−.37***	−.19*	—			
Harsh and inconsistent discipline: FA	−.28**	−.16*	.60***	—		
Sons' global distress	−.16*	−.07	.36***	.23**	—	
Sons' cognitive self-worth	.31***	.29**	−.30***	−.16*	−.43***	—
Sons' self-restraint	.49***	.33***	−.23**	−.29***	−.18*	.32***

*p < .05; **p < .01; ***p < .001.

predictor variables were conducted to determine direct paths between parenting, global distress, cognitive self-worth, self-restraint, and achievement. Next, to investigate the mediational role of sons' self-restraint, cognitive self-worth, and global distress in linking parenting and achievement, additional models were built to predict first, sons' self-restraint, then cognitive self-worth, and finally, global distress. The standardized beta weights (part correlations) derived from these simultaneous regression equations describe the unique relationship between variables and control for their relationship with other variables. Separate models were built for mothers and fathers.

Table 2 shows results from the multiple regression analyses for both the mother and father models. Figure 2 depicts these relations among parents' harsh and inconsistent discipline, sons' distress, cognitive self-worth, self-restraint, and GPA. Standardized beta weights are reported in Figure 2 where there were significant, independent relations between variables as predicted in Figure 1. In both mother and father models, cognitive self-worth and sons' self-restraint were related directly and positively to GPA. Cognitive self-worth was related indirectly to GPA because of its positive association with classroom self-restraint when controlling for the effects of parenting and global distress.

As shown in the mothers' model, mothers' harsh and inconsistent parenting was related directly to low classroom grades and had an additional negative relationship with classroom performance by way of its positive relationship with sons' distress and cognitive self-worth. Mothers' parenting had no relation with sons' self-restraint independent of its association with sons' global distress and cognitive self-worth. The mothers' model explained

TABLE 2: Results of Multiple Regressions on Sons' Distress, Cognitive Self-Worth, Distress, Restraint, and Academic Achievement (GPA)

Predictor Variables	Distress	Cognitive Self-Worth	Restraint	GPA
		Outcome Variables		
Mothers' Model				
Harsh & inconsistent discipline	.37***	−.18†	−.17	−.24*
Sons' distress	—	−.38***	.03	.08
Cognitive self-worth	—	—	.23*	.21*
Sons' restraint	—	—	—	.40***
Fathers' Model				
Harsh & inconsistent discipline	.28*	.07	−.27**	−.11
Sons' distress	—	−.42***	.04	.06
Cognitive self-worth	—	—	.24*	.23*
Sons' restraint	—	—	—	.41***

NOTE: Standardized beta weights are shown.
$†p < .10$; $*p < .05$; $**p < .01$; $***p < .001$.

34% of the variance in GPA (F [4, 81] = 10.49, $p < .001$), 9% of the variance in sons' self-restraint (F[3, 82] = 2.94, $p < .05$), 22% of the variance in cognitive self-worth (F[2, 83] = 11.9, $p < .001$), and 14% of the variance in sons' global distress (F[1, 84] = 13.63, $p < .001$).

To assess the indirect effects of the predictor variables on GPA (paths with mediating variables as shown in Figure 1), the standardized beta weights for each path were multiplied with each other and then the products were summed to yield a total indirect effect score. Summing effects across the four indirect paths (parenting → distress → self-worth → GPA; parenting → self-worth → GPA; self-worth → self-restraint → GPA; parenting → distress → self-worth → self-restraint → GPA), the total indirect effect of mothers' harsh and inconsistent discipline on GPA was .10.

In contrast to mothers' parenting, perceived fathering was only indirectly related to GPA. As with mothers' parenting, fathers' harsh and inconsistent discipline was related to poor classroom performance by way of its relationship with global distress. In addition, fathers' harsh and inconsistent discipline was related independently to low grades by way of its negative relation with sons' classroom self-restraint. This finding is consistent with previous reports that self-restraint explains part of the relation between observed interactions of fathers and their sons in the home and sons' classroom grades (Feldman & Wentzel, 1990). The fathers' model explained 31% of the

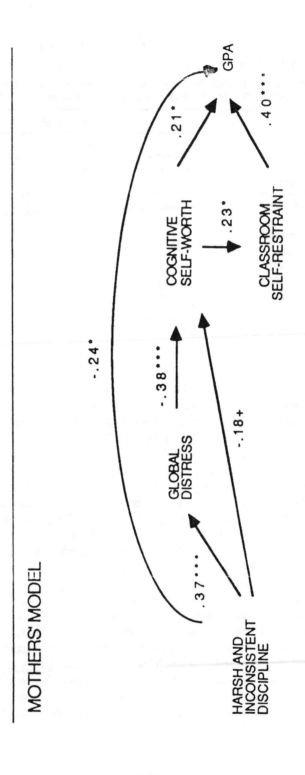

MOTHERS' MODEL

FATHERS' MODEL

Figure 2: Relations Among Parents' Child Rearing, Sons' Global Distress, Cognitive Self-Worth, Classroom Self-Restraint, and GPA.

267

variance in GPA $(F[4, 77] = 8.41, p < .001)$, 14% of the variance in sons' self-restraint $(F[3, 78] = 4.32, p < .01)$, 20% of the variance in cognitive self-worth $(F[2, 79] = 9.70, p < .001)$, and 8% of the variance in sons' global distress $(F[1, 80] = 6.93, p < .01)$. Summing across the three indirect paths (parenting → distress → self-worth → GPA; parenting → distress → self-worth → self-restraint → GPA; parenting → self-restraint → GPA), the total indirect effect of fathers' harsh and inconsistent discipline on GPA was .15.

Similar analyses were carried out using standardized test scores as the achievement outcome of interest. In this case, the direct effects were similar to those shown in Figure 2 with two exceptions. First, in the case of standardized test scores, mothers' harsh and inconsistent discipline was no longer directly related to sons' achievement. Second, the strength of the relation between sons' self-restraint and achievement decreased ($\beta = .24$, $p < .05$, for both mothers' and fathers' models). The relation between cognitive self-worth and achievement remained essentially the same ($\beta = .24$ and .23, $p < .05$, for fathers' and mothers' models, respectively).

In sum, correlational findings indicated significant relations among sons' achievement outcomes, perceived child-rearing practices, sons' distress, cognitive self-worth, and self-restraint. When multiple regression techniques were employed, findings were similar to those shown in Figure 1. However, mothers' harsh and inconsistent discipline was related to academic outcomes directly and via global distress and cognitive self-worth. Fathers' harsh and inconsistent discipline was related indirectly to sons' achievement by way of its negative association with sons' classroom self-restraint as well as the two affective variables. In general, these results were replicated when standardized test scores were substituted into the model.

DISCUSSION

The purpose of this study was to identify nonintellectual factors that contribute to relations between parenting and academic achievement in early adolescent boys. Correlational results indicated that classroom self-restraint, global distress, and cognitive self-worth were related significantly to sons' perceptions of mothers' and fathers' harsh and inconsistent parenting as well as to academic outcomes. Results of multiple regression techniques suggest that boys' classroom self-restraint and emotional adjustment are noncognitive correlates of intellectual competence that partly explain the relation between the quality of parenting and academic outcomes. Specifically, the negative relationship between fathers' harsh and inconsistent discipline and sons' achievement can be partly explained by a negative relationship between fathers' parenting and their sons' classroom self-restraint and global distress. The negative relation between mothers' harsh and inconsistent parenting and sons' achievement can be explained partly by the association between mothers' negative parenting and sons' global distress and lower cognitive self-worth. Finally, self-restraint also explains part of the relation between cognitive self-worth and academic achievement in that boys with high cognitive self-worth also display relatively high levels of restraint in the classroom.

These findings are noteworthy in several respects. First, relations between sons' self-restraint, cognitive self-worth, and achievement were replicated when standardized test scores were substituted for classroom grades as the index of intellectual achievement. Thus the indirect effects of harsh and inconsistent parenting on achievement were evident in two quite different evaluation contexts. In light of the literature cited earlier, it was expected that positive affect supports achievement on standardized tests as well as in the classroom. With respect to self-restraint, however, one could argue that teachers reward students for socially competent behavior as well as for intellectual skills (Rosenholtz & Simpson, 1984; Sivan, 1986). For this reason, one would expect a stronger relationship between classroom self-restraint and GPA but not test scores. The significant, positive relation between self-restraint and standardized test scores suggests that social competence in the classroom is adaptive not only in terms of earning positive rewards in the form of grades, but also in terms of actual learning, intellectual development, or test-taking skills.

Second, as in earlier work (Feldman & Wentzel, 1990), maladaptive forms of father-son relationships were negatively related to GPA by way of sons' low self-restraint in the classroom. In addition, however, sons' emotional adjustment also seems to mediate the relation between the quality of parenting and sons' achievement. Indeed, the harsh and inconsistent discipline of both mothers and fathers was related directly and positively to sons' global distress and in the case of mothers, to low cognitive self-worth as well. The precise mechanisms by which emotional adjustment and self-restraint influence academic achievement were not the primary focus of this study (see Wentzel et al., 1990). Nevertheless, the path linking cognitive self-worth to academic outcomes by way of self-restraint indicates the complexity of such mechanisms.

In general, the affective component of cognitive self-worth is believed to influence achievement outcomes by generating either positive or negative motivational orientations toward learning (Harter, 1983, in press). The results of the present study suggest that one way in which these affective motivators may be expressed is by restraint-related behavior in the classroom. Although not typically discussed as a motivational outcome relevant to achievement, restraint-related behavior indicates a willingness to learn on the part of the student, is clearly valued by teachers (Helton & Oakland, 1977; Kedar-Voivodas, 1983), and can influence the quality of instruction that an individual student receives (Brophy & Good, 1974; see also Wentzel, 1991).

As in previous research, the mediational role of self-restraint was evident for father-son relationships but not for mother-son relationships. Fathers are typically perceived both by parents and early adolescent boys as showing concern with sons' achievement of future goals and academic success (Power & Shanks, 1989; Youniss & Smollar, 1985). One can speculate that nurturant fathers accentuate links between sons' present behavior and the achievement of long-term goals. As such, positive father-son relationships may support the development of restraint-related skills necessary to achieve future success, whereas harsh and inconsistent fathering may result in sons' behavior that is low in restraint and less adaptive for achieving long-term goals.

The direct relation between mothers' harsh and inconsistent discipline and sons' achievement is interesting in two respects. First, it suggests that other mediators not assessed in this study may be important in linking the quality of mother-son relationships to school performance. Although speculative, such mediators may take the form of mothers' power over sons' decision-making or mothers' relationships with their husbands. Both of these factors have been linked with early adolescent boys' psychological functioning (Gehring, Wentzel, Feldman, & Munson, 1990; Feldman & Wentzel, 1990). Second, the absence of a significant relation between mothers' parenting and sons' performance on standardized achievement tests suggests that maternal influences on achievement may be highly specific. For instance, mothers may have a stronger influence on boys' day-to-day academic activities and corresponding motivational aspects of achievement than on more stable, intellectual aspects of performance assessed by standardized tests.

Two potential limitations of this study also deserve comment. First, parenting, global distress, and cognitive self-worth were assessed with self-report measures. Thus one can only conclude that sons who are emotionally distressed and have low levels of cognitive self-worth also tend to perceive their parents' discipline as being harsh and inconsistent. Alternative procedures would be to observe parenting or to obtain reports of parenting from parents themselves. However, the use of children's reports of parenting behavior is a desirable complement to observational data in that observational data represent only a small, situationally specific sample of behavior. In contrast, self-reports can provide a broader sampling of prototypic parental behavior because they reflect mental representations that have been aggregated over diverse contexts and developed over long periods of time. In addition, children's reports of family functioning have been found to be related to observers' ratings somewhat more strongly than parental reports (Feldman, Wentzel, & Gehring, 1989; Schwartz, Barton-Henry, & Pruzinsky, 1985).

In addition, the correlational nature of these data requires recognition that relations among academic outcomes, child behavior, and parents' harsh and inconsistent discipline are undoubtedly more reciprocal than the pathways represented in Figure 1. For instance, low cognitive self-worth and high levels of distress at school may be the result of actual failure experiences in the classroom (Harter, 1983). Similarly, teacher or peer reactions to low self-restraint may eventually lead to feelings of low self-worth. Finally, parenting of early adolescents may partly reflect mothers' and fathers' reactions to sons' distress or reports of behavior problems at school (Patterson, Bank, & Stoolmiller, 1990).

Nonetheless, even in preschoolers who have had no school-related experience, emotional distress characterized by general apathy and withdrawal predicts later academic problems in the elementary grades (Kohn & Rosman, 1974). In addition, research has demonstrated a causal link between boys' academic self-concept and later achievement outcomes (Byrne, 1984; Marsh, 1987). From a developmental perspective, good parenting is expected to precede competent child behavior in the classroom. Clearly, however, the immediate as well as long-term effects of a child's social, emotional, and academic functioning on parenting needs to be examined in future research.

Finally, this research was conducted with a sample composed of middle-class boys. Thus conclusions that generalize to children from other socioeconomic or ethnic groups need to be made with caution. Parenting styles and patterns of parent-child interactions can vary dramatically as a function of a family's ethnic and cultural background (see Maccoby & Martin, 1983). In addition, the quality of parent-daughter relationships may yield quite different social and academic outcomes for early adolescent girls. Future studies will be needed to investigate these important issues.

In sum, the results of this study suggest that social and emotional adjustment skills are important noncognitive factors that explain at least part of the link between parenting and sons' academic competence. In particular, findings suggest that both mothers' and fathers' harsh and inconsistent discipline is linked to cognitive outcomes through its joint association with sons' emotional adjustment. Fathers' harsh and inconsistent discipline is linked indirectly to achievement by way of its association with sons' self-restraint. These findings underscore the critical contribution of social and emotional development to academic and intellectual achievements, and the key role of parenting in influencing such development.

REFERENCES

Achenbach, T. M., & Edelbrock, C. (1978). The classification of child psychopathology: A review and analysis of empirical efforts. *Psychological Bulletin, 85,* 1275-1302.

Armentrout, J. A. (1971). Parental child-rearing attitudes and preadolescents' problem behaviors. *Journal of Consulting and Clinical Psychology, 37,* 278-285.

Baumrind, D. (1973). The development of instrumental competence through socialization. In A. Pick (Ed.), *Minnesota symposium on child development, Vol. 7* (pp. 3-45). Minneapolis: University of Minnesota Press.

Bing, E. (1963). Effects of child-rearing practices on development of differential cognitive abilities. *Child Development, 34,* 631-648.

Brophy, J. E., & Good, T. L. (1974). *Teacher-student relationships: Causes and consequences.* New York; Holt, Rinehart & Winston.

Byrne, B. M. (1984). The general/academic self-concept nomological network: A review of construct validation research. *Review of Educational Research, 54,* 427-456.

Byrne, B. M., & Shavelson, R. J. (1986). On the structure of adolescent self-concept. *Journal of Educational Psychology, 78,* 474-481.

Clarizio, H. F., & McCoy, G. F. (1983). *Behavior disorders in children.* New York: Harper & Row.

Cole, D. A., & Rehm, L. P. (1986). Family interaction patterns and childhood depression. *Journal of Child Psychology, 14,* 297-314.

CTB/McGraw-Hill (1983). *Comprehensive Tests of Basic Skills.* Monterey, CA: Author.

Dornbusch, S., Ritter, P., Leiderman, P. H., Roberts, D. F., & Fraleigh, M. J. (1987). The relation of parenting styles to adolescent school performance. *Child Development, 58,* 1244-1257.

Dweck, C. S., & Leggett, E. L. (1988). A social-cognitive approach to motivation and personality. *Psychological Review, 95,* 246-273.

Emery, R. E. (1982). Interparental conflict and the children of discord and divorce. *Psychological Bulletin, 92,* 310-330.

Emery, R. E., & O'Leary, D. (1982). Children's perceptions of marital discord and behavior problems of boys and girls. *Journal of Abnormal Child Psychology, 10,* 11-24.

Feldman, S. S., & Wentzel, K. R. (1990). The relationship between family interaction patterns, classroom self-restraint, and academic achievement. *Journal of Educational Psychology, 82,* 813-819.

Feldman, S. S., Wentzel, K. R., & Gehring, T. M. (1989). A comparison of the views of mothers, fathers, and preadolescents about family cohesion and power. *Journal of Family Psychology, 3,* 39-60.

Feldman, S. S., Wentzel, K. R., Weinberger, D. A., & Munson, J. (1990). Marital satisfaction of parents of preadolescent boys and its relationship to family and child functioning. *Journal of Family Psychology, 4,* 211-232.

Gehring, T. M., Wentzel, K. R., Feldman, S. S., & Munson, J. (1990). Conflict in families of adolescents: The impact on cohesion and power structures. *Journal of Family Psychology, 3,* 290-309.

Harter, S. (1982). The perceived competence scale for children. *Child Development, 53,* 87-97.

Harter, S. (1983). Developmental perspectives on the self-system. In P. H. Mussen (Ed.), *Handbook of child psychology, Vol. 4* (pp. 275-385). New York: Wiley.

Harter, S. (in press). The relationship between perceived competence, affect, and motivational orientation within the classroom: Process and pattern of change. In A. K. Boggiano & T. Pittman

(Eds.), *Achievement and motivation: A social-developmental perspective.* New York: Cambridge University Press.

Harter, S., & Connell, J. P. (1984). A model of children's achievement and related self-perceptions of competence, control, and motivational orientation. In M. L. Maehr (Ed.), *Advances in motivation and achievement, Vol. 3* (pp. 219-250). Greenwich, CT: JAI Press.

Helton, G. B., & Oakland, T. D. (1977). Teachers' attitudinal responses to differing characteristics of elementary school students. *Journal of Educational Psychology, 69,* 261-265.

Hess, R. D., & Holloway, S. D. (1984). Family and school as educational institutions. In R. D. Parke (Ed.), *Review of child development research, Vol. 7* (pp. 179-222). Chicago: University of Chicago Press.

Hess, R. D., Holloway, S. D., Dickson, W. P., & Price, G. G. (1984). Maternal variables as predictors of children's school readiness and later achievement in vocabulary and mathematics in sixth grade. *Child Development, 55,* 1902-1912.

Hess, R. D., & McDevitt, T. M. (1984). Some cognitive consequences of maternal intervention techniques: A longitudinal study. *Child Development, 55,* 2017-2030.

Kedar-Voivodas, G. (1983). The impact of elementary children's school roles and sex roles on teacher attitudes: An interactional analysis. *Review of Educational Research, 53,* 415-437.

Klinger, E. (1975). Consequences of commitment to and disengagement from incentives. *Psychological Review, 82,* 1-25.

Kohn, M., & Rosman, B. L. (1974). Social-emotional, cognitive, and demographic determinants of poor school achievement: Implications for a strategy of intervention. *Journal of Educational Psychology, 66,* 267-276.

Kovacs, M. (1980). Rating scales to assess depression in school-aged children. *Acta Paedopsychiatrica, 46,* 305-315.

Leung, K., & Drasgow, F. (1986). Relation between self-esteem and delinquent behavior in three ethnic groups: An application of item response theory. *Journal of Cross-Cultural Psychology, 17,* 151-167.

Litovsky, V. G., & Dusek, J. B. (1985). Perceptions of child rearing and self-concept development during the early adolescent years. *Journal of Youth and Adolescence, 14,* 373-387.

Maccoby, E. E., & Martin, J. A. (1983). Socialization in the context of the family: Parent-child interaction. In P. H. Mussen (Ed.), *Handbook of child psychology, Vol. 4* (pp. 1-101). New York: Wiley.

Marsh, H. W. (1987). The big-fish-little-pond effect on academic self-concept. *Journal of Educational Psychology, 79,* 280-295.

Meece, J. L., Blumenfeld, P. C., & Hoyle, R. H. (1988). Students' goal orientations and cognitive engagement in classroom activities. *Journal of Educational Psychology, 80,* 514-523.

Ney, P., Colbert, P., Newman, B., & Young, J. (1986). Aggressive behavior and learning difficulties as symptoms of depression in children. *Child Psychiatry and Human Development, 17,* 3-14.

Paikoff, R. L., & Brooks-Gunn, J. (in press). Biological processes during adolescence: What role do they play in socio-emotional development? In R. Montemayor, G. Adams, & T. Gullotta (Eds.), *Advances in adolescent development: The transition from childhood to adolescence, Vol. 2.* Beverly Hills, CA: Sage.

Papini, D., & Sebby, R. (1987). Adolescent pubertal status and affective family relationships: A multivariate assessment. *Journal of Youth and Adolescence, 16,* 1-15.

Patterson, G. R., Bank, L., & Stoolmiller, M. (1990). The preadolescent's contributions to disrupted family process. In R. Montemayor, G. R. Adams, & T. P. Gullota (Eds.), *From *childhood to adolescence: A transitional period? Vol. 2* (pp. 107-133). Newbury Park, CA: Sage.

Petersen, A., & Taylor, B. (1980). The biological approach to adolescence: Biological change and psychological adaptation. In J. Adelson (Ed.), *Handbook of adolescent psychology* (pp. 117-155). New York: Free Press.

Power, T. G., & Shanks, J. A. (1989). Parents as socializers: Maternal and paternal views. *Journal of Youth and Adolescence, 18*, 203-217.

Pyszczynski, T., & Greenberg, J. (1986). Evidence for a depressive self-focusing style. *Journal of Research in Personality, 20*, 95-106.

Radin, N. (1972). Father-child interaction and the intellectual functioning of four-year-old boys. *Developmental Psychology, 6*, 353-361.

Radin, N. (1973). Observed paternal behaviors as antecedents of intellectual functioning in young boys. *Developmental Psychology, 8*, 369-376.

Rosenholtz, S. J., & Simpson, C. (1984). The formation of ability conceptions: Developmental trend or social construction? *Review of Educational Research, 54*, 31-64.

Schaefer, E. (1965). Children's reports of parental behavior: An inventory. *Child Development, 36*, 413-424.

Schludermann, E., & Schludermann, S. (1970). Replicability of factors in Children's Report of Parental Behavior (CRPBI). *The Journal of Psychology, 76*, 239-249.

Schwartz, J. C., Barton-Henry, M. L., & Pruzinsky, T. (1985). Assessing child-rearing behaviors: A comparison of ratings made by mother, father, child, and sibling on the CRPBI. *Child Development, 56*, 462-479.

Seligman, M. E., & Garber, J. (1980). *Human helplessness: Theory and research*. New York: Academic Press.

Sivan, E. (1986). Motivation in social constructivist theory. *Educational Psychologist, 21*, 209-233.

Smetana, J. G. (1988). Concepts of self and social convention: Adolescents' and parents' reasoning about hypothetical and actual family conflicts. In M. R. Gunnar (Ed.), *21st Minnesota Symposium on Child Psychology* (pp. 79-122). Hillsdale, NJ: Lawrence Erlbaum.

Spielberger, C. (1973). *State-trait anxiety for children: Preliminary manual*. Palo Alto, CA: Consulting Psychologists Press.

Steinberg, L. (1987). Impact of puberty on family relations: Effects of pubertal status and pubertal timing. *Developmental Psychology, 23*, 451-460.

Steinberg, L., Elman, J., & Mounts, N. (1989). Authoritative parenting, psychosocial maturity, and academic success among adolescents. *Child Development, 60*, 1424-1436.

Tanner, J. M. (1962). *Growth at adolescence*. Springfield, IL: Thomas.

Walker, L. S., & Greene, J. W. (1986). The social context of adolescent self-esteem. *Journal of Youth and Adolescence, 15*, 315-322.

Weinberger, D. A. (1989). *Social-emotional adjustment in older children and adults: I. Psychometric properties of the Weinberger Adjustment Inventory*. Unpublished manuscript.

Weinberger, D. A., Feldman, S. S., & Ford, M. E. (1989). *Validation of the Weinberger Parenting Inventory for Preadolescents and their Parents*. Unpublished manuscript.

Weinberger, D. A., & Schwartz, G. E. (1990). Distress and restraint as superordinate dimensions of self-reported adjustment: A typological perspective. *Journal of Personality, 58*, 381-417.

Weinberger, D. A., Tublin, S. K., Ford, M. E., & Feldman, S. S. (1990). Preadolescents' social-emotional adjustment and selective attrition in family research. *Child Development, 61*, 1374-1386.

Wentzel, K. R. (1991). Social competence at school: The relationship between social responsibility and academic achievement. *Review of Educational Research, 61,* 1-24.

Wentzel, K. R., Weinberger, D. A., Ford, M. E., & Feldman, S. S. (1990). Academic achievement in preadolescence: The role of motivational, affective, and self-regulatory processes. *Journal of Applied Developmental Psychology, 11,* 179-193.

Yee, D. K., & Flanagan, C. (1985). Family environments and self-consciousness in early adolescence. *Journal of Early Adolescence, 5,* 59-68.

Youniss, J., & Smollar, J. (1985). *Adolescent relations with mothers, fathers, and friends.* Chicago: University of Chicago Press.

Requests of reprints should be addressed to: Kathryn R. Wentzel, 3304 Benjamin Building, Department of Human Development, University of Maryland, College Park, MD 20742.

The Relation of Parenting Style to Adolescent School Performance

Sanford M. Dornbusch, Philip L. Ritter, P. Herbert Leiderman, Donald F. Roberts, and Michael J. Fraleigh

Stanford Center for the Study of Youth Development

DORNBUSCH, SANFORD M.; RITTER, PHILIP L., LEIDERMAN, P. HERBERT; ROBERTS, DONALD F.; and FRALEIGH, MICHAEL J. *The Relation of Parenting Style to Adolescent School Performance.* CHILD DEVELOPMENT, 1987, 58, 1244–1257. This article develops and tests a reformation of Baumrind's typology of authoritarian, permissive, and authoritative parenting styles in the context of adolescent school performance. Using a large and diverse sample of San Francisco Bay Area high school students ($N = 7,836$), we found that both authoritarian and permissive parenting styles were negatively associated with grades, and authoritative parenting was positively associated with grades. Parenting styles generally showed the expected relation to grades across gender, age, parental education, ethnic, and family structure categories. Authoritarian parenting tended to have a stronger association with grades than did the other 2 parenting styles, except among Hispanic males. The full typology best predicted grades among white students. Pure authoritative families (high on authoritative but not high on the other 2 indices) had the highest mean grades, while inconsistent families that combine authoritarian parenting with other parenting styles had the lowest grades.

A recent review of research on the family and school as educational institutions notes an increasing emphasis on "process" studies that seek to identify those features of the family environment through which socioeconomic and cultural background have an impact on mental development and school achievement. Hess and Holloway (1984) analyzed results from studies of preschool, primary, and middle-school children and identified five processes linking family and school achievement: (1) verbal interaction between mother and children, (2) expectation of parents for achievement, (3) positive affective relationships between parents and children, (4) parental beliefs and attributions about the child, and (5) discipline and control strategies. Among these various processes, discipline and control strategies appeared to have a major influence on school achievement (Baumrind, 1973; Hess & McDevitt, 1984; Marjoriebanks, 1979).

The research of Baumrind is particularly pertinent because she attempts to link components of family interaction to cognitive competence. She postulates three family parenting styles (authoritative, authoritarian, and permissive) that have consequences for the development of cognitive and social competence. These three family types differ in the values, behaviors, and standards that children are expected to adopt; in the ways these values, behaviors, and standards are transmitted; and in parental expectations about the behavior of children. In this study we extend Baumrind's typology to a large and ethnically diverse sample of adolescents.

Baumrind, in a series of studies of preschool children and their families (Baumrind & Black, 1967), and later in studies of somewhat older children, delineated three modes of family interaction that we will reformulate for use in this study of adolescents and their

This research was supported by the Hewlett Foundation, the Irvine Foundation, the Bank of America Foundation, individual trustees of the California Family Foundation, the Stanford Center for the Study of Youth Development, and Father Flanagan's Boys' Home. It was part of the joint project known as the Study of Stanford and the Schools. The principals of the six cooperating schools participated actively at every stage, from project design to analysis: Verdis Crockett, Samuel Johnson, Jr., Gary McHenry, Robert Palazzi, Charles Perotti, Gary Poulos, Joyce Rosenstiel, and Jesus Sanchez. We are indebted to Lee J. Cronbach, Helena Kraemer, Steven H. Chaffee, Michael W. Kirst, Michael Garet, W. Richard Scott, Robert C. Calfee, Shirley Feldman, Eleanor E. Maccoby, Martin Ford, and Albert H. Hastorf for their suggestions and criticisms. Jean Kanerva, Barbara Prescott, Lindsay White, Lisa Shaffer, Fox Vernon, Robert Macaulay, Ivan Fukumoto, Angela Valenzuela, and Worku Negash assisted in data collection and analysis. Send requests for reprints to the first author at The Stanford Center for the Study of Youth Development, Stanford University, Stanford, CA 94305.

parents. (We will not describe the harmonious and nonconforming patterns, which we do not use.)

The authoritarian style of parenting had the following characteristics: parents attempted to shape, control, and evaluate the behavior and attitudes of their children in accordance with an absolute set of standards; parents emphasize obedience, respect for authority, work, tradition, and the preservation of order; verbal give-and-take between parent and child is discouraged. Baumrind's study of preschool children found that such a mode of family interaction was associated with low levels of independence and social responsibility.

Baumrind later described the authoritarian pattern, somewhat more formally, as being high in demandedness on the part of the parents and low in parental responsiveness to the child. She continued her studies of children, this time with children 8–9 years old (Baumrind, 1971, 1973). She found that the authoritarian pattern, high in demandedness and low in parental responsiveness, had different consequences for girls and for boys. Girls, but not boys, who came from authoritarian families were more socially assertive. For both sexes, intrusive-directiveness was associated with lower cognitive competence (Baumrind, in preparation).

A second pattern is permissive parenting, in which parents are tolerant and accepting toward the child's impulses, use as little punishment as possible, make few demands for mature behavior, and allow considerable self-regulation by the child. In the study of preschool children, Baumrind found the children of permissive parents were immature, lacked impulse control and self-reliance, and evidenced a lack of social responsibility and independence. In the follow-up studies at 8–9 years of age, these children were low in both social and cognitive competence.

Authoritative parenting is the third type described by Baumrind. This pattern contains the following elements: an expectation of mature behavior from the child and clear setting of standards by the parents; firm enforcement of rules and standards, using commands and sanctions when necessary; encouragement of the child's independence and individuality; open communication between parents and children, with encouragement of verbal give-and-take; and recognition of the rights of both parents and children.

Female children of authoritative parents in the preschool sample were socially responsible and more independent than other children. Male children were as independent as the other children were, and they appeared to be socially responsible. At ages 8 and 9, both male and female offspring of authoritative parents were high in social and cognitive competence (Baumrind, in preparation).

The studies of Baumrind and others have focused on preschool children and children in elementary school. Studies of family processes and school achievement beyond childhood are rare. A recent study showed that the effect of parental control processes persisted in school performance among children 12 years of age (Hess & McDevitt, 1984). In addition, there is suggestive evidence that high achievement in the adolescent years is associated with at least one family process, high identification with parents (Kandel & Lesser, 1969; Morrow & Wilson, 1961; Rickberg & Westby, 1967; Shaw & White, 1965; Swift, 1967; Weinhert & Trieber, 1982).

This article develops and tests Baumrind's conceptualization of family processes in the context of adolescent school performance. The study is unusual in that it extends Baumrind's typology of authoritative, authoritarian, and permissive parenting to a very large and diverse sample of adolescents, using high school grades as the criterion variable. A large-scale questionnaire study of adolescents, in high schools was used to derive indirect measures of the style of parenting. In assigning scores on the three parenting styles, we relied on the face validity of questions and response categories. The reliability of two of our three measures and the consistency of our findings increase our confidence in the utility of this approach.

Sources of Data

The major source of data for this study is a questionnaire completed by 7,836 adolescents enrolled in six high schools in the San Francisco Bay area, approximately 88% of the total enrollment of those schools, in Spring 1985. The questionnaire contained numerous items. Those used in this article include student background characteristics, self-reported grades, perceptions of parental attitudes and behaviors, and family communication patterns. From this questionnaire we used perceptions of family processes to construct indices of parenting style, background variables to serve as controls, and self-reported grades as the dependent variable.

Some questionnaire items were not answered by all students. Small variations in sample size across tables reflect this fact. We chose to present all the available data rather than including only those cases where the data were complete.

The data from that questionnaire are augmented by information on parental education from two additional sources. First, a student questionnaire had been administered in Spring 1983 to a sample of students at five of the six participating schools. The students who participated in both surveys gave us a substantial pool of students for whom we had parental education. Second, parental responses to a family questionnaire mailed to the homes of all students in our sample provided information on parental education for additional cases in our sample. For those analyses, such as multiple regressions, which required the inclusion of parental education as a measure of social stratification, a substantial portion of our cases had to be excluded because of the absence of information on parental education.

For one school in our sample we had current grade point averages for every student. Those data enabled us to assess the validity of the self-reported grades that we used as a dependent variable.

Measures

Demographic Variables

Ethnicity.—Each high school student was asked to select one of nine categories for ethnic identification: Asian, black, Filipino, Pacific Islander, American Indian, Latino or Hispanic, white, and other. Vietnamese respondents were combined with the Asian subgroup. Sample sizes provide sufficient cases for the analysis in this article of responses from four groups: Asian, black, Hispanic, and (non-Hispanic) white.

Parental education.—Our measure of parental status or social class was parental education. There was no information on parental education in the student questionnaire used as the basis for most of this article. Two other sources, responses to a questionnaire mailed to parents and responses to a previous student questionnaire, were used to determine parental education for a subset of the total sample. Together, these two additional sources provided information on parental education for 4,053 cases, or 52% of the total sample.

The parental education categories used in the previous student questionnaire were: (1) not a high school graduate; (2) high school graduate; (3) vocational, trade, or business school; (4) some college; (5) 4-year college de-

gree; (6) graduate or professional degree; and (7) don't know. The question that was used in the parent survey had slightly finer gradations, and was recoded to match the breakdown shown here. Mother's education and father's education were then averaged to create a single parental education measure for each family. Finally, for qualitative analyses, mean parental education was trichotomized so as to produce categories of clear social meaning: up to 3.5 = low education, 4 to 4.5 = middle education, and 5 and above = high education. Families whose mean education did not reach attendance at a college were in the low-education group; the middle-education group included college attendance but not receiving a 4-year degree; the high group had at least a 4-year college degree.

Family structure.—Our measure of family structure came from student reports of who is present in the household. In the analyses presented here, family structure consists of five categories: two natural parents, single mother, mother and stepfather, single father, and father and stepmother. All other family forms were too infrequent to provide a sample large enough for analysis.

Measures of Parenting Style

Three parenting style indices were developed to roughly conform with Baumrind's three styles of parenting (authoritarian, permissive, and authoritative). Twenty-five items or sets of items were identified in the student questionnaire as closely reflecting one of the three styles, and each index was constructed by taking the means of the appropriate items. No question was allowed to contribute to more than one of the indices, so that the three scores are not forced to be correlated with each other.

The authoritarian index was based on the mean response to the following eight questions concerning the frequency of certain family behaviors: in their family communication, the parents tell the youth not to argue with adults, that he or she will know better when grown up, and that the parents are correct and should not be questioned; as a response to poor grades, the parents get upset, reduce the youth's allowance, or "ground" the youth; as a response to good grades, parents tell the youth to do even better, and note that other grades should be as good.

The permissive index was the mean of eight responses: hard work in school is not important to the parents (the mean for four academic subjects), the parents don't care if the student gets bad grades, they don't care if the student gets good grades, there are no rules concerning watching television, and (using the highest involvement of the possible parent figures) the parents are not involved in education, they do not attend school programs for parents, they do not help with homework, and they do not check the child's homework.

The authoritative index was calculated from the mean frequency of nine responses concerning family behavior: in their family communication, parents tell the youth to look at both sides of issues, they admit that the youth sometimes knows more, they talk about politics within the family, and they emphasize that everyone should help with decisions in the family; as a response to good grades, parents praise the student, and give more freedom to make decisions; as a response to poor grades, they take away freedom, encourage the student to try harder, and offer to help.

These three indices of parental style were used as continuous variables throughout the article as the main measures for the three parenting styles.

The reliability of these three quantitative indices of parenting style was assessed using Cronbach's alpha. The alpha coefficients were .70 for the eight items of the authoritarian index, .60 for the eight items of the permissive index, and .66 for the nine items of the authoritative index. The alphas for the authoritarian and authoritative indices were moderately high and satisfactory, and the alpha for the permissive index was only slightly lower.

The slightly lower reliability for the index of permissive parenting may be a product of the limited nature of the indicators of permissiveness within our questionnaire. The concept of permissiveness may be tapping two distinct and identifiable parental attitudes. Permissiveness may refer to a parenting attitude that is essentially neglectful and uncaring, or it may refer to parenting that is caring and concerned but ideologically genuinely permissive. It is impossible to disentangle these differing orientations in our permissiveness scale. Ideally, researchers should construct scales and measure these two separable orientations. In the meantime, we urge caution in interpreting those portions of our results that feature indicators of permissiveness.

In addition to these quantitative measures, types of families were constructed based on the scores on the three indices. In particular, three "pure" styles of families

were defined, with a family included in a pure family style category if it scored in the top one-third on one parenting style index and not in the top one-third on either of the other two indices.

Half of the families (50%) could not be characterized as having a pure parenting style, while 18% (1,321) were categorized as pure permissive, 17% (1,218) were pure authoritative and 15% (1,064) were pure authoritarian. Thus, pure parenting styles apply to only half of the families in the total sample.

In addition, we created a variable in which every family was assigned to one of the possible combinations of pure parenting styles. These combinations range from being high on all three pure parenting styles to being high on none of them.

Measures of Student Performance
Self-reported grades.—The measure of student performance used throughout this article is the response by the student to a question that asks for the selection of a category that represents the usual grade the student receives. The categories were: mostly A's, about half A's and half B's, mostly B's, about half B's and half C's, mostly C's, about half C's and half D's, mostly D's, and mostly below D. A numerical scale of self-reported grades was then related to these responses, with 4.0 representing the top category.

We have consulted with educators about the use of grades as a measure of school performance. Their consensus was that grades, unlike scores on intelligence tests and measures based on standardized achievement tests, provide the most appropriate measure of current school performance. Grades have their difficulties as a measure of intellectual performance, for they often represent relatively arbitrary assessments by a teacher. But the typical grade, usual grade, or mean grade is the summation of many judgments about the extent to which a student is responding to the school curriculum.

Grade-point averages.—We found that grade-point averages were available in most of our schools only for seniors approaching graduation. One school had up-to-date grade-point averages for all its students. We therefore compared the questionnaire response, the self-reported grade, to the grade-point average for each student in that school.

The correlation between grade-point averages and self-reported grades was .76 ($N = 1,146$). We were concerned that there might be a systematic inflation of self-reported grades for students whose academic performance was low. Accordingly, we examined the responses of students at each grade level. There was only a slight tendency to overstate grades when one reached grades near the bottom of the distribution—mean grades of C and below.

Accordingly, throughout this article we will use a single measure of school performance that was available for almost all students in the sample. Self-reported grades give a close approximation to the distribution of grades on the transcript and will be used as the measure of school performance in all analyses.

Results

Parenting Style

In Table 1 we report the mean on each of the three parenting style indices by sex, age, ethnicity, parental education, and family structure. The extent to which different groups were reported by their children to employ each style of parenting is interesting in itself, in addition to its relation to high school grades. Since each index is based on a different set of questions, scores on one index should not be compared with scores on another. Rather, comparisons should focus on group differences in the means for a single index.

There were small sex differences in the parenting styles reported by the students. Females, compared to males, reported a slightly lower level of authoritarian parenting, a difference that was statistically significant. There was no gender difference in the reports of permissive parenting. These small gender differences in means will not be discussed further. Most of our analyses relating grades to parenting styles will not show gender differences in the results.

Family parenting style does appear to be related to the age of the adolescent. There was a decline in the mean score on the authoritarian index with increased age; permissiveness, on the other hand, was higher in the older age groups. The authoritative index did not show a clear relation to age. This suggests that, while there may be shifts in the level of authoritarian or permissive parenting as maturation takes place, the authoritative style may represent an ideological commitment that does not readily change as children grow up.

In Table 1, the mean on each parenting index for each ethnic-sex group is compared to the appropriate mean for whites. Differences among ethnic groups are seen in that analysis. Asian, black, and Hispanic families were higher on the authoritarian index for both sexes than were white families. Families of Asians, Hispanics, and black females were lower on the authoritative index than were white families. For permissiveness, the ethnic differences were more complex. Compared to whites, blacks were lower on permissiveness, Hispanics were higher, and Asians were slightly higher. Sixteen of the 18 differences were statistically significant.

The means on each parenting index in Table 1 also showed a clear relation to parental. education. Comparing within each sex, families with higher parental education tended to be somewhat lower in authoritarian and permissive parenting and higher on authoritative parenting. These differences in parenting styles among parental education groups are interesting in themselves, even though the association of parenting styles with grades will be shown to apply across all parental education groups.

With respect to family structure, single mothers showed a higher level of permissive parenting than did two natural parents. For their sons only, single mothers showed lower levels of authoritarian parenting when compared to households containing both natural parents. Single fathers were also more permissive for both sexes, while they were less authoritarian for females and less authoritative for males than families containing both natural parents. Step-families, compared to families with two natural parents, tended to be more authoritarian and more permissive, and, for males only, less authoritative. Of the 24 comparisons between two-natural-parent families and other types of families, 12 were statistically significant.

Parenting Styles and Grades

For both sexes, the correlations between grades and the three indices of parenting style strongly support earlier studies on the cognitive impact of parenting styles. The negative correlation of authoritarian parenting to grades was $-.18$ for males and $-.23$ for females. For permissive parenting, the correlations were $-.09$ for males and $-.17$ for females. Finally, authoritative parenting had positive correlations with grades of .08 for males and .13 for females. All correlations were significant at the .001 level. The relation of authoritarian parenting to grades was the strongest of the three correlations for both sexes.

One question that could be asked about these relations of parenting styles to grades is whether they apply equally well within groups that differ on age, ethnicity, family structure, or education. Correlational analyses within categories provide a series of independent tests of the relation between parenting styles and grades. We will later present multiple regressions for the total sample and within ethnic groups, but here we will assess the consistency of these relations in specific categories of students.

The bulk of the literature on parenting styles is based on studies of young children. In that younger age group, the age of each child is more likely to be a central variable than in our studies of an adolescent population in high school. We did not expect that the relations between parenting style and grades would be highly dependent on the age of the student, but we tested the possibility by looking at the relation between parenting style and grades for males and females in each of the five largest age groups in our sample: 14, 15, 16, 17, and 18. There were no important fluctuations among age groups in the association between parenting style and grades. All 30 correlations (three scores by five ages and two sexes) were in the expected direction, and 29 were statistically significant.

The Baumrind typology was developed from the intensive analysis of parenting in largely middle-class, white families. We can take advantage of the size of our sample and its diversity to see whether, controlling for the sex of the child, the four main ethnic groups in our study show similar relations between each style of parenting and grades, and thus examine the extent to which a conceptualization developed in one cultural arena applies to groups with possibly divergent norms and values.

The data indicate that, across ethnic groups, authoritarian and permissive styles were associated with lower grades, and an authoritative style was associated with higher grades. All eight correlation coefficients for the two sexes and four ethnic groups were negative when the authoritarian parenting style was related to grades, and the same was true when the permissive parenting style was related to grades. For the authoritative style the correlation to grades was positive in seven out of eight ethnic-sex groups, with the only failure among Asian females. Thirteen of the 24 correlations were statistically significant at the .05 level.

There were, however, ethnic differences in the strength of the correlations between parenting styles and grades. For Asians, the correlations of grades with both the authoritative and the permissive styles were near zero. For Hispanic males, authoritarian parenting showed almost no relation to grades ($-.03$), even though the relation was strongly negative among Hispanic females ($-.26$). Among whites, our largest ethnic group, and blacks, our smallest, all correlations were as expected. Asians appear to be the ethnic group for whom our typology applies least well. Although our approach does not seem to be limited in application to only a single ethnic group, data from Asians appear to offer support only for the relation of authoritarian parenting to grades.

Although we have only a smaller sample of students for whom we know the education of their parents, it seems appropriate to use that information to see whether our parenting style indices relate to grades across social classes. There are low, middle, and high parental education families within each sex, making six independent subgroups within which to examine the relation of the three parenting styles to grades. All 18 correlations were in the expected direction, with 11 statistically significant. All correlations of authoritarian parenting with grades were statistically significant. The data support the view that the parenting style typology applies fairly well across the social classes.

We can simultaneously control for ethnicity and parental education and thereby produce numerous correlations of parenting style with grades, although many were based on a small number of cases. There are four ethnic groups, three parental education groups, two sexes, and three styles of parenting. Excluding groups with fewer than 10 students, there were 63 remaining correlation coefficients to examine. Of the 63, 48 were in the expected direction (positive for the authoritative index and negative for the authoritarian and permissive indices) and 15 in the opposite direction, a ratio better than three to one. Looking only at correlations that were statistically significant, 21 were in the predicted direction and only one (authoritative parenting for sons of low-education Asians) was in the opposite direction. These correlations supported the hypothesized relations between each parenting style and grades.

As American society has exhibited a decline in the proportion of children living with both natural parents, we wish to see if our reformulation of Baumrind is applicable to

TABLE 1
MEAN ON EACH PARENTING STYLE INDEX, BY SEX, AGE, ETHNICITY, PARENTAL EDUCATION, AND FAMILY STRUCTURE

	MALE				FEMALE			
	Authoritarian	Permissive	Authoritative	N	Authoritarian	Permissive	Authoritative	N
Total	3.41 (.64)	2.95 (.62)	3.55 (.60)	4,047	3.34*** (.61)	2.96 (.57)	3.56 (.55)	3,789
Age:								
14	3.43 (.64)	2.75 (.57)	3.63 (.59)	455	3.38 (.60)	2.82 (.54)	3.54 (.57)	550
15	3.41 (.63)	2.87 (.62)	3.54 (.61)	1,032	3.38 (.60)	2.87 (.57)	3.57 (.55)	1,069
16	3.47 (.63)	2.94 (.59)	3.55 (.57)	1,085	3.38 (.60)	2.98 (.55)	3.55 (.55)	974
17	3.35 (.63)	3.07 (.61)	3.56 (.61)	896	3.27 (.60)	3.08 (.55)	3.59 (.54)	758
18	3.35 (.66)	3.14 (.63)	3.49 (.62)	461	3.21 (.62)	3.12 (.58)	3.56 (.55)	347
Ethnicity:								
White	3.33 (.61)	2.95 (.57)	3.58 (.58)	2,314	3.25 (.59)	2.94 (.53)	3.61 (.52)	2,239
Asian	3.52*** (.63)	3.02* (.63)	3.45*** (.63)	418	3.45*** (.58)	2.97 (.58)	3.51*** (.53)	382
Black	3.65*** (.70)	2.70*** (.70)	3.62 (.68)	230	3.54*** (.59)	2.84* (.59)	3.51* (.64)	196
Hispanic	3.55*** (.65)	3.02* (.71)	3.49** (.63)	549	3.47*** (.63)	3.08*** (.63)	3.46*** (.60)	525

Parental education:								
Low	3.43*** (.64)	3.01*** (.60)	3.49*** (.58)	3.35*** (.60)	715	3.03*** (.55)	3.48*** (.54)	679
Middle	3.33 (.58)	2.85 (.55)	3.63* (.56)	3.25+ (.58)	947	2.87 (.51)	3.65** (.50)	939
High	3.31 (.56)	2.84 (.51)	3.71 (.49)	3.18 (.56)	353	2.83 (.49)	3.73 (.46)	325
Family structure:								
Two natural parents	3.41 (.62)	2.92 (.59)	3.58 (.60)	3.33 (.59)	2,432	2.92 (.54)	3.58 (.53)	2,241
Single mother	3.33** (.63)	3.06*** (.61)	3.54 (.58)	3.33 (.60)	635	3.03*** (.58)	3.54 (.58)	716
Mother and stepfather ...	3.48+ (.64)	2.99+ (.61)	3.54 (.61)	3.40*** (.60)	321	3.02*** (.52)	3.56 (.56)	367
Single father	3.39 (.64)	3.06** (.62)	3.47* (.61)	3.08*** (.69)	158	3.09** (.63)	3.58 (.62)	101
Father and stepmother ...	3.63*** (.66)	3.01 (.65)	3.47* (.64)	3.44+ (.65)	158	3.07** (.59)	3.56 (.57)	114

NOTE.—Numbers in parentheses are standard deviations. Within the Total row, tests of significance compare the mean on each index for females with the mean on the same index for males. Within the analysis for Ethnicity, tests of significance compare the mean on each index for a sex within an ethnic group with the mean on the same index for the same sex among whites. Within the analysis for Parental education, tests of significance compare the mean on each index for a sex within either the low or middle parental education group with the mean on the same index for the same sex within the high parental education group. Within the analysis for Family structure, tests of significance compare the mean on each index for a sex within each of the single-parent or stepparent groups with the mean on the same index for the same sex within families containing two natural parents.

+ $p < .10$, two-tailed.
* $p < .05$, two-tailed.
** $p < .01$, two-tailed.
*** $p < .001$, two-tailed.

283

children living in other types of families. For five types of family structure, the three parenting styles were related to grades for both sexes. Of those 30 correlations, only two failed to be in the hypothesized direction. The two failures occurred in the least common family structure—the child living with a male single parent—where sampling fluctuation is greatest. Within the more frequent family structures—two natural parents, a single mother, or a mother and stepfather in the household—15 of the 18 correlations were statistically significant at the .05 level using a two-tail test. Since all 17 statistically significant correlations were in the predicted direction, the evidence suggests that diverse

family structures do not limit the scope of application of parenting styles.

Multiple Regressions

Table 2 contains two multiple regressions in which a series of structural variables are combined, in the first regression, with the indices of parenting style, or, in the second regression, with a set of measures of pure parenting style (in the top one-third on one parenting style index and not in the top one-third on either of the other two indices) in order to predict grades. In a separate article we will show that family processes, of which parenting style is just one element, are more powerful than structural variables in the ex-

TABLE 2

DETERMINANTS OF GRADES, USING STRUCTURAL VARIABLES AND EITHER PARENTING STYLE INDICES OR
PURE PARENTING STYLES

	WITH PARENTING STYLE INDICES			WITH PURE PARENTING STYLES		
	b	Beta	F	b	Beta	F
Female	.084***	.054	13.2***	.093***	.060	15.8***
	(.023)			(.024)		
Parental education	.117***	.171	112.2***	.125***	.183	126.9***
	(.011)			(.011)		
Black	−.188**	−.045	8.9**	−.205**	−.049	10.3**
	(.063)			(.064)		
Hispanic	−.117*	−.040	6.4*	−.122**	−.042	6.7**
	(.047)			(.047)		
Asian	.485***	.186	151.6***	.466***	.179	137.4***
	(.039)			(.040)		
Age	−.023*	−.037	5.9*	−.023*	−.036	5.6*
	(.010)			(.010)		
Single parent	−.213***	−.107	48.6***	−.200***	−.100	42.3***
	(.031)			(.031)		
Stepparent	−.163***	−.064	17.6***	−.175***	−.068	19.8***
	(.039)			(.039)		
Authoritarian	−.303***	−.230	227.7***	...	...	...
	(.020)					
Permissive	−.127***	−.088	26.9***	...	...	...
	(.025)					
Authoritative	.053*	.037	5.0*	...	...	...
	(.024)					
Pure Authoritarian	...	...	...	−.295***	−.177	134.2***
				(.025)		
Pure Permissive	...	...	...	−.143***	−.083	27.0***
				(.027)		
Pure Authoritative	...	...	...	.045+	.027	3.2+
				(.025)		
Constant	3.941	...	...	2.825	...	...
R^2		.176			.156	
N		3,752			3,752	

NOTE.—Numbers in parentheses are standard errors.
+ $p < .10$, two-tailed.
* $p < .05$, two-tailed.
** $p < .01$, two-tailed.
*** $p < .001$, two-tailed.

planation of variability in grades. Indeed, the proportion of variance explained in that analysis was surprisingly high, .34 to .38, given that no measure of intellectual performance or previous school performance was used as a predictor.

In Table 2, the only family processes used as predictors are those related to our measures of parenting styles, so that we are not expecting to explain a high proportion of the variance in grades. The utility of the multiple regression technique is that it permits the simultaneous operation and statistical control of all the structural variables we have used in the preceding analyses, and that it enables us to assess the relative strength of the relation between grades and each of the three parenting styles when the structural variables are all taken into account.

The first finding we note in Table 2 is that the proportion of the variance in grades explained by the predictors was slightly lower when the pure parenting styles were substituted for the scores on the parenting style indices. One explanation of this result will be discussed in our presentation of Table 4.

The standardized beta weights provide a means for assessing the relative contribution of each of the predictor variables. Focusing first on the structural variables, we note that the most powerful ethnic predictor in both equations was Asian. This gives further support to our conclusion that the parenting styles we have studied do little to explain the high grades of the Asians in our sample.

Parental education was also a relatively powerful predictor, with betas averaging approximately .18. Other relatively powerful structural predictors were our two measures of family structure. Being in a single-parent household or in a household containing a step-parent was negatively associated with grades. (A separate article will examine the processes within those family structures that produced these results.) In addition, female students tended to get higher grades than males, and black, Hispanic, and older students tended to get lower grades.

Turning to the parenting style indices in the first regression, we note once again the relatively stronger relation of the authoritarian index to grades, with a beta weight higher than the betas for the permissive and authoritative indices. Moreover, that the authoritarian index is stronger than parental education as a predictor indicates that this process variable was a better predictor than the usual measure of social status.

Using measures of pure parenting style produced similar results in the second equation. Pure authoritarian parenting showed a stronger relation to grades than either of the other two parenting types. In this equation, pure authoritarian parenting was approximately equal to parental education in strength as a predictor of grades. The relations between the pure parenting variables and grades were in the expected directions.

We also examined ethnic differences in the impact of parenting styles. Table 3 presents multiple regressions within each ethnic group, using the same structural variables and parenting indices that were used in the first equation of Table 2. (We also did regressions within each of the three most frequent family structures. We do not present the tables of results, but the findings show the same pattern in each family structure, with authoritarian and permissive parenting negatively associated with grades, and with authoritative parenting positively associated with grades.)

Within the Asian group, authoritarian parenting was the strongest predictor of grades, but the other parenting indices were not significantly related to grades. Within blacks, the group with the smallest number of cases, no parenting index was significantly associated with grades.

Among Hispanics, an interesting result emerged. Being female was significantly associated with high grades. Yet the interaction of females and authoritarian parenting was associated with low grades, significant if a one-tail test was used, and with the same magnitude of beta weight as being female. This interaction of gender and authoritarian parenting reversed the relation of authoritarian parenting itself to grades within the Hispanic sample. The failure of authoritarian parenting to affect Hispanic males was noted earlier. This may partially explain why, among Hispanics, females were only slightly higher than males in mean grades, while the difference was much more substantial in the other ethnic groups.

We can speculate on the reasons that authoritarian parenting is gender-specific in its impact on Hispanics. Perhaps this reflects cultural orientations that produce major gender differences within the Hispanic population. For example, Hispanic informants suggest that disobedience is expected among male children in authoritarian households but not expected from females. Males see themselves as future heads of households; their subordination is only temporary. Others suggest the importance of considering the lifelong orien-

TABLE 3

DETERMINANTS OF GRADES, USING STRUCTURAL
VARIABLES AND PARENTING STYLE WITHIN
ETHNIC GROUPS

	b	Beta	F
Asians:[a]			
Female	.001	.001	.0
	(.069)		
Parental education........	.086**	.139	7.7**
	(.031)		
Age	−.070*	−.129	6.3*
	(.028)		
Single parent....	−.269*	−.125	6.4*
	(.107)		
Stepparent......	−.654***	−.186	14.3***
	(.173)		
Authoritarian....	−.228***	−.190	14.6***
	(.060)		
Permissive......	−.073	−.057	1.0
	(.074)		
Authoritative....	−.089	−.070	1.5
	(.073)		
Blacks:[b]			
Female	.354**	.266	9.5**
	(.115)		
Parental education........	.076	.128	1.9
	(.054)		
Age	.017	.029	.1
	(.053)		
Single parent....	−.019	−.013	.0
	(.123)		
Stepparent......	.131	.065	.5
	(.180)		
Authoritarian....	−.142	−.127	2.2
	(.095)		
Permissive......	.076	.064	.5
	(.109)		
Authoritative....	−.001	−.001	.0
	(.097)		
Hispanics:[c]			
Female	1.070*	.662	3.87*
	(.544)		
Parental education........	.037	.059	.95
	(.038)		
Age	−.007	−.010	.03
	(.038)		
Single parent....	−.167	−.085	2.06
	(.116)		
Stepparent......	−.209	−.078	1.73
	(.159)		
Authoritarian....	.117	.088	.24
	(.240)		
Permissive......	−.048	−.039	.33
	(.085)		
Authoritative....	.170[+]	.125	3.19[+]
	(.095)		
Authoritarian × female	−.280[+]	−.666	3.28[+]
	(.155)		

TABLE 3 (Continued)

	b	Beta	F
Whites:[d]			
Female	.080**	.053	8.5**
	(.028)		
Parental education........	.140***	.188	103.0***
	(.014)		
Age	−.025*	−.041	4.7*
	(.011)		
Single parent....	−.240***	−.123	44.0***
	(.036)		
Stepparent......	−.138**	−.058	9.7**
	(.044)		
Authoritarian....	−.344***	−.262	200.7***
	(.024)		
Permissive......	−.142***	−.096	22.2***
	(.030)		
Authoritative....	.073*	.050	6.4*
	(.029)		

[a] Intercept = 5.534; N = 370; R^2 = .141.
[b] Intercept = 1.777; N = 135; R^2 = .121.
[c] Intercept = 1.624; N = 285; R^2 = .082.
[d] Intercept = 3.993; N = 2,592; R^2 = .157.
[+] $p < .10$, two-tailed.
[*] $p < .05$, two-tailed.
[**] $p < .01$, two-tailed.
[***] $p < .001$, two-tailed.

tations of Hispanic females, emphasizing femininity and family. Whatever the explanation, we have here clear additional evidence of difficulty in directly applying the parenting typology across diverse cultures.

Finally, looking at the results for whites in Table 3, we note how well the pattern of findings reflects the original formulation. Authoritarian and permissive parenting are associated with low grades, and authoritative parenting is associated with high grades. The typology derived from a predominantly white sample of children obviously continues to fit the white adolescent population fairly well.

Pure and Inconsistent Parenting Styles

All families in our sample can be categorized as either predominantly practicing one form of parenting or practicing a combination of parenting styles. The data in Table 4 include the mean grades of students from the families that could be categorized as pure authoritarian, pure permissive, and pure authoritative. We find that, for both sexes, the mean grades of the children from pure authoritative families were much higher than the mean grades of children from pure authoritarian or pure permissive families (all differences significant at the .001 level).

Looking at the same three pure family parenting styles, we examined mean grades

TABLE 4

MEAN GRADE OF EACH COMBINATION OF HIGH ON PARENTING STYLE INDICES, BY SEX

INDICES ON WHICH HOUSEHOLD IS HIGH	MALE		FEMALE		TOTAL	
	Mean Grade	N	Mean Grade	N	Mean Grade	N
All indices high	2.34	92	2.42	54	2.37	146
	(.73)		(.79)		(.75)	
Authoritarian and permissive	2.42	349	2.49	328	2.45	677
	(.82)		(.83)		(.83)	
Authoritarian and authoritative ...	2.54	444	2.65	303	2.58	747
	(.77)		(.77)		(.77)	
Permissive and authoritative	2.84	129	2.94	133	2.89	262
	(.76)		(.69)		(.72)	
Authoritarian only (pure)	2.62	555	2.68	509	2.65	1,064
	(.79)		(.79)		(.79)	
Permissive only (pure)	2.61	673	2.70	648	2.66	1,321
	(.90)		(.85)		(.87)	
Authoritative only (pure)	2.96	552	3.08	666	3.02	1,218
	(.77)		(.72)		(.75)	
No index high	2.80	917	3.00	908	2.90	1,825
	(.82)		(.74)		(.79)	

within ethnic, parental education, and family structure categories. For both sexes, within the four ethnic groups, three parental education groups, and the three most common family structures, there were no exceptions to the ordering of mean grades for the pure forms. Pure authoritative families always had the highest mean grades.

Table 4 also includes, for the two sexes and the total sample, mean grades for students coming from families exhibiting each possible combination of high scores on the three parenting style indices. Our definition of a family with a pure parenting style was that the family be in the top one-third on one parenting style index and not be in the top one-third on the other two indices. In Table 4, every family is thus assigned to one of the following groups: high on all three indices; high on two indices (authoritarian and permissive, authoritarian and authoritative, or permissive and authoritative); high on only a single index (our pure authoritarian, pure permissive, and pure authoritative families); and not high on any index.

The mean grades in Table 4 exhibit a pattern that helps to explain the slightly lower predictive power of the equation using pure parenting styles in Table 2. The mean grades of students from pure authoritative families were clearly the highest. But the mean grades of students in pure authoritarian or pure permissive families were not the lowest. The lowest grades were found among students

whose family parenting style is inconsistent, especially with combinations that include authoritarian parenting. The combination of authoritarian, permissive, and authoritative parenting (all indices high) and the combination of authoritarian and permissive parenting were associated with the lowest mean grades. Authoritarian combined with authoritative parenting was also associated with low grades. Only the combination of authoritative and permissive parenting (not including authoritarian parenting) had mean grades higher than pure authoritarian or pure permissive.

Thus, inconsistency, when including a high index on authoritarian parenting, is associated with the lowest grades. We speculate that inconsistency in the home environment creates anxiety among children, and that anxiety reduces the relation between the student's effort in school and the grade received. We have examined some other data from our sample and note a slight tendency for inconsistent communications from parents to be associated with a lower correlation between hours of homework and grades.

Discussion

This article has provided evidence that Baumrind's typology of parenting styles, originally formulated to explain social and cognitive development among young children, can successfully be applied to adolescents and related to their academic performance in high school. Students from a wide range of backgrounds tended to get lower grades when their descriptions of family behavior indicated more authoritarian parenting, more permissive parenting, or less authoritative parenting. The association between grades and the index of authoritarian parenting was stronger than the association between grades and the indices of the other styles of parenting.

The measurement of parenting styles from data derived from the child's perceptions creates a potential problem. For example, if students who are more estranged from their parents do less well in school and also tend to assign negative authoritarian characteristics to their parents, that might explain some of our findings. But some of our results do not fit this explanation focused on bias in reporting. First, some combinations of parenting styles, such as a highly authoritarian style mixed with high levels of permissiveness, were associated with lower grades than a pure authoritarian style. That students reporting such mixed or inconsistent parenting styles did less well in school suggests that the reports are more a reflection of attitudes toward parents. Second, families of different ethnic background or different parental education markedly diverged in their use of parenting styles. Yet, without any allowance for the values and norms of each group with respect to authoritarian parenting, it continued to be negatively associated with grades across diverse groups. Such results suggest that we are dealing with more than a global positive or negative perception of parents and their behavior. Nevertheless, a survey such as this one cannot answer objections to using such perceptual data. Observational data, preferably longitudinal, are needed to check on these results.

Even as we stress the applicability of this typology of parenting styles across a variety of social groups, there are numerous findings that call for further investigation. For example, the mean level of authoritarianism was about the same in families of Hispanic males and of Hispanic females, yet authoritarianism was much more associated with poor school performance among the Hispanic females.

Similarly, our data show clearly that the success of Asian children in our public schools cannot be adequately explained in terms of the parenting styles we have studied. Compared to whites, Asian high school students of both sexes reported that their families were higher on the index of authoritarian parenting and lower on the index of authoritative parenting. Yet, counter to the general association of such parenting patterns

to grades, the Asians as a group were receiving high grades in school. In addition, while authoritarian parenting was significantly associated with lower grades among Asians, there was no significant relation between grades and the other two parenting styles. This article concludes with more questions than answers in examining Asian parenting practices and school performance.

The typology of parenting styles that we have adapted was primarily devised for the study of middle-class white families and their children. Indeed, the parenting typology did tend to be more associated with grades among whites than among the other ethnic groups. Yet, with the exception already noted for Hispanic males, in all ethnic groups authoritarian parenting showed the expected relation to grades. Permissive and authoritative parenting were not as consistently related to grades across ethnic lines.

It is impressive that the diverse measures of parenting styles were associated with grades across a wide variety of social categories. The two sexes, the five age groups, the five types of family structure, and the three parental education groups all exhibited the same predicted pattern. The families that were high in authoritarian or permissive parenting tended to have students who did less well in high school, and the families that were high in authoritative parenting had children who got higher grades in school. There were major differences between the sexes, among the age groups, among the family structures, and among the parental education groups in the extent to which the different styles of parenting were employed. Yet, regardless of each group's mean scores on the parenting styles, the relation of each style to school performance exhibited the predicted pattern within each group.

There is a need for further investigations that will help increase our understanding of these parenting styles and their consequences. Certainly, longitudinal studies that can unscramble the causal pattern are crucial. To some extent, parental behavior is a product of school performance by children, and that relation probably is inflating our correlational analysis. In addition, determining which parent or step-parent is engaging in which type of parenting style may help us to delineate the meaning of various parenting behaviors. Finally, careful studies of the meanings of specific behaviors as interpreted by members of various social groups, particularly ethnic groups, could produce a major advance in our knowledge. Both better data and better conceptualizations are needed to advance our knowledge of parent-adolescent relationships.

References

Baumrind, D. (1971). Current patterns of parental authority. *Developmental Psychology Monograph, 4,* 1–103.

Baumrind, D. (1973). The development of instrumental competence through socialization. In A. D. Pick (Ed.), *Minnesota symposium on child psychology* (Vol. 7, pp. 3–46). Minneapolis: University of Minnesota Press.

Baumrind, D., & Black, A. E. (1967). Socialization practices associated with dimensions of competence in preschool boys and girls. *Child Development, 38,* 291–327.

Hess, R. D., & Holloway, S. D. (1984). Family and school as educational institutions. In R. D. Parke (Ed.), *Review of child development research* (Vol. 7, pp. 179–222). Chicago: University of Chicago Press.

Hess, R. D., & McDevitt, T. M. (1984). Some cognitive consequences of maternal intervention techniques: A longitudinal study. *Child Development, 55,* 2017–2030.

Kandel, D. B., & Lesser, G. S. (1969). Parental and peer influences on educational plans of adolescents. *American Sociological Review, 34,* 213–223.

Marjoriebanks, K. (1979). Family environments. In H. J. Walberg (Ed.). *Educational environments and effects* (pp. 15–37). Berkeley: McCuthan.

Morrow, W. R., & Wilson, R. C. (1961). Family relations of bright high achieving and underachieving high school boys. *Child Development, 32,* 501–510.

Rickberg, R. A., & Westby, D. L. (1967). Parental encouragement, occupation, education and family size: Artifactual or independent determinants of adolescent educational expectations. *Social Forces, 49,* 362–374.

Shaw, M. E., & White, D. L. (1965). Relationship between child parent identification and academic underachievement. *Journal of Clinical Psychology, 21,* 10–13.

Swift, D. F. (1967). Family environment and 11 + success: Some basic preconditions. *British Journal of Educational Psychology, 37,* 10–12.

Weinhert, F. E., & Trieber, B. (1982). School socialization and cognitive development. In W. Hartup (Ed.), *Review of child development research* (Vol. 6, pp. 704–758). Chicago: University of Chicago Press.

JOURNAL OF RESEARCH ON ADOLESCENCE, 5(2), 147–172
Copyright © 1995, Lawrence Erlbaum Associates, Inc.

Full Service Schools:
Revolution or Fad?

Joy G. Dryfoos

Hastings-on-Hudson, New York

During the past decade, a plethora of new school-based models for enhancing the life chances of adolescents have emerged. The term *full service schools* encompasses school-based primary health clinics, youth service programs, community schools, and other innovative efforts to improve access to health and social services. These programs have in common the use of school facilities for delivering services through partnerships with community agencies; a shared vision of youth development; and financial support from sources outside school systems, particularly states and foundations. Organizing a school-based initiative requires careful planning to involve school personnel, community agencies, parents, and students. Evaluation is still preliminary; scattered results are encouraging in regard to utilization of and access to needed health and mental health care; dropout, substance abuse, and pregnancy prevention; and improved attendance. This evolving field of school-based intervention creates new opportunities for research on outcomes and impacts, operational components, and cost benefits. Observers see the development of full service schools as a significant step toward the integration of the movements for quality education and the drive for healthy youth development.

Two important strands of social intervention began to come together during the resource-strained 1980s. The drive to meet the urgent health and social support needs of growing numbers of disadvantaged children, youth, and families was linked to the movement toward educational reform that would lead to more successful futures for these people. A variety of new institutional arrangements were created by

---

Requests for reprints should be sent to Joy G. Dryfoos, 20 Circle Drive, Hastings-on-Hudson, NY 10706.

innovative practitioners and educators. School-based clinics, school-linked clinics, family resource centers, community schools, caring communities, youth service centers, and such programs as Cities-in-Schools, Schools of the 21st Century, New Beginnings, and Beacons all used school buildings as places for integrating programs to assist poor and troubled people. The term that best describes this emerging phenomenon is *full service schools,* a phrase first encountered in the Florida's innovative legislation to support comprehensive school-based programs (Florida Department of Health and Rehabilitative Services and Department of Education, 1991):

> A Full Service School integrates education, medical, social and/or human services that are beneficial to meeting the needs of children and youth and their families on school grounds or in locations that are easily accessible. Full Service Schools provide the types of prevention, treatment, and support services children and families need to succeed ... services that are high quality and comprehensive and are built on interagency partnerships ... among state and local and public and private entities ... [including] education, health care, transportation, job training, child care, housing, employment, and social services. (p. 1)

This article is based on a recently published book by Joy Dryfoos, *Full Service Schools: A Revolution in Health and Social Services for Children, Youth, and Families* (Dryfoos, 1994). Here current research, commentary, and observations about the concept of full service schools are summarized, with particular focus on programs for adolescents. The rationale for the linkage of educational and health efforts is presented along with precedents for bringing support services into school buildings. Various school-based models are reviewed, showing how states and foundations have shaped the development of this emerging field. Consideration is given to organizational issues such as governance, "turf," controversy, and financing. A summary of evaluation research findings is offered along with suggestions about the potential of this field for new studies. Finally, the future prospects for integrated school-based health and social services are addressed. Are full service schools the wave of the future or is the concept merely another fad in demonstration projects that will rapidly be supplanted by something else?

RATIONALE

Why the accelerated movement toward comprehensive school-based services for adolescents? The plight of young people growing up in inner cities or poor rural areas has been well documented. The dire statistics of the new morbidities—adverse effects of modern-age sex, drugs, violence, depression, and stress—account for a vast number of youths who will never make it without immediate intervention. My own estimate is that one in four young people growing up in the United States today is in grave jeopardy (Dryfoos, 1990). These disadvantaged young people, living in run-down, resource-poor communities, cannot overcome the odds without substantial assistance. Some lack family nurturing and require individual attention from other caring adults. Many go to schools in which they are expected to fail. Both the health system and the educational system are called upon to respond to these social deficiencies. Thus, the rationale for creating new kinds of institutional arrangements crosses several domains: health, education, and social services integration.

Health

Although adolescents are generally healthy, youth in disadvantaged communities are much less likely to have access to primary health care and more likely to rely on emergency rooms for treatment of illnesses and accidents than their advantaged peers (Office of Technology Assessment [OTA], U.S. Congress, 1991). Even in middle-class communities, few private physicians are equipped to deal with the psychosocial problems that are so prevalent during the teen years. Teenagers, in general, are less likely to be covered by any form of health insurance, and for those poor teenagers eligible for Medicaid, coverage is tied to parental enrollment, reducing the prospects for confidentiality. The OTA, U.S. Congress (1991), when charged by Congress to review the health status of American adolescents and present options for congressional consideration, strongly recommended comprehensive school health clinics as the most promising recent innovation to improve access to health care. They added a note of caution, however, pointing out that systematic evidence that school centers improve health outcomes is limited.

Along with the OTA report, some 25 other major reports have been published recently that address the relation between young people's health status and their educational experience, call for a comprehensive approach to health, and support the placement of health promotion and health service programs in schools (Lavin, Shapiro, & Weill, 1992).

Education

Schools cannot educate children who are too "stressed out" to concentrate. Teachers are not trained as social workers and cannot possibly attend to their jobs if they must spend all of their time trying to remedy problems. The challenge for schools is to be allowed to concentrate on teaching. Even if all the necessary support services are in place, disadvantaged young people cannot succeed unless they attend schools with quality educational programs. Educational experts have excellent ideas about how to improve the educational outcomes of disadvantaged children, with extensive research and demonstration models that work in low-income communities (Comer, 1989; Slavin, Karweit, & Wasik, 1994; Wehlage, Rutter, Smith, Lesko, & Fernandez, 1989). Consensus is building among educators about the importance of bringing support services into schools that will strengthen their efforts at restructuring (United States Government Accounting Office, 1993; Usdan, 1994). Organizations such as the National Association of State Boards of Education, the National Association of School Boards, and the Council of Chief State School Officers have been in the vanguard of task forces and commissions that call for comprehensive school-based service programs.

Need for Integrated Services

Service integration—the establishment of linkages between agencies—is a hardy perennial that reappears whenever there are a plethora of categorical programs and overwhelming needs but little new money to address the problem. The subject is of interest to advocates of full service schools because of the necessity of welding together fragmented health and social service agencies with educational systems, often a challenging experience. Much has been written about the fragmentation that results from the development of specialized programs to address each category of need as it gains visibility in a very competitive funding and media environment (Schorr, 1988). This categorization has been particularly marked in regard to adolescent problems, with each year's crisis ending in a new wave of limited grants and program development: delinquency, substance abuse, teen pregnancy, HIV/AIDS, and the latest, violence/conflict resolution. But families also experience difficulty gaining access to health, social, welfare, housing, and employment services that are operated separately with different regulations, eligibility, and geographic location.

Growing recognition based on recent research findings that these categorical programs have only limited and short-term effects has fed the demand for integration of services, reducing the fragmentation of existing service systems for families (Kahn & Kammerman, 1992). Many of the new family-centered programs are being placed in schools to facilitate "one-stop-shopping" for whatever families and their children need to overcome the enormous odds they are up against in disadvantaged communities. Much of the service integration rhetoric calls for *systems changes*—new ways of organizing administrative structures that are more responsive to consumers (Melaville, Blank, & Asayesh, 1993). In this literature, considerable attention is being directed toward the involvement of the community and the importance of a sense of ownership by parents and other residents, recalling the language of the community action programs of the 1960s.

Historical Precedents

The idea of bringing health and social services into schools has been around for more than a century. At the turn of the century, settlement house workers and social activists led the movement toward attending to the critical needs of disadvantaged immigrants pouring into city schools. Both the demand and the supply have fluctuated over the years, reflecting changing social conditions and social attitudes. In periods of poverty, epidemics, and unrest, provision of school-based primary health services and extensive health inspection by physicians has been allowed, but whenever school services have loomed as competition to the private sector, approval has been withdrawn.

The history of social services in schools mirrors that of health services. Early on, social activists stimulated the development of vocational guidance, home visiting, vacation schools, school breakfasts and lunches, and after-school recreation programs, largely through voluntary efforts. As these initiatives formalized, schools began to become the employers and providers, and the programs were left to the vagaries and budgets of school boards and electorates. After World War II, school systems generally incorporated more pupil personnel services, including guidance counselors, social workers, and psychologists, but the primary thrust came from middle-class families who wanted assurance that their children would do well and get into college. Beginning in 1975, with the passage of legislation that called for special education, schools were made responsible for caring for physically and emotionally handicapped children, including everything from physical and speech therapy and psychological services to intensive nursing care and case management. Today, almost half of school workers are noninstructional employees (Tyack, 1992). Yet school systems cannot meet all the needs of their students with the existing personnel. During the final decade of this century, the pendulum is swinging back to bringing outside health and social service programs into schools in response to contemporary crises growing from poverty, immigration, and community decay. Currently, every major national social and health organization supports the concept that community agencies should bring services into schools.

VISION OF A FULL SERVICE SCHOOL

My vision of a full service school integrates the best of school reform with all other services that children, youth, and their families need, most of which can be located in a school building. This concept expands the Florida (1991) definition and, like a big umbrella, encompasses the educational mandate that places responsibility on school systems to reorganize and innovate. Restructured schools attend to individual differences, give staff a wide range of choices regarding teaching methods, organize curricula that are stimulating and relevant, and eliminate tracking and suspensions. The charge to community agencies is to bring the support side into the school: health, mental health, family planning, employment services, child care, parent education, case management, recreation, cultural events, welfare, community policing, and whatever else may fit into the picture. The result is a new kind of "seamless" institution, a community school with a joint governance structure that allows maximum responsiveness to families and communities and promotes accessibility and continuity for those most in need of services.

Table 1 presents an idealized model of the full service school, listing in the left column some of the components that might be incorporated

TABLE 1
Components of Full Service Schools Institutions

Quality Education Provided by Schools	Services Provided by Schools or Commnity Agencies	Support Services Provided by Community Agencies
Effective basic skills	Comprehensive health	Health screening and services
Individualized instruction	education	Dental services
Team teaching	Health promotion	Family planning
Cooperative learning	Social skills training	Individual counseling
School-based management	Preparation for the world	Substance abuse treatment
Healthy school climate	of work (life planning)	Mental health services
Alternatives to tracking		Nutrition/weight management
Parent involvement		Referral with follow-up
Effective discipline		Basic services: Housing, food, clothes
		Recreation, sports, culture
		Mentoring
		Family welfare services
		Parent education, literacy
		Child care
		Employment training/jobs
		Case management
		Crisis intervention
		Community policing

into a quality education initiative and, in the right column, those support services that could be provided by community agencies. The support items are drawn from research on the common components of successful prevention programs in the separate fields of substance abuse, teen pregnancy, delinquency, and school failure (Dryfoos, 1990) or based on observations of school-based services demonstration projects (Cahill, 1993; Children's Aid Society, 1993; Florida Department of Health and Rehabilitative Services and Department of Education, 1991). Several components, such as social skills training, health education and promotion, and career training, could be placed in either column. Whereas these health education efforts are currently implemented by school systems, it is also feasible for community agency staff on the support side of the model to provide those services in the school.

CURRENT STATUS

Everywhere in the United States, the school house doors have opened. At least 40 different types of personnel have been identified in school-based programs, including nurse practitioners, substance abuse counselors, mediation trainers, legal advisors, volunteer senior citizens, case managers, community police, and clergy. Almost none of these people are paid by school systems; rather, they work for health departments, neighborhood health centers, mental health and social service agencies, hospital/medical schools, youth agencies, mayors' offices, employment agencies, labor unions, or universities. The funds for these programs derive from an assortment of state and federal categorical funding sources, foundation grants, and local contributions. With few exceptions, schools do not lay out their own scarce resources for these support services.

Many different models of full service schools are being promoted by states, foundations, universities, and individual practitioners. School-based and school-linked health clinics have been organized by all of those entities. However, some states have also developed comprehensive school-based services programs for youth in which health services are only one of many components. Other states have supported youth centers in schools that are primarily for the purposes of coordination and that do not include health clinics. Several states have initiatives that give school districts a choice from a menu of on-site and referral services, and the result is a mixture of models. Finally, around the country, a few models have been identified that appear to be on the way to fulfilling the vision of the full service school, with attention to both sides of the education/support services equation.

One further distinction is between family-focused initiatives and those that center on adolescents. My concern here is with the latter, with heavy emphasis on changing the school environment to enable students to learn. Whereas parental involvement is one objective, it is not always possible or feasible. However, within the domain of full service schools are many different family-centered programs that begin with the needs of parents, helping them get their children off to a good start. Head Start programs are moving in this direction, extending their hours and adding more services. Excellent family-centered programs are emerging at the elementary-school level. The two proto-types intersect in middle schools, during the developmental stage for young adolescents prior to separation from family influences. I do not focus on family service centers here; however, their importance in the movement toward the development of full service schools must not be overlooked.

School-Based Clinics

A school-based clinic is a primary medical care facility located in a school building typically operated by a health agency, hospital, or other community group. (School-linked clinics are located near schools and connected to them through formal referral systems.) The model is more easily described than other kinds of full service schools (such as family resource centers) because practitioners have made an effort to standardize it. Most recently, a national working group of providers and foundations has produced a set of principals of operation and standards of service provision. They have called for a multidiscipli-nary team to provide comprehensive medical, social, mental health, and health education services in a well-equipped school clinic with assurance of 24-hr backup by a medical institution.[1] A typical clinic in a large high school might employ two nurse practitioners (or physician assistants), two or more social workers, a health educator, a reception-ist, and a part-time physician. In school clinics, the most heavily uti-lized services are for acute illnesses and accidents, mental health counseling, and physical examinations and screenings, but clinics may also provide family planning; treatment for sexually transmitted dis-eases; dental care; counseling regarding nutrition, substance abuse, and chronic disease management; immunizations; treatment for acne; prenatal and postnatal care; and child care. A survey of school-based

---

[1]Information provided by the National Work Group on School-Based Health Care, Columbia University School of Public Health, Center for Population and Family Health.

and school-linked health centers showed that 70% offer on-site individual counseling, over 30% provide group counseling, and more than half currently offer health information and prevention education within the classroom regarding substance abuse, reproductive health care, nutrition, and HIV/AIDS (McKinney & Peak, 1994).

In 1984, only 10 school-based clinics could be identified. Today, more than 600 school-based clinics have been organized, mostly in junior and senior high schools in low-income communities. The most significant support for school-based clinics has come from state budgets and from Maternal and Child Health departments in at least 20 states that have made the decision to use federal block granted funds to support local school health initiatives. For example, in Connecticut, a state Adolescent Health Coordinator actively works with schools and community groups to plan and maintain clinics in schools covering most parts of the state. New York uses state funds to support 140 school-based primary health clinics in inner city and poor rural neighborhoods. Across the country, at least 35 school clinics have been organized by community health centers with support from the Bureau of Primary Health Care in Washington.

Youth Service Centers

New Jersey's School-Based Youth Services Program is frequently cited as the model for the nation. Beginning in 1986, grants were awarded by the Department of Human Services for proposals that combined the resources of schools and community agencies to prevent teen pregnancy, dropout, and other high-risk behaviors. Each of the 29 school-based programs has a different configuration. Local community mental health centers are the operators of five of the school-based efforts, bringing mental health counselors into the school center along with other prevention, health, and recreational activities. New York City's Beacons are "lighted" schools kept open all hours with additional services offered by local community-based organizations. Each program is different depending on the capabilities of the local groups to address neighborhood interests.

In Kentucky, every school with more than 20% of the students eligible for free lunch can apply for a grant to open a Youth Service Center or a Family Resource Center. Several hundred junior and senior high schools have received funds to designate a space in the school as a center, staffed by a full-time coordinator, who develops a menu of ancillary services depending on an assessment of the needs of the students and the resources in the community. Employment counseling and job placement, after-school recreation, family counseling, and referral for health services are typically provided.

In California's Healthy Start initiative, the Department of Education is empowered to award grants to low-income school districts to create innovative, comprehensive, school-based or school-linked health, social, and academic support services. To receive funding, school systems must submit evidence of a working collaborative partnership with health, mental health, social services, drug and alcohol, probation, and other public and nonprofit agencies.

The range in size of grants is significant. In Kentucky, the average grant is about $75,000, only enough to fund a full-time coordinator, whereas New Jersey's annual grants have been about $250,000, adequate to contract for center staff and professional services. In Florida, full service schools are receiving as much as $400,000 a year, and, in some communities, new building grants for comprehensive centers equal more than a million dollars.

Full Service Schools

Only a few schools have been identified that could be labeled "full service," covering all the components listed in Table 1. Yet across the country, one finds remarkable examples of very comprehensive demonstration models. In New York City and Modesta, California are two, quite similar innovative schools that provide quality educational experiences to disadvantaged junior high school students and bring in everything else that is needed to lead toward successful achievement. In New York City, the Children's Aid Society, in conjunction with Community School District 6 has created a true settlement house in a school (Children's Aid Society, 1993). The Hanshaw Middle School in Modesta, California is also open most of the time to serve the needs of a deprived, largely Hispanic neighborhood (Hanshaw Middle School, 1992). With support from California's Healthy Start initiative, a center has been constructed on the campus to house an interagency case management team and a primary health care and dental clinic. The Hanshaw program results from many partnerships between the school system and mental health, social services, public assistance, public health, and nonprofit health and service agencies.

Foundations

In 1987, the Robert Wood Johnson Foundation awarded grants to launch health centers in 24 schools and, building on that experience, has created the Making the Grade initiative, supporting 10 states to create state-level offices for school-based services and model clinics in two local sites. The Carnegie Corporation is supporting states in its Turning Point initiative to help middle schools link students to comprehensive health and social services as one component of middle-school reorganization. The Hogg Foundation for Mental Health has been instrumental in creating The Schools of the Future, changing schools into primary neighborhood institutions for promoting child and family development, building on the Comer School Development Program, Zigler's Schools of the 21st Century, school-based clinics, programs for community renewal, and family preservation.

A major new foundation-supported effort will attempt to reproduce in elementary schools the thrust of school-based initiatives for adolescents. Under the auspices of the National Health/Education Consortium (1993), a national demonstration project will be undertaken with 50 elementary school-based health centers in five geographic areas. Grants will be awarded to replicate a demonstrationl model based on research in existing elementary school clinics.

ORGANIZATIONAL ISSUES

Governance

The concept of full service schools calls for a joint governance structure whereby partners agree to pursue a shared vision and have common goals, expect to share resources, participate in joint decision making, and use their personal and institutional power to change systems (Melaville et al., 1993). This implies a formal process that leads to the establishment of a new kind of governing body, such as a nonprofit coordinating agency or a new mayor's office initiative with the authority to oversee the whole comprehensive program. Program experience to date has shown little structural change. More typically, partners—schools and community agencies—have agreed on goals and signed contracts or memoranda of understanding that leave the status quo of the organizations entirely intact. The agreement may specify policies regarding fiscal responsibility, client–student data collection, confidentiality, and other administrative issues.

Most school-based health clinics are funded by grants directly to health agencies who then contract with school systems to provide services. This is a matter of policy for some state health departments and foundations who believe that the school system should not be burdened with the responsibility for providing primary health and social services to the students. Observers of the Robert Wood Johnson initiative concluded that the way to strengthen health services provided in schools was to make those services an integral part of a community's health care delivery system (Lear, Gleicher, St. Germaine, & Porter, 1991). Community health agencies are already positioned to collect third party reimbursements (Medicaid), carry their own liability insurance, arrange medical referrals, protect medical confidentiality, and provide medical backup when the school health centers are closed.

In states with initiatives that start with school restructuring, such as Kentucky, the grants go directly to school systems with the proviso that they collaborate with human services providers at the local level. In Florida, where the grants also go to the school system, the proposals must show evidence of formal partnerships with community agencies, particularly the local public health agency. Whether the school or the health agency takes the fiscal lead in the development of a full service school project, whatever transpires in a school building must be approved by the school authorities.

Moving Into a School

Whereas the superintendent and the school board must sign off on arrangements and policies for full service schools, the building principal facilitates the partnership with extensive planning for obtaining parental consent and releasing students from classrooms for clinic appointments, arranging hours of operation, and dealing with emergencies. Existing school personnel may perceive the transaction as the school environment being infiltrated with a new staff who work for a different organization, often with a higher pay scale and always with a different union. Scarce space, classrooms, or the old band room is converted into a primary care facility with freshly painted walls, new furniture, and attractive posters. Or, as in Florida, prefab units are added to the campus.

Full service school programs often encounter opposition from teachers and others who are not convinced that health and social services should be provided on school sites (even though the school system is rarely the actual provider). Competition often arises between existing pupil personnel services (school nurses, guidance counselors, social workers, school psychologists) and full service staff over the question of who is in charge of working with the student and the family. School-based clinics have accommodated school nurses by incorporating their services into the new delivery system and discerning principals create student service teams to coordinate the work of the school personnel and the clinic personnel. It has been observed that within a short period of time, all parties agree that the growing needs of troubled students and their families far outweigh the joint capacities of the partnerships and they join together to advocate for additional services.

Full service school coordinators are a new category of personnel. Often nurse practitioners or social workers, they must know how to integrate with school personnel and promote a sense of "ownership" throughout the school community. Programs report increasing referrals from teachers who want help in dealing with problems. School-based practitioners, because they are heavily exposed to the day-to-day stresses of urban schools, perceive that schools must undergo dramatic changes if they are to improve the outcomes for the students. They can help school administrators move toward restructuring by arranging for consultants, conducting staff retreats, fostering continuing education, and joining in the dialogue about healthy school environments.

Controversy

The phrase *school-based clinic* is like a red flag for conservative groups waiting for an excuse to raise community tensions over sexuality issues. The most highly publicized school-based clinics in the early 1980s were heralded as pregnancy prevention programs, leading to attacks from the opposition that schools were opening sex clinics and abortion mills. When later replications of these models were shown to have little effect on pregnancy rates because they did not include family planning services, the attack shifted and the opposition organized against bringing any kind of services into school buildings, even into elementary schools. At the time that the Kentucky Youth and Family Service Centers were first proposed, the Eagle Forum put out brochures referring to the program proponents as child snatchers. In reality, few programs have been suppressed because of organized opposition. In accounts of these events, parents and medical providers invariably surface as the most articulate and credible advocates for school-based services (Rienzo & Button, 1993).

Many of the state programs were authorized by legislation that prohibited the distribution of contraceptives and referral for abortions on school premises. Other "comprehensive" programs issued from the school–community planning process, with the distribution of birth control omitted—the price for avoiding controversy. As a result, only about 20% of all school-based health clinics provide contraceptives, although most conduct reproductive health care examinations and referral, pregnancy tests, and screening and treatment for sexually transmitted diseases (McKinney & Peak, 1994). Nationally, only 10% to

20% of visits to school-based clinics are for family planning, suggesting that the expectation of controversy has a cooling effect on service provision. In the few clinics that have more assertive efforts to provide sexuality education and counseling, and offer contraceptives, the utilization rates for family planning are much higher (Kirby & Waszak, 1989). In recent years, school systems have been changing their policies to allow the distribution of condoms in schools, as long as parents do not object. Typically, the local health department comes into the school to hand out the condoms, relieving the school system of the responsibility (Samuels & Smith, 1993).

Public acceptance of the concept of full service schools is much higher than might be expected. The 1992 Gallup Poll reported that 77% of respondents favored using public school buildings in their communities to provide health and social services to students, administered and coordinated by various government agencies (Elam, Gallup, & Rose, 1992). Contrary to the conventional wisdom about how conservative the American public is, a majority of respondents (68%) approved of condom distribution in their local public schools, although one in four of them would require parental consent. A 1993 sample survey of North Carolina registered voters showed that 73% believe that health care centers offering prevention services should be located at high schools—with the strongest support from African-Americans and 18 to 34 year olds—and no differences by gender, religion, or parental status. More than 60% favored providing birth control at the centers (The North Carolina Coalition on Adolescent Pregnancy, 1993).

Financing

In every discussion of full service schools, the proverbial bottom line is money. Where will the resources come from to support the wide replication of these various models? Program development thus far has been heavily dependent on state initiatives and a few foundation efforts. Many agreements have been made between schools and public health, mental health, and social services agencies to relocate staff in school centers, resulting in substantial amounts of "in-kind" contributions from local agencies. A few communities have passed special taxes to support school-health services. In addition, knowledgeable program developers have found ways to tap into categorical funding sources that fit into a menu of comprehensive services. The most frequently mentioned sources are Drug Free Schools, Chapter 1 (Elementary and Secondary School Funds), Title X Family Planning, special mental health, and juvenile delinquency initiatives (Dryfoos, 1994). However, categorical funding is difficult to access; each has its own funding periods, accountability procedures, regulations, and administrative bodies. No program has permanence. Finally, a few school-based programs have attempted to establish a fee structure, charging small amounts for services rendered, but, generally, this has not proven efficient because collections are low and needy students are deterred from utilization. As a result, almost all of the programs are free.

It is not anticipated that many states can significantly increase their level of participation in light of continuing budget squeezes in state governments. Prior to the talk of health reform and managed care, Medicaid was looked to as a funding solution, with the goal of certifying low-income schools as eligible for reimbursement from medical assistance. A few schools are already partners with managed care providers, and others are devising ways to operate under the proposed health reform.

Practitioners, educators, and advocates are now looking to the federal government to play a role in moving these initiatives from demonstration projects in a few school communities to broad institutionalization across the country. Does this mean a center in every school? One estimate of the potential demand for full service schools can be based on the number of schools where more than 50% of the students are eligible for free lunch. About 1 in 5 of the 80,000 public elementary and secondary schools fall into that category, suggesting that as many as 16,000 sites should be set up as rapidly as possible. However, the concept of full service schools applies to every school in which the present staff cannot attend to all the needs of the student population. Community agencies can be invited in to fill the gaps.

The prospects for an expanded role in the advancement of full service schools would have been greatly enhanced by the Clinton administration's health reform proposals. Funds were included for community partnerships in disadvantaged areas to provide school-based health and social services and health education (103rd Congress, 1993). The 1994 Crime Bill also contained provisions for supporting community-schools, modeled after the Beacon program (Portner, 1994). With the advent of the 104th Congress in early 1995, the outlook is less optimistic. The issue of health reform has been bypassed by budget-cutting, with responsibility for such issues as adolescent health promotion and crime prevention remanded to states and localities. Nevertheless, the first federal grants for school-based clinics were awarded under a "Healthy Schools, Healthy Communities" program through the Bureau of Primary Health Care ("News in Brief," 1994). The administration's educational reform package does require state education agencies to demonstrate how they will coordinate access to social services, health care, nutrition, and child care. Reauthorization of Chapter 1—the Elementary and Secondary Education Act—calls for similar actions at the local school level which will help light up schools in disadvantaged communities and bring in needed support services (Independent Commission on Chapter 1, 1994).

EVALUATION AND RESEARCH

The first question that is raised by researchers is "do full service schools work?" Do they make any difference in the outcomes for adolescents, specifically, do schools with clinics and other support services have lower dropout and teen pregnancy rates, higher attendance and achievement? The answer is a tentative *yes*. A review of the data currently available about school-based clinics and full service schools suggests that these new programs have shown some potential.[2] Both the quality and the quantity of the research to date have severe limitations, but scattered returns from preliminary studies are encouraging. In addition to studies of behavioral change, several research efforts have been directed toward analyzing the process of organizing and implementing school-based programs.

Utilization and Outcomes

Based on the current state of the art, a number of observations can be made about school-based health clinics. Programs are generally located in the communities and schools with the greatest needs. A number of studies confirm that school clinics are being utilized most by the highest risk students who report the greatest number of problems. Practitioners report early detection of physical problems, such as heart murmurs and asthma, and frequent identification of psychosocial problems resulting from sexual abuse, neglect, and parental drug abuse. Utilization figures show that the characteristics of students who use the centers mirror the school population, with slightly higher usage by female students, younger students, and African-American students. Many of the school health clinic users have no other source of routine medical care and no health insurance. Use of emergency

---

[2]In my book, *Full Service Schools* (1994), Chapter 6 is devoted to evaluation findings. More than 30 different sources are cited. For this article, I have referenced only the research studies that were not included in Chapter 6.

rooms has declined in areas with school clinics. Because minor illnesses, such as headaches, menstrual cramps, and accidents on school property, can be treated in school, absences and excuses to go home have decreased in schools with on-site health services.

In centers with mental health personnel, substantial numbers of students and their families are gaining access to psychosocial counseling that was not available to them within the community. The demand is overwhelming. Scattered evidence shows that a few school-based clinics have had an impact on delaying the initiation of intercourse, upgrading the quality of contraceptive use, and lowering pregnancy rates, but only in programs that offer comprehensive family planning services. Programs are just beginning to produce data on other effects. Clinic users in a few schools have been shown to have lower substance use and dropout rates and better school attendance. School-based clinics have the capacity to respond to particular needs in a community, to conduct immunization campaigns or do screening for tuberculosis.

In addition to individual counseling, center staff have an impact on students' behavior through health education and health promotion in classrooms and group counseling covering a range of youth problems, such as substance use, family relations, sexuality, nutrition, conflict resolution, and peer relationships. Students, parents, teachers, and school personnel report a high level of satisfaction with school clinics and centers and appreciate their accessibility, convenience, and caring attitudes. Students particularly value confidentiality. The Office of the Inspector General (1993) recently surveyed state health officials and reported "overwhelming" (p. 8) agreement that school-based health centers improved access to health care by going "where the kids are" (p. 8). They also found that, in addition to primary health care, the centers were providing specialized services aimed at adolescents, not only in clinics but in classrooms and through outreach. This quality was attributed to the presence of staff who were specially trained in attending to adolescents.

Brindis, Morales, McCarter, Dobrin, and Wolfe (1993) reported on a cost–benefit analysis of three California school-based clinics comparing the costs for the school services with the estimated cost in the absence of the school clinic. They factored in reduced emergency room use, pregnancies avoided, early pregnancy detection, and detection and treatment of chlamydia, a prevalent sexually transmitted disease. The ratios of savings to costs ranged from \$1.38 to \$2.00 in savings per \$1.00 costs, suggesting that the school clinic services were a good investment for the health system.

Almost all of the research compiled has been conducted in school-based health and social service settings. We can only speculate about the potential impact of a thoroughly implemented full service school based on preliminary observations of a few demonstration projects. The two schools mentioned earlier (IS218 and Hanshaw), after their first years, are reporting very high attendance rates, improved achievement, and a vastly improved school climate. Visits to exceptional schools can leave powerful impressions, encouraging the viewer to believe that it is possible to create new kinds of responsive institutions that are full of light and the joy of learning. As one student said, "Everybody here treats you with respect" (Dryfoos, 1994, p. 119).

Common Attributes of Full Service Schools

Although the models mentioned here (clinics, centers, community schools) have many differences, research on the support side (health, mental health, and social services) has yielded a number of common components of successful programs (Brellochs & Fothergill, 1993; Brindis et al., 1993; Godin, Woodhouse, Livingwood, & Jacobs, 1993; The School-Based Adolescent Health Care Program, 1993):

1. A planning process starts off with a needs assessment to insure that the design of the new institutional arrangements are responsive to the requirements of the students and their families.
2. The configuration of support services brought in from the outside is dependent on what already exists in the school in the way of health, social services, and counseling.
3. An Advisory Board includes school and agency personnel, parents and community leaders (and occasionally students). Parental consent is required for receipt of services.
4. If primary health care is to be provided, adequate space is designated in or near a school building for a medical clinic with examining rooms, a lab, an area for confidential counseling, and arrangements for record keeping and referrals.
5. If medical services are not provided on site, a special space is designated within the school as a center for individual and group counseling, parent education, career information, offices for case managers, kitchen, play space, clothes/food distribution, and arrangements for referrals.
6. The building principal is instrumental in the implementation and smooth operation of full service schools. Schools provide space, maintenance, and security.
7. School doors are open before and after school, weekends, and over the summer. Classrooms, gyms, and computer facilities are open for community use.

8. A full-time coordinator or program director runs the support services in conjunction with school and community agencies. Personnel are trained to be sensitive to issues related to youth development and cultural diversity.
9. A data system is in place, preferably a computerized management information system that can process record keeping and billing as well as evaluation data.

Needed Research

The emergence of these diverse school-based programs creates a rich territory for researchers interested in tracking complex models. However, they should be wary of the many pitfalls in the search for causal explanations and measures of long-term program effectiveness. Cook, Anson, and Walchli (1993) called for adolescent health studies that are based on strong theoretical constructs, random assignment, valid outcome measures, long time periods, powerful and well-defined interventions, high statistical power, and large heterogeneous samples. Millstein (1988), in an earlier monograph on school-linked services, summarized the methodological problems in conducting school-based research dealing with high-risk populations. First, the difficulty in establishing appropriate comparison groups was emphasized, particularly in light of the sizable attrition rate in many inner city schools. If an appropriate matching school cannot be found, she suggests doing cohort analyses, comparing ninth graders in Year 1, prior to the program, to ninth graders in Year 2, after the program has been implemented. Millstein also notes the limited effects that can be measured in small samples and warns against using an entire school population as a base when only a small proportion of the students actually utilize the services. Few of these problems have been addressed in the evaluations completed to date. The cost for such research would be high, and it is probably not possible to assign students to school service programs randomly. Nevertheless, evaluation should clearly receive high priority, to gain a more consistent fix on outcomes, and to track the longitudinal effects of these efforts. Millstein (1988) called for a major evaluation study, including comparison schools and matched subjects.

Operational research on full service schools is also a challenging area, for example, studies of the cost effectiveness of providing health and social services in schools compared to other means of providing services to adolescents, such as private physicians' offices, community health centers, health maintenance organizations, hospital outpatient and emergency departments, and cost–benefits of providing preventive and health promotion services in schools compared to not providing those services anywhere. Much more needs to be known about the operational management of school-based centers, including the most efficient staffing mix, costs and financing, the appropriate roles of pediatricians, nurse practitioners, social workers, physician's assistants, psychologists, health educators, aides, and other personnel, and the most efficient scheduling and arrangements between backup referral agencies and school centers. Studies are needed on the quality of the services and follow-up provided and how well they measure up to the standards being promulgated by advocacy and practitioner groups. We must dig into school systems and determine the appropriate delineation of responsibilities between schools and outside organizations; for example, who should conduct health education and health promotion?

One important research tool, *School Health Care—Online* (Kaplan, 1994), developed by David Kaplan of the University of Colorado School of Medicine, was designed as a data collection and management information tool for school-based clinics. Currently, the software program is designed to collect individual physical and mental health, health screening, risk behaviors, epidemiologic, administrative, billing, and program outcome data. The computer system is set up to produce over 100 preprogrammed reports including "tickler" files listing referrals and follow-up information and statistical reports on users, immunizations, case management, and health screening. Several hundred providers are using this system, but no central clearinghouse has been designated to process and analyze the reports. It would greatly enhance our understanding of the potential of full service schools if a comprehensive census could be conducted along with data collection that would help define the different models and their capabilities. Inclusion of questions about utilization of school-based health and social services in national surveys, such as the National Health Interview, National Youth Risk Behavior Survey, and other such instruments, would also strengthen this research.

The United States Government Accounting Office (GAO; 1993) was recently asked by Senator Ted Kennedy of Massachusetts to review studies and evaluations of multiservice, school-linked programs. The GAO reported that some comprehensive school-linked programs prevent dropout through effects on absenteeism and academic achievement. However, they asserted that among the research issues yet to be addresssed are the short- and long-term costs and benefits of various types of school-linked programs and the relative cost effectiveness of these programs compared with other prevention strategies. The report strongly urged the federal government to provide funding for planning comprehensive school-linked programs, long-term program support, and technical assistance with developing and evaluating programs.

DISCUSSION

The proliferation of models that fit under the full service schools umbrella has resulted from many forces: demand from school systems for help in dealing with the "new morbidities," recognition of the necessity to shelter children for longer hours, bubbling up of unique creative models for working with high-risk youth, dedication of youth workers to bringing their services into the schools, movement at the community level to integrate services, commitment of foundations to the creation of comprehensive service systems, and support from innovative state government initiatives.

Does all of this activity add up to a revolution? Implementation of the concept of full service schools would surely lead to a major transformation in the use of school facilities for improving the lives of disadvantaged children, youth, and families. This metamorphosis is still in an early stage. However, programs exist whereby requisite services are located together in one place, in a school-based center that welcomes its clientele, promises them confidential and caring services, and demonstrates a high level of concern about what happens to them. In today's beleaguered communities, this is a profound departure from the fragmented nonsystems upon which people are expected to rely to help them get through their troubled lives. Even in middle-class communities, young people experience stressful circumstances and appreciate access to caring adults on the school premises.

The concept of full service schools fits well with what we have learned from research about today's young people, who may lack parental support, go to endangered schools, live in troubled communities, and face many barriers to achievement. The idea embraces partial solutions to many of these problems, simultaneously addressing the need for individual support, comprehensive services, parent involvement, and community improvement, in the context of school restructuring. The concept incorporates the discourse on service integration, pushing toward the combination of health, mental health, and family services, along with recreation and culture in one site—the school—open from early in the morning until late at night, weekends, and summers.

Although a strong consensus has emerged across educational and social support domains in support of full service schools, critics raise valid questions about the various models that we have reviewed. Perhaps the most powerful argument can be made that all of this will not make much difference in the lives of disadvantaged youth. By the time they are adolescents, this may be "too little, too late." For some very troubled young people, no matter what goes on behind the schoolhouse door, they still must return to dangerous households or the streets. No one would quarrel with the point that early intervention is essential, but this should not be used as a justification for ignoring the millions of teenagers who can still be assisted. At the same time, in communities with school-based services, attention is turning toward the development of more sites in elementary schools. The preferred arrangement is the "cluster," tracking youngsters from kindergarten (or even preschool) through high school with related support services at each school along the way.

Questions have also been raised about placing the locus of full service programs in schools in communities that are distrustful of the educational establishment. Some school systems are so resistant to change that community leaders have little confidence that the quality education part of the full service vision will ever materialize. Chaskin and Richman (1992) proposed an alternative model that places services in buildings run by community-based organizations in which families feel comfortable and are assured larger roles in decision making. The service integration theory still holds, but the locus of services is placed firmly in the neighborhood, directly operated under local control. The school board has no place in this model, obviating the difficult negotiations that can be stressful and time-consuming. Michigan's experience with its 19 teen health centers (11 school-based or school-linked and 8 in the community) suggested that community-based centers had greater flexibility, especially in regard to the provision of family planning; could more easily assure confidentiality; serve more dropouts; were free to set their own parental consent protocols; and avoided the (unfounded) suspicion that school funds were being used for nonacademic services (Miller, 1991). However, the school-based centers were found to have reduced the necessity for outreach; more readily involved school personnel; and served students on site. They were perceived to have more direct access to teens (increasing the likelihood of foundation support); took on the function of health promotion in the schools; and were able to garner in-kind resources from the school system, such as space, maintenance, utilities, and supplies.

Concern has been raised about the viability of full service schools as sites for dealing with young people who no longer attend school. Some of the existing school-based centers do serve out-of-school youth as well as siblings and parents of current students. Others do not. For two major youth-serving organizations in New York City (El Puente and the Door), the transformation into full service schools started with the community organizations that added basic educational components to their rosters of services and obtained certification as part of the public school system (Cahill, 1994). This community youth center–school model offers an approach for working with school dropouts who are often youth agency clients. The disaffected youth are drawn back into the school system through the efforts of trusted youth service agency staff.

Much of the rhetoric in support of the full service schools concept has been presented in the language of *systems change*, calling for radical reform of the way educational, health, and welfare agencies provide services. Consensus has formed around the goals of one-stop, seamless service provision whether in a school- or community-based agency, along with empowerment of the target population. This review of current models shows that most of the programs have moved services from one place to another; for example, a medical unit from a hospital or health department relocates into a school through a contractual arrangement, or staff of a community mental health center is reassigned to a school, or a grant to a school creates a coordinator in a center. As the program expands, the center staff work with the school to draw in additional services, fostering more contracts between the schools and community agencies. But few of the schools systems or the agencies have changed their governance. The outside agency is not involved in school restructuring or school policy, nor is the school system involved in the governance of the provider agency. The result is not yet a new organizational entity, but the school is an improved institution and on the path to becoming a different kind of institution that is significantly more responsive to the needs of the community.

That few full service school models have been able to overcome the barriers to the formation of new kinds of governance should not be perceived as a deterrent to further service integration efforts. Past attempts at systems reform have shown that it is much more difficult to alter the way that entrenched administrators operate across agencies than to make incremental changes in the existing systems they run (Kusserow, 1991). The movement toward service integration as exemplified in full service schools has clearly had an èffect on cutting red tape in some programs, but practitioners are still confronted with the conflicting eligibility criteria and restrictions that go along with categorical programs.

The concept of full service schools is an appealing and popular one. Implementation acts as a catalyst between educational initiatives and the drive for improved social supports. But enthusiasm could fade rapidly if the support services programs are too weak to make a difference. Having an understaffed clinic or inadequate arrangements for after-hours backup crisis care may produce expectations that can never be met. Poorly trained practitioners may fail to connect with today's teenagers, whose lives are complex and troubled. Outside staffs may never communicate with school personnel, setting up expensive parallel systems of care that duplicate the services for some and never cover all the needs in a school. Even the best school-based program is politically vulnerable because of the high turnover in elected officials and school administrators. More than money is required to move toward wide replication. Technical assistance and training is essential to help schools and communities build strong programs, recruit well-qualified personnel, and establish strong accountability for these programs. The models are in the early stages of documentation and standard setting, ready for substantive evaluation and replication.

ACKNOWLEDGMENTS

This work was supported by the Carnegie Corporation as part of a long-term Youth at Risk project. The conclusions are those of Joy G. Dryfoos and do not necessarily represent those of the foundation.

REFERENCES

Brellochs, C., & Fothergill, K. (1993). *Special report: Defining school-based health center services.* New York: Columbia University, School of Public Health.

Brindis, C., Morales, S., McCarter, V., Dobrin, C., & Wolfe, A. (1993). *An evaluation study of school-based clinics in California: Major findings, 1986–1991.* San Francisco: University of California, Institute for Health Policy Studies.

Cahill, M. (1993). *A documentation report on the New York City Beacons initiative.* New York: The Youth Development Institute, The Fund for the City of New York.

Cahill, M. (1994). *Schools and communities: A continuum of relationships.* New York: The Youth Development Institute, The Fund for the City of New York.

Chaskin, R., & Richman, H. (1992). Concerns about school-linked services: Institution-based versus community-based models. *The Future of Children: School-Linked Services, 2*(1), 107–117.

Children's Aid Society. (1993). *Building a community school: A revolutionary design in public education.* New York: Author.

Comer, J. (1989). Educating poor minority children. *Scientific American, 259*(5), 42–48.

Cook, T., Anson, A., & Walchli, S. (1993). From causal description to causal explanation: Improving three already good evaluations of adolescent health programs. In S. Millstein, A. Peterson, & E. Nightengale (Eds.), *Promoting the health of adolescents: New directions for the twenty-first century* (pp. 339–374). New York: Oxford University Press.

Dryfoos, J. (1990). *Adolescents-at-risk: Prevalence and prevention.* New York: Oxford University Press.

Dryfoos, J. (1994). *Full service schools: A revolution in health and social services for children, youth, and families.* San Francisco: Jossey-Bass.

Elam, S., Gallup, A., & Rose, L. (1992, September). The 24th annual Gallup/Phi Delta Kappa poll of public's attitude toward the public schools. *Phi Delta Kappan,* pp. 42–53.

Florida Department of Health and Rehabilitative Services and Department of Education. (1991). *Request for program designs for supplemental school health programs (Instructions).* Tallahassee: State of Florida.

Godin, S., Woodhouse, L., Livingwood, W., & Jacobs, H. (1993). Key factors in successful school-based clinics. *NMHA Prevention Update, 4*(1), 3.

Hanshaw Middle School. (1992). *Health start support services for children act* (SB620; operational grant proposal). Modesto, CA: Modesto City Schools.

Independent Commission on Chapter 1. (1994). *Legislative Update.* Washington, DC: Author.

Kahn, A., & Kammerman, S. (1992). *Integrating service integration: An overview of initiatives, issues, and possibilities.* New York: National Center for Children in Poverty.

Kaplan, D. (1994).*The school health care—online system.* (Available from David Kaplan, The Childrens' Hospital, 1056 East 19th Avenue, Denver, CO   80218)

Kirby, D., & Waszak, C. (1989). *An assessment of six school-based clinics: Services, impact and potential.* Washington, DC: Center for Population Options.

Kusserow, R. (1991). *Services integration: A twenty-year perspective.* Washington, DC: Office of the Inspector General, Department of Health and Human Services.

Lavin, A., Shapiro, G., & Weill, K. (1992). *Creating an agenda for school-based health promotion: A review of selected reports.* Cambridge, MA: Harvard School of Public Health.

Lear, J., Gleicher, H., St. Germaine, A., & Porter, P. (1991). Reorganizing health care for adolescents: The experience of the school-based adolescent health care program. *Journal of Adolescent Health, 12,* 450–458.

McKinney, D., & Peak, G. (1994). *School-based and school-linked health centers: Update 1993.* Washington, DC: Center for Population Options.

Melaville, A., Blank, M., & Asayesh, G. (1993). *A guide for crafting a profamily system of education and human services.* Washington, DC: U.S. Government Printing Office.

Miller, K. (1991). School and community-based teen health centers: Michigan's experience. *Clinic News, 6*(4), 4–5.

Millstein, S. (1988). *The potential of school-linked centers to promote adolescent health and development.* Washington, DC: Carnegie Council on Adolescent Development.

National Health/Education Consortium. (1993). *Elementary school-based clinics: A summary of a feasibility study.* Washington, DC: Author.

News in brief. (1994, February 2). *Education Week,* p. 2.

The North Carolina Coalition on Adolescent Pregnancy. (1993). *We the people.* Charlotte, NC: Author.

Office of the Inspector General. (1993). *School-based health centers and managed care* (OEI-05-92-00680). Washington, DC: Department of Health and Human Services.

Office of Technology Assessment, U.S. Congress. (1991). *Adolescent health: Vol. I. Summary and policy options* (OTA-H-468). Washington, DC: U.S. Government Printing Office.

103rd Congress. (1993). *Health security act.* Washington, DC: U.S. Government Printing Office.

Portner, J. (1994, March 30). Ounce of prevention threatens to hold up crime measure. *Education Week,* p. 17.

Rienzo, B., & Button, J. (1993). The politics of school-based clinics: A community-level analysis. *Journal of School Health, 63*(6), 266–272.

Samuels, S., & Smith, M. (1993). *Condoms in the schools.* Menlo Park, CA: The Henry J.

Kaiser Family Foundation.

The School-Based Adolescent Health Care Program. (1993). *The answer is at school: Bringing health care to our students.* Washington, DC: Robert Wood Johnson Foundation.

Schorr, L. (1988). *Within our reach.* New York: Doubleday.

Slavin, R., Karweit, N., & Wasik, B. (1994). *Preventing early school failure: Research on effective strategies.* Boston, MA: Allyn & Bacon.

Tyack, D. (1992). Health and social services in public schools: Historical perspectives. *The Future of Children: School-Linked Services, 2*(1), 19–31.

United States General Accounting Office. (1993). *School-linked human services: A comprehensive strategy for aiding students at risk of school failure* (GAO/HRD-94-21). Washington, DC: Author.

Usdan, M. (1994, January). The relationship between school boards and general purpose government. *Phi Delta Kappan,* pp. 374–377.

Wehlage, G., Rutter, R., Smith, G., Lesko, N., & Fernandez, R. (1989). *Reducing the risk: Schools as communities of support.* New York: Falmer Press.

Received February 1, 1994
Revision received April 25, 1994
Accepted April 28, 1994

Effects on Students of an Interdisciplinary Program Linking Social Studies, Art, and Family Volunteers in the Middle Grades

Joyce L. Epstein
Johns Hopkins University
Susan L. Dauber
Northwestern University

This study explored several components of middle grades reform including school and family partnerships, interdisciplinary units of work, and student outcomes to increase art awareness, appreciation, and criticism. The case study was an empirical evaluation of the effects on student learning of the Teachers Involve Parents in Schoolwork (TIPS) Social Studies and Art Volunteers program in an urban middle school. The program organized parent and other volunteers in order to create opportunities for students to study interdisciplinary connections between art and social studies curricula in the middle grades. The volunteers prepared and presented discussions of prints of well-known art in students' social studies. Data were collected from over 400 students in Grades Six through 8 in a Baltimore City middle school to evaluate the effects of the TIPS Social Studies and Art Volunteers program. Results show that students increased their awareness of art, developed attitudes toward and preferences for different styles of art, and were able to express their likes and dislikes. Students' comments reflect variations in early adolescents' transitions from concrete to abstract thinking. The data support the viability of the program as one that may help other middle grades schools organize volunteers as part of a comprehensive program of six major types of school, family, and community partnerships.

The development of the TIPS Social Studies and Art process benefited from the work of many people, including Principal Gloria Pegram, Social Studies Department Chairs Avis Terry and the late Tatiana Charchalis, and all of the social studies teachers at Fallstaff Middle School in Baltimore, Maryland, between 1987-1989. We also thank the numerous parents, grandparents, other volunteers, and students who participated in the program and who helped us evaluate and improve the program. This project was supported with funding from the Office of Educational Research and Improvement, U.S. Department of Education, National Endowment for the Arts, and a National Science Foundation Graduate Fellowship to the second author. The opinions are the authors' and are not necessarily the positions or policies of the funding agencies.

Journal of Early Adolescence, Vol. 15, No. 1, February 1995 114-144
© 1995 Sage Publications, Inc.

School and family partnerships are on nearly every agenda for improving education in the middle grades. One problem has been that few middle grades teachers and administrators have an understanding of how to design, organize, and implement a program of partnerships (Epstein & Dauber, 1991).

Interdisciplinary units of work also are on nearly every agenda for middle grades reform. This goal, too, is easy to say, but difficult to accomplish, in part because it is necessary to provide teachers with time to work and think together to create lessons that link subjects in meaningful ways (Epstein & Mac Iver, 1990).

This case study explored the results of a program that is designed to combine these two components of middle grades reform—school and family partnerships, and curricular reform linking social studies and art education. First, we discuss the "big picture" of school and family partnerships, and the particular questions about volunteers in middle schools that this study addressed. Then we examine how new directions in Discipline Based Art Education (DBAE) help us think about and use interdisciplinary connections of social studies and art. These orientations are followed by a description of the program, the research questions, data, results, and implications.

School and Family Partnerships

Recent studies that include adolescents and their families provide an important knowledge base on which to build useful programs to increase family and school partnerships (Baker & Stevenson, 1986; Bauch, 1988; Becker & Epstein, 1982; Dauber & Epstein, 1993; Dornbusch & Ritter, 1988; Epstein, 1986; Epstein & Dauber, 1991). These and other studies of family environments and school and family connections have suggested that involving parents in their children's education is important for student success in school, for parents' effectiveness, and for strengthening school programs. One common result across surveys has been that parents of elementary, middle, and high school children report that they want to be informed and involved, but that they are not guided each year by the schools to help them know how to assist at school or to help their children at home. (For two comprehensive reviews of this literature see Epstein, 1992; Swap, 1993.)

Our studies in the elementary and middle grades and the research of others led to the development of a framework to identify six major types of involvement that create a comprehensive program of school and family partnerships (Epstein, 1992). In short form the six types are

- Type 1: Basic obligations of families including parenting skills and home conditions for learning at each age and grade level;
- Type 2: Basic obligations of schools including school-to-home and home-to-school communications about school programs and children's progress;
- Type 3: Volunteers and audiences at the school or in other locations to support the school and students;
- Type 4: Involvement of families in learning activities at home;
- Type 5: Participation by families in decision making, governance, and advocacy; and
- Type 6:.Collaborations with community groups and agencies to strengthen school programs, family practices, and student learning and development.

All six types of involvement decline in the middle grades, as compared to the involvement of parents in the elementary grades (Dauber & Epstein, 1993; Epstein & Dauber, 1991; Stevenson & Baker, 1987; 1991; 1993). This general decline can be reversed, however, if schools begin to work to develop or select practices on each of the six types of involvement (Epstein & Connors, in press; Epstein & Herrick, 1991; Epstein, Herrick, & Coates, in press). Efforts by educators demonstrate that it is possible to design comprehensive programs to involve families of adolescents in productive ways in all types of involvement, as documented in special issues of *Educational Horizons* (1988) on "Parents and Schools" and *Phi Delta Kappan* (1991) on "Paths to Partnership."

Most of the practical approaches to involve families have not been evaluated. Although educators' program development activities are essential, their best guesses are only an interim step to understanding best practices. One topic for research over the next several years is to focus on the design, implementation, and evaluation of specific practices of parent involvement for differing grade levels, student and parent populations, and subject areas. Only when teachers and administrators have a "menu" of tested techniques will family involvement be more widely incorporated into regular teaching practice.

A Closer Look at Type 3 — Volunteers

As middle grades schools work to develop their comprehensive programs of six types of involvement, they may meet barriers that delay or block progress in designing and implementing particular practices to fulfill one type of involvement or another. For example, volunteers (Type 3) tend to be greater in number in the elementary than in the middle grades (Dauber & Epstein, 1993; Epstein & Dauber, 1991). In part, this is because middle grades schools have not developed procedures to recruit and train volunteers to assist teachers or to enrich students' programs. These and other schools will benefit from research on viable approaches for organizing and using productive volunteers.

For many teachers at all grade levels, the bottom line is whether school and family partnerships increase student learning and success in school. Although many studies have reported connections between parent involvement and student achievement (e.g., see the Henderson, 1987 annotated review), there is considerable confusion about how particular practices of involvement help students increase their skills and scores. Not every practice to involve families affects student learning in the short term (Epstein, in press). For most Type 3 activities, simply having volunteers assist teachers or administrators at school or in classrooms will not directly or immediately increase student learning. If, however, volunteers bring curricular content directly to students, there should be a measurable link between the volunteer program and an increase in student skills or knowledge.

Creating an Integrated, Interdisciplinary Curriculum

Although most middle grades educators talk about integrating curricula, few schools have implemented such programs, mainly because it is very hard work (Epstein & Mac Iver, 1990). Interdisciplinary units require that teachers on teams or in various departments have common planning time to work together to develop and test materials and procedures. In most schools, common planning time is limited. Most middle grades students still study one subject after another without an awareness of the connections between and among subjects. In the current study, the TIPS Social Studies and Art process integrated social studies units of work with information on artists' lives and with displays of art work. Other interdisciplinary connections may be made by using ideas from TIPS lessons that suggest topics for discussion, writing across the curriculum (e.g., writing assignments in social studies on reactions to the art work that the students see), and art activities for classwork or homework.

For several years, educators have been debating the need for curricular reform in art education. Although most reports about curricular reform ignore art because it is not a basic or core or academic subject, several recognize art as an essential subject and as a versatile subject for interdisciplinary connections (Bennett, 1986; Boyer, 1983; Goodlad, 1984; and see numerous articles in two special sections of the *Phi Delta Kappan*, April, 1992, and February, 1994).

Discipline-based art education (DBAE) has been discussed as a strategy to help correct weaknesses in present programs by increasing art awareness, art history, and art criticism at all levels of schooling (Clark, Day, & Greer, 1987; Darby & Catterall, 1993; Eisner, 1987, 1988; Getty Center for Education in the Arts, 1986; Jackson, 1987; McLaughlin, Thomas, & Peterson, 1984). One aim of DBAE is to provide greater exposure to, and experiences with, art so that all students—not just the few who take electives in high school—develop a strong cultural literacy in art that characterizes well-educated people. It is expected that a rigorous program will help students examine, analyze, interpret, and discuss works of art, and that students also will improve these analytic, cognitive skills (Getty Center for Education in the Arts, 1986; Darby & Catterall, 1993). Because the arts tend to be interesting and motivating to students, students may become more engaged in learning other subjects that include art.

Linking School and Family
Partnerships and Interdisciplinary Studies

Many middle grades schools are struggling to include the arts in students' education and to create feasible interdisciplinary units of work. The struggles are particularly difficult in schools where budget cuts coldly remove the arts from the curriculum. Many middle grades schools also are struggling to involve families at school and at home in ways that strengthen school programs, and that increase students' chances for success.

In a sense, the arts are a natural interdisciplinary connector *and* a viable way to mobilize family and community partnerships with schools. Parents and other volunteers may be comfortable introducing art to students in places where this is not the "teacher's curriculum." That is, teachers may welcome the assistance of parents in introducing students to a topic that enriches the standard curriculum. There is a level of comfort, too, in that there are no right answers about one's preferences or criticisms in art. There also is room for multicultural perspectives and the expression of the many voices of parents, students, and teachers, when art is introduced in social studies.

TEACHERS INVOLVE PARENTS IN SCHOOLWORK (TIPS) VOLUNTEERS IN SOCIAL STUDIES AND ART

The Teachers Involve Parents in Schoolwork (TIPS) Volunteers in Social Studies and Art program addresses these issues with an organized approach to increase productive volunteers in the middle grades by linking social studies curricula with art awareness, appreciation, and criticism (Epstein & Salinas, 1991).

What Is It?

The Teachers Involve Parents in Schoolwork (TIPS) Social Studies and Art program provides middle grades teachers with a structure to organize parents and other volunteers to bring art appreciation, history, and criticism to middle school social studies classes. The volunteers prepare (at home) and present (at school) discussions on prints of well-known paintings that are linked to social studies units in American history, world cultures, government and citizenship, or other topics. The process emphasizes bringing volunteers to the middle grades school in productive roles, and providing opportunities for parents who cannot come to the school building to participate in the program by preparing some of the information at home that will be used by the classroom volunteers, teachers, and students. In these ways, parents and other volunteers help teachers develop interdisciplinary lessons for classroom discussions to enrich the instructional program.

What Are the Goals of the Program?

TIPS Social Studies and Art aims to (a) establish productive partnerships among teachers and parent volunteers; (b) demonstrate interdisciplinary linkages of art with history, geography, and social issues in social studies; (c) extend and enrich students' education through exposure to, and discussions about, art in social studies classes; and (d) increase students' knowledge, understanding, and appreciation of art.

Increasing volunteers and interdisciplinary work. In most middle schools, volunteers pose a particular problem; they all but disappear in the middle grades. Middle grades teachers believe that students do not want their parents at the school. We found that this was not true if parents were not required to have close, frequent, or familiar contact in school with their *own* children. To assist middle grades schools in developing age-appropriate volunteer programs, we worked with a middle school and its staff over several years to design, implement, and test the TIPS Social Studies and Art Volunteers program. The goal was to create productive partnerships between parents and social studies teachers to enrich the curriculum for students, and to assist teachers who typically do not have time to do research and develop materials to integrate art with social studies. The program provides important roles for parents of middle grades students, without requiring a great deal of parents' or teachers' time.

Increasing the awareness of middle grades students of artists and their work. There often is a severe shortage of art experiences at the middle level, especially in urban school systems. Required or elective art courses are often short-term "exploratory" experiences in art techniques and media. These are necessary, but insufficient experiences for students, as most short courses do little to connect art with other subjects or to emphasize art history, criticism, and appreciation.

What Are the Components of the Program?

The TIPS Social Studies and Art process organizes regular monthly presentations, providing broad and continuing opportunities to extend all students' understanding about art in history and in the human experience. A TIPS Social Studies and Art manual is available to guide teachers and parents to organize, implement, and evaluate the program. Sets of prototype materials also are available that provide examples of discussions of over 30 art prints in American history, world cultures, and government and citizenship (Epstein & Salinas, 1991). The manual also includes guidelines for field trips to art museums, and sample quizzes to assess students' knowledge and students', teachers', and volunteers' reactions to the program.

For example, in American History students are introduced to American artists. Prototype presentations include discussions of work by Frederick Remington, Currier and Ives, Edward Hicks, Horace Pippin, Georgia O'Keeffe, Romare Bearden, Robert Rauchenberg, Andy Warhol, and others representing a range of artists from different eras with differing styles and differing backgrounds. Similarly diverse prints are discussed in prototype lessons for social studies units on World Cultures (DaVinci to Picasso) and Government and Citizen Participation (Vermeer to Mondrian).

324

Each teacher selects eight paintings for the year from a set of prints linked to the social studies curriculum. Presentations and discussions are conducted monthly, from October to May. Each presentation about an artist and print includes sections on the artist's life, style, and technique, the specific art work, connections to social studies, connections among two or more artists and prints, where to see original work by the artist, and topics for class discussion, writing, and art work. Other supplementary activities that are provided with each presentation may be conducted by the teacher as classwork or assigned as homework.

Over three middle grades (e.g., 6-8 or 7-9), students are introduced to at least 24 artists, their styles, their work, and their contributions in history. The presentations were designed by parents, other volunteers, and the researchers, and tested in social studies classrooms for 3 years by volunteers and middle grades teachers and students. Although the demonstration project was conducted by linking art with social studies, other interdisciplinary connections (e.g., art or music with English, math, science, or foreign language) also may be developed from the TIPS process.

How Is It Implemented in Middle Grades Schools?

The steps required to implement the TIPS Social Studies and Art process include (a) selecting a teacher-coordinator and parent-coordinator to cooperatively organize the program in conjunction with social studies (or another school subject); (b) selecting and ordering art prints; (c) recruiting and training parents or others in the school community as volunteers; (d) setting up schedules for presentations by volunteers; and (e) evaluating the effects of the process on students, teachers and volunteers. Volunteers and all teachers are provided with the "write-ups" that guide the presentations and discussions of the artists and prints.

There must be a teacher coordinator, a parent coordinator, and a parent assistant coordinator for the program. The teacher may be the department chair, a team leader, or another teacher with a particular interest in integrating social studies with art. The teacher coordinator must be willing to take responsibility for working with the parent coordinator and helping to recruit volunteers. The parent coordinator *and* assistant coordinator must assume responsibility for recruiting and training parents and other volunteers, scheduling their visits to the classrooms, and working with the teacher coordinator and other teachers as necessary. The parent leaders could volunteer or be appointed or elected as an ongoing committee chair by the PTA or other parent organization. The assistant one year becomes the chief coordinator the next year, with a new assistant, to assure the continuity of leadership of the program. The activity requires only a few hours each month of the coordinator's time, once the program is under way.

Who Are the Volunteers?

Parents (or grandparents or other volunteers from the school community) are involved in the TIPS Social Studies and Art process in two ways. They do research on an artist and art print to prepare a presentation for discussion with students, and/or they conduct the 20-minute presentation in the social studies classroom once a month. Volunteers may choose to do the research only, the presentation only, or both. They do not have to be expert in art, but they do have to enjoy talking about art with middle grades students.

In all, there must be at least one volunteer for each social studies teacher. At best, there would be one volunteer for each scheduled class of each social studies teacher. In classes that are not covered by volunteers, the social studies teachers conduct the discussions with the students, just as do the volunteers.

THE DEMONSTRATION SCHOOL

The study was conducted in a middle school in Baltimore City whose staff is known for its high quality and openness to new ideas. The school serves a diverse student body that is about 80% African American and 20% White. About 40% of the students are low income, eligible for free or reduced lunch, and close to 20% of the students are "chronically absent," missing more than 20 days of school per year. In a 1992 assessment, the school met the state's functional test and performance standards in reading, but did not meet the state's standards for satisfactory skills in math, writing, or attendance. Compared to other middle schools in the city, this school scores higher than most, but compared to state standards, the school falls short in basic math, writing, and student attendance.

Despite the challenges of helping all students succeed, there is a "can do" spirit among the faculty and students at this school. The school has been consistently innovative since its opening as a middle school in the mid-1970s. It was, for example, the only school in the city organized with mixed-age and mixed-ability groups in most classes. It was a good partner in the development and testing of the TIPS Social Studies and Art program.

EVALUATION OF TIPS
SOCIAL STUDIES AND ART VOLUNTEERS

In our work with schools on the development and evaluation of specific practices of school and family partnerships, we follow a two-step approach (Epstein, Herrick, & Coates, in press). The first step is to assess whether a practice actually is implemented, how teachers, students, and parents react to it, and how the program's design should be improved. The second step—after implementation is confirmed—is to study whether the practice (as implemented and improved) has measurable *effects* on students, families, or teaching practice.

Can the Program Be Implemented?

The TIPS Social Studies and Art process was developed and monitored in the demonstration school for 3 years. In the first 2 years, researchers and teachers were interested in the implementation of the program. Informal interviews and surveys were conducted on questions such as How is the program going? How are the volunteers working out? How do the teachers, volunteers, and students like the program? What should be changed and improved? What should be kept?

Teachers were asked whether they liked the program, how the volunteers were doing, and whether they wanted the program to continue the next school year. Volunteers were surveyed to determine whether they felt comfortable with the program, and with the children and teachers. At least one class of every social studies teacher was visited for group discussions with over 120 students about their reactions to the program. The classes included classes of sixth, seventh, and eighth graders, that were heterogeneous in ability, and one special education class. From these interviews and surveys we learned

- The TIPS Social Studies and Art process was successfully implemented in the middle grades school. Parent and other volunteers were systematically recruited, trained, and regularly visited their assigned classrooms. Students in all social studies classes were engaged monthly throughout the school year in discussions that connected social studies and famous art. The parent coordinator, teacher coordinator, cooperating teachers, and volunteers were highly committed to the program.

- Teachers gave the program very positive ratings. The teachers reported that if there were no volunteers for particular classes, they were able to conduct the discussions based on the volunteer's presentations in other classes. Without exception, the teachers welcomed volunteers back to continue the program the next school year.
- Parents and other volunteers (including mothers, fathers, grandparents, other relatives, and adult friends of the school) successfully fulfilled, with few exceptions, their obligations to make monthly visits to their social studies classrooms. The volunteers gave the program very positive ratings. Volunteers were equally positive about and faithful to the program whether or not they were linked to their child's teacher or another teacher. Several continued as volunteers for more than one year, even some who needed special permission from an employer to participate as a volunteer during the school day.
- Contrary to previous ideas on the subject, the middle grades students gave the program very positive ratings, and were also positive about the parents and other volunteers.

What Are the Effects on Students?

The thorough but informal assessments over 2 years indicated that the program was being implemented well, and that all social studies teachers were participating enthusiastically. The teachers and researchers agreed that it was time to frame questions about the effects of the program on student learning and attitudes. This study explored whether and how much the students learned from the program in its third full year of implementation in the demonstration school.

DATA

Data were collected from over 400 students in Grades 6 through 8 in the demonstration middle school. Short surveys were administered in the fall and in the spring of the school year in regular classes by social studies teachers as part of the daily "drill" that students take to review some aspect of their classwork. Questionnaires measured students' recognition of, and reactions to, American artists and paintings that they saw monthly in their social studies classes.

We wanted to know whether males or females responded to the program differently; whether brighter students, students who liked the program, or students who were artistic themselves remembered more about the paintings they saw. Measures included gender, grade in school, report card grades, attitude toward the program, preferences for the pictures, the frequency with which students looked at the pictures while they were in the classroom, whether the student likes to draw, and the fall pre-test of prior knowledge of the artists and prints. We also asked whether students who were in the program in previous years were more interested in the program or remembered more artists or prints.

Limitations of the data. In this collaborative study with the school, the teachers administered the pretests and posttests. We encountered several real-world problems that affected the quality of the sample and data. The fall sample excluded one teacher whose class was involved with other projects when the pretest was given. The spring sample excluded another teacher whose special education class was involved in other projects when the post test was given. The students in the spring sample included relatively few eighth graders because many were already involved in planning and rehearsing for graduation exercises. Finally, in the spring sample, one teacher's classes' responses were suspiciously high on one of the measures. These students were omitted from analyses when the suspect measure was the focus of attention.

Despite these fall and spring vagaries, statistical checks on fall, spring, and longitudinal samples show that the mean scores and standard deviations on all measures were stable and consistent. The samples of 495 students (fall), 404 students (spring), and 270 students (longitudinal, fall and spring) were useful for evaluating the effects of the TIPS Social Studies and art process. A subset of the longitudinal sample of 123 seventh- and eighth-grade students who returned to the school in the fall was useful for exploring students' recall of information gained in previous years. In this school, sixth graders, new to the school, had not had the program the previous year.

RESULTS

Six research questions were addressed with the measures collected from students to understand the effects of the program. We wanted to

TABLE 1: Summary of Means and Standard Deviations on Key Measures From Fall and Spring Samples

	Fall Sample n = 495		Spring Sample n = 404	
	Mean	Standard Deviation	Mean	Standard Deviation
Gender (male = 1; female = 2)	1.54	0.50	1.55	0.50
Report card grades (A = 1 . . . mostly D/F = 5)	3.68	1.58	3.69	1.75
Enjoy art program (not at all = 1 . . . a lot = 5)	3.79	0.91	3.68	1.14
Number of pictures liked (spring only) (none = 1. . .all = 5)	—	—	2.84	1.15
Like to draw (a lot = 1. . .not at all = 5)	1.92	0.96	2.02	1.05
Look at pictures (spring only) (daily = 1. . .never = 5)	—	—	2.98	1.19
Tried: Match painting with artist (8)	2.62	2.77	5.08[a]	3.47
Correct: Match painting with artist (8)	1.11	1.00	1.61[a]	1.87
Tried: match painting with content (8) (Spring only)	—	—	6.28	2.44
Correct: Match painting with content (8) (spring only)	—	—	4.35	2.94

a. Spring means based on $n = 308$, excluding one class with high outlier/ suspect scores.

know (a) Who are the students in the sample? (b) What did they learn over one year about the artists and their work? Which students gained in knowledge or skills? (c) Which students recalled information from previous years? (d) Which students enjoyed the program? (e) What were the attitudes of the least successful students? (f) How did the students express their likes and dislikes of the art they saw?

Question A: Who are the students in the sample? What are students' scores on the measures for this study?

Table 1 presents the means and standard deviations on key measures for students in the fall and spring surveys. There were about equal numbers of males and females among the students. Average report card grades were mostly Cs. Most students enjoyed the program, liked some of the pictures (about 3 to 4 out of 8) that they saw, liked to draw "a little," and looked at the pictures "sometimes" during the weeks that the art prints remained in the classroom. The means and standard deviations show a basic acceptance and participation in the program, and considerable variation on all student characteristics and attitudes.

The descriptive statistics in Table 1 show that by the spring of the school year, students recognized more names of art work, on average, even if they did not always know the correct answers to match the names of artists, prints, and content. Other analyses reveal that in the fall, 18% tried to answer all 8 matching questions and 22% tried none. In the fall, 0.4% had 5 correct, and no students had 6, 7, or 8 answers correct. By contrast, in the spring, 53% tried to answer all 8 of the matching questions and 22% tried none. In the spring, 8% had between 5 and 8 correct responses of paintings and artists. Thus students tried more and got more correct in the spring than in the fall. Overall, the program helped students become familiar with and identify artists and prints that they did not previously know.

> Question B: Which students gained most from the program? What did the students remember about the artists and prints they saw?

Two measures were used to learn if students remembered the artists or prints that they saw from fall to spring of the school year. One measure— painting and artist required students to match an artist with the title of a painting. For example, students who saw the print *The Apache* had to match it to the artist—Remington. The second measure—painting and content—required students to match the title of a painting with a description about the painting. For example, students who saw the painting *Summertime* had to match it with the description "Life in the city is shown as a mix of humor and problems for Black Americans." Every class saw 8 art prints, but not necessarily the same ones. The questions on the assessments were tailored to measure each class's experiences with particular prints through the school year. Multiple regression analyses were conducted with the data from 270 students for whom fall and spring scores were available.

TABLE 2:   Effects on Students' Awareness and Knowledge of Paintings
(longitudinal sample)

	Number Correct Match Painting and Artist	Number Correct Match Painting and Content
	Standardized Regression Coefficients	
Gender	.031	−.024
Report card grades (−)	−.245*	−.282*
Enjoy program (+)	.097	.157*
Number correct in fall[a]	.071	−.005
N	172	257
R^2	.09	.14

a. Other variables in the model were not significant. These included how often the student looked at the pictures, whether the student liked to draw, and the number of pictures the student saw and liked.
* Significant beyond .05 level.

Matching paintings and artists. Most students found it difficult to re-call which artists painted which pictures. On average, students correctly matched 2 of 8 prints and artists ($X = 1.60$; standard deviation = 1.72). The first column of Table 2 summarizes the analyses of effects on student knowledge of paintings and artists. Only students' report card grades sig-nificantly explained the number of correct matching. As might be ex-pected on a standard matching test, better students got more answers correct. Because the fall pre test scores were low and had little variance, prior knowledge of art was not a factor for explaining what students learned over the year.

Matching paintings and content. Students found it easier to match the titles of the paintings with descriptions of what they were about. On av-erage, students correctly matched 5 of 8 prints with their content (mean = 4.83; sd = 2.78). The second column of Table 2 shows that two vari-ables—report card grades and enjoyment of the program—significantly and independently explained the number of correct matchings of paint-ings with content. Better students again had more correct answers, but, with report card grades statistically controlled, students who enjoyed the program more had more correct matchings of paintings and content.

TABLE 3:   Average Correct Matchings by Student Report Card Grades

Report Card Grades	Matching Artist and Print	Matching Print and Content
A, As and Bs	2-3 correct	4-5 correct
Bs and Cs, C	1-2 correct	4 correct
C, D, F	1 correct	3-3.5 correct

Other variables were not important for explaining the students' knowledge of the paintings that they saw.

Table 3 shows the connections between report card grades and the two measures of recall. Students with higher report card grades were more able to remember the paintings and artists by name, and the contents of the paintings. Students with low grades were mainly able to recall paintings and contents, and not the artists' names.

Question C: Over the long term, which students recalled pictures they saw in previous school years?

A second gauge on knowledge gained and participation or engagement in the program was based on students' recall of art prints they saw in earlier school years. In the fall survey, 55% of the students who were previously in the program were able to recall at least one painting that they had seen the year before. Sometimes they wrote the artist's name, sometimes the title of the painting, and sometimes a descriptive phrase about the painting. Seventh and eighth graders who had been in the school for 1 or 2 years and who participated in the TIPS Social Studies and Art program were included in this analysis (n = 123). Table 4 presents the effects on students' recall in the fall of a print from the previous year.

The only significant explanatory variable was student grade level. Eighth graders who were older students and who may have been in the TIPS program for 2 previous years were more able to recall and write down something they remembered about a painting or artist from the previous year. Students with better report card grades tended to recall a painting more successfully than other students, but the coefficient ($\beta = -.159$) was not significant.

Question D: Which students enjoyed the program most?

333

TABLE 4: Effects on Remembering Pictures From Previous Years
(Fall Sample)

	Remember Painting From Last Year (standardized regression coefficients)
Gender	−.043
Grade in school	.215*
Report card grades (−)	−.159
Enjoy art program	−.016
Like to draw	−.019
R^2	.07

a. Includes only the seventh-and-eighth grade students in the fall sample who attended the school the previous year ($n = 123$).
* Significant at or beyond .05 level.

Table 5 presents an analysis of student attitudes toward the program. Students were asked "Do you like having a new picture in your social studies class each month?" The responses were coded from 1 (*no, not at all*) through 5 (*yes, a lot*). Enjoyment of the program was significantly affected by three variables—liking the particular pictures they saw, looking more frequently at the pictures in the classroom, and knowing and remembering the pictures.

Students who liked more of the 8 pictures that they saw, liked the program more overall ($\beta = .442$), and students who could remember more of the paintings also liked the program more ($\beta = .125$). It is logical that there are strong connections between liking parts of a program and liking the program, in general. Neither gender nor school report card grades significantly influenced student enjoyment of the program.

Students who looked more often at a picture while it was in their classroom said they enjoyed the program more ($\beta = -.174$). Students who paid more attention to the print during the weeks it remained in their classrooms liked the program more, independent of their ability to remember the prints or their liking of the pictures. Interestingly, students who said they like to draw, paint, or sketch tended to look at the prints more frequently while they were in the classroom ($r = .143$).

Question E: What are the attitudes toward the program of the least successful students?

TABLE 5: Effects on Student Attitudes Toward Art Program of Student
          Sample

	Enjoy Program (standardized regression coefficients)
Gender	−.044
Report card grades (−)	−.017
Like pictures (+)	.442*
Look at pictures (−)	−.174*
Like to draw (−)	−.082
Number correct in Fall	−.010
Number correct match of painting and content (spring)	.125*
N	257
R^2	.32

*Significant at or beyond .05 level.

We examined the responses of students who did not try to answer any of the matching questions on one or both of the tests on the spring assessment ($n = 90$), but who did answer other questions on the survey. We can learn something about these students whose scores were zero tried, zero correct. They included more seventh graders, more boys, and more students with low grades. On average, students who tried none of the matching questions, liked fewer pictures and reported that they rarely looked at the pictures when they were in the classroom. Nevertheless, over 50% of these students said they liked the program. Also, over 72% of these students commented on pictures they liked, disliked, or would hang in their living rooms. Thus, although some students did not take the tests that required them to demonstrate traditional or "test" knowledge, they did not tune out of the program completely. They were able to relate to the program and make personal choices of paintings.

Question F: How did the students express their likes and dislikes of the art they saw?

In the spring, students were asked to name particular pictures that they liked, disliked, would hang in their living rooms at home, and to give reasons for their choices. Many more students answered these questions which, unlike the matching items, did not look like a test. Of the 404 students in the spring sample,

- 78% commented on a picture they saw and Liked
- 70% commented on a picture they saw and Did not like
- 76% commented on a picture they would Hang in their living room.

Some of the students thought all of the paintings they saw were beautiful. Others wrote that all were ugly. Some selected pictures because "I like his/her work." Others disliked pictures because "It is not my style," or "It doesn't suit me." Some commented on the artists' purposes (e.g., "the way an artist just takes a person's mind and persuades it to perceive what he wants them to"). Although most students liked colorful pictures, some ignored color and focused on story or style. Other comments focused on texture, brushwork, and collage techniques. Their written comments showed how they related to the variety of prints they saw each month during the year.

The students' words also document the diversity of characteristics, abilities, and attitudes of early adolescents. The written comments particularly vividly illustrate different reactions to abstract and realistic art. Early adolescents are at different phases in a transition from concrete manipulatory thinking to greater facility with abstract concepts (Lipsitz, 1980; Wiles & Bondi, 1986). Those who have progressed further in their development of abstract thinking skills should be more comfortable with abstract or symbolic art.

WHAT STUDENTS LIKED

Most students liked realistic art. Boys tended to comment on the excitement of a picture like *Turn Him Loose, Bill* by Remington. Many were looking for "excitement" or "action" in all paintings and were disappointed that some were "dull" or "dark" or "showed no action." Others, boys and girls, were looking for pictures that were "calm," "cool," "settled," or "pleasant." However, some students strongly preferred abstract art.

In this section, students' average report card grades are shown in parentheses to illustrate that a preference for abstract or realistic art is not solely determined by school ability. Rather, the diversity in preferences for abstract or realistic art may reflect differing stages of facility with abstract thinking. Of course, the comments also reflect other personal judgments (not just a stage of concrete or abstract thinking), as students may, for a variety of reasons, come to prefer one style of art or another.

The following written comments from students illustrate their reasons for *liking* a particular painting.

Preference for Abstract/Symbolic Art

High Achievers — What They Said:

Mondrian's *Composition* because I like modern painting. I like figuring out what the artist tried to show us (artist from prior year). I also like *Retroactive I*. (A)

The art with Kennedy (in it) because it showed freedom and advancement in our society and planet. (A/B)

Average or Low Achievers — What They Said:

Three Flags because it looked like it was in 3-D. (C)
Three Flags. It looks real good. If I were rich I would buy it. (C/D)
Rancho Church. I liked how it was a little abstract. I thought it was interesting. (B/C)
O'Keeffe (sic) because you can put what you want in the picture to make it up yourself. (C)
Mondrian—whom I didn't see this year but I like his work anyway. (artist from prior year) (C)
The one that had President Kennedy because it showed peace. (F)

Preference for Realistic Art

High Achievers — What They Said:

I liked *Christina's World* because of Wyeth's method of painting. It was so realistic. (A)

The Apache and *Turn Him Loose, Bill* because it showed the life of the cowboys and Indians in the Wild West. (A/B)

The Domino Players because they seemed to relate to life today. (A/B)

Stuart because of the way he painted *George Washington* as if he took a picture of him by surprise. (A/B)

Average or Low Achievers — What They Said:

Peaceable Kingdom because the world should be as it is in the painting. (B/C)
Christina's World because it showed a disabled girl and it made me think. (D/F)

WHAT STUDENTS WOULD
CHOOSE FOR THEIR LIVING ROOMS

Liking a print and putting it in your living room reflect two levels of preferences. Students were more particular about what they would hang up at home than what they said they liked. Their explanations sometimes reflected the growing independence, or some say *orneriness* of early adolescents. For example, the same student who commented that Winslow (Homer) "captivated my imagination" wouldn't select a picture to hang in his living room because "people should not force something on students (like art) ." Several selected a print, but explained that they would put it in their dining room or bedroom because that is where it would look better. The following comments illustrate reasons that students give for choosing paintings to hang in their living rooms that again contrast preferences for symbolic or realistic art.

Selections of Abstract/Symbolic Art

> I would like to have *Three Flags* in my house because when people saw it they would be into it, like What does it mean? It is different.
> Not the boring scenes with the buffaloes and mountains. I like more interesting paintings like *Retroactive I*.
> I would probably like to hang *Composition* in my living room because everyday I could find something new in it. (print from prior year)
> *Summertime*—nobody would know exactly what it was. Everyone would have their own point of view. Great conversation piece.

Selections of Realistic/Concrete Art

> *Peaceable Kingdom* because it was really beautiful. It had a lot of animals that were really well drawn.
> *Across the Continent* because it matches the furniture.
> The one with the little town with a train coming in and the tracks were going to pass a lake and go into the mountains. (*Across the Continent*)
> The picture with the buffalo where it is about to rain because it's not too wild or crazy.
> *The Domino Players* because of a family game. Really because of the family participating.

OTHER CHARACTERISTICS OF EARLY ADOLESCENCE

Also, students' choices and comments reflected other characteristics of early adolescents, such as increasing empathy:

> *Christina's World* because it tells of a lovely girl and when I get older I am going to teach handicapped children.

. . . and increasing humor:

> The one about the girl that couldn't walk because she looks like she needs help and so does my living room.
>
> Some picked none of the prints they saw, but for different reasons:
> None. I like Poblo Picosso (sic) better. (artist from previous year)
> None, because my mom wouldn't let me hang anything in her living room.

WHAT STUDENTS DID NOT LIKE

Most students' comments about paintings that they did not like concerned the colors, dullness, or style of work. Some students described as ugly the same paintings that others thought beautiful. The following comments illustrate reasons the students gave for *not* liking a painting.

Dislike of Abstract/Symbolic Art

> The one with President Kennedy and all the other stuff, because it didn't look like art to me.
> *Mural*—the splashes and drips made me dizzy. (print from prior year)
> The abstract prints because I feel those painters are liars and that I could paint that stuff myself.

Dislike of Realistic/Concrete Art

> The painting on George—it looked boring and not exciting enough.
> *The Last of the Molhekins* (sic) because it showed the Indians as violent people and they were just protecting their land.
> Henry's painting because the blacks were slaves. (*Wedding of the 1830s*)
> The mother of an artist—her colors were not showing any movement or excitement.

BRIDGING CONCRETE AND ABSTRACT THINKING

Some students found symbolism in realistic art, and representation in symbolic art. These comments seemed to bridge the abstract versus realistic distinction, indicating the dynamic nature of this transition in thinking skills. The bridging was evidenced in several ways. For example, some students liked the picture *Wedding of the 1830s* because it was pretty or because it was a wedding—a happy event. Others disliked it for the image of African Americans portrayed in the picture. The symbolism in this realistic picture was noted by many students, suggesting a bridge between abstract and concrete thinking. Some took a symbolic print and interpreted it literally:

> Rauschenberg because it was very pretty to me and it was like it was saying something about the '60s.

Others took realistic prints and interpreted them symbolically for both likes and dislikes:

> *George Washington* to add patriotism to my living room.
> The way that some of them use dark colors that make a picture look sad, lonely, and angry.

Some students liked the same print, but focused on its concrete or symbolic qualities:

> *The Buffalo Trail* painting because of the motion it showed. It made the observer realize the cold and darkness of the place and the wild running buffalo

compared with

> *Buffalo Trail* because of the way the clouds and trees were painted.

Early adolescents first may feel more comfortable finding symbolism or thinking abstractly about concrete or realistic images, before they feel comfortable with fully abstract images and ideas; or, they may find it comfortable thinking abstractly about realistic images. These data suggest some intriguing areas for systematic study of the development, bridging, and expression of concrete and abstract thinking in early adolescence.

SUMMARY AND DISCUSSION

In this study, we took a two-step approach to evaluation. First, informal interviews with students, and surveys and interviews of teachers and volunteers were conducted over 2 years to assess whether the TIPS Social Studies and Art Volunteer program was successfully implemented in the middle grades. Second, with evidence of the systematic implementation of the program in all social studies teachers' classes, we proceeded to evaluate the effects of the program on student learning and attitudes. The main results help us better understand middle grades students, schools, family involvement, and ways to improve the program.

- Middle grades students increased their awareness of artists and paintings. Particularly, many students increased their familiarity with and recall of names of paintings and their topics.

Students found it easier to remember the paintings than the artists. Although students with higher report card grades did better on the matching tests, report card grades were not the only important explanatory variable. Positive attitudes about the program, regardless of report card grades or success in school, independently explained the number of correct matchings of the titles of paintings and their descriptions.

There are several reasons why students were more successful in linking painting and content, than painting and artist. The TIPS Social Studies and Art program is introduced to students as one that should make their social studies classes more enjoyable. It was stressed that the discussions in class were not part of the students' report card grades. Not grading students for their reactions and opinions may be a good idea. For example, many students who were reluctant to participate in other classes, participated actively in the discussions of the art prints. However, some students may have paid less attention to the details of the art and artists, knowing that the information would not determine their grades.

Also, by design, most class time is focused on the paintings and not the artists. In a typical 20-minute presentation, the volunteer introduces the artist and something about the artist's life (2 to 4 minutes), discusses the technique and style of painting (2 to 4 minutes), gives the story behind the particular picture (4 to 6 minutes), and makes connections to social studies (2 to 4 minutes). Then, students discuss their reactions to the picture and their likes and dislikes for the last 5 to 8 minutes of class time. The students mainly are asked to examine the art work, form impressions, and express their attitudes toward art. They then "live" with the art print for 3 or 4 weeks while it is in the classroom. The volunteer may spend 1-2 minutes at the start of each session reviewing the names of the artists and prints the students had seen previously. The majority of time, however, is spent by the volunteer and by the students on the painting, its content, and students' reactions. It is not surprising, then, that students were better able to match pictures and content more than pictures and artist's name.

The data indicate that in the fall of the school year, students had little or no knowledge about the artists or paintings, but that in the spring many had made real gains in awareness and understanding. They were better able to match prints with content, much the way adults would if exposed to art work that they had not seen before. Students were not drilled to remember the names of the artists. Some students remembered some names, particularly of paintings they liked or disliked. Most students remembered the images they saw—the first step toward greater familiarity with art.

In discussions with teachers about these results, several suggested that they should guide the volunteers more closely in order to standardize some of the most important information that the students receive in all classes. The teachers believe that this is one way to help more students remember more of the art prints that they are shown.

- Students who enjoyed the program remembered more about the paintings.
- Students who looked at the pictures while they were in their classrooms, and liked more of them, liked the program more overall.

Because students who liked the pictures more liked the program more overall, it is important that teachers include presentations on a variety of artists and styles of art, and that the information and discussions be pertinent and interesting to early adolescents. In one discussion with students, they suggested that they should help pick which pictures to study. This might increase the number of students who are interested in particular prints.

Because students with high and low report card grades who enjoy the program remember more content, it is particularly important for educators and volunteers to capture the interest and participation of students when they begin each school year, and to maintain their interest with good presentations, discussions, and high rates of student participation.

The findings suggest that students might benefit from greater use by the teachers of the numerous activities included with each presentation that require students to observe and react to the art work while it is in their classrooms each month. The suggested activities include discussions, writing assignments, art activities for classwork, extra credit, or for homework.

These activities also could expand the program significantly. Presently, the TIPS Social Studies and Art process is designed to increase the number of students who are exposed to visual art, art history, and art criticism. The program does not directly address art making or production—another aspect of comprehensive art education (Getty, 1986; Eisner, 1988; Jackson, 1987). However, the TIPS presentations include suggestions for art production for classwork, homework, or extra-credit activities. Also, the social studies teachers could collaborate on this goal with regular art teachers to link their curricula of social studies, art appreciation, and art production more formally.

- Students who were in the program longer were able to recall more art work.

The analyses indicate that maturity and experience in the program increased students' recall over time. The results suggest the benefits of carrying the interdisciplinary theme of "social studies and art" through the middle grades to build familiarity with art work, and to provide many opportunities for students to identify some paintings (and drawings or sculpture) that they like. TIPS Social Studies and Art Volunteers is designed as a 3-year middle grades program, not an incidental activity to conduct for only one year.

- Students developed and expressed their attitudes and preferences for different styles of art.
- Despite some students' inability to identify pictures or artists in test-like matching items, nearly 80% were able and willing to convey their likes and dislikes.

In this program, students are encouraged to form their own reactions and opinions to the art they see. They are told that there are no "right" answers when it comes to likes and dislikes of art prints. In this study, the students' written reasons for their preferences reflected their diverse levels of comfort with realistic and symbolic pictures and concrete and abstract thinking. For some students, the TIPS Social Studies and Art program offered their first experiences with nonrepresentational, symbolic, and abstract art.

Most who disliked abstract prints rejected all or most of the abstract work. By contrast, most who disliked some realistic or representational prints usually liked some others. These patterns reveal the dynamic quality of the development of concrete and abstract thinking skills, with some students moving quickly and others more slowly in their abilities or willingness to relate to symbolism. The written comments also demonstrated various bridging qualities in students' thinking, such as finding symbolism in representational work or representations of feelings and form in abstract work.

In addition to the differences in students' preferences for abstract or realistic art, students' comments also illustrated the emergence of other characteristics of early adolescents. Students looked to the art prints for emotions more than for history. They tended to look past facts to find feelings. Middle grades students are people-people, filled with energy and empathy when given an opportunity to hear about others. When they could not find much emotion in a picture, they searched for it. One year a student suggested, "We should have been told more about the boy in *Blue Boy*—who he was and what he felt like." This and similar reactions from students lead to including anecdotes about the artist, subject, or historic times in the presentations. At the same time, the students' natural tendency to look for feelings makes it important for volunteers and teachers to emphasize the interesting facts about the artists, art, and historic times in order to increase students' understanding.

- Multiple measures, including test-like matching questions to measure student knowledge, and open-ended reactions to obtain students' recall and reactions were important for fully understanding the effects of the program.

The various measures used in this study show that test-like matching exercises are not the only useful techniques to measure student achievement in an enrichment program like TIPS Social Studies and Art. The matching tests provided important quantitative results that statistically accounted for gender, grades, attitudes, and experience with the program. However, it also was important to collect students' written reactions to the program and the art work they saw. These responses illuminated students' personalities, preferences, and several of the developmental characteristics of early adolescents.

Combined, the quantitative results and comments raise new questions for studies of students' changing relationships with art and other subjects. For example, the combined results show that, overall, most students liked realistic pictures; a smaller proportion preferred abstract art work. These preferences were not exclusively related to students' grades or success in school, as students with high and low report card grades were found in both camps. Their preferences, or levels of comfort, may reflect students' different stages of development of abstract thinking, including their bridging of concrete and abstract concepts. As they increase their ability to think abstractly, more students may be more open to new styles of art. A good question for new research (that also requires a combination of quantitative and qualitative data) is whether the length of time that students have been at particular levels of abstract thinking, formally measured, affect their readiness and preferences for abstract or symbolic art (or literature, music, or puzzles).

- The TIPS Social Studies and Art volunteers program contributes to the development of a program of school and family partnerships, increasing the number of productive volunteers in a middle school.

Middle grades schools have placed parent involvement on their agendas for improving student success, but have not figured out how to organize effective and comprehensive programs that include practices of six major types of partnership activities. One of the six types of involvement—volunteers—has, historically, been low in the middle grades. In part, this was due to a lack of viable strategies to organize productive volunteers who assist teachers, students, and administrators in ways that are appropriate for the middle grades. The TIPS Volunteers program illustrates one process that recruits, trains, and schedules volunteers to help educators increase students' experiences with interdisciplinary connections of subjects that inform each other well.

- Variety is important for the success of an interdisciplinary program linking social studies and art in the middle grades.

Collectively, the main results point to the importance of including a variety of artists, prints, media, and styles to expand early adolescents experiences in art. The students seem to be "trying on" their new thinking skills for size. One student one year asked for more abstract pictures. He said, "You know, like that one about war with the eyes and arms and heads going in all directions," referring to Picasso's *Guernica*.

One year, the teacher coordinator noticed that some teachers selected only realistic pictures (teachers have personal preferences, too), omitted women artists, or included too few African American artists. The coordinator negotiated with the teachers to select their final choices of 8 prints to provide students with opportunities to see and study a more varied collection.

Also, one year, one of the volunteers personally disliked several of the pictures that were assigned to the class. She was alerted that when she gave her own ideas she needed to identify them, and to present others' opinions about the merits of the "masterpieces" so the students could make their own judgments.

It will never be the case that all students like all of the pictures that they see. Indeed, in order to build a capacity to express likes and dislikes, students need to see pictures that will prompt strong positive and negative feelings. It is expected, however, that a wide variety of prints will permit all students to find some during the year that they can relate to, enjoy, and from which they will extend their creative and critical thinking.

CONCLUSION

Jackson (1987, p. 42) wrote, "Let us assume that it makes sense for students to be introduced to great works of art. . . When and where should this kind of instruction go on?" The TIPS Social Studies and Art Volunteers program gives one workable answer to that question.

The present study indicates that with this program, students begin to identify major artists, major styles of art, and set the artist and work in historic context. The program enables many students to describe and discuss art with greater insight and sophistication than they had before.

When time in school is limited, when teachers trained in art education are scarce, and when school budgets are low, it is difficult for middle grades schools (or schools at other levels) to include art in all students' education. The TIPS Social Studies and Art Volunteers process offers a useful tool for meeting the diverse goals of involving families, integrating subjects, and providing students with a cultural background in art awareness, appreciation, and criticism in the middle grades.

REFERENCES

The arts in education Special issue. (1994). *Phi Delta Kappan, 75,* 6.
Baker, D. P., & Stevenson, D. L. (1986). Mothers' strategies for children's school achievement: Managing the transition to high school. *Sociology of Education, 59,* 156-166.

Bauch, P. A. (1988). Is parent involvement different in private schools? *Educational Horizons, 66*, 78-82.

Becker, H. J., & Epstein, J. L. (1982). Parent involvement: A study of teacher practices. *Elementary School Journal, 83*, 85-102.

Bennett, W. (1986). *First lessons: A report on elementary education in America.* Washington, DC: U.S. Government Printing Office.

Boyer, E. (1983). *High school.* New York: Harper & Row.

Clark, G. A., Day, M. D., & Greer, W. D. (1987). Discipline-based art education: Becoming students of art. *Journal of Aesthetic Education, 21 (2), 129-193.*

Darby, J. T., & Catterall, J. S. (1993). *The fourth R: The arts and learning* (mimeo). Los Angeles: UCLA *and the Galef Institute.*

Dauber, S. L., & Epstein, J. L. (1993). Parents' attitudes and practices of involvement in inner-city elementary and middle schools. In N. Chavkin (Ed.), *Families and schools in a pluralistic society* (pp. 53-71). Albany, NY: SUNY Press.

Dornbusch, S. M., & Ritter, P. L. (1988). Parents of high school students: A neglected resource. *Educational Horizons, 66,* 75-77.

Eisner, E. W. (1987). Discipline-based art education: A reply to Jackson. *Educational Researcher, 16 (9), 50-52.*

Eisner, E. W. (1988). *DBAE: The role of Disciplined Based Art Education in America's schools.* Los Angeles: Getty Center for Education in the Arts.

Epstein, J. L. (1986). Parents' reactions to teacher practices of parent involvement. *Elementary School Journal, 86,* 277-294.

Epstein, J. L. (1992). School and family partnerships. In M. Alkin (Ed.), *Encyclopedia of educational research* (6th ed., pp. 1139-1151). New York: Macmillan.

Epstein, J. L. (in press). *School and family partnerships: Preparing educators and improving schools.* Boulder: Westview.

Epstein, J. L., & Connors, L. C. (in press). School and family partnerships in the middle grades. In B. Rutherford, (Ed.), *Creating school/family partnership.* Columbus, OH: National Middle School Association.

Epstein, J. L., & Dauber, S. (1991). School programs and practices of parent involvement in inner-city elementary and middle schools. *Elementary School Journal, 91,* 289-303.

Epstein, J. L., & Herrick, S. C. (1991). *Improving school and family partnerships in urban middle grades schools: Orientation days and school newsletters* (Report No. 20). Baltimore: The Johns Hopkins University Center for Research on Effective Schooling for Disadvantaged Students.

Epstein, J. L., Herrick, S. C., & Coates, L. (in press). Effects of summer home learning packets on student achievement in language arts in the middle grades. *School Effectiveness and School Improvement.*

Epstein, J. L., & Mac Iver, D. J. (1990). *Education in the middle grades: National practices and trends.* Columbus, OH: National Middle School Association.

Epstein, J. L., & Salinas, K. C. (1991). *Teachers manual: TIPS Social Studies and Art Volunteers proces*; Prototype Activities for TIPS Social Studies and Art in American Art, World Cultures, and Urban Life, Baltimore: The Johns Hopkins Center on Families, Communities, Schools and Children's Learning.

Getty Center for Education in the Arts. (1986). *Beyond creating: The place for art in America's schools.* Los Angeles: Author.

Goodlad, J. (1984). *A place called school.* New York: McGraw-Hill.

Henderson, A. (1987). *The evidence continues to grow: Parent involvement improves student achievement.* Columbia, MD: National Committee for Citizens in Education.

Jackson, P. W. (1987). Mainstreaming art: An essay on discipline-based art education. *Educational Researcher, 16 (6), 39-43.*

Lipsitz, J. (1980). *The forgotten years.* New Brunswick, NJ: Transaction Books.

McLaughlin, M. W., Thomas, M. A., & Peterson, J. (1984). *Art history, art criticism, and art production: An examination of art education in selected school districts.* (Report No. R-3161/3-JPG) Santa Monica, CA: RAND Corporation.

Parent involvement [Special issue]. (1991). *Phi Delta Kappan, 72* (5).

Parents and schools [Special issue]. (1988). *Educational Horizons, 66*(2).

The role of the arts in education [Special issue]. (1992). *Phi Delta Kappan, 73*(8).

Stevenson, D., & Baker, D. (1987). The family-school relation and the child's school performance. *Child Development, 58,* 1348-1357.

Swap, S. (1993). *Developing home-school partnerships: From concepts to practice.* New York: Teachers College Press.

Wiles, J., & Bondi, J. (1986). *Making middle schools work.* Alexandria, VA: Association for Supervision and Curriculum Development.

Requests for reprints should be addressed to Joyce L. Epstein, Codirector of the Center on Families, Communities, Schools and Children's Learning at Johns Hopkins University.

Developmental Psychology
1991, Vol. 27, No. 4, 644–655

Out-of-School Care of Young Adolescents and Self-Reported Behavior

Nancy L. Galambos and Jennifer L. Maggs
University of Victoria, Victoria, British Columbia, Canada

Sixth graders in adult care during out-of-school hours were contrasted with 6th graders in self-care situations, on 2 occasions, winter and summer ($N = 112$). Hierarchical multiple regression analyses examined how well out-of-school care situations predicted 3 dimensions each of peer experience and self-image, concurrently and longitudinally. Additional analyses assessed the role of parent-adolescent relations in moderating the relation between self-care and adolescent behavior. Results revealed no differences between adolescents in adult care and those in self-care at home. Self-care girls who were more distant from adult supervision (e.g., they spent unsupervised time hanging out), however, reported more problem behavior and contact with more deviant peers in relation to other girls and to boys. Parental acceptance and firm control, however, appeared to buffer girls from engaging in problem behavior when in self-care away from home. Orthogonal contrasts between groups showed that girls and boys in self-care away from home were more involved with peers than those in self-care at home or in adult care.

With the majority of mothers of school-age children now in the labor force, there is much concern about the supervision of these children when parents are at work and school is out. Of particular concern is the phenomenon of children who regularly care for themselves after school—some 7% of American children between the ages of 5 and 13 (U.S. Bureau of the Census, 1987). Children in self-care are often called "latchkey children." Although the term refers mainly to children who stay home after school, many children in self-care spend their time in places other than home (Rodman, Pratto, & Nelson, 1988; Steinberg, 1988).

There are two contrasting perspectives about children in self-care (see Galambos & Dixon, 1984). On the one hand, many writers have claimed that self-care has deleterious consequences for the psychosocial development of the child (Baker & Gore, 1989; Huff, 1982; Long & Long, 1983). On the other hand, writers have argued that self-care may be beneficial with respect to learning responsibility and independence (Dullea, 1981; Kieffer, 1981; Langway, 1981).

Little systematic research, however, has addressed the negative or positive consequences of self-care. Most studies conducted in suburban or rural neighborhoods have found that on measures of self-esteem, academic achievement, personality adjustment, peer relations, and locus of control, children in self-care do not differ from children in adult care (Galambos & Garbarino, 1985; Gold & Andres, 1978a, 1978b; Rodman, Pratto, & Nelson, 1985; Vandell & Corasaniti, 1988). In contrast, the earliest study, conducted with a sample of Black inner

city children in the fifth grade, found that girls in self-care showed poorer cognitive, personality, and social adjustment than did adult-care girls (Woods, 1972). More recently, a large-scale study conducted in the Los Angeles and San Diego metropolitan areas found a significant positive relationship between level of substance use among eighth-grade girls and boys and time spent in self-care after school (Richardson et al., 1989). Galambos and Garbarino (1985) suggested that self-care might have potentially negative consequences in an urban environment, which may be more physically dangerous than a suburban or rural environment.

Steinberg (1986) focused concern on the after-school ecology of children, that is, where and with whom children spend time when school is out. He criticized extant research on two grounds: First, most earlier comparisons between self- and adult-care children failed to consider the variation in self-care situations (i.e., some children stay home, some go to a friend's house, and others "hang out" in public places). These studies merely contrasted two groups of children: those who were cared for by adults and those who were frequently in self-care. Second, Steinberg argued that the dependent measures selected in these past studies were largely global indices of adjustment that are less likely to be directly affected by the self-care situation than are other behaviors such as involvement with peers, conformity to peer pressure, and problem behavior. After all, the immediate consequence of self-care is that it may place on the child decisions about where to spend time, with whom, and what to do.

To improve on previous research, Steinberg (1986) contrasted suburban adolescents (fifth, sixth, eighth, and ninth graders) in adult-care with adolescents in several self-care situations (e.g., those who stay home, those who go to a friend's house, and those who just hang out). Steinberg found that self-care adolescents who hung out were more likely to conform to antisocial peer pressure (as measured by responses to hypothetical situations) than were self-care adolescents who went to a friend's house; and those who went to a friend's house were more con-

Completion of this article was supported by Social Sciences and Humanities Research Council of Canada and University of Victoria Faculty Research Grants to Nancy L. Galambos. We are indebted to the families and schools who participated in this project and to three anonymous reviewers for their valuable suggestions on this article.

Correspondence concerning this article should be addressed to Nancy L. Galambos, Department of Psychology, University of Victoria, Victoria, British Columbia, Canada V8W 3P5.

forming than those in self-care who stayed home after school. This research thus pointed to the necessity for considering different self-care situations as well as for examining behaviors that might be directly linked with these situations, such as experiences with peers.

Moreover, Steinberg (1986) found that parental permissiveness was associated with the self-care situation. Boys in self-care came from more permissive homes than boys in adult-care. Among self-care girls, there was a positive relationship between parental permissiveness and distance from adult supervision (i.e., self-care at home, at a friend's house, or hanging out). The results showed that parental permissiveness explained a small, but significant, portion of variance in girls' and boys' susceptibility to antisocial peer pressure. In addition, authoritative parental control (i.e., high responsiveness and high demandingness) was a buffer against susceptibility to peer pressure among self-care boys and girls. Self-care adolescents who came from authoritative homes were less conforming than self-care adolescents who came from less authoritative homes. Parental practices and the nature of the parent–adolescent relationship, therefore, are important to examine when considering the association between self-care and adolescent behavior.

Given the limited research on self-care children, several issues remain. First, although Steinberg (1986) found that some adolescents in self-care seemed likely to conform to antisocial peer pressure, his study did not examine whether they were, in fact, engaging in problem behavior. Second, Steinberg (1988) argued that it is far more important to study problem behavior than enduring personality traits such as self-esteem, but others believe it is too soon to dismiss personality traits in the study of self-care children (Galambos & Maggs, in press; Rodman et al., 1988). Third, to date, self-care has only been studied during the school year, but what happens to children who are in self-care during the summer and have a potentially larger number of hours during which they may go unsupervised? Fourth, no published study has used longitudinal data to assess whether there are longer term effects of self-care on children's behavior. Fifth, further exploration is needed to clarify the role of parent–adolescent relations in linking self-care to adolescent behavior.

The purpose of this study is to consider these issues using longitudinal data from a study of two-earner families with sixth-grade children. Sixth graders in several out-of-school care arrangements were examined on two occasions of measurement, one in the winter and one in the summer. The following questions were asked:

1. To what extent is variation in out-of-school care predictive of experiences with peers (i.e., peer involvement, deviant peers, and problem behavior) and the more global construct of self-image (i.e., impulse control, mastery, and emotional tone) concurrently and 6 months later?
2. Does the seasonal context of the out-of-school care situation (winter afternoons vs. summer days) bear on the relations among self-care, peer experience, and self-image?
3. How are three selected aspects of parent–adolescent relations—parental acceptance, lax control, and parent–adolescent conflict—linked to self-care, peer experience, and self-image?

Method

Subjects

The subjects were sixth graders (mean age in January 1988: 11 years, 7 months) participating in the Two-Earner Family Study, a longitudinal study of young adolescents in two-parent families in which both parents were employed on a part- or full-time basis. Data for this study were obtained on two occasions (winter 1988 and summer 1988). Data on out-of-school care arrangements were available for 112 subjects on Occasion 1 (winter 1988) and for 100 of these subjects on Occasion 2 (summer 1988). The schools from which the subjects were drawn were small (with one or two classrooms of sixth graders) and were located in primarily suburban areas of a city in Canada.

The mothers of the subjects worked for an average of 30.9 hours per week ($SD = 11.2$), and fathers worked an average of 42 hours per week ($SD = 10.3$). The mothers had been employed for an average of 6.5 years ($SD = 5.4$); fathers had been employed an average of 17.2 years ($SD = 7.4$). The mean number of children per family was 2.4 ($SD = 0.9$), and the mean number of years married was 14.7 ($SD = 4.5$). Mothers and fathers had achieved similar levels of education (mothers: $M = 13.1$ years, $SD = 2.2$; fathers: $M = 13.8$ years, $SD = 3.1$). The mean age of the mothers was 37.4 years old ($SD = 3.9$), and the mean age of the fathers was 40 ($SD = 5.5$).

With respect to occupations held by the parents, 25% of the fathers were in professional/technical occupations; 35% were in managerial, sales, or clerical occupations; and 39% were in service, unskilled, or skilled labor occupations. The corresponding figures for mothers were 18%, 73%, and 10%, respectively. Mean family socioeconomic status (SES) was 50.01 ($SD = 15.18$), as assessed by the father's score on the Blishen and McRoberts (1976) occupational index for Canadian samples. Examples of occupations and their SES scores are motor vehicle repair (32.8), real estate sales (50.1), and accounting (67.4).

Procedure

To obtain the sample, we sent letters soliciting participants home with all sixth graders in 19 schools. Sixth graders were targeted because the focus of the study was on parental work, family stress, and the transition to adolescence. Criteria for participation were that the households contained two parents (not necessarily biological parents) who were employed (i.e., they identified themselves as having jobs) and all three family members (both parents and sixth grader) wished to participate. Families returned prestamped postcards indicating their desire to take part in the study. Although the schools had no information on the percentage of sixth graders in dual-earner families, we estimated, using census statistics (Statistics Canada, 1984), that at least 50% of two-earner families responded to the letter. This response rate is in line with other studies in which adolescents and their parents participated (see e.g., Parsons, Adler, & Kaczala, 1982; Smetana, 1989). In addition, advertisements requesting families meeting the same criteria were run in local newspapers.

Questionnaires were mailed to each parent and child individually. Family members were requested not to discuss the questionnaires with one another and were given separate return envelopes. Each family member received a token payment for participation: $5 on Occasion 1 and $10 on Occasion 2. Ninety-three percent of the families who participated on Occasion 1 also participated on Occasion 2.

Measures

Supervision Status

On Occasion 1, the sixth graders were separated into four supervision categories on the basis of their responses to a series of questions designed by Steinberg (1986) to assess the after-school care situation.

The four categories were adult care (supervised by a parent or other adult at home or in another setting, such as at school), self-care at home, self-care at a friend's home, and self-care hanging out. Steinberg's results indicated that these four care situations discriminated most among adolescents with respect to susceptibility to antisocial peer pressure. The validity of this measure in the present sample is supported by the finding that all 28 sixth graders who had at least one parent home during after-school hours reported that they were in adult care and not self-care.

For Occasion 2, during the summer, the series of questions were revised to shorten the number of items needed to determine supervision status and to reflect supervision status during the summer day (e.g., "There is usually at least one adult around where I spend my time during the day" and "During the day where do you spend MOST of your time?"). As supporting evidence for the validity of this measure, we examined cases in which at least one parent was off work all day during the summer. The majority of parents in the sample worked day shifts, but all 8 subjects who did have one parent home all day reported being in adult care.

Table 1 presents the percentage of boys and girls in each of the four supervision categories in the winter and summer. The percentage of boys and girls in self-care ranged from 33% to 47%. A cross-tabulation of supervision status in winter and summer (collapsed into two groups: adult care and self-care) showed that 63% of the sixth graders maintained the same status. The remaining subjects shifted from adult care in the winter to self-care in the summer (15%), or vice versa (22%).

Although Steinberg (1986) treated the after-school care situation categorically, one goal of this study was to predict adolescent behavior from a continuous measure of supervision, using a 4-point scale: adult care (1), self-care home (2), self-care at friend's (3), and self-care hanging out (4). These points on the continuum represent increasing psychological, if not physical, distance from supervision by parents or other adults. For example, a child in self-care at home would feel the reach of parental authority less than the child who is in the actual presence of an adult but more than the self-care child who spends time at a friend's home. Indeed, Steinberg's (1986) results pointed to successively higher levels of susceptibility to antisocial peer pressure as the adolescent's distance from adult supervision increased (e.g., moving from adult care to self-care away from home), thereby supporting a graduated ordering of the supervision variable. In addition, Cohen and Cohen (1983) argued that continuous variables are preferred over categorical variables because of the greater amount of variance that can be explained and the greater power of the statistical test that can be associated with continuous variables. Thus, there were conceptual and empirical bases for treating supervision status as a continuous variable as well as statistical advantages to doing so. However, questions remained as to whether some self-care children (i.e., those at home) differ from adult-care children and whether different groups of self-care children differ on dimensions of peer experience and self-image. Thus, a second set of regression

analyses used planned orthogonal contrasts (Pedhazur, 1982) to test specific assumptions about differences between groups.

Adolescent Behavior

Six self-report measures were used to determine the nature of the sixth grader's peer experiences (i.e., peer involvement, deviant peers, and problem behavior) and self-image (i.e., impulse control, mastery and coping, and emotional tone). The peer experience measures were selected because of their relevance to what the sixth grader was doing when out of school. Although the Problem Behavior Scale is not a measure of peer experience, it is included because most problem behaviors probably occur in the presence of peers. The self-image measures were selected because of their similarity to measures used in previous research on self-care (Galambos & Garbarino, 1985; Rodman et al., 1985). One goal of the study was to assess whether the out-of-school situation was more relevant to peer experience than to self-image, as argued by Steinberg (1986, 1988). The six measures were available for the winter and summer occasions.

Peer involvement. The mean monthly frequency of engaging in typical activities with friends was assessed with a six-item scale devised by Brown, Clasen, and Eicher (1986). Subjects were asked to indicate "How many times in the past month" they engaged in six activities with friends (e.g., went to a movie or a concert, or out to eat; attended a school event; talked on phone for half hour or more; went somewhere or did something after school). Responses were rated on a 5-point scale ranging from *never* (1) to *almost every day* (5). Higher scores represented more involvement in social activities with peers. Cronbach's coefficient alpha was .75 and .73 for winter and summer. Given the content of the items, a higher score, however, does not necessarily represent negative or undesirable behavior. Although higher scores on supervision status indicate that the adolescent spends afterschool time in the company of peers, the peer involvement measure appears to be unlike supervision status in that first, it is composed of items that do not assess whether there are adults present (in fact, some of the activities would require the presence of adults), and second, many of the peer involvement activities take place in the evening or on weekends and not after school.[1]

Deviant peers. This measure assessed the extent to which the sixth grader's friends engaged in misconduct or problem behavior, such as shoplifting or damaging property. The scale consists of the mean of four items (e.g., "My friends often get into trouble with adults") rated on a 4-point scale ranging from *disagree strongly* (1) to *agree strongly* (4). The items were similar to those on a scale used by Galambos and Silbereisen (1987a, 1987b). Higher scores indicated contact with more deviant peers. Cronbach's coefficient alpha was .69 and .74 for winter and summer, respectively.

Problem behavior. The frequency of misconduct by the sixth grader in the past month was measured with 8 items obtained from a misconduct scale developed by Brown et al. (1986) and an additional 17 items taken from Kaplan's (1978) deviant response scale. The 25 items were chosen because they represented a wide range of problem behaviors, including minor acts that might be typical for a sixth grader (e.g.,

Table 1
Percentage of Sixth Graders in Various Out-of-School Supervision Arrangements

	Winter		Summer	
Supervision	Boys ($n = 50$)	Girls ($n = 62$)	Boys ($n = 45$)	Girls ($n = 55$)
Adult care	58	53	62	67
Self-care, home	18	26	18	13
Self-care, friend's	10	8	4	9
Self-care, hanging out	14	13	16	11

[1] To further investigate the possible overlap between the measures of supervision status and peer involvement, we eliminated two items in the peer involvement measure regarding after-school time and then reran our major analyses predicting peer involvement from supervision status (the analyses presented in Tables 3, 4, 5, and 6). In four of the five reanalyses, the results were the same. Although these reanalyses minimized the overlap between the peer involvement and supervision status variables, some caution in interpreting the relationship between peer involvement and supervision status may be warranted.

looked for trouble, did something that parents said not to do) and more serious actions (e.g., took things worth between $2 and $50, used drugs). Subjects were asked "How many times in the past month" they participated in misbehavior, and they then rated each item on a 5-point scale from *never* (1) to *almost every day* (5). The mean of all 25 items was computed to form the score for problem behavior, with a higher score indicating more frequent misbehavior. Cronbach's coefficient alpha was .82 on both occasions.

Impulse control. The impulse control subscale from the Self-Image Questionnaire for Young Adolescents (SIQYA; Petersen, Schulenberg, Abramowitz, Offer, & Jarcho, 1984) measured the sixth grader's resistance to impulsive, violent, or angry behavior. Eight items (e.g., "Even under pressure I manage to remain calm") were rated on a 6-point scale ranging from *does not describe me at all* (1) to *describes me very well* (6). A mean scale score was computed with higher scores indicating more impulse control. The Cronbach's coefficient alpha was .66 during the winter and .74 during the summer.

Mastery and coping. The mastery and coping subscale from the SIQYA (Petersen et al., 1984) assessed the sixth grader's confidence in coping. This measure consisted of 10 items (e.g., "When I decide to do something, I do it") rated in a manner identical to that of the impulse control measure. A mean scale score was computed, with higher scores representing higher feelings of mastery. The Cronbach's coefficient alpha was .73 in the winter and .71 in the summer.

Emotional tone. This subscale from the SIQYA measured the degree of positive affect in the sixth grader. It consisted of 11 items (e.g., "Most of the time I am happy"). The mean scale score was used, with more happiness indicated by higher scores. Cronbach's coefficient alpha was .81 for the winter and .79 for the summer measurement.

Parent–Adolescent Relations

Three aspects of parent–adolescent relations were measured: parental acceptance of the adolescent (the degree of warmth and understanding directed toward the adolescent), lax control of the adolescent (the degree to which rules and limits on behavior are not consistently enforced), and parent–adolescent conflict (the level of disagreement present in the parent–adolescent relationship). These measures were selected because they are global dimensions of parent–adolescent relations that have been implicated as important predictors of adolescent behavior (Maccoby & Martin, 1983; Montemayor, 1983), and we hypothesized that adolescents who do not feel accepted, have lax discipline at home, or experience conflict may be more likely to be found in unsupervised situations outside of the home. These are also relatively independent dimensions. In our sample, parental acceptance was correlated with lax discipline at $-.07$ (ns) and with parent–adolescent conflict at $-.21$ ($p < .05$); lax discipline and parent–adolescent conflict were correlated at .15 (ns).

Parental acceptance. The Acceptance subscale of the 56-item version (Burger & Armentrout, 1971) of the Child's Report of Parental Behavior Inventory (CRPBI; Schaefer, 1965) was used to assess the degree of warmth and acceptance directed toward the adolescent by the mothers and fathers. The subscale consists of the mean of 24 items (e.g., "she [mother] almost always speaks to me in a warm and friendly voice") with responses on a 5-point scale ranging from *very much unlike her* (1) to *very much like her* (5). (We expanded the response scale from the traditional 3-point scale to a 5-point scale to increase variability.) For both the winter and summer data collections, the adolescents completed the subscale about their mothers and fathers separately; the mothers and fathers rated the same 24 items with respect to their own behavior toward the adolescent. Cronbach's coefficient alphas were in the .90s for all informants across both occasions. The psychometric adequacy of this scale has been supported (Litovsky & Dusek, 1985; Margolies & Weintraub, 1977). Aggregate scores were formed by calcu-

lating the mean of the eight subscale scores (i.e., for the two occasions, the adolescent's report of mother acceptance and father acceptance, the mother's report of acceptance, and the father's report of acceptance). The purpose of combining scores from diverse informants was to eliminate as much systematic error variance as possible and to obtain a valid assessment of parental acceptance (see, e.g., Schwarz, Barton-Henry, & Pruzinsky, 1985). Scores across time and raters were positively intercorrelated. The internal consistency (Cronbach's coefficient alpha) of this 8-item aggregate measure was .78. Higher scores indicate more parental acceptance ($M = 3.78$; $SD = 0.36$).

Lax control. The Lax Control subscale of the 56-item version (Burger & Armentrout, 1971) of the CRPBI (Schaefer, 1965) was used to measure the amount of permissiveness and inconsistent discipline experienced by the adolescent at home. This subscale consisted of the mean of 16 items (e.g., "he [father] lets me get away with a lot of things"; "he does not bother to enforce rules") with responses rated on a 5-point scale ranging from *very much unlike him* (1) to *very much like him* (5). The adolescents rated their mothers and fathers, separately, and each parent rated themselves. The Cronbach's coefficient alphas were .80 and above for all three informants for winter and summer. This measure has been used with success in previous research (Litovsky & Dusek, 1985; Margolies & Weintraub, 1977). Aggregate scores were formed by calculating the mean of the eight subscale scores. Cronbach's coefficient alpha for this 8-item aggregate measure was .74. Higher scores indicate more permissiveness and lax control ($M = 2.18$; $SD = 0.32$).

Parent–adolescent conflict. The Issues Checklist (IC; Prinz, Foster, Kent, & O'Leary, 1979) was used to measure the amount of disagreement between parents and adolescent. Versions of the IC have proven to be useful for research with adolescents (Prinz et al., 1979; Steinberg, 1987). The IC asks parents and adolescents whether they discussed any of 44 specific topics (e.g., "cleaning up bedroom" or "time for going to bed") in the last 2 weeks. For each topic discussed, respondents indicated the intensity of the discussion on a 5-point scale ranging from *very calm* (1) to *very angry* (5). Although mothers and fathers completed the IC with reference to their adolescent, the adolescents completed the IC with reference to the parents as a unit. Frequency of conflict was computed by summing the number of topics with an intensity rating of (2) or above (cf. Steinberg, 1987). Intensity of conflict was computed by calculating the mean level of intensity of all topics discussed. The intensity and frequency scores were standardized separately for mothers, fathers, and adolescents. Aggregate scores were computed by obtaining the mean for the set of 12 scores (intensity and frequency scores for mothers, fathers, and adolescents on two occasions). Cronbach's coefficient alpha was .81. Higher scores indicate a higher level of conflict between parents and adolescent ($M = 0.00$; $SD = 0.58$).

Results

Table 2 presents the means and standard deviations of the peer experience and self-image measures. Correlations among these variables are also presented, with boys and girls combined (there were no significant sex differences between the correlations). Among the peer experience measures, deviant peers and problem behavior are related; higher peer involvement is associated with more problem behavior. The self-image scales are all positively interrelated. In addition, higher scores on deviant peers and problem behavior are associated with lower scores on the three self-image measures.

Preliminary Analyses

An extensive set of analyses was run to examine SES as a predictor of adolescent behavior, alone and in interaction with

Table 2
Means, Standard Deviations, and Intercorrelations of Peer Experience and Self-Image Measures, Winter and Summer 1988

	Winter		Summer		Measure					
Measure	M	SD	M	SD	1	2	3	4	5	6
Peer experience										
1. Involvement	2.45	0.74	2.34	0.74	—	.06	.43*	−.07	−.05	−.07
2. Deviant peers	1.74	0.64	1.66	0.65	.05	—	.34*	−.43*	−.30*	−.34*
3. Problem behavior	1.17	0.18	1.15	0.18	.43*	.34*	—	−.43*	−.27*	−.12
Self-image										
4. Impulse control	4.34	0.75	4.39	0.75	−.07	−.44*	−.45*	—	.49*	.56*
5. Mastery and coping	4.79	0.68	4.86	0.62	−.04	−.29*	−.28*	.48*	—	.58*
6. Emotional tone	4.56	0.83	4.74	0.72	−.08	−.38*	−.16	.57*	.67*	—

Note. $N = 97–111$. Winter intercorrelations are above the diagonal; summer intercorrelations are below.
* $p < .05$.

supervision status. SES alone explained up to 6% of the variance in the dependent measures, but the effects of supervision status did not differ by level of SES (as determined by largely insignificant interactions). In addition, because the omission of SES as a predictor did not change the nature of the results, it was excluded from the analyses reported here.

Another set of regressions examined the total number of hours that both parents were simultaneously at work during after-school hours in the winter (the 3:00–6:00 p.m. time slot) and daytime hours in the summer (the 9:00 a.m. to 6:00 p.m. time slot). The aim was to determine whether parental work hours alone or in interaction with supervision status were predictive of adolescent behavior. Because the number of significant effects was no more than that expected by chance, parental work hours were dropped from further analysis.

Supervision Status as a Continuous Measure

Hierarchical multiple regression analyses were conducted in order to examine how well the continuous measure of supervision status predicted peer experience and self-image concurrently and longitudinally. Supervision × Sex interaction effects were tested in order to determine whether supervision status had different consequences for boys and girls. Previous research (Steinberg, 1986; Woods, 1972) suggested such a possibility.

Winter Results

In the first set of analyses, sex of the sixth grader, supervision status (winter), and the Supervision × Sex interaction were entered as predictors in the first, second, and third steps, respectively. The dependent variables were the six self-report measures (winter). Table 3 presents the results of these analyses. Supervision status was a significant predictor of all three peer experience measures, alone or in interaction with the sex of adolescent. Peer involvement was higher among sixth graders who were further from adult supervision. This was true for boys and girls. The significant Supervision × Sex interaction for deviant peers indicated that, among girls, greater distance from adult supervision (e.g., self-care hanging out) was linked to more contact with friends who got into trouble. Similarly, the results for problem behavior indicated that girls' greater distance from

adult supervision was associated with a higher number of problem behaviors.

Although the Supervision × Sex interaction did not reach conventional levels of significance for the self-image measures, the results showed a tendency for girls further away from adult supervision to report less impulse control and lower feelings of mastery.

Summer Results

The second set of analyses was identical to the first but pertained to supervision status during the summer (see Table 4). For the most part, the findings of the summer measurement replicated those of the winter. With respect to peer involvement, boys and girls further away from adult supervision were more likely to report engaging in peer activities, in relation to their counterparts closer to adult authority. Again, there were significant Supervision × Sex interactions for deviant peers and problem behavior: Among girls, greater distance from adult supervision was associated with more contact with deviant peers and a higher number of problem behaviors. Supervision status was not related to any of the self-image measures.

Longitudinal Results

Next, longitudinal analyses were conducted to determine the extent to which winter and summer supervision status predicted summer peer experiences and self-image. Hierarchical multiple regressions were computed in which there were five steps, with the following predictors: sex; supervision status (winter); Sex × Supervision (winter); supervision status (summer); Sex × Supervision (summer). These analyses were useful in determining whether supervision status in the summer explained the variance in the dependent measures above and beyond that which was explained by earlier supervision status.

The results are presented in Table 5. Summer supervision status was a significant predictor of peer involvement in the summer (R^2 change = .04), with involvement higher among adolescents who were further away from adult supervision. There were no significant predictors for deviant peers (summer), although there was a tendency for girls further away from adult supervision in the summer to report contact with more deviant peers (R^2 change = .03, $p < .10$). The regression for problem

Table 3
Standardized and Unstandardized Regression Coefficients for Prediction of Peer Experience and Self-Image (Winter 1988)

Step and predictor	Peer experience						Self-image					
	Peer involvement		Deviant peers		Problem behavior		Impulse control		Mastery and coping		Emotional tone	
	Stan-dardized	Unstan-dardized	Stan-dardized	Unstan-dardized	Stan-dardized	Unstan-dardized	Stan-dardized	Unstan-dardized	Stan-dardized	Unstan-dardized	Stan-dardized	Unstan-dardized
1. Sex	.03	.05	-.05	-.07	.13	.05	.05	.07	-.11	-.15	.11	.18
Step R^2	.00		.00		.02		.00		.01		.01	
2. Supervision	.30	.20**	.06	.04	.10	.02	-.09	-.07	-.09	-.06	-.07	-.06
Step R^2	.09**		.00		.01		.01		.01		.01	
3. Supervision × Sex	-.19	-.08	-.59	-.22**	-.83	-.09**	.56	.24**	.55	.22*	.23	.11
Step R^2	.00		.03**		.07**		.03*		.03*		.01	
Final R^2	.09**		.04		.10**		.04		.05		.02	

Note. $N = 110$–111.
*$p < .10$. **$p < .05$.

Table 4
Standardized and Unstandardized Regression Coefficients for Prediction of Peer Experience and Self-Image (Summer 1988)

Step and predictor	Peer experience						Self-image					
	Peer involvement		Deviant peers		Problem behavior		Impulse control		Mastery and coping		Emotional tone	
	Stan-dardized	Unstan-dardized	Stan-dardized	Unstan-dardized	Stan-dardized	Unstan-dardized	Stan-dardized	Unstan-dardized	Stan-dardized	Unstan-dardized	Stan-dardized	Unstan-dardized
1. Sex	.04	.06	-.04	-.05	.15	.06	.13	.20	-.08	-.10	.12	.19
Step R^2	.00		.00		.02		.02		.01		.02	
2. Supervision	.23	.16*	.03	.02	.24	.04*	-.05	-.04	-.08	-.10	.14	.10
Step R^2	.05*		.00		.06*		.00		.00		.02	
3. Supervision × Sex	.29	.12	-.70	-.26*	-.65	-.07*	.42	.18	.35	.13	.06	.03
Step R^2	.01		.05*		.04*		.02		.01		.00	
Final R^2	.06		.05		.12*		.04		.02		.04	

Note. $N = 98$–100.
*$p < .05$.

Table 5
Standardized and Unstandardized Regression Coefficients for Prediction of Peer Experience and Self-Image (Summer 1988) from Winter and Summer Supervision

| | Peer experience (summer 1988) | | | | | | Self-image (summer 1988) | | | | | |
| | Peer involvement | | Deviant peers | | Problem behavior | | Impulse control | | Mastery and coping | | Emotional tone | |
Step and predictor	Stan-dardized	Unstan-dardized	Stan-dardized	Unstan-dardized	Stan-dardized	Unstan-dardized	Stan-dardized	Unstan-dardized	Stan-dardized	Unstan-dardized	Stan-dardized	Unstan-dardized
1. Sex	.04	.06	-.04	-.05	.15	.06	.13	.20	-.08	-.10	.12	.19
2. Supervision (winter)	.07	.05	.09	.05	.05	.01	-.13	-.09	-.14	-.08	-.11	-.08
3. Supervision (winter) × Sex	-.20	-.09	-.42	-.16	-.72	-.08**	.70	.32**	.62	.24**	.20	.09
4. Supervision (summer)	.22	.15**	-.03	-.02	.19	.03*	.03	.02	.11	.07	.21	.14**
5. Supervision (summer) × Sex	.35	.15	-.60	-.22*	-.61	-.06*	.18	.08	.10	.04	-.16	-.07
Final R^2	.06		.06		.14**		.09		.08		.07	

Note. $N = 98-100$. In cases for which the individual predictor is significant, the step R^2 is also significant.
* $p < .10$. ** $p < .05$.

behavior showed a significant Sex × Supervision (winter) interaction (R^2 change = .05), indicating that girls who were further from adult supervision in the winter engaged in more problem behavior the following summer.

Supervision status was implicated in the longer term prediction of self-image. With respect to impulse control, the Sex × Supervision (winter) interaction was a significant predictor (R^2 change = .05); girls who were further from adult supervision after school in the winter reported lower levels of impulse control the following summer. Similarly, girls who were further from adult supervision after school in the winter reported lower mastery scores the following summer (R^2 change = .04). The regression for emotional tone found that supervision status (summer) was a significant predictor (R^2 change = .04), such that boys and girls who were more distant from adult supervision in the summer felt happier than those who were more closely supervised.

These longitudinal analyses were rerun, controlling for the Occasion 1 score on the dependent variable (i.e., testing whether changes in the dependent variable were related to supervision status in the winter or summer). For predicting changes in problem behavior, the Sex × Supervision (summer) interaction was significant ($\beta = -.69$, R^2 change = .04, $p < .05$), indicating that girls whose problem behavior increased from winter to summer were more distant from adult supervision in the summer.

Comparisons of Supervision Groups

The next set of analyses used planned orthogonal contrasts to examine differences among young adolescents in various out-of-school care arrangements. Previous literature (Rodman et al., 1985; Steinberg, 1986) pointed to three unresolved questions that needed further examination: (a) Are self-care children who stay in the home during out-of-school hours different from adult-care children? (b) Are self-care children who spend time in places other than home (e.g., at a friend's or hanging out) different from children who are closer to parental authority (i.e., those in adult care and self-care children who stay at home)? (c) Are self-care children who hang out different from those who go to a friend's? The corresponding set of orthogonal contrasts translate into (a) adult care versus self-care at home, (b) adult care plus self-care at home (two groups combined into one) versus self-care at a friend's plus self-care hanging out (two groups combined), and (c) self-care at a friend's versus self-care hanging out.

Three variables were orthogonally coded to represent these three contrasts weighted for unequal group sizes (Pedhazur, 1982). In hierarchical multiple regressions, sex of adolescent was entered in the first block. The set of three orthogonal contrasts was entered in the second block. The interactions of each of these contrasts with sex of adolescent were entered in the third block. Table 6 presents the results of these group comparisons.

Winter Results

Peer involvement and problem behavior were the only two dependent variables for which any contrast was significant. With respect to peer involvement, one significant contrast emerged, indicating that the group of adolescents who were in

Table 6
Summary of Results of Planned Orthogonal Contrasts

Dependent variable	Significant contrast and direction of difference	β	Step R^2	Final R^2
	Peer experience			
Peer involvement				
Winter	AC + SC home < SC friend's + SC hanging out	.27**	.09**	.10
Summer	AC + SC home < SC friend's + SC hanging out	.23**		
	SC friend's < SC hanging out	.29**	.15**	.19**
Deviant peers	No contrasts significant at either time			
Problem behavior				
Winter	AC + SC home < SC friend's + SC hanging out[a]	−.74**	.08**	.12*
Summer	AC + SC home < SC friend's + SC hanging out	.25		
	SC friend's < SC hanging out	.25	.14**	
	AC + SC home < SC friend's + SC hanging out[a]	−.62**		
	SC friend's < SC hanging out[a]	−.62**	.08**	.25**
	Self-image			
Impulse control	No contrasts significant at either time			
Mastery and coping	No contrasts significant at either time			
Emotional tone	No contrasts significant at either time			

Note. $N = 98–111$. AC = adult care. SC = self-care.
[a] This was a significant interaction between the contrast and sex (result applies to girls only).
* $p < .10$. ** $p < .05$.

self-care away from home (e.g., at a friend's or hanging out) were more involved with their peers than the adult-care and self-care home adolescents. With respect to problem behavior, a significant interaction with sex revealed that self-care girls who were away from the home (e.g., at a friend's or hanging out) reported more problem behavior than the adult-care and self-care home girls. There was no difference in the winter (on any of the dependent measures) between adolescents in adult care and those in self-care at home, or between adolescents in self-care at a friend's and those in self-care hanging out.

Summer Results

In the summer, the orthogonal contrasts were significant predictors only of peer involvement and problem behavior. Similar to the winter results, the self-care at a friend's plus self-care hanging out adolescents were significantly more involved with their peers than the adult-care plus self-care at home adolescents. In addition, the contrast between self-care at a friend's and self-care hanging out was significant, with hanging-out adolescents more involved with peers than were those in self-care at a friend's. With respect to problem behavior, the self-care away from home group (e.g., at a friend's and hanging out) reported more problem behavior than the adult-care and self-care at home groups; and the self-care hanging-out group reported more problem behavior than the self-care at a friend's group. These results, however, were qualified by significant interactions of these two contrasts with sex of adolescent. That is, it was only among girls that self-care away from home was associated with more problem behavior in relation to the combined grouping of adult care and self-care at home. It was also only among girls that self-care hanging out was associated with more problem behavior than self-care at a friend's.

Longitudinal Results

We next examined whether changes in the dependent measure were related to winter or summer supervision status (dichotomized as adult care plus self-care at home vs. self-care at a friend's plus self-care hanging out). The major finding of significance was that girls who increased their level of problem behavior from winter to summer were more likely to be in self-care away from home during the summer, in relation to girls whose problem behavior did not increase ($\beta = -.90$, R^2 change = .07, $p < .05$).

Parent–Adolescent Relations

Given that Steinberg (1986) reported the self-care situation to be associated with parental permissiveness, we hypothesized that adolescents further from adult supervision would experience lax control by their parents. Additionally, we assumed that adolescents who felt less accepted by and had more conflict with parents would be more apt to be found unsupervised away from home. To test these hypotheses, we performed three 5-step regression analyses on the dependent variables of lax control, parental acceptance, and parent–adolescent conflict. The five steps and predictors were sex, supervision status (winter), Sex × Supervision Status (winter), supervision status (summer), and Sex × Supervision Status (summer). In winter and summer, supervision status was dichotomized as adult care plus self-care at home versus self-care at a friend's plus self-care hanging out. There were no significant predictors for lax control, although there was a tendency for boys whose parents were more controlling to be in self-care away from home in the winter ($\beta = -.56$, R^2 change = .03, $p < .10$). With respect to parental acceptance, there was a significant interaction between sex and summer supervision ($\beta = .73$, R^2 change $= .05$, $p < .05$). This interaction indicated that self-care girls away from home had less accepting parents than other girls, but the reverse was true for self-care boys away from home. There was a significant interaction between winter supervision status and sex in predicting parent–adolescent conflict ($\beta = -.86$, R^2 change $= .07$, $p < .05$), indicating that parent–adolescent conflict was higher among self-care girls (and not boys) who were away from home. A total of 14% of the variance was explained in parent–adolescent conflict.

Next we asked, to what extent does the quality of parent–adolescent relations moderate the relation between supervision status and adolescent behavior? Because Steinberg (1986) found that authoritative parenting buffered the self-care adolescent from susceptibility to antisocial peer pressure, it seemed reasonable to predict in our sample that among self-care girls away from home, parental acceptance and firm control would work to lessen their problem behavior. Greater parent–adolescent conflict, on the other hand, might accentuate the relation between distance from adult supervision and adolescent behavior. To test these assumptions, we performed regression analyses within sex in which there were two blocks of predictors. The dependent variables were the six peer experience and self-image variables measured in the summer. The predictors in the first block were summer supervision status (dichotomized as adult care plus self-care at home vs. self-care at a friend's plus self-care hanging out) and the three parent–adolescent relations measures. In the second block were the two-way interactions of supervision status with the three parent–adolescent relations measures. Significant interactions would indicate a moderating effect of parent–adolescent relations.

The results of the regressions are presented in Table 7. There were no significant predictors of girls' peer involvement. Supervision status was not a significant predictor of deviant peers, but as lax control increased, so did girls' contact with deviant peers. With respect to problem behavior, self-care away from home was associated with more problem behavior, but this was qualified by significant interactions of supervision with lax control and parental acceptance. These interactions indicated that for self-care girls who spent time away from home, firm control and parental acceptance mitigated problem behavior. Supervision status was unrelated to impulse control. Among self-care girls away from home, there was a tendency for less parental acceptance and less conflict to be associated with lower feelings of mastery. No significant predictors were found for emotional tone.

The same set of regressions was performed for boys. In the absence of clear relations between supervision status and the dependent measures among boys, we thought it possible that parent–adolescent relations might be more important than supervision for explaining variation in peer experience and self-image. Indeed, the parent–adolescent relation measures explained up to 45% of the variance in the dependent measures. Boys in self-care away from home were more involved with peers than were other boys. Greater parent–adolescent conflict predicted association with more deviant peers, and there was a tendency for self-care away from home to be associated with more deviant peers. Greater parent–adolescent conflict was also associated with higher levels of problem behavior, lower impulse control, and less mastery. The results for emotional tone suggested that less parent–adolescent conflict was associated with more positive affect in boys; there was a tendency for greater parental acceptance and self-care away from home to be related to more positive affect.

Discussion

The results of this study lead to several conclusions about the nature of out-of-school supervision, peer experience, and self-image in early adolescence. Self-care, when it takes place out of the home, may provide the opportunity for experiences that are distinct from those encountered by adolescents in adult care or in self-care at home. First, self-care girls and boys not at home after school seem to be more generally involved with peers. Second, in early adolescence, girls who are more distant from adult supervision, and particularly those who hang out, may be at some risk for problem behavior, associating with more deviant peers, and developing a poorer self-image. More accepting and less permissive parenting, however, appears to mitigate this risk. Third, the relationship between supervision status and self-reported behavior is similar in the winter and summer, but with supervision status explaining more of the variance in peer experience in the summer (see Table 6). Fourth, although boys in general evidenced no clear risk from self-care, poor parent–adolescent relations (low acceptance and more conflict) were significantly associated with potentially troublesome peer behaviors and self-images.

Finally, the results of the orthogonal contrasts demonstrated that self-care adolescents who stayed in the home were not different on any variable studied from those adolescents in adult care. These results replicate those of Rodman et al. (1985) and Steinberg (1986), who also found no differences between children in adult care and those in self-care at home.

The pattern of results provides support for the argument that it is important in the study of self-care children to focus on peer experience (Steinberg, 1986, 1988), and given that among girls there was a distinct tendency for supervision status to be associated with self-image (e.g., impulse control and mastery), further research needs to examine self-image as well (Rodman et al., 1985, 1988). Correlations showed that lower impulse control and lower mastery were associated with more deviant peers and more problem behavior. Perhaps among girls, self-care out of the home affects self-image indirectly by setting up the opportunity for engaging in problem behaviors with friends, which in turn, help shape the adolescent's experience of self. This interpretation is merely speculative, for we must be cautious regarding inferences about the direction of effects in this study. Self-care out of the home, for instance, does not necessarily lead to problem behavior. It is just as likely that certain adolescents (e.g., those who are risk taking, adventure seekers, or socially inclined) select themselves into self-care situations in which they spend time with their peers.

Support is provided in this study for Steinberg's (1986, 1988) insistence on the importance of assessing where unsupervised adolescents spend time. Self-care, per se, seemed to be problematic only when adolescents ventured out of the home territory. Perhaps future studies with larger sample sizes might be able to differentiate further the types of settings in which self-care adolescents spend time. It is also important to consider parent–adolescent relations in future research on self-care. Although the self-care situation was not associated with any clear pattern of

Table 7

Summary of Regressions Predicting Adolescent Peer Experience and Self-Image Measures From Supervision Status and Parent–Adolescent Relations (Summer 1988)

Dependent variable	Significant predictors	β	Step R^2	Final R^2
	Girls			
Peer experience				
Peer involvement	None			
Deviant peers	Lax control	.46**	.29**	.32**
Problem behavior	Supervision	.42**	.27**	
	Supervision × Lax Control	2.69**		
	Supervision × Acceptance	−2.31**	.25**	.53**
Self-image				
Impulse control	Acceptance	.26*	.20**	.26*
Mastery and coping	Supervision × Acceptance	1.73*		
	Supervision × P–A Conflict	.46**	.13*	.20
Emotional tone	None			
	Boys			
Peer experience				
Peer involvement	Supervision	.35**	.19*	.31*
Deviant peers	P–A conflict	.41**		
	Supervision	.27*	.23**	.23
Problem behavior	P–A conflict	.46**	.28**	.36**
Self-image				
Impulse control	P–A conflict	−.60**	.42**	.45**
Mastery and coping	Acceptance	.28*		
	P–A conflict	−.34**	.26**	.27
Emotional tone	Supervision	.27*		
	Acceptance	.27*		
	P–A conflict	−.29**	.25**	.28

Note. For girls, $N = 48$–49. For boys, $N = 40$–42. P–A = parent–adolescent. Dependent variables and supervision status (dichotomized as adult care + self-care home vs. self-care friend's + self-care hanging out) measured in summer.
* $p < .10$. ** $p < .05$.

parent–adolescent relations in boys' families, self-care girls away from home were more likely to experience more conflict and less acceptance.

Why were the sixth-grade girls who were unsupervised away from home more likely to associate with deviant peers and to engage in problem behavior? This was somewhat unexpected, given that Hoffman (1980) argued that girls might benefit from less supervision and boys may need more supervision than they are typically given. On the other hand, in two studies, self-care girls as a group scored less favorably on outcome measures than did self-care girls (Steinberg, 1986; Woods, 1972).

We suspect that the unsupervised girls who were not at home were hanging out with older peers. After all, self-care away from home was associated, in both boys and girls, with higher peer involvement, but it was self-care girls away from home who reported that their friends sometimes got into trouble. Inspection of the actual problem behaviors of the group of self-care girls who were hanging out showed that they were engaging in some behaviors that would probably require the availability of older friends (e.g., cruising, smoking, and drinking). Perhaps these were early-maturing girls who believed they deserved and could handle more autonomy (cf. Magnusson, Stattin, & Allen, 1986). These were also the girls who had higher levels of conflict with and less acceptance from parents than did other girls. It is

possible that their behavior with peers might be a source of parent–adolescent tension. Boys' relatively later physical development, on the other hand, might make it less likely that they associate with older and more physically mature adolescents who are experimenting with some problem behaviors.

An examination of the mean level of problem behavior across sex and supervision groups showed that among supervised adolescents, boys had higher rates of problem behavior than did girls. It was only when girls were unsupervised away from home that their rate of problem behavior equaled, and even surpassed, the rate among boys. It may be that some subgroups of girls will reach their peak in problem behavior earlier than will other girls and boys and that self-care away from home may play a part in this process. Again, we cannot rule out the possibility that girls who might engage in problem behavior are more likely to be placed, by themselves or by other circumstances, in self-care out of the home.

The results for the winter and summer occasions were more alike than different. The total amount of variance explained in peer involvement and problem behavior was higher in the summer than in the winter, as demonstrated in the group differences (orthogonal contrasts) analysis. The divergence between the self-care at a friend's and self-care hanging-out girls may be attributable to the larger amount of time to fill in the summer.

Presumably, a larger selection of time-consuming activities are available when at a friend's house than when hanging out (e.g., games and TV). The finding that showed that distance from adult supervision was associated with feeling happier (only in the summer) suggests that some adolescents might become bored if they are "stuck at home" or are with adults during the summer.

In general, our results should not be overgeneralized or over-interpreted, given the absolute amounts of variance that were explained by supervision status alone or in interaction with sex (up to 25%). What this means, of course, is that supervision status is only one aspect of the adolescent's experience and that there are other important variables that would explain some of the variance as well. In fact, parent–adolescent relations, and not supervision status, explained a substantial portion of variance in peer experience and self-image among boys.

Another limitation to this study is that it involves a largely suburban sample of Canadian sixth graders with two parents. The results might differ for older or younger samples, children with single parents, American youth, or children growing up in large cities. In fact, it could be hypothesized that the effects of self-care away from home might be magnified in an inner city where crime and delinquency are common or in single-parent families in which continual adult supervision might be more difficult to achieve.

One implication of this study is that placing a child in self-care is not necessarily associated with negative outcomes. However, it should also be noted that no study has clearly indicated that self-care is related to positive outcomes, either. If that child spends unsupervised time away from home, however, the risk of problem behavior may be higher, at least among girls. At the same time, parents cannot imprison their children at home but can minimize risks by being attentive, warm, and firm in discipline. Whether a parent chooses self-care should depend on a host of considerations, including the ability to monitor the child's activities and to provide authoritative control (Crouter, MacDermid, McHale, & Perry-Jenkins, 1990; Steinberg, 1986); assessment of the child's age, responsibility, and previous relations and activities with peers; and knowledge about possible alternatives, including after-school care programs.

References

Baker, S., & Gore, T. (1989, May 29). Some reasons for 'wilding.' *Newsweek*, pp. 6–7.

Blishen, B. R., & McRoberts, H. A. (1976). A revised socio-economic index for occupations in Canada. *Canadian Review of Sociology and Anthropology, 13*, 71–79.

Brown, B. B., Clasen, D. R., & Eicher, S. A. (1986). Perceptions of peer pressure, peer conformity dispositions, and self-reported behavior among adolescents. *Developmental Psychology, 22*, 521–530.

Burger, G. K., & Armentrout, J. A. (1971). Comparative study of methods to estimate factor scores for reports of parental behaviors. *Proceedings of the 79th Annual Convention of the American Psychological Association, 6*, 149–150.

Cohen, J., & Cohen, P. (1983). *Applied multiple regression/correlation analysis for the behavioral sciences* (2nd ed.). Hillsdale, NJ: Erlbaum.

Crouter, A. C., MacDermid, S. M., McHale, S. M., & Perry-Jenkins, M. (1990). Parental monitoring and perceptions of children's school performance and conduct in dual- and single-earner families. *Developmental Psychology, 26*, 649–657.

Dullea, G. (1981, March 9). Schools help the latchkey children cope. *New York Times*, p. 87.

Galambos, N. L., & Dixon, R. A. (1984). Toward understanding and caring for latchkey children. *Child Care Quarterly, 13*, 116–125.

Galambos, N. L., & Garbarino, J. (1985). Adjustment of unsupervised children in a rural setting. *Journal of Genetic Psychology, 146*, 227–231.

Galambos, N. L., & Maggs, J. L. (in press). Children in self-care: Figures, facts, and fiction. In J. V. Lerner & N. L. Galambos (Eds.), *Employed mothers and their children*. New York: Garland Press.

Galambos, N. L., & Silbereisen, R. K. (1987a). Influences of income change and parental acceptance on adolescent transgression proneness and peer relations. *European Journal of Psychology of Education, 1*, 17–28.

Galambos, N. L., & Silbereisen, R. K. (1987b). Substance use in West German adolescents: A longitudinal study of adolescents' use of alcohol and tobacco. *Journal of Adolescent Research, 2*, 161–174.

Gold, D., & Andres, D. (1978a). Comparisons of adolescent children with employed and nonemployed mothers. *Merrill-Palmer Quarterly, 24*, 243–253.

Gold, D., & Andres, D. (1978b). Developmental comparisons between ten-year-old children with employed and nonemployed mothers. *Child Development, 49*, 75–84.

Hoffman, L. W. (1980). The effects of maternal employment on the academic attitudes and performance of school-aged children. *School Psychology Review, 9*, 319–335.

Huff, K. (1982, September 20). In their own words. *People*, pp. 83–84, 87–88.

Kaplan, H. B. (1978). Deviant behavior and self-enhancement in adolescence. *Journal of Youth and Adolescence, 7*, 253–277.

Kieffer, E. (1981, February). The latchkey kids: How are they doing? *Family Circle*, pp. 28, 31, 34–35.

Langway, L. (1981, February 16). The latchkey children. *Newsweek*, pp. 96–97.

Litovsky, V. G., & Dusek, J. B. (1985). Perceptions of child rearing and self-concept development during the early adolescent years. *Journal of Youth and Adolescence, 14*, 373–387.

Long, L., & Long, T. (1983). *The handbook for latchkey children and their parents*. New York: Berkley Books.

Maccoby, E. E., & Martin, J. A. (1983). Socialization in the context of the family: Parent-child interaction. In E. M. Hetherington (Ed.), *Handbook of child psychology: Vol. 4. Socialization, personality, and social development* (pp. 1–101). New York: Wiley.

Magnusson, D., Stattin, H., & Allen, V. L. (1986). Differential maturation among girls and its relation to social adjustment: A longitudinal perspective. In P. B. Baltes, D. L. Featherman, & R. M. Lerner (Eds.), *Life-span development and behavior* (Vol. 7, pp. 135–172). Hillsdale, NJ: Erlbaum.

Margolies, P. J., & Weintraub, S. (1977). The revised 56-item CRPBI as a research instrument: Reliability and factor structure. *Journal of Clinical Psychology, 33*, 472–476.

Montemayor, R. (1983). Parents and adolescents in conflict: All families some of the time and some families most of the time. *Journal of Early Adolescence, 3*, 83–103.

Parsons, J. E., Adler, T., & Kaczala, C. (1982). Socialization of achievement attitudes and beliefs: Parental influences. *Child Development, 53*, 310–321.

Pedhazur, E. J. (1982). *Multiple regression in behavioral research: Explanation and prediction* (2nd ed.). New York: Holt, Rinehart & Winston.

Petersen, A. C., Schulenberg, J. E., Abramowitz, R. H., Offer, D., & Jarcho, H. D. (1984). A self-image questionnaire for young adolescents (SIQYA): Reliability and validity studies. *Journal of Youth and Adolescence, 13*, 93–111.

Prinz, R., Foster, S., Kent, R., & O'Leary, K. (1979). Multivariate assessment of conflict in distressed and nondistressed mother-adolescent dyads. *Journal of Applied Behavioral Analysis, 12,* 691–700.

Richardson, J. L., Dwyer, K., McGuigan, K., Hansen, W. B., Dent, C., Johnson, C. A., Sussman, S. Y., Brannon, B., & Flay, B. (1989). Substance use among eighth-grade students who take care of themselves after school. *Pediatrics, 84,* 556–566.

Rodman, H., Pratto, D. J., & Nelson, R. S. (1985). Child care arrangements and children's functioning: A comparison of self-care and adult-care children. *Developmental Psychology, 21,* 413–418.

Rodman, H., Pratto, D. J., & Nelson, R. S. (1988). Toward a definition of self-care children: A commentary on Steinberg (1986). *Developmental Psychology, 24,* 292–294.

Schaefer, E. (1965). Children's reports of parental behavior: An inventory. *Child Development, 36,* 413–424.

Schwarz, J. C., Barton-Henry, M. L., & Pruzinsky, T. (1985). Assessing child-rearing behaviors: A comparison of ratings made by mother, father, child, and sibling on the CRPBI. *Child Development, 56,* 462–479.

Smetana, J. G. (1989). Adolescents' and parents' reasoning about actual family conflict. *Child Development, 60,* 1052–1067.

Statistics Canada. (1984). *The labour force.* Ottawa, Ontario: Minister of Supply and Services Canada.

Steinberg, L. (1986). Latchkey children and susceptibility to peer pressure: An ecological analysis. *Developmental Psychology, 22,* 433–439.

Steinberg, L. (1987). Impact of puberty on family relations: Effects of pubertal status and pubertal timing. *Developmental Psychology, 23,* 451–460.

Steinberg, L. (1988). Simple solutions to a complex problem: A response to Rodman, Pratto, and Nelson (1988). *Developmental Psychology, 24,* 295–296.

U.S. Bureau of the Census. (1987). *After-school care of school-age children: December 1984* (Current Population Reports, Series P-23, No. 149). Washington, DC: U.S. Government Printing Office.

Vandell, D. L., & Corasaniti, M. A. (1988). The relation between third graders' after-school care and social, academic, and emotional functioning. *Child Development, 59,* 868–875.

Woods, M. B. (1972). The unsupervised child of the working mother. *Developmental Psychology, 6,* 14–25.

Received September 14, 1989
Revision received October 1, 1990
Accepted February 14, 1991 ■

Acknowledgments

Piaget, J. "Intellectual Evolution from Adolescence to Adulthood." *Human Development* 15 (1972): 1–12. Reprinted with the permission of S. Karger, AG.

Elkind, David. "Egocentrism in Adolescence." *Child Development* 38 (1967): 1025–34. Reprinted with the permission of the Society for Research in Child Development.

Kuhn, Deanna, Victoria Ho, and Catherine Adams. "Formal Reasoning Among Pre- and Late Adolescents." *Child Development* 50 (1979): 1128–35. Reprinted with the permission of the Society for Research in Child Development.

Overton, Willis F., John H. Steidl, Diana Rosenstein, and Harvey A. Horowitz. "Formal Operations as Regulatory Context in Adolescence." *Adolescent Psychiatry* 18 (1992): 502–13. Reprinted with the permission of the University of Chicago Press.

Keating, Daniel P., and Lawrence V. Clark. "Development of Physical and Social Reasoning in Adolescence." *Developmental Psychology* 16 (1980): 23–30. Copyright 1980 by the American Psychological Association. Reprinted by permission.

Kohlberg, Lawrence. "Revisions in the Theory and Practice of Moral Development." *New Directions for Child Development* 2 (1978): 83–87. Reprinted with the permission of Jossey-Bass Publishers.

Smetana, Judith G., Melanie Killen, and Elliot Turiel. "Children's Reasoning About Interpersonal and Moral Conflicts." *Child Development* 63 (1991): 629–44. Reprinted with the permission of the Society for Research in Child Development.

Eisenberg, Nancy, Gustavo Carlo, Bridget Murphy, and Patricia Van Court. "Prosocial Development in Late Adolescence: A Longitudinal Study." *Child Development* 66 (1995): 1179–97. Reprinted with the permission of the Society for Research in Child Development.

Eisenberg, Nancy, and Sandra McNally. "Socialization and Mothers' and Adolescents' Empathy-Related Characteristics." *Journal of Research on Adolescence* 3 (1993): 171–91. Reprinted with the permission of Lawrence Erlbaum Associates Inc.

Damon, William, and Anne Gregory. "The Youth Charter: Towards the Formation of Adolescent Moral Identity." *Journal of Moral Education* 26 (1997): 117–30. Reprinted with the permission of Carfax Publishing Co.

Eccles, Jacquelynne S., and Allan Wigfield. "In the Mind of the Actor: The Structure of Adolescents' Achievement Task Values and Expectancy-Related Beliefs." *Personality and Social Psychology Bulletin* 21 (1995): 215–25. Reprinted with the permission of the author.

Jovanovic, Jasna, and Richard M. Lerner. "Individual-Contextual Relationships and Mathematics Performance: Comparing American and Serbian Young Adolescents." *Journal of Early Adolescence* 14 (1994): 449–70. Reprinted with the permission of Sage Publications, Inc.

Steinberg, Laurence, Sanford M. Dornbusch, and B. Bradford Brown. "Ethnic Differences in Adolescent Achievement: An Ecological Perspective." *American Psychologist* 47 (1992): 723–29. Copyright 1992 by the American Psychological Association. Reprinted by permission.

Taylor, Ronald D., Robin Casten, Susanne M. Flickinger, Debra Roberts, and Cecil D. Fulmore. "Explaining the School Performance of African-American Adolescents." *Journal of Research on Adolescence* 4 (1994): 21–44. Reprinted with the permission of Lawrence Erlbaum Associates, Inc.

Rosenthal, Doreen A., and S. Shirley Feldman. "The Influence of Perceived Family and Personal Factors on Self-Reported School Performance of Chinese and Western High School Students." *Journal of Research on Adolescence* 1 (1991): 135–54. Reprinted with the permission of Lawrence Erlbaum Associates Inc.

Sameroff, Arnold J., Ronald Seifer, Alfred Baldwin, and Clara Baldwin. "Stability of Intelligence from Preschool to Adolescence: The Influence of Social and Family Risk Factors." *Child Development* 64 (1993): 80–97. Reprinted with the permission of the Society for Research in Child Development.

Leadbeater, Bonnie J. "School Outcomes for Minority-Group Adolescent Mothers at 28 to 36 Months Postpartum: A Longitudinal Follow-Up." *Journal of Research on Adolescence* 6 (1996): 629–48. Reprinted with the permission of Lawrence Erlbaum Associates, Inc.

Wentzel, Kathryn R., S. Shirley Feldman, and Daniel A. Weinberger. "Parental Child Rearing and Academic Achievement in Boys: The Mediational Role of Social-Emotional Adjustment." *Journal of Early Adolescence* 11 (1991): 321–39. Reprinted with the permission of Sage Publications, Inc.

Dornbusch, Sanford M., Philip L. Ritter, P. Herbert Leiderman, Donald F. Roberts, and Michael J. Fraleigh. "The Relation of Parenting Style to Adolescent School Performance." *Child Development* 58 (1987): 1244–1257. Reprinted with the permission of the Society for Research in Child Development.

Dryfoos, Joy G. "Full Service Schools: Revolution or Fad?" *Journal of Research on Adolescence* 5 (1995): 147–72. Reprinted with the permission of Lawrence Erlbaum Associates, Inc.

Epstein, Joyce L., and Susan L. Dauber. "Effects on Students of an Interdisciplinary Program Linking Social Studies, Art, and Family Volunteers in the Middle Grades." *Journal of Early Adolescence* 15 (1995): 114–44. Reprinted with the permission of Sage Publications, Inc.

Galambos, Nancy L., and Jennifer L. Maggs. "Out-of-School Care of Young Adolescents and Self-Reported Behavior." *Developmental Psychology* 27 (1991): 644–55. Copyright 1991 by the American Psychological Association. Reprinted by permission.

ISS.5/ADO
N/L